Shojo Beat

love★com

Story & Art by
Aya Nakahara

15

love ★ com

contents 15

The Story So Far...

Risa and Ôtani are their class's lopsided comedy duo...and they've become a couple! Ôtani has been accepted into a teachers' college while Risa plans to become a fashion stylist.

Risa's grandfather doesn't approve of Ôtani, so he hires a hottie to lead him astray. It doesn't work—because Ôtani is already entangled with an even more dangerous woman, the scheming Hitomi! Risa and Ôtani brave Hitomi's yakuza friends to get their relationship back on track and win Grandpa's grudging approval.

Then Haruka and his fangirls ruin the couple's concert date by kidnapping Ôtani, but Risa and Ôtani's love remains strong...

♥ To really get all the details, check out *Lovely Complex* volumes 1-14, available at bookstores everywhere!!

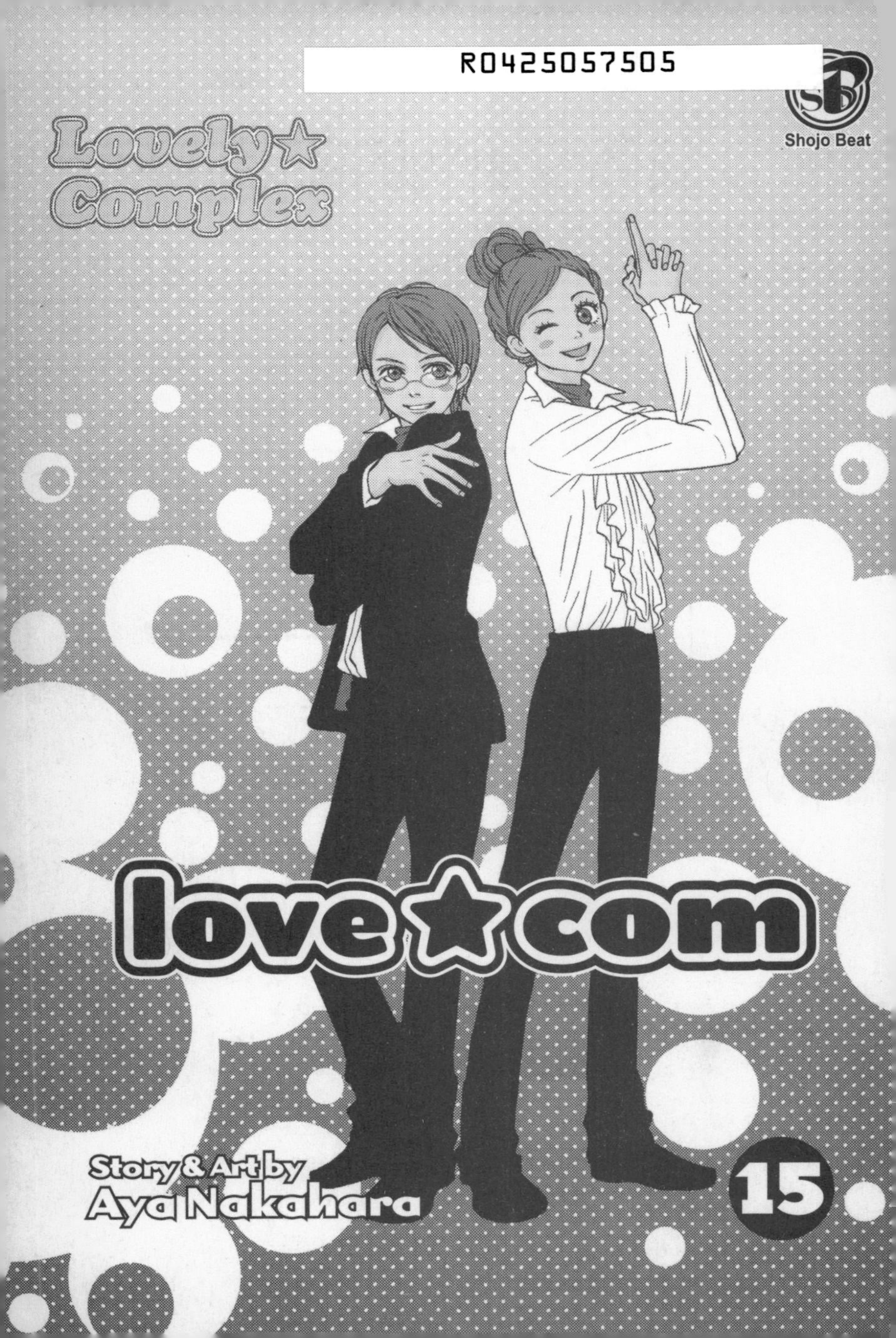
Shojo Beat
Lovely★Complex
love★com
Story & Art by
Aya Nakahara
15

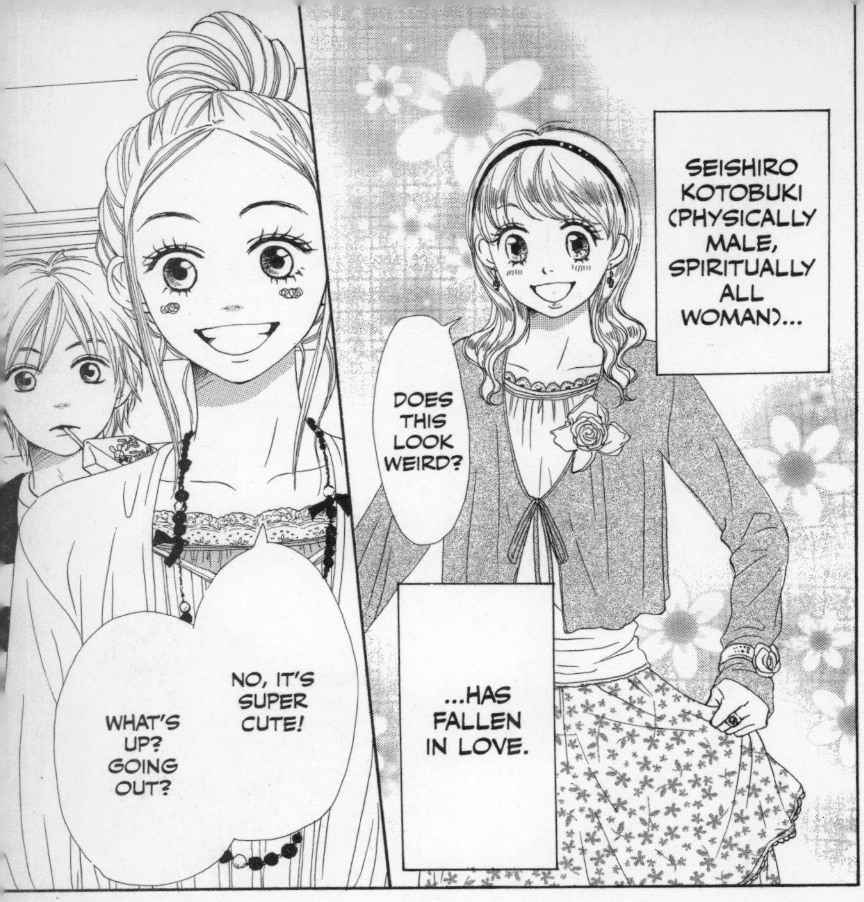
SEISHIRO KOTOBUKI (PHYSICALLY MALE, SPIRITUALLY ALL WOMAN)...
DOES THIS LOOK WEIRD?
...HAS FALLEN IN LOVE.
NO, IT'S SUPER CUTE!
WHAT'S UP? GOING OUT?

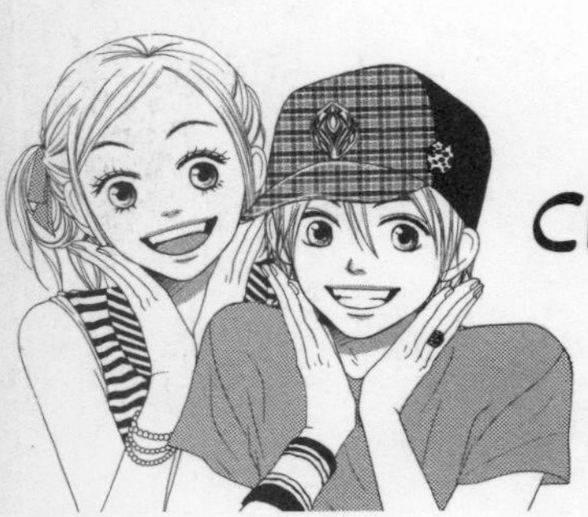

CHAPTER 56

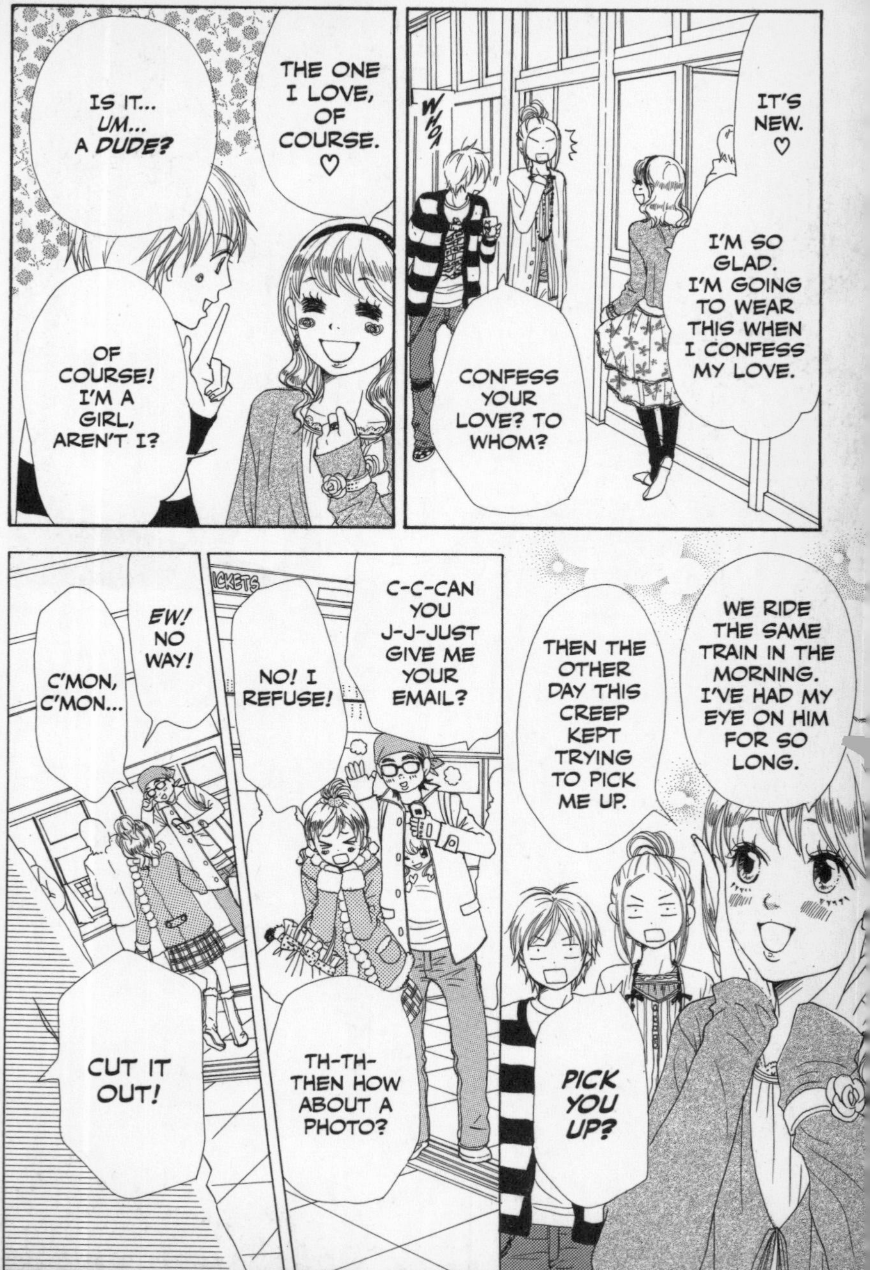
IT'S NEW. ♡
I'M SO GLAD. I'M GOING TO WEAR THIS WHEN I CONFESS MY LOVE.
WHOA
CONFESS YOUR LOVE? TO WHOM?
THE ONE I LOVE, OF COURSE. ♡
IS IT... *UM*... A *DUDE?*
OF COURSE! I'M A GIRL, AREN'T I?
WE RIDE THE SAME TRAIN IN THE MORNING. I'VE HAD MY EYE ON HIM FOR SO LONG.
THEN THE OTHER DAY THIS CREEP KEPT TRYING TO PICK ME UP.
PICK YOU UP?
TICKETS
C-C-CAN YOU J-J-JUST GIVE ME YOUR EMAIL?
NO! I REFUSE!
TH-TH-THEN HOW ABOUT A PHOTO?
EW! NO WAY!
C'MON, C'MON...
CUT IT OUT!

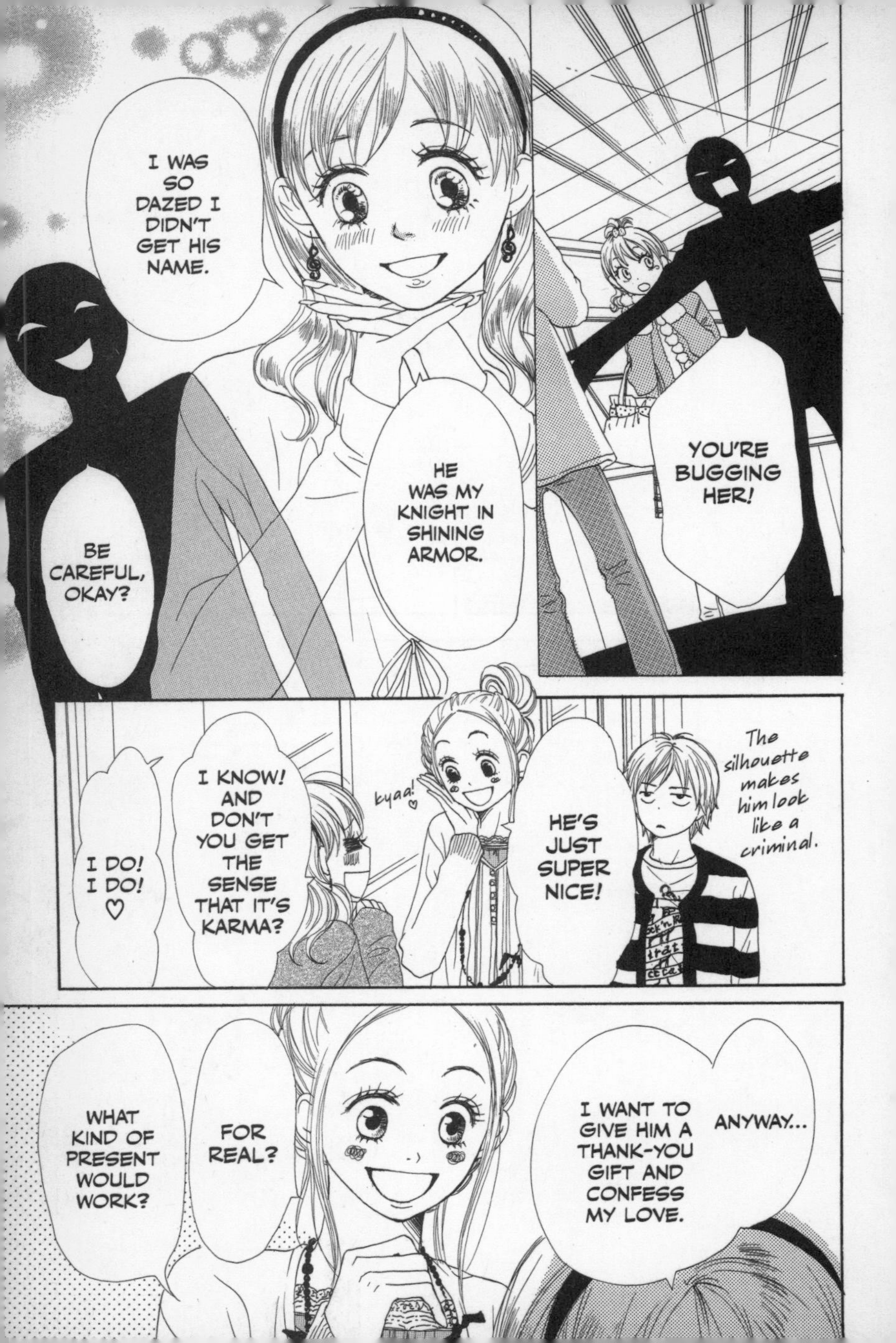
YOU'RE BUGGING HER!
I WAS SO DAZED I DIDN'T GET HIS NAME.
HE WAS MY KNIGHT IN SHINING ARMOR.
BE CAREFUL, OKAY?
The silhouette makes him look like a criminal.
HE'S JUST SUPER NICE!
kyaa! ♡
I KNOW! AND DON'T YOU GET THE SENSE THAT IT'S KARMA?
I DO! I DO! ♡
ANYWAY...
I WANT TO GIVE HIM A THANK-YOU GIFT AND CONFESS MY LOVE.
FOR REAL?
WHAT KIND OF PRESENT WOULD WORK?

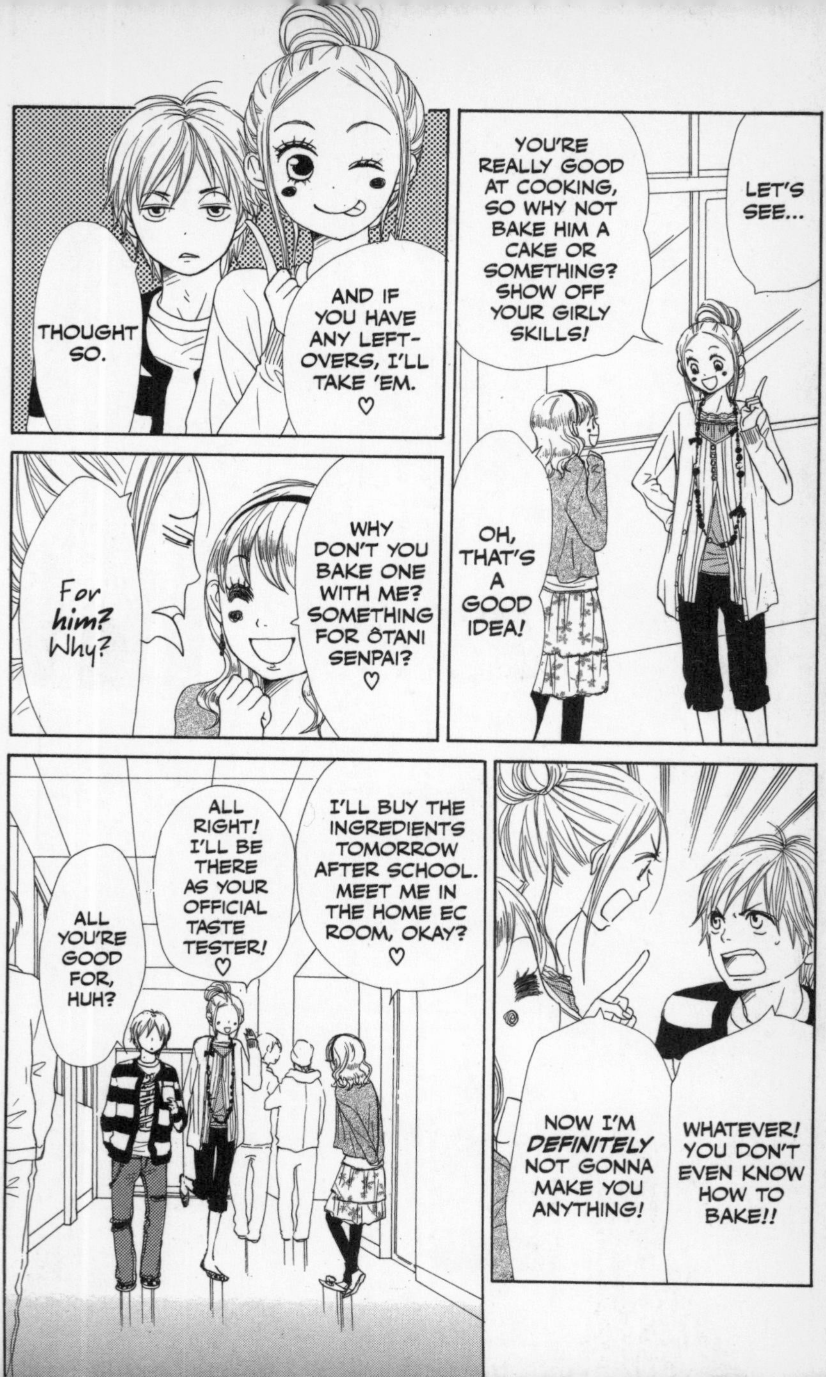
LET'S SEE...
YOU'RE REALLY GOOD AT COOKING, SO WHY NOT BAKE HIM A CAKE OR SOMETHING? SHOW OFF YOUR GIRLY SKILLS!
OH, THAT'S A GOOD IDEA!
AND IF YOU HAVE ANY LEFT-OVERS, I'LL TAKE 'EM. ♡
THOUGHT SO.
WHY DON'T YOU BAKE ONE WITH ME? SOMETHING FOR ÔTANI SENPAI? ♡
For *him?* Why?
WHATEVER! YOU DON'T EVEN KNOW HOW TO BAKE!!
NOW I'M *DEFINITELY* NOT GONNA MAKE YOU ANYTHING!
I'LL BUY THE INGREDIENTS TOMORROW AFTER SCHOOL. MEET ME IN THE HOME EC ROOM, OKAY? ♡
ALL RIGHT! I'LL BE THERE AS YOUR OFFICIAL TASTE TESTER! ♡
ALL YOU'RE GOOD FOR, HUH?

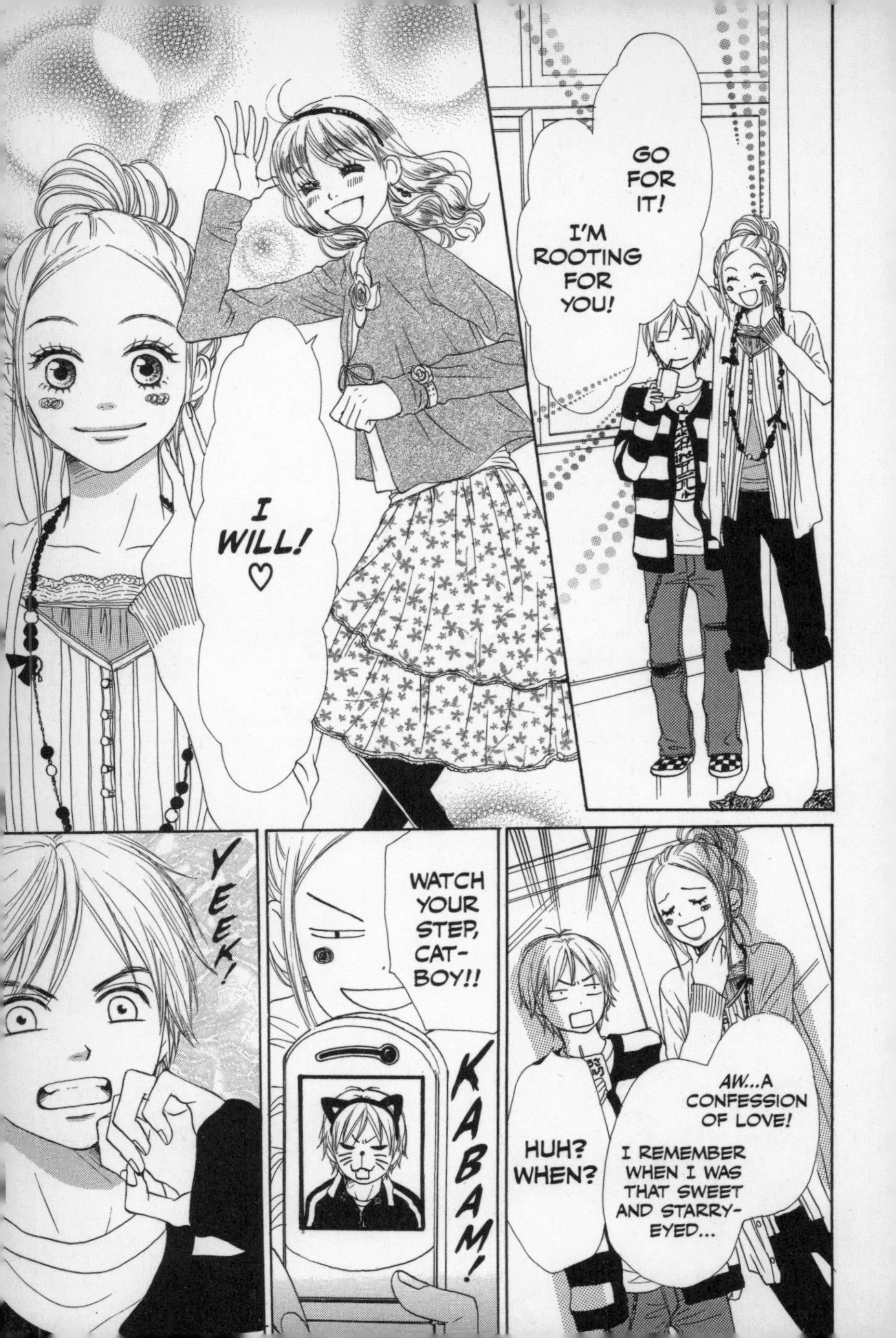
GO FOR IT!
I'M ROOTING FOR YOU!
I WILL! ♥
AW...A CONFESSION OF LOVE!
I REMEMBER WHEN I WAS THAT SWEET AND STARRY-EYED...
HUH? WHEN?
WATCH YOUR STEP, CAT-BOY!!
KABAM!
YEEK!

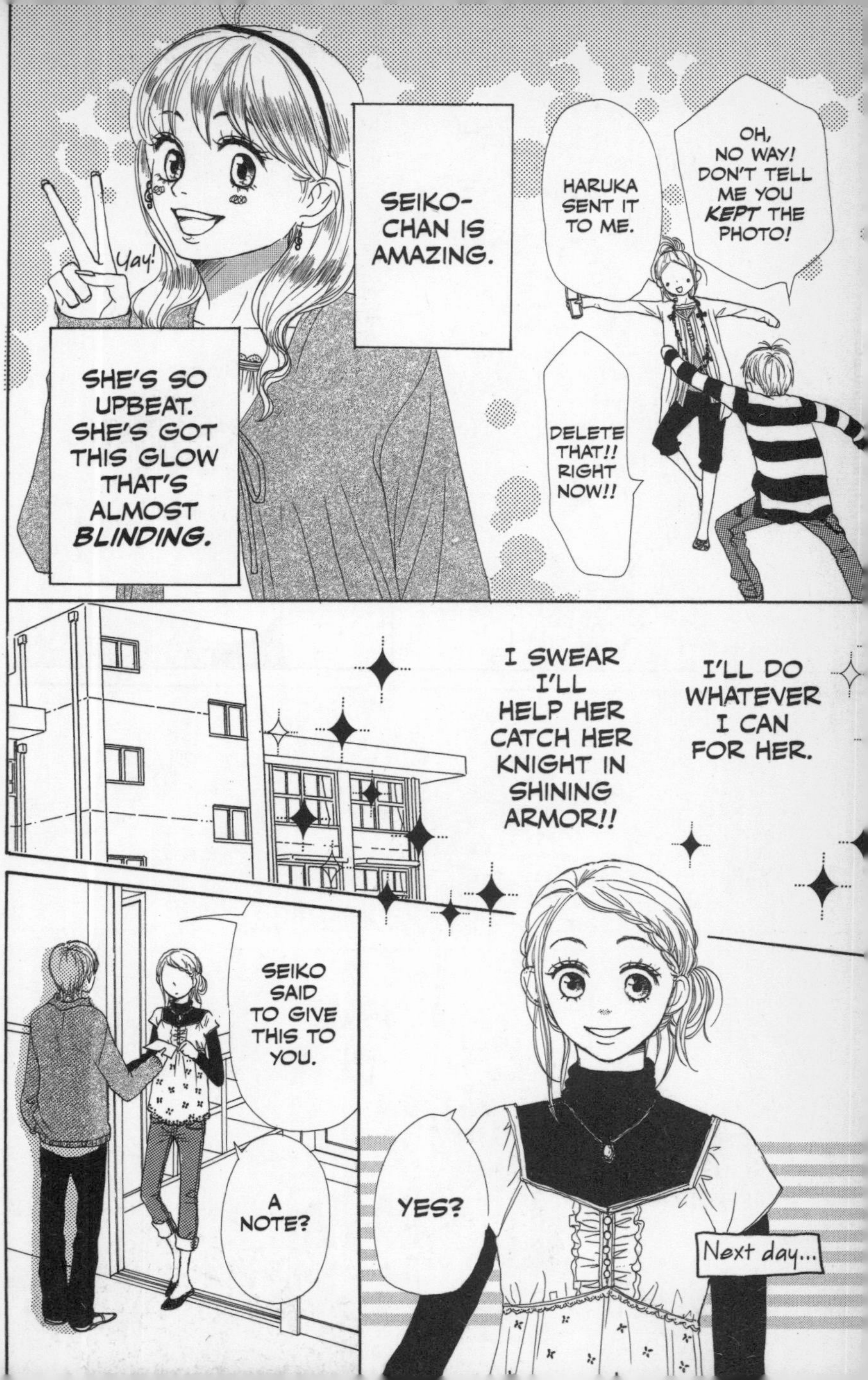
OH, NO WAY! DON'T TELL ME YOU *KEPT* THE PHOTO!
HARUKA SENT IT TO ME.
SEIKO-CHAN IS AMAZING.
DELETE THAT!! RIGHT NOW!!
Yay!
SHE'S SO UPBEAT. SHE'S GOT THIS GLOW THAT'S ALMOST *BLINDING.*
I'LL DO WHATEVER I CAN FOR HER.
I SWEAR I'LL HELP HER CATCH HER KNIGHT IN SHINING ARMOR!!
Next day...
YES?
SEIKO SAID TO GIVE THIS TO YOU.
A NOTE?

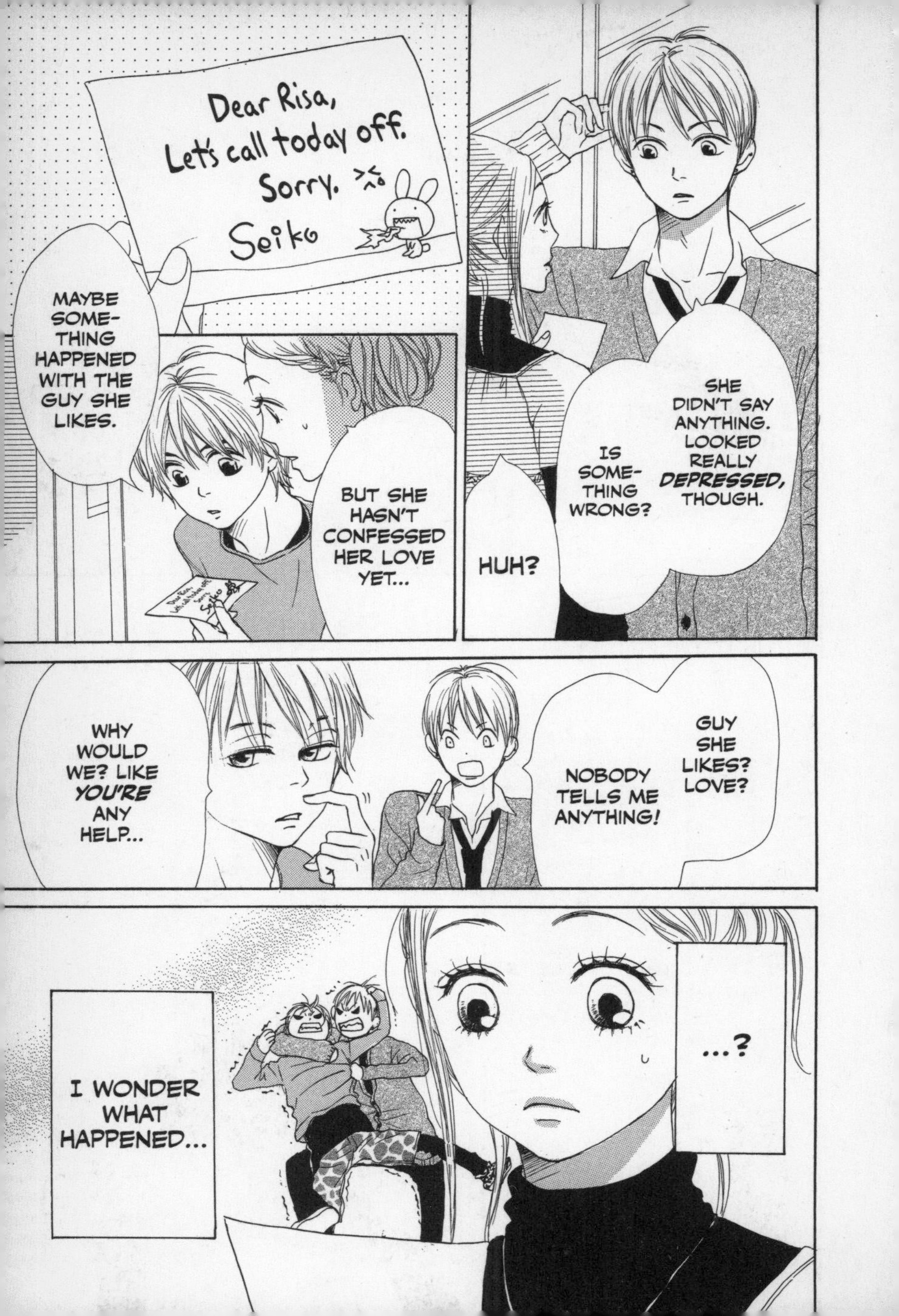
SHE DIDN'T SAY ANYTHING. LOOKED REALLY DEPRESSED, THOUGH.
IS SOMETHING WRONG?
HUH?
Dear Risa,
Let's call today off.
Sorry.
Seiko
MAYBE SOMETHING HAPPENED WITH THE GUY SHE LIKES.
BUT SHE HASN'T CONFESSED HER LOVE YET...
GUY SHE LIKES? LOVE?
NOBODY TELLS ME ANYTHING!
WHY WOULD WE? LIKE YOU'RE ANY HELP...
...?
I WONDER WHAT HAPPENED...

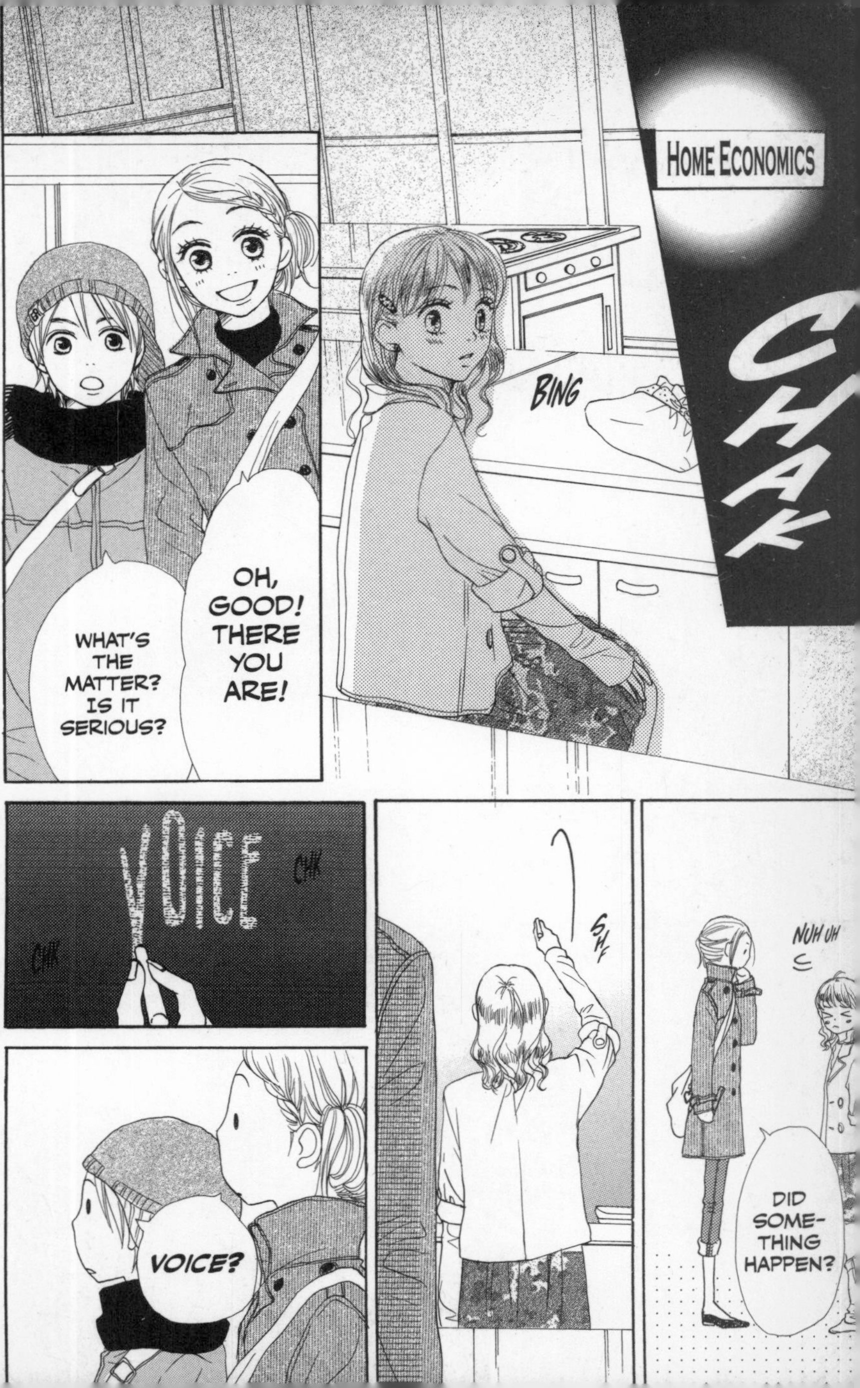

HOME ECONOMICS
CHAK
BING
OH, GOOD! THERE YOU ARE!
WHAT'S THE MATTER? IS IT SERIOUS?
NUH UH
DID SOMETHING HAPPEN?
SHF
CHK
VOICE
CHK
VOICE?

VOICE CHANGE

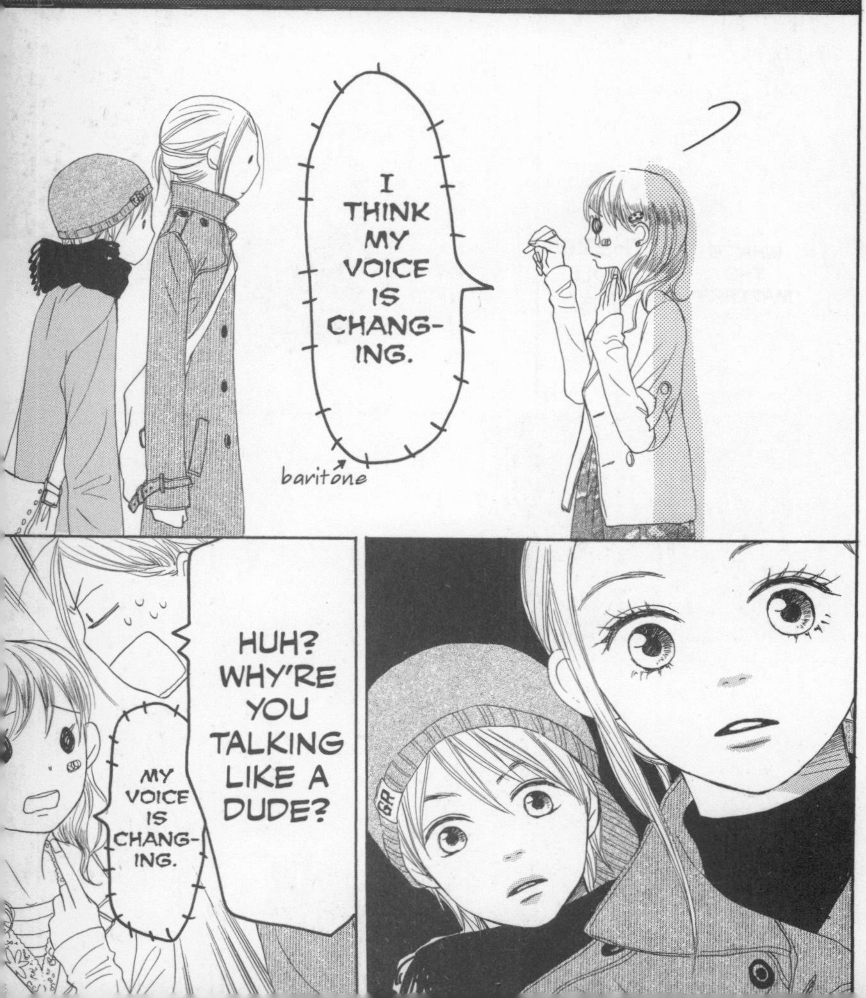
I THINK MY VOICE IS CHANGING.
baritone
HUH? WHY'RE YOU TALKING LIKE A DUDE?
MY VOICE IS CHANGING.

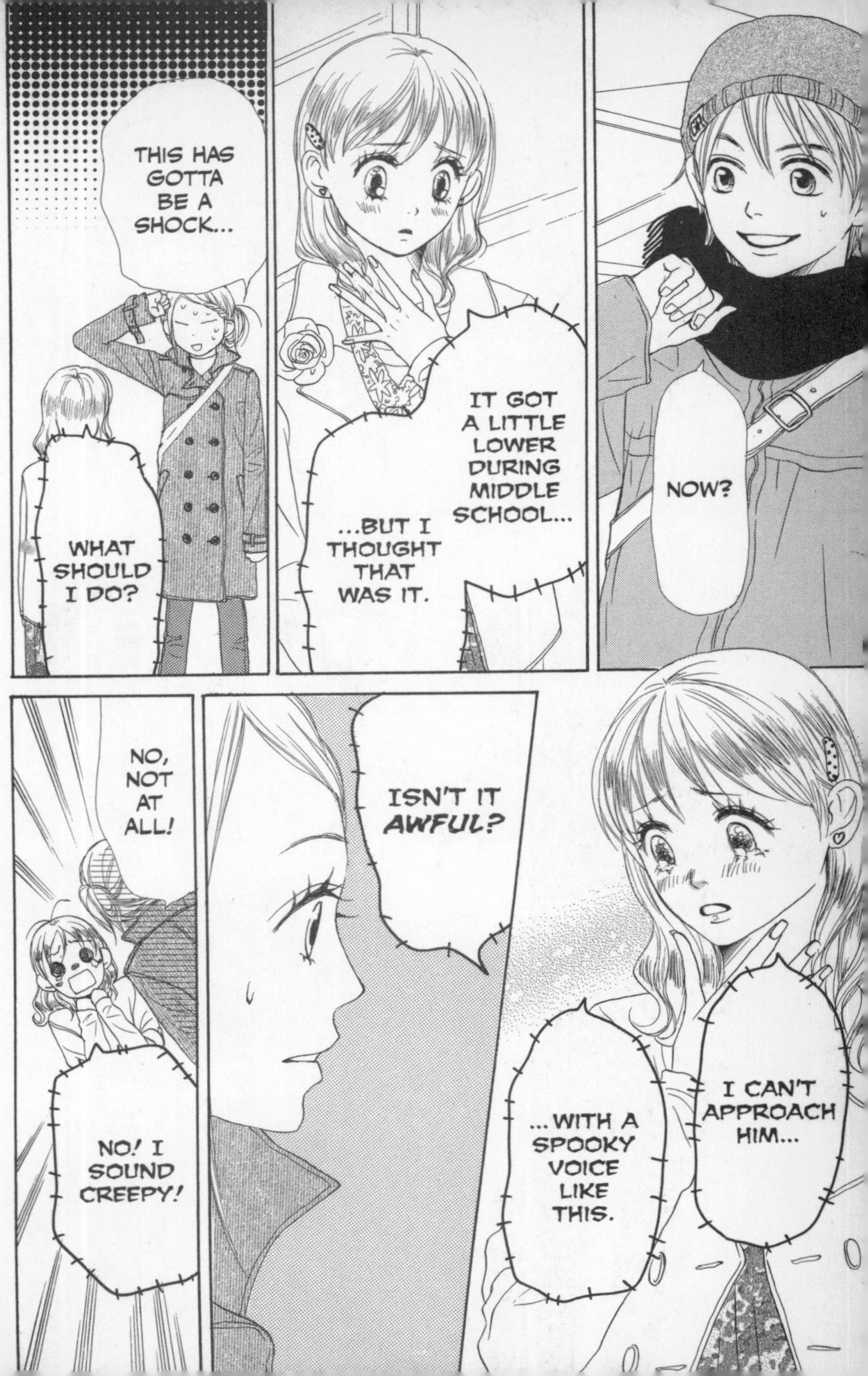
NOW?
IT GOT A LITTLE LOWER DURING MIDDLE SCHOOL...
...BUT I THOUGHT THAT WAS IT.
THIS HAS GOTTA BE A SHOCK...
WHAT SHOULD I DO?
I CAN'T APPROACH HIM...
...WITH A SPOOKY VOICE LIKE THIS.
ISN'T IT *AWFUL?*
NO, NOT AT ALL!
NO! I SOUND CREEPY!

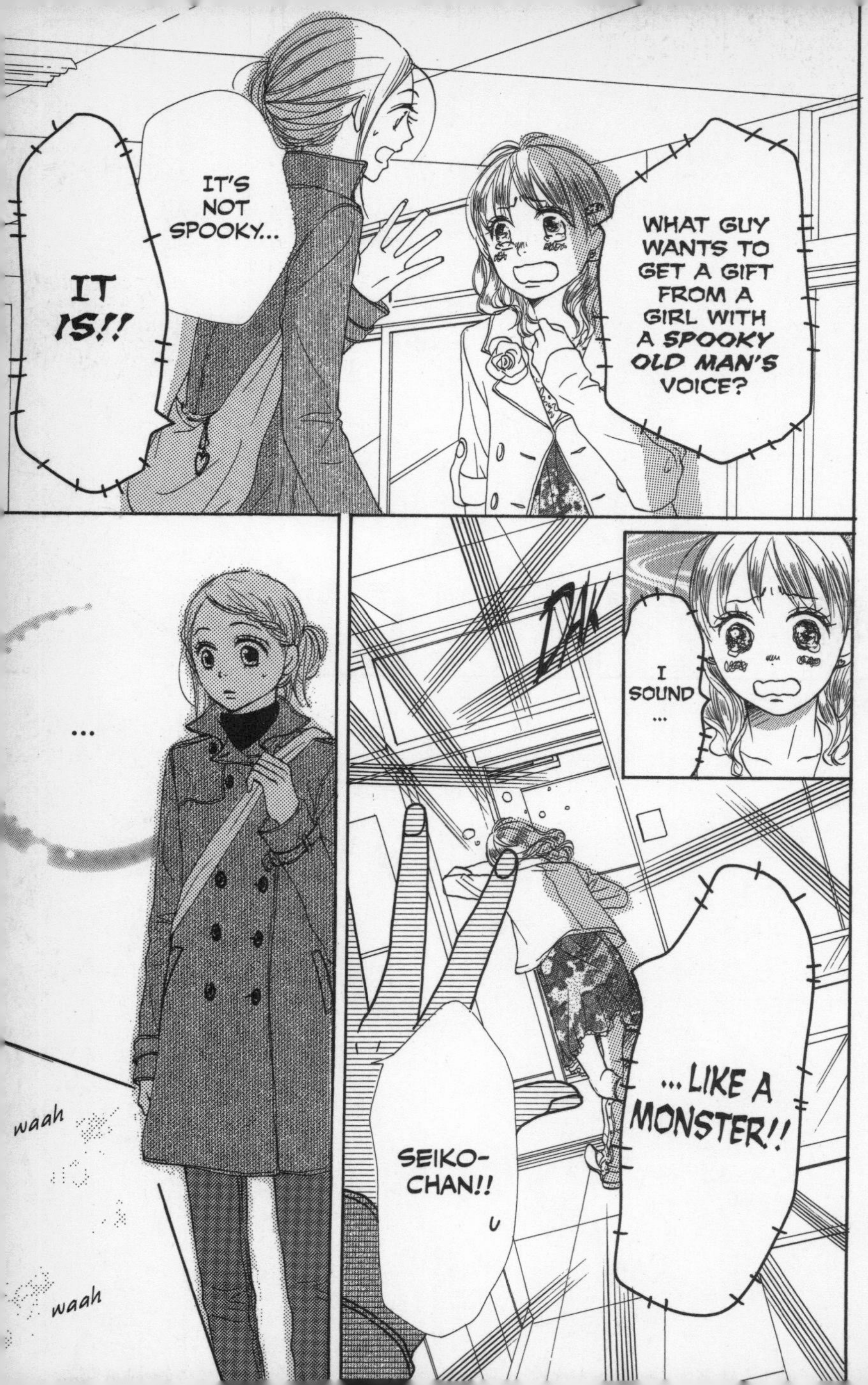
WHAT GUY WANTS TO GET A GIFT FROM A GIRL WITH A SPOOKY OLD MAN'S VOICE?
IT'S NOT SPOOKY...
IT IS!!
I SOUND ...
DAK
...LIKE A MONSTER!!
SEIKO-CHAN!!
u
...
waah
waah

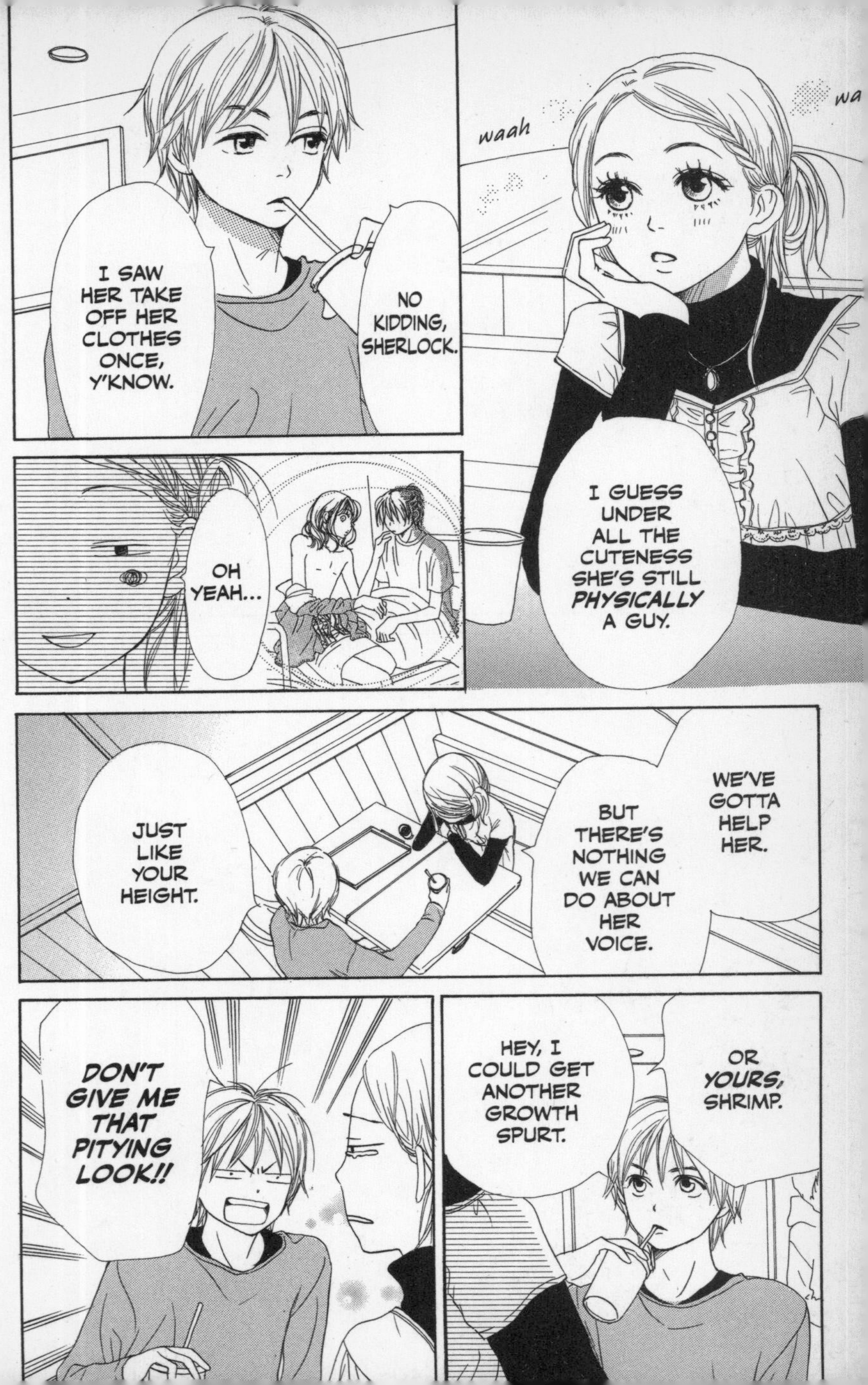
wa
waah
I GUESS UNDER ALL THE CUTENESS SHE'S STILL *PHYSICALLY* A GUY.
NO KIDDING, SHERLOCK.
I SAW HER TAKE OFF HER CLOTHES ONCE, Y'KNOW.
OH YEAH...
WE'VE GOTTA HELP HER.
BUT THERE'S NOTHING WE CAN DO ABOUT HER VOICE.
JUST LIKE YOUR HEIGHT.
OR *YOURS,* SHRIMP.
HEY, I COULD GET ANOTHER GROWTH SPURT.
DON'T GIVE ME THAT PITYING LOOK!!

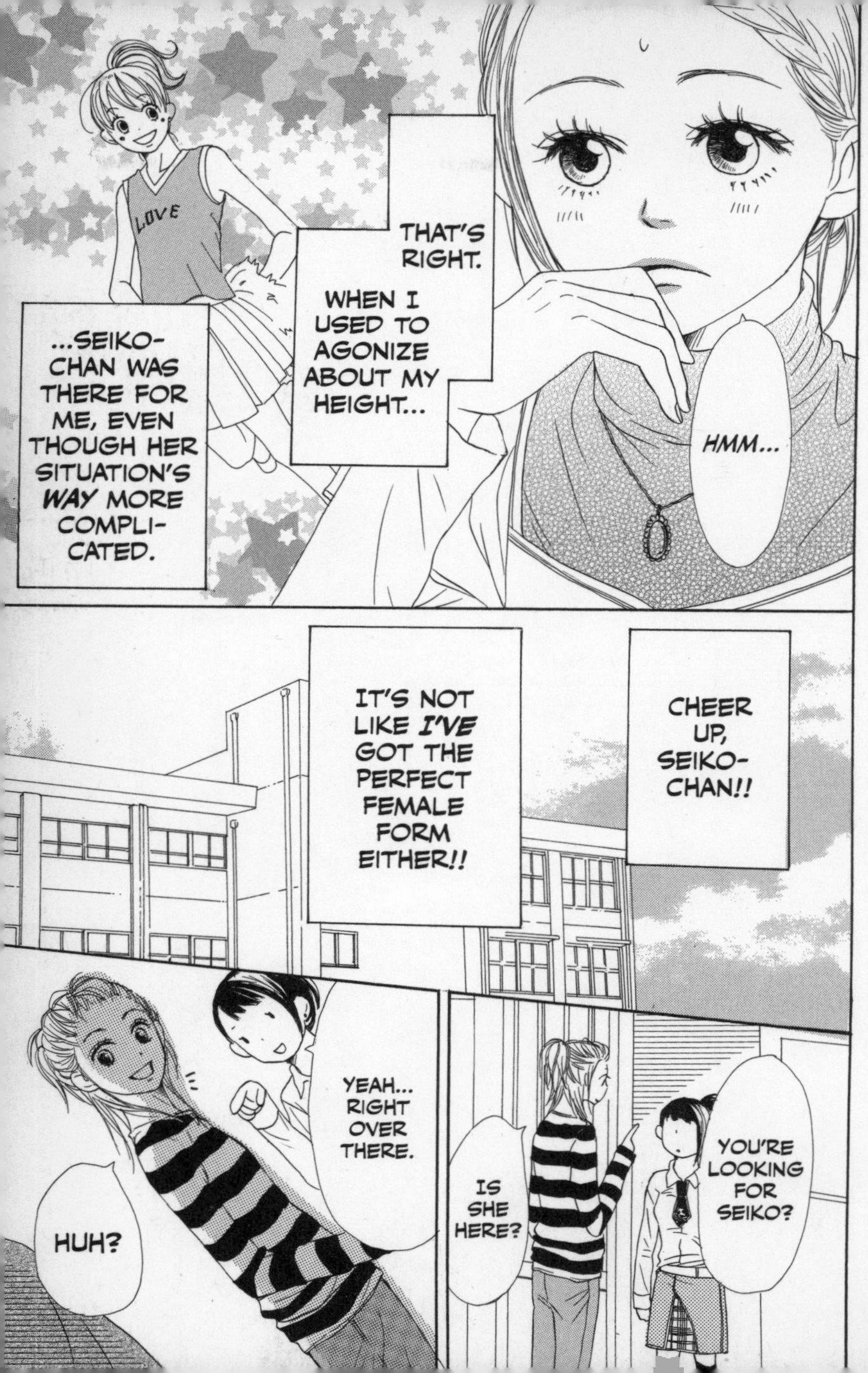
HMM...
THAT'S RIGHT.
WHEN I USED TO AGONIZE ABOUT MY HEIGHT...
...SEIKO-CHAN WAS THERE FOR ME, EVEN THOUGH HER SITUATION'S *WAY* MORE COMPLICATED.
LOVE
CHEER UP, SEIKO-CHAN!!
IT'S NOT LIKE *I'VE* GOT THE PERFECT FEMALE FORM EITHER!!
YOU'RE LOOKING FOR SEIKO?
IS SHE HERE?
YEAH... RIGHT OVER THERE.
HUH?

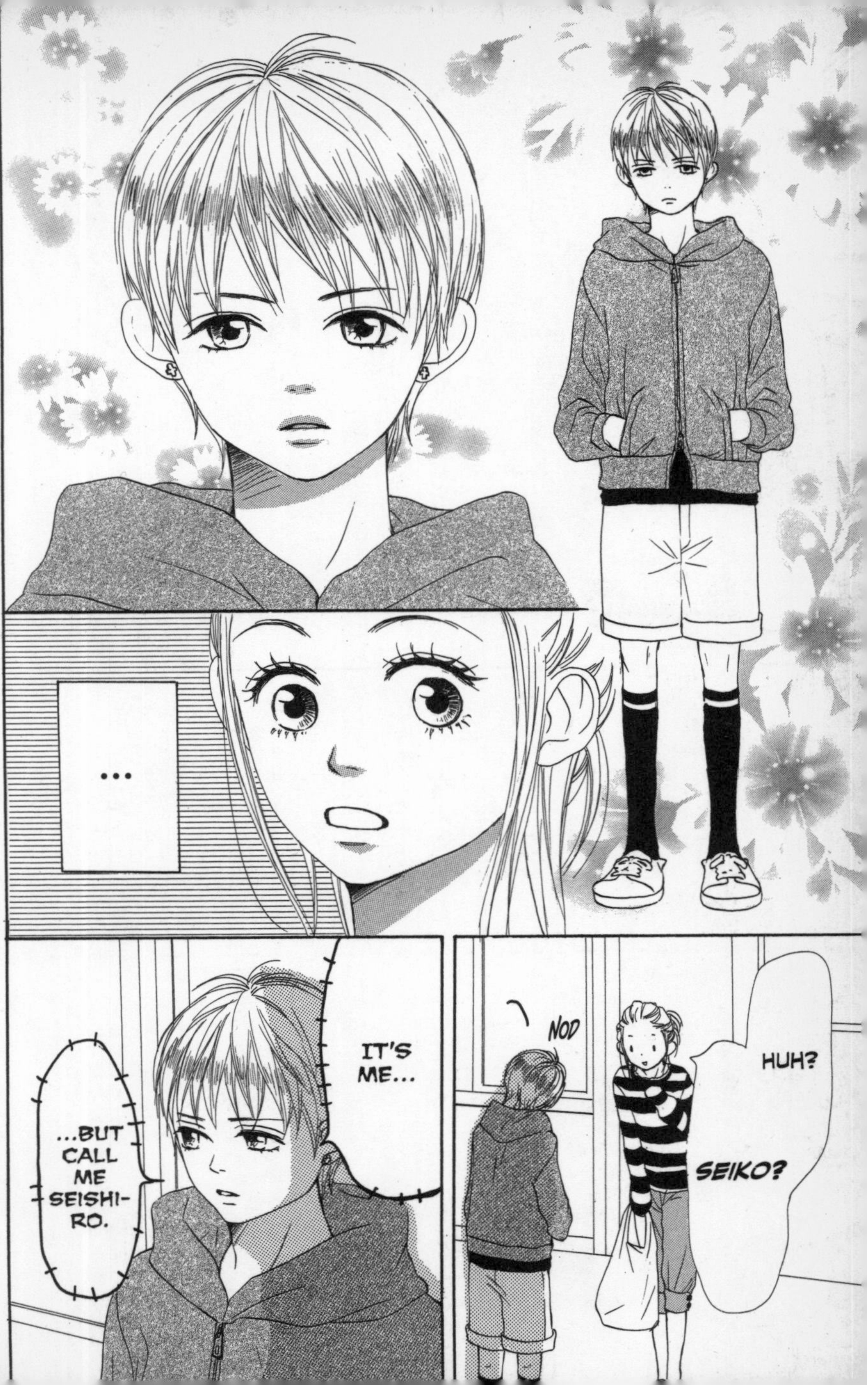
...
HUH?
SEIKO?
NOD
IT'S ME...
...BUT CALL ME SEISHIRO.

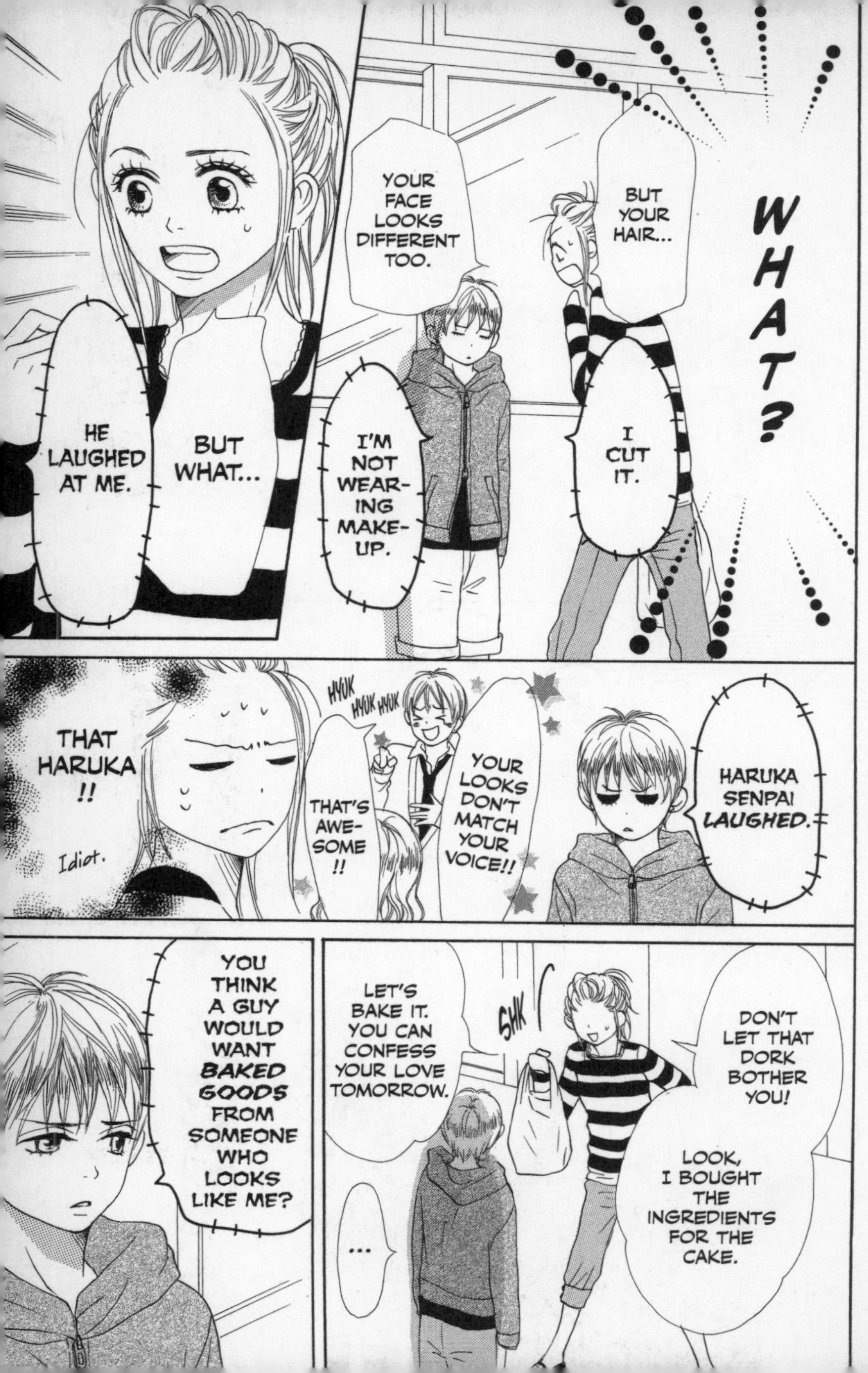
BUT YOUR HAIR...
I CUT IT.
YOUR FACE LOOKS DIFFERENT TOO.
I'M NOT WEARING MAKE-UP.
WHAT?
BUT WHAT...
HE LAUGHED AT ME.
HARUKA SENPAI LAUGHED.
YOUR LOOKS DON'T MATCH YOUR VOICE!!
HYUK HYUK HYUK
THAT'S AWESOME!!
THAT HARUKA!!
Idiot.
DON'T LET THAT DORK BOTHER YOU!
LOOK, I BOUGHT THE INGREDIENTS FOR THE CAKE.
SHK
LET'S BAKE IT. YOU CAN CONFESS YOUR LOVE TOMORROW.
...
YOU THINK A GUY WOULD WANT BAKED GOODS FROM SOMEONE WHO LOOKS LIKE ME?

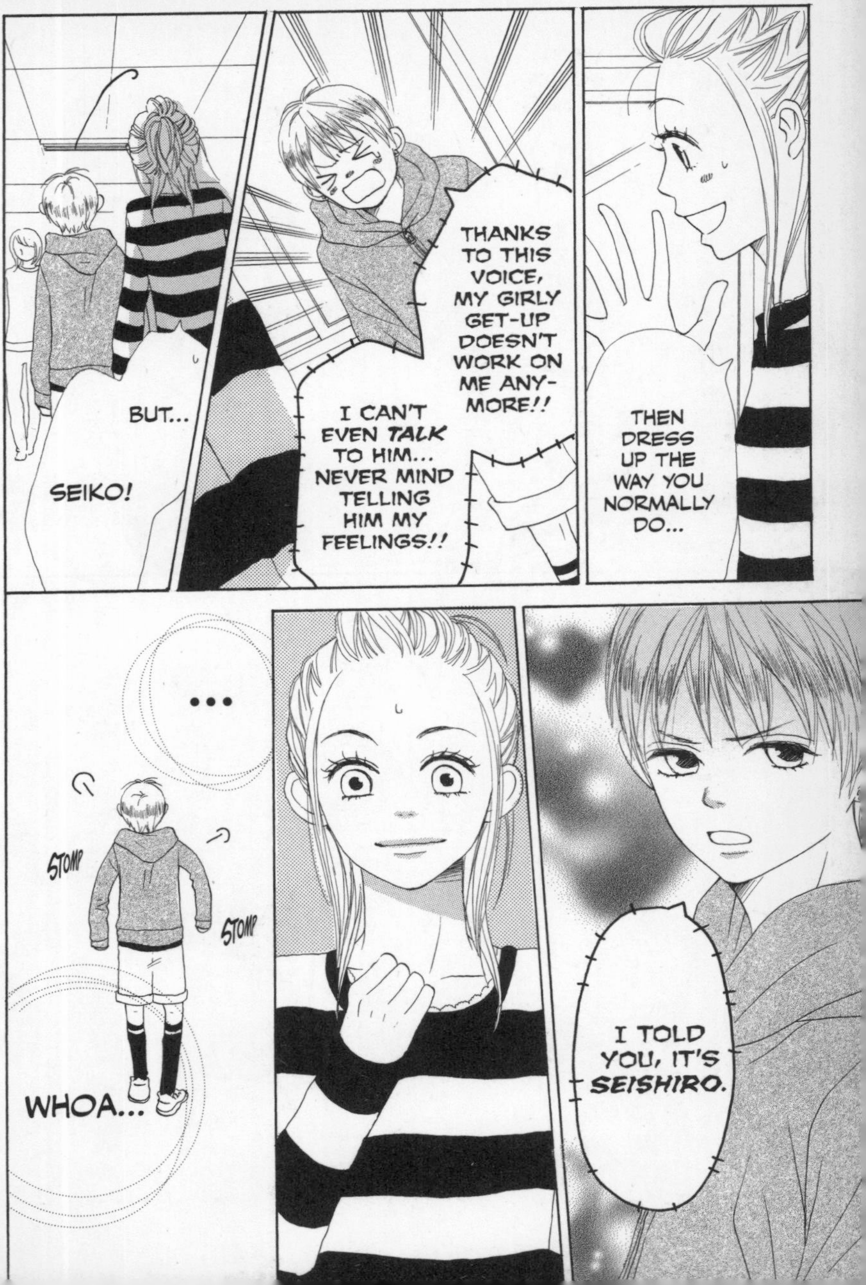
THEN DRESS UP THE WAY YOU NORMALLY DO...
THANKS TO THIS VOICE, MY GIRLY GET-UP DOESN'T WORK ON ME ANY-MORE!!
I CAN'T EVEN TALK TO HIM... NEVER MIND TELLING HIM MY FEELINGS!!
BUT...
SEIKO!
I TOLD YOU, IT'S SEISHIRO.
...
STOMP
STOMP
WHOA...

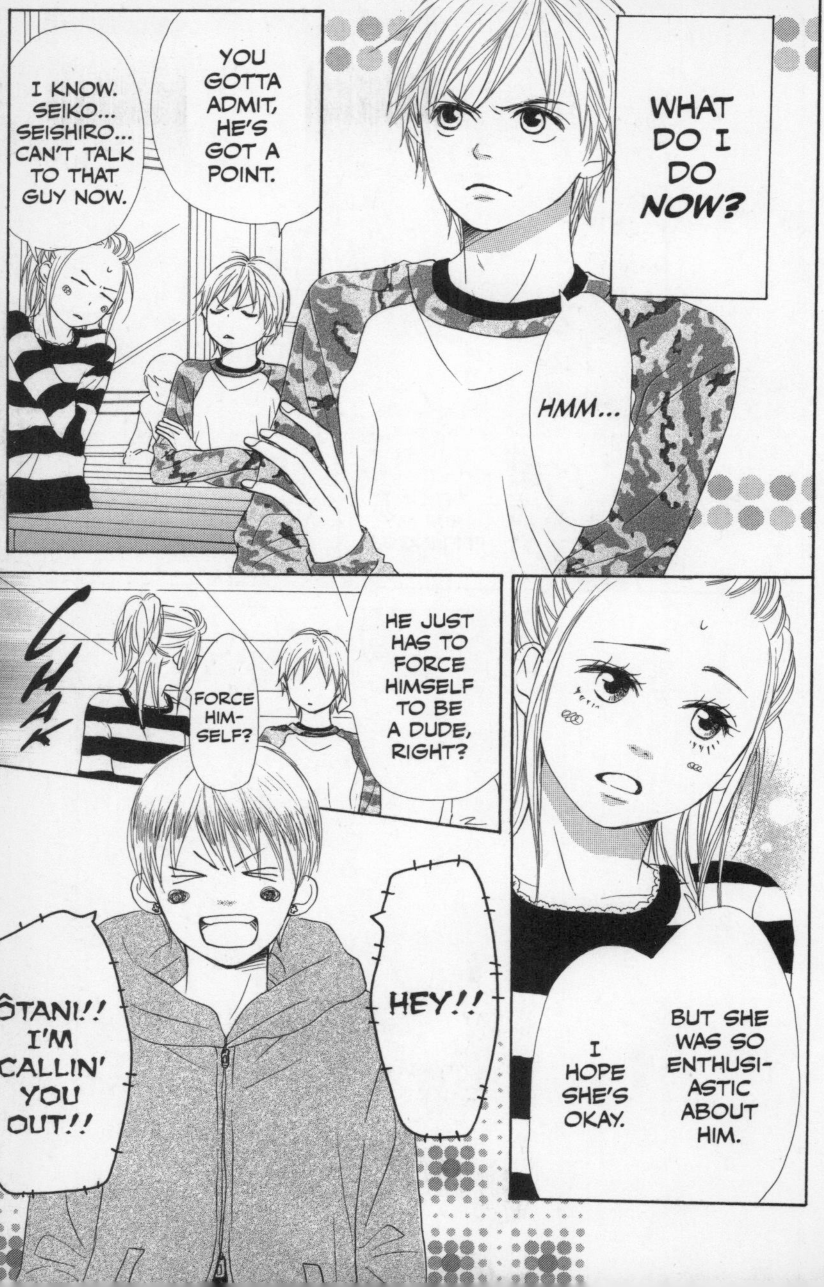
WHAT DO I DO NOW?
YOU GOTTA ADMIT, HE'S GOT A POINT.
I KNOW. SEIKO... SEISHIRO... CAN'T TALK TO THAT GUY NOW.
HMM...
BUT SHE WAS SO ENTHUSI-ASTIC ABOUT HIM.
I HOPE SHE'S OKAY.
HE JUST HAS TO FORCE HIMSELF TO BE A DUDE, RIGHT?
FORCE HIM-SELF?
CHAK
HEY!!
ÔTANI!! I'M CALLIN' YOU OUT!!

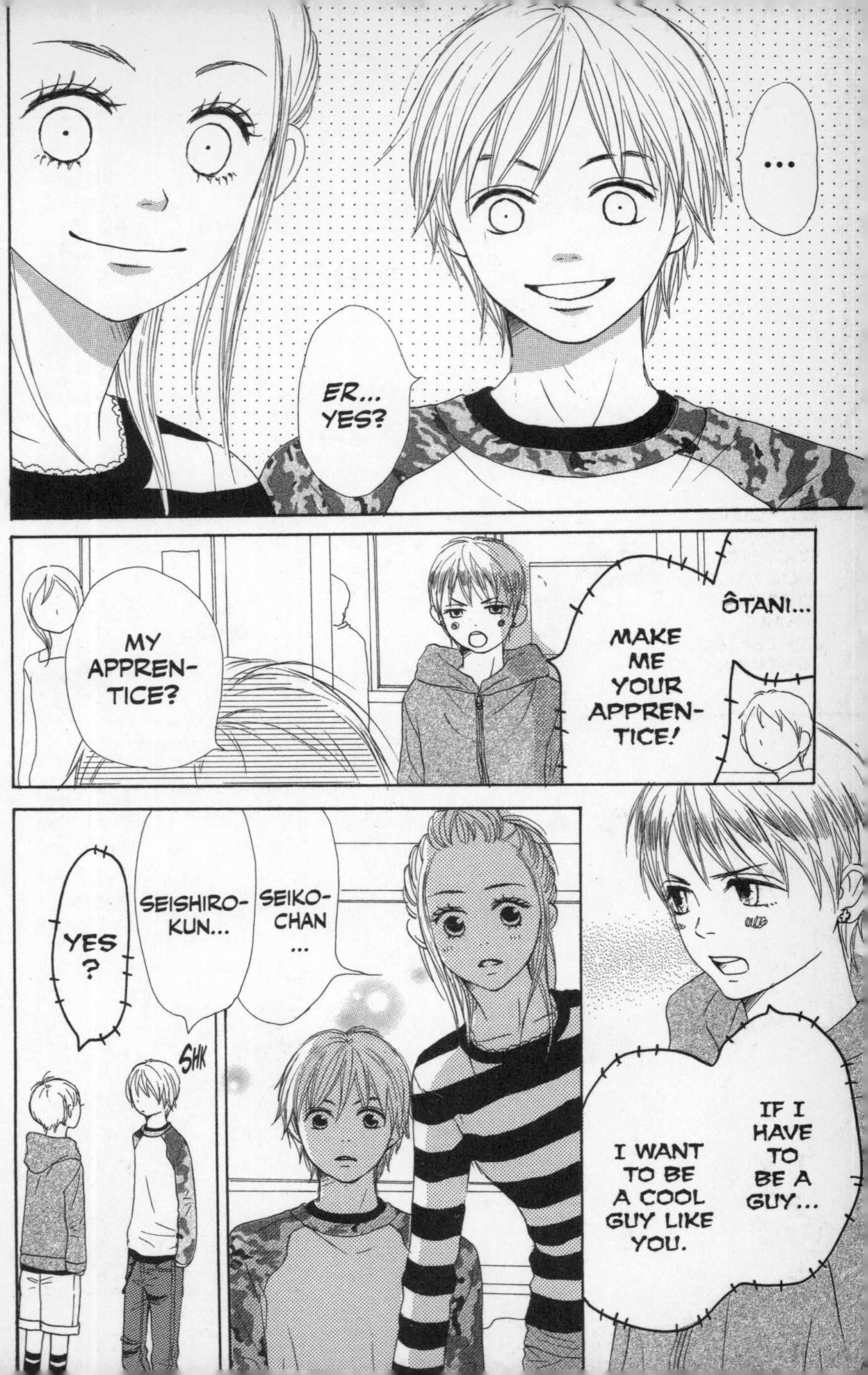
...
ER... YES?
ÔTANI...
MAKE ME YOUR APPREN-TICE!
MY APPREN-TICE?
IF I HAVE TO BE A GUY...
I WANT TO BE A COOL GUY LIKE YOU.
SEIKO-CHAN ...
SEISHIRO-KUN...
YES ?
SHK

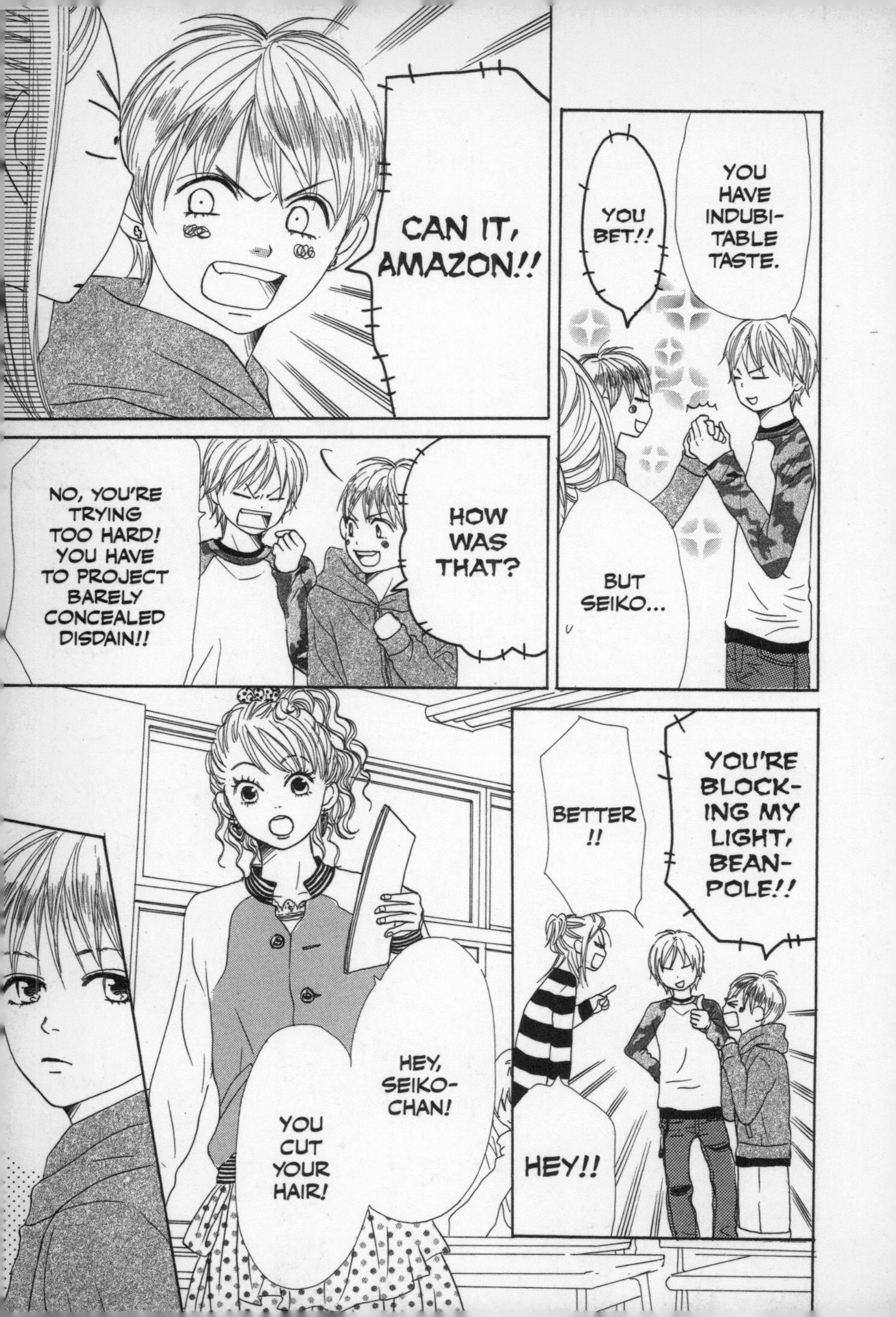
YOU HAVE INDUBITABLE TASTE.
YOU BET!!
BUT SEIKO...
CAN IT, AMAZON!!
HOW WAS THAT?
NO, YOU'RE TRYING TOO HARD! YOU HAVE TO PROJECT BARELY CONCEALED DISDAIN!!
YOU'RE BLOCKING MY LIGHT, BEANPOLE!!
BETTER!!
HEY!!
HEY, SEIKO-CHAN!
YOU CUT YOUR HAIR!

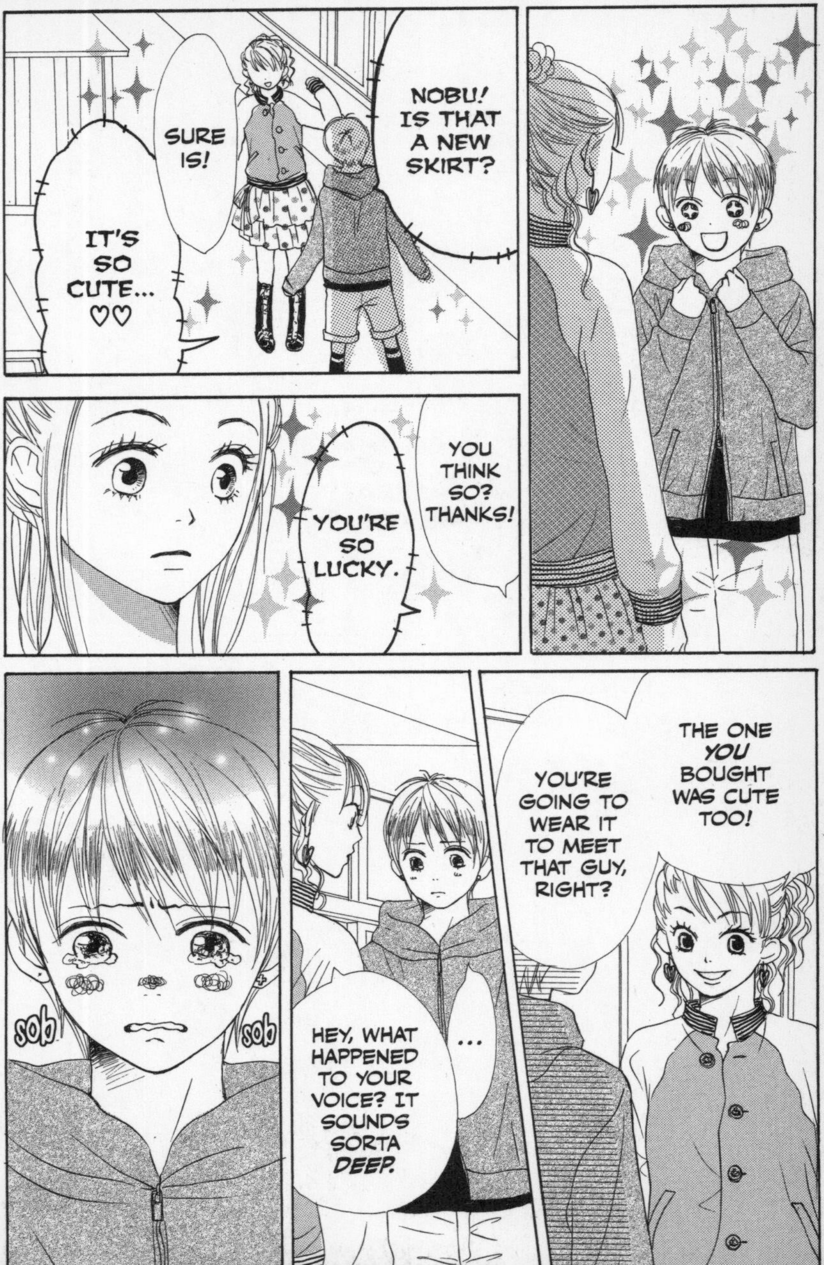
NOBU! IS THAT A NEW SKIRT?
SURE IS!
IT'S SO CUTE... ♡♡
YOU THINK SO? THANKS!
YOU'RE SO LUCKY.
THE ONE *YOU* BOUGHT WAS CUTE TOO!
YOU'RE GOING TO WEAR IT TO MEET THAT GUY, RIGHT?
...
HEY, WHAT HAPPENED TO YOUR VOICE? IT SOUNDS SORTA *DEEP*.
sob
sob

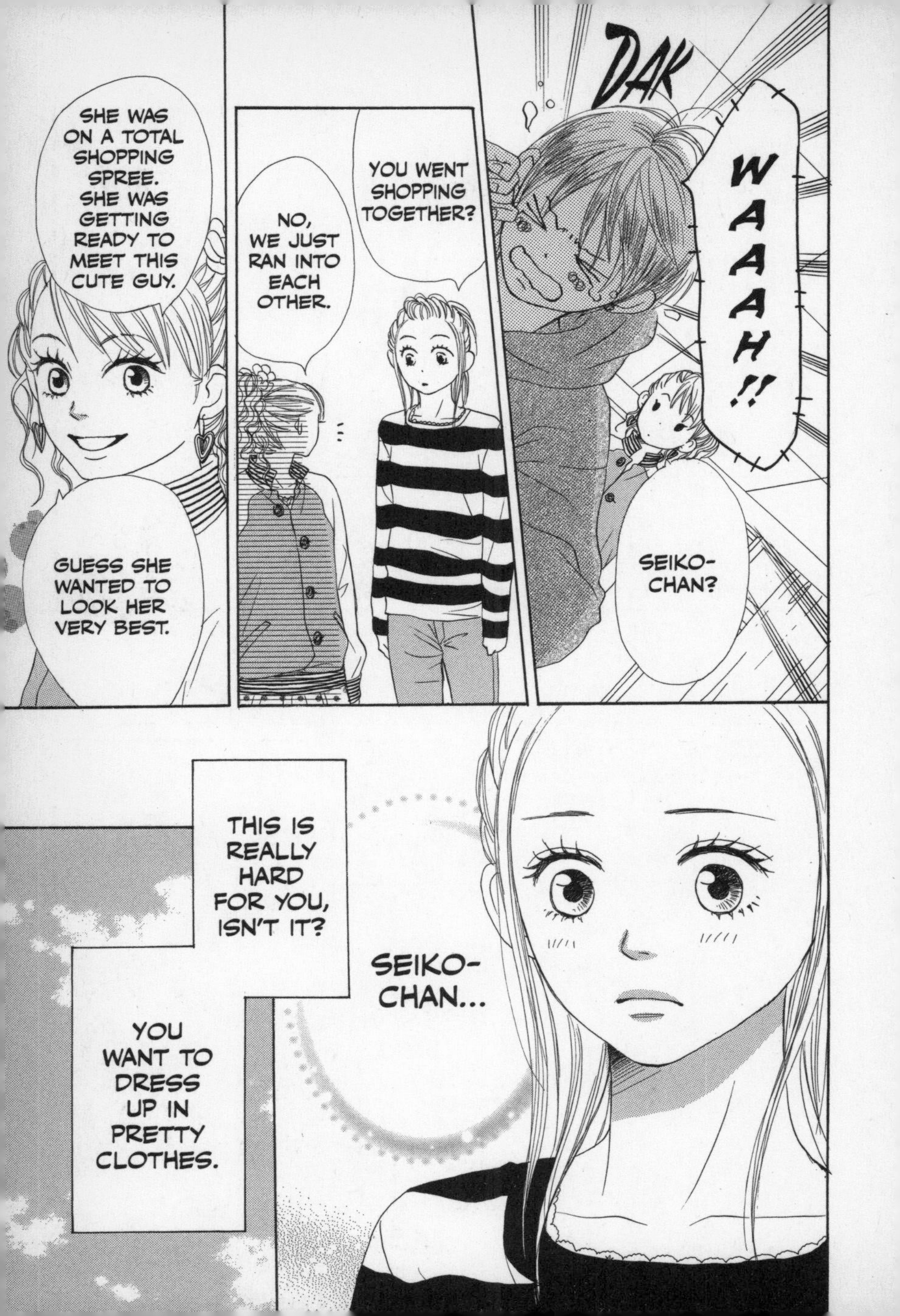
DAK
WAAAAH!!
SEIKO-CHAN?
YOU WENT SHOPPING TOGETHER?
NO, WE JUST RAN INTO EACH OTHER.
SHE WAS ON A TOTAL SHOPPING SPREE. SHE WAS GETTING READY TO MEET THIS CUTE GUY.
GUESS SHE WANTED TO LOOK HER VERY BEST.
SEIKO-CHAN...
THIS IS REALLY HARD FOR YOU, ISN'T IT?
YOU WANT TO DRESS UP IN PRETTY CLOTHES.

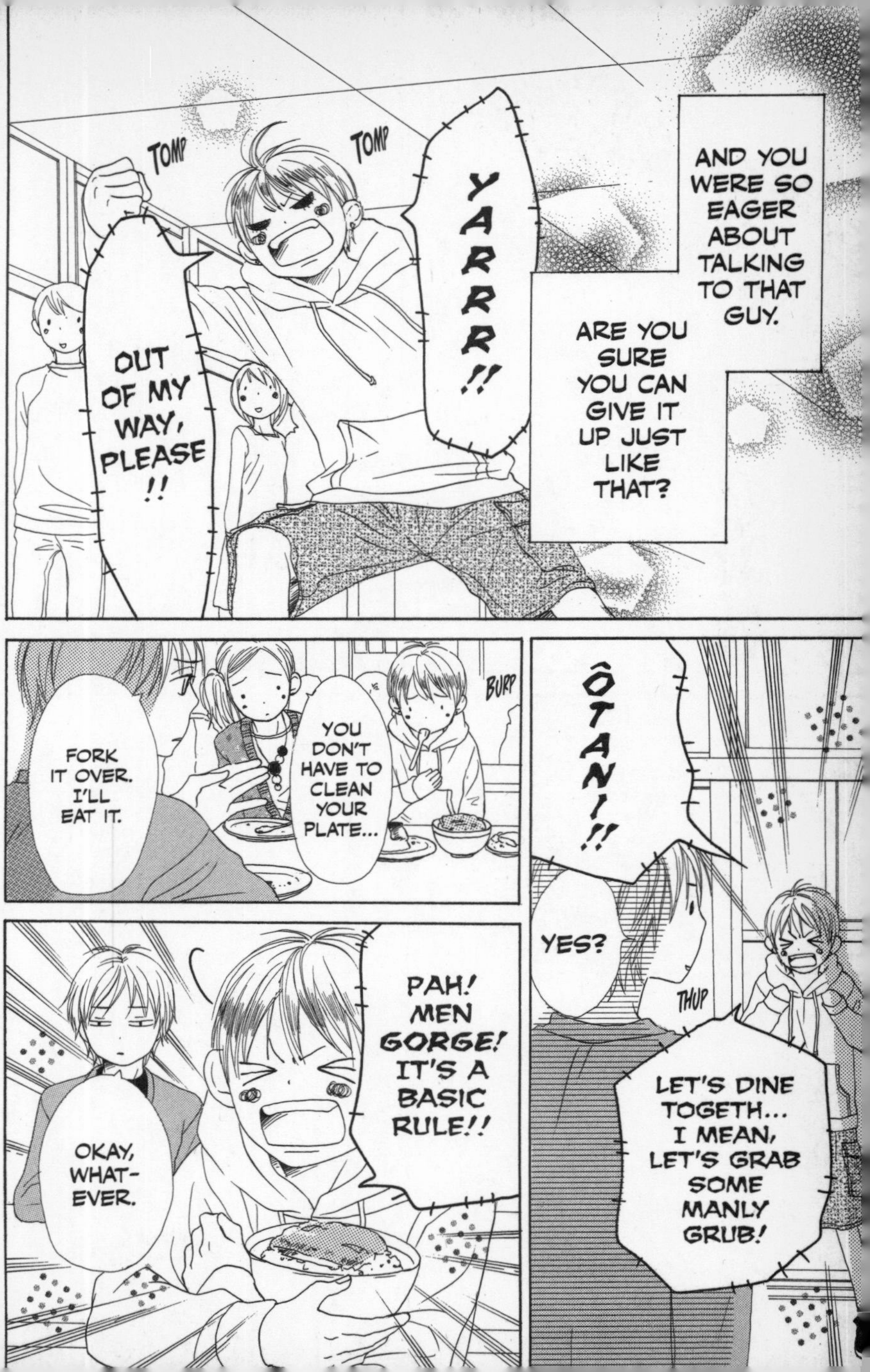
AND YOU WERE SO EAGER ABOUT TALKING TO THAT GUY.
ARE YOU SURE YOU CAN GIVE IT UP JUST LIKE THAT?
TOMP
TOMP
YARRR!!
OUT OF MY WAY, PLEASE!!
ÔTANI!!
YES?
THUP
LET'S DINE TOGETH... I MEAN, LET'S GRAB SOME MANLY GRUB!
BURP
YOU DON'T HAVE TO CLEAN YOUR PLATE...
FORK IT OVER. I'LL EAT IT.
PAH! MEN GORGE! IT'S A BASIC RULE!!
OKAY, WHAT-EVER.

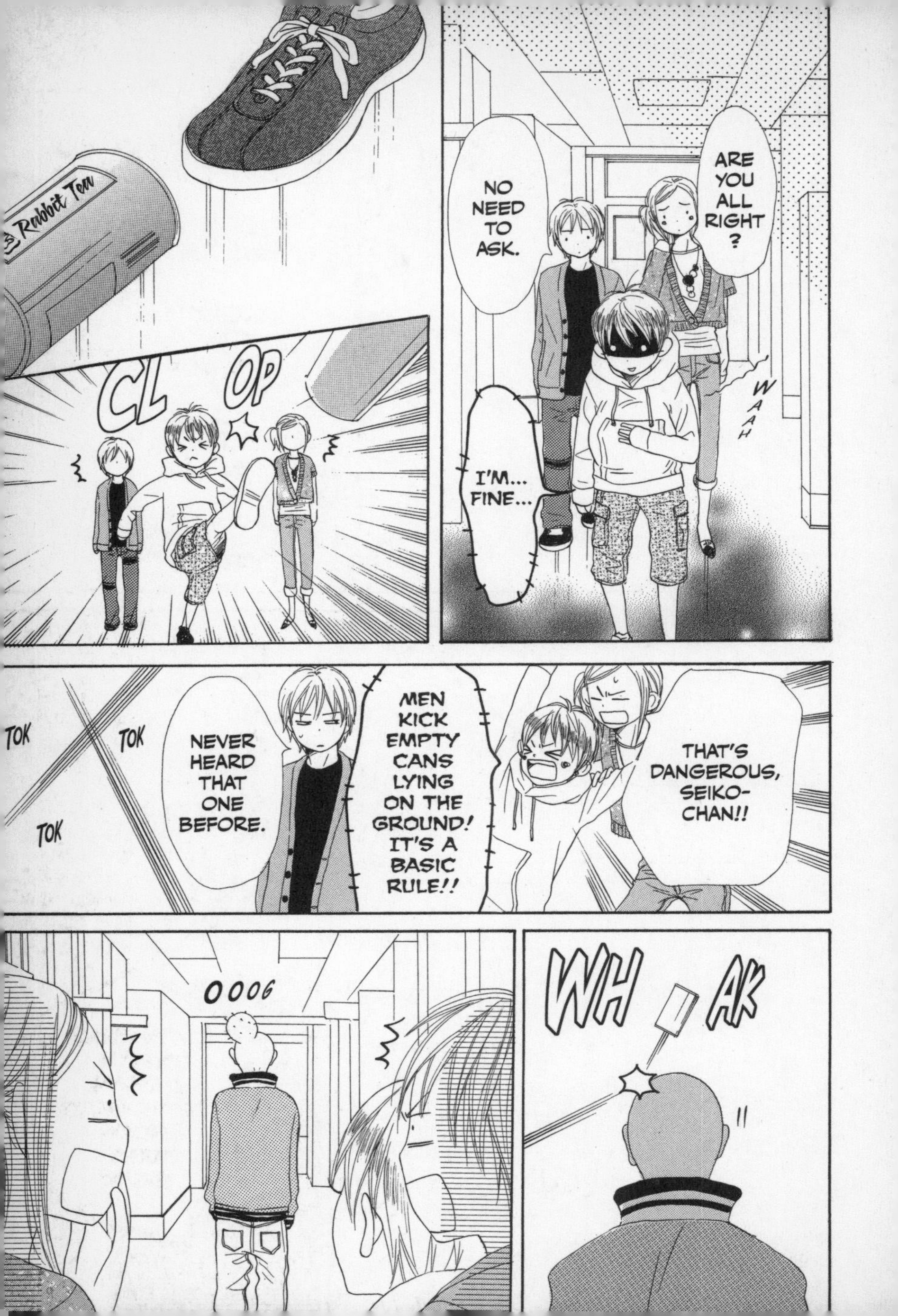
ARE YOU ALL RIGHT?
NO NEED TO ASK.
WAAH
I'M... FINE...
Rabbit Tea
CL OP
THAT'S DANGEROUS, SEIKO-CHAN!!
MEN KICK EMPTY CANS LYING ON THE GROUND! IT'S A BASIC RULE!!
NEVER HEARD THAT ONE BEFORE.
TOK
TOK
TOK
WH AK
OOOG

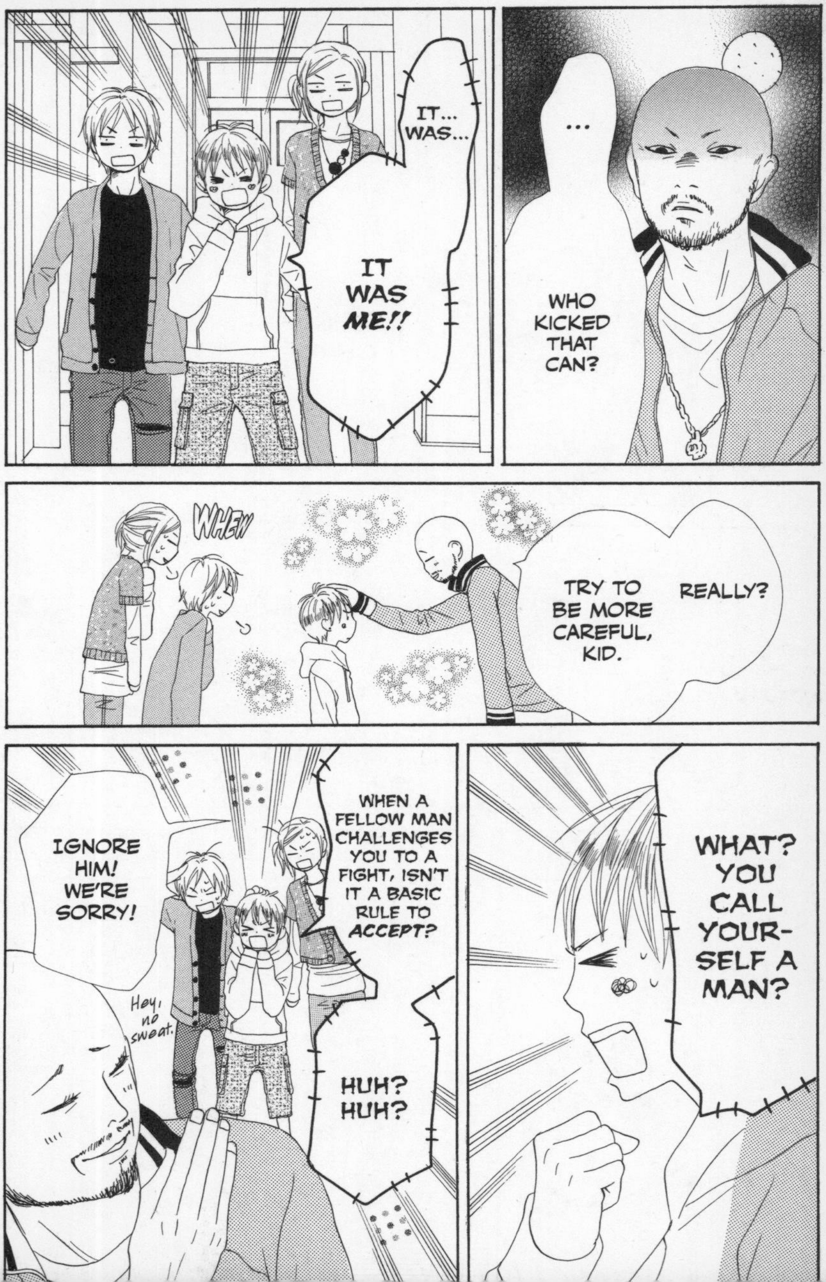
...
WHO KICKED THAT CAN?
IT... WAS...
IT WAS *ME!!*
REALLY?
TRY TO BE MORE CAREFUL, KID.
WHEW
WHAT? YOU CALL YOURSELF A MAN?
WHEN A FELLOW MAN CHALLENGES YOU TO A FIGHT, ISN'T IT A BASIC RULE TO *ACCEPT?*
HUH? HUH?
IGNORE HIM! WE'RE SORRY!
Hey, no sweat.

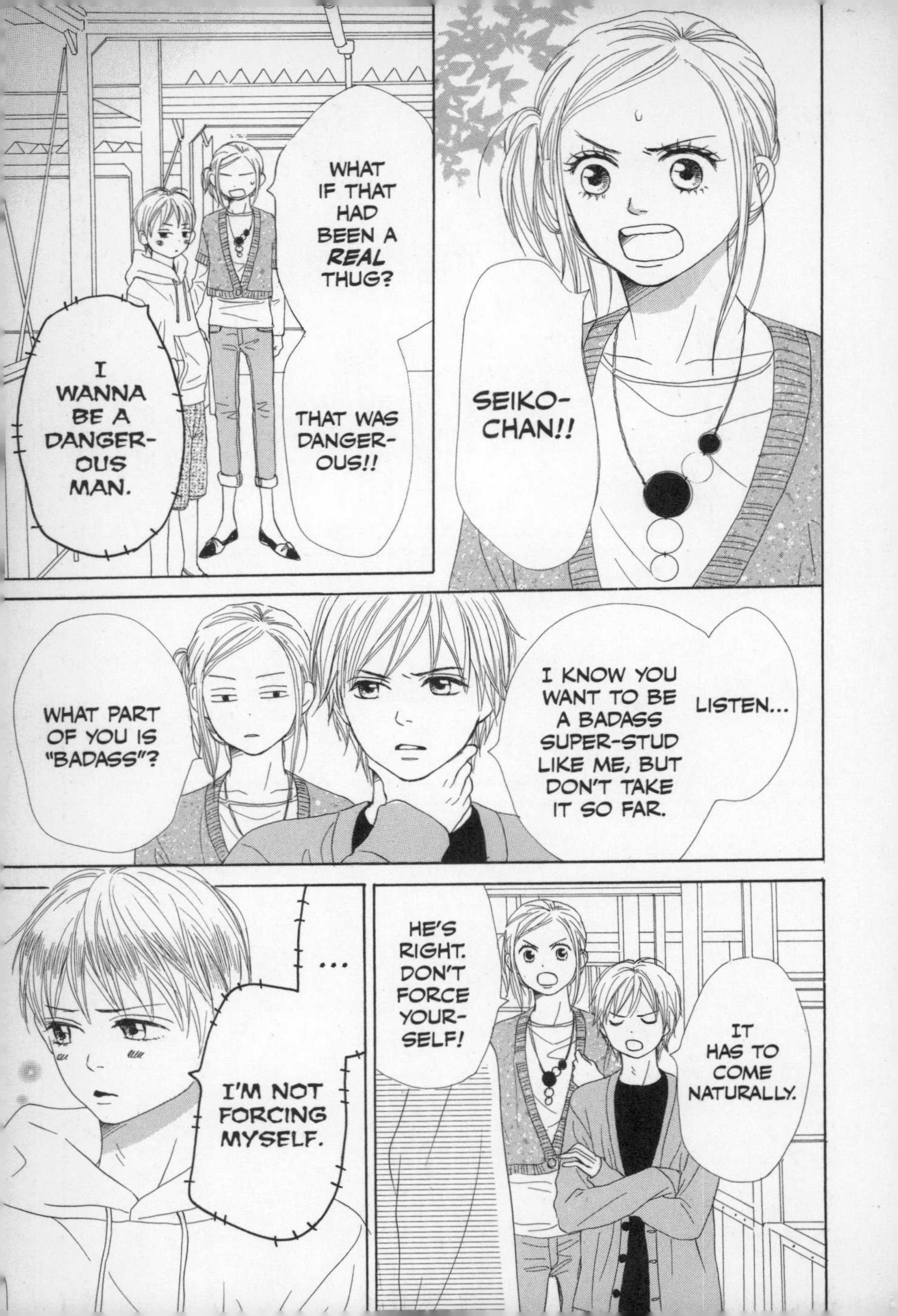
SEIKO-CHAN!!
WHAT IF THAT HAD BEEN A *REAL* THUG?
THAT WAS DANGEROUS!!
I WANNA BE A DANGEROUS MAN.
LISTEN...
I KNOW YOU WANT TO BE A BADASS SUPER-STUD LIKE ME, BUT DON'T TAKE IT SO FAR.
WHAT PART OF YOU IS "BADASS"?
IT HAS TO COME NATURALLY.
HE'S RIGHT. DON'T FORCE YOURSELF!
...
I'M NOT FORCING MYSELF.

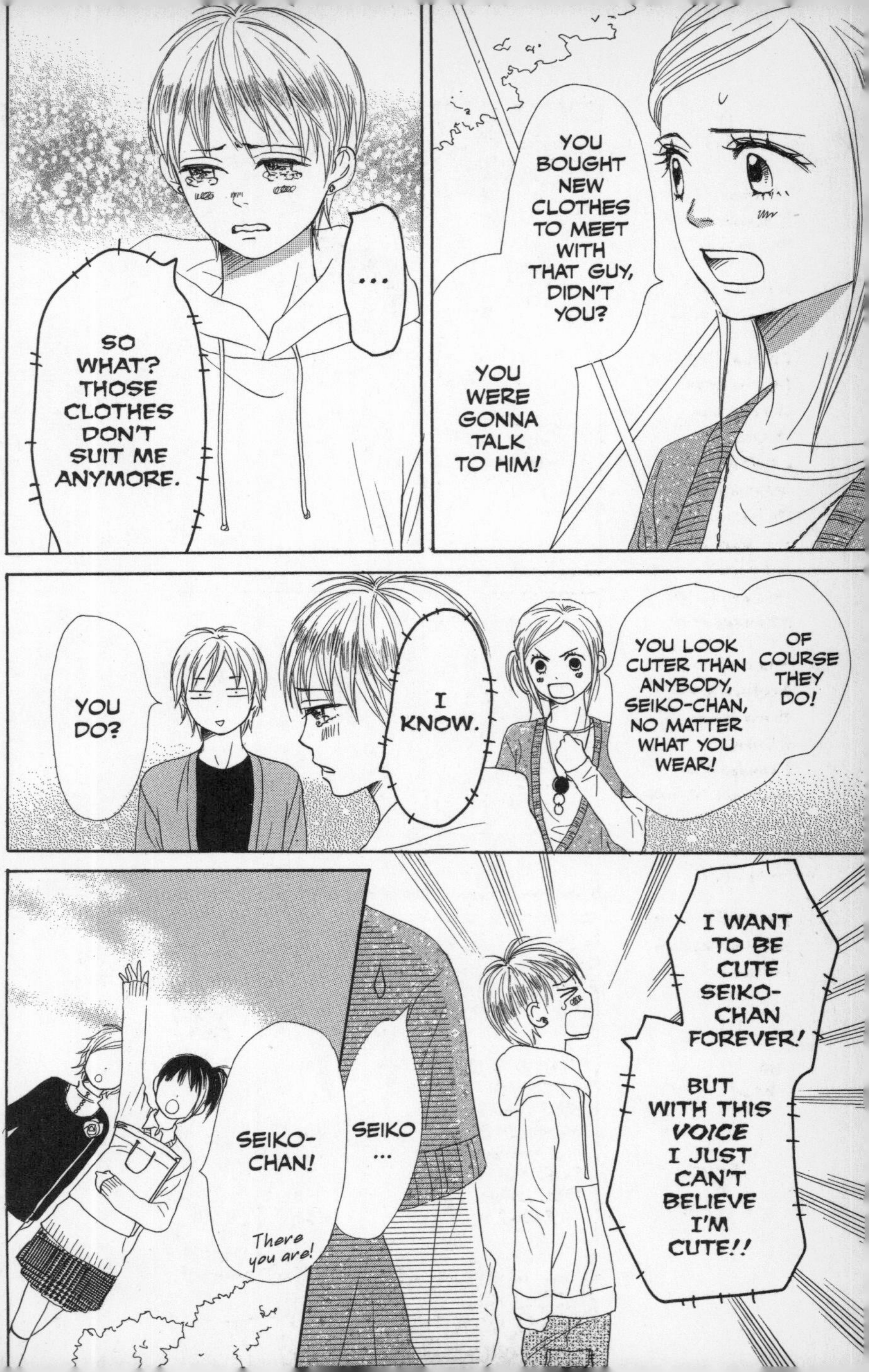
YOU BOUGHT NEW CLOTHES TO MEET WITH THAT GUY, DIDN'T YOU?
YOU WERE GONNA TALK TO HIM!
...
SO WHAT? THOSE CLOTHES DON'T SUIT ME ANYMORE.
OF COURSE THEY DO!
YOU LOOK CUTER THAN ANYBODY, SEIKO-CHAN, NO MATTER WHAT YOU WEAR!
I KNOW.
YOU DO?
I WANT TO BE CUTE SEIKO-CHAN FOREVER!
BUT WITH THIS VOICE I JUST CAN'T BELIEVE I'M CUTE!!
SEIKO...
SEIKO-CHAN!
There you are!

Hi! Nakahara here. It's been a while. How are you?

We're up to volume 15. Wow.

I actually just finished drawing the very last chapter of Love♥Com for the magazine. But since I have this graphic novel collection to work on, I don't feel like it's ended at all.

And even after this book is out, there are two volumes left. I wonder when I'll finally get to think, "Wow, it's over. What a long trip it's been..."

I guess I'll wait and save the nostalgia for later.

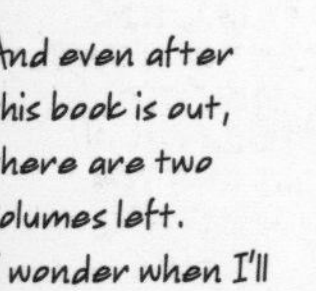
ha
ha

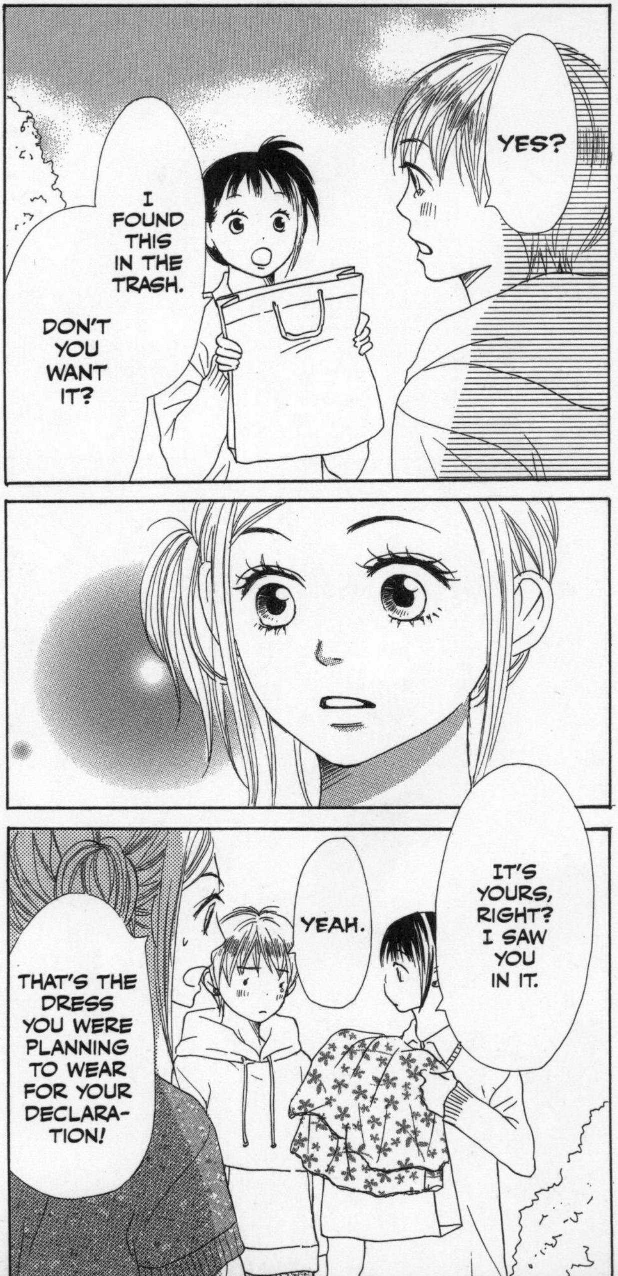
YES?
I FOUND THIS IN THE TRASH.
DON'T YOU WANT IT?
IT'S YOURS, RIGHT? I SAW YOU IN IT.
YEAH.
THAT'S THE DRESS YOU WERE PLANNING TO WEAR FOR YOUR DECLARA-TION!

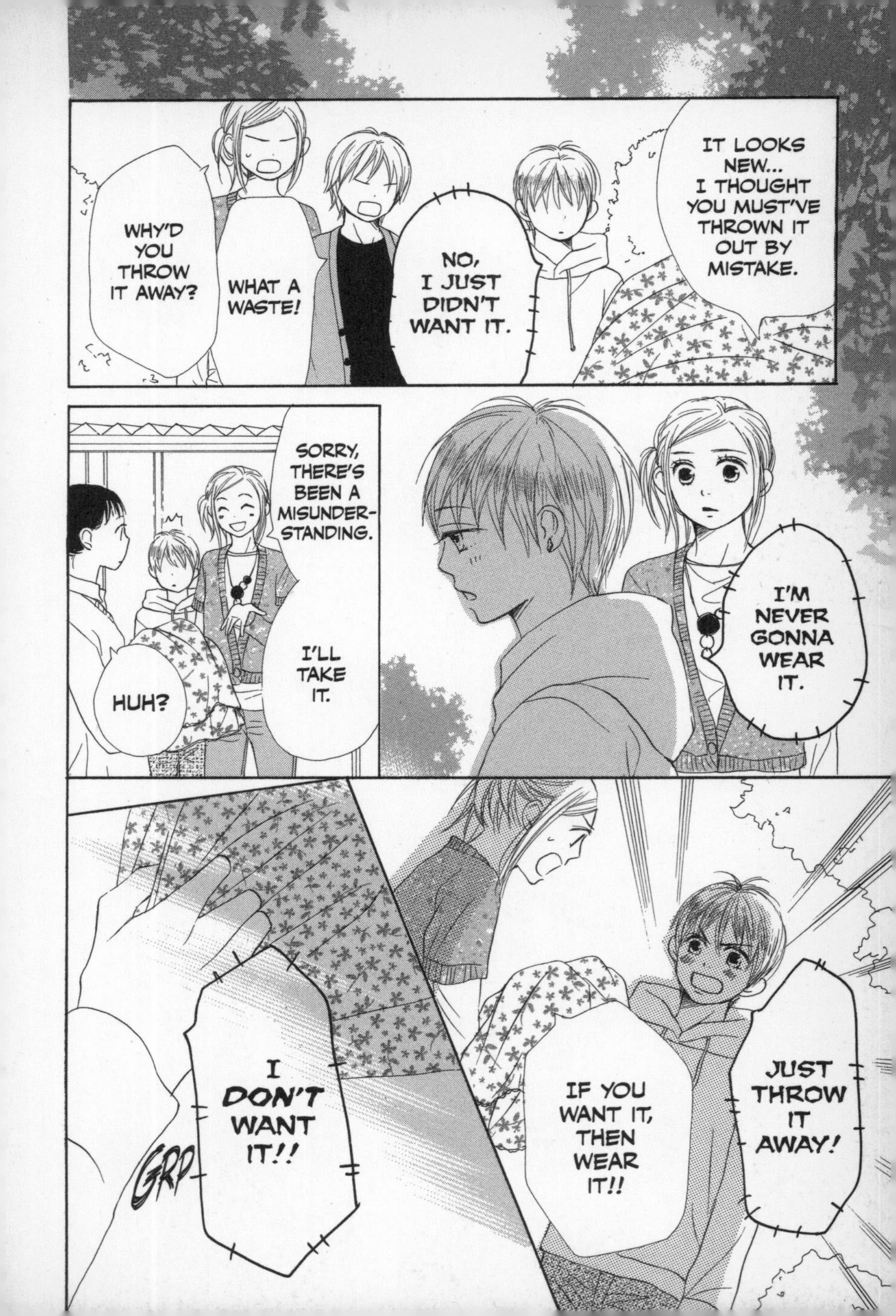
IT LOOKS NEW... I THOUGHT YOU MUST'VE THROWN IT OUT BY MISTAKE.
NO, I JUST DIDN'T WANT IT.
WHAT A WASTE!
WHY'D YOU THROW IT AWAY?
I'M NEVER GONNA WEAR IT.
SORRY, THERE'S BEEN A MISUNDER-STANDING.
I'LL TAKE IT.
HUH?
JUST THROW IT AWAY!
IF YOU WANT IT, THEN WEAR IT!!
I *DON'T* WANT IT!!
GRP

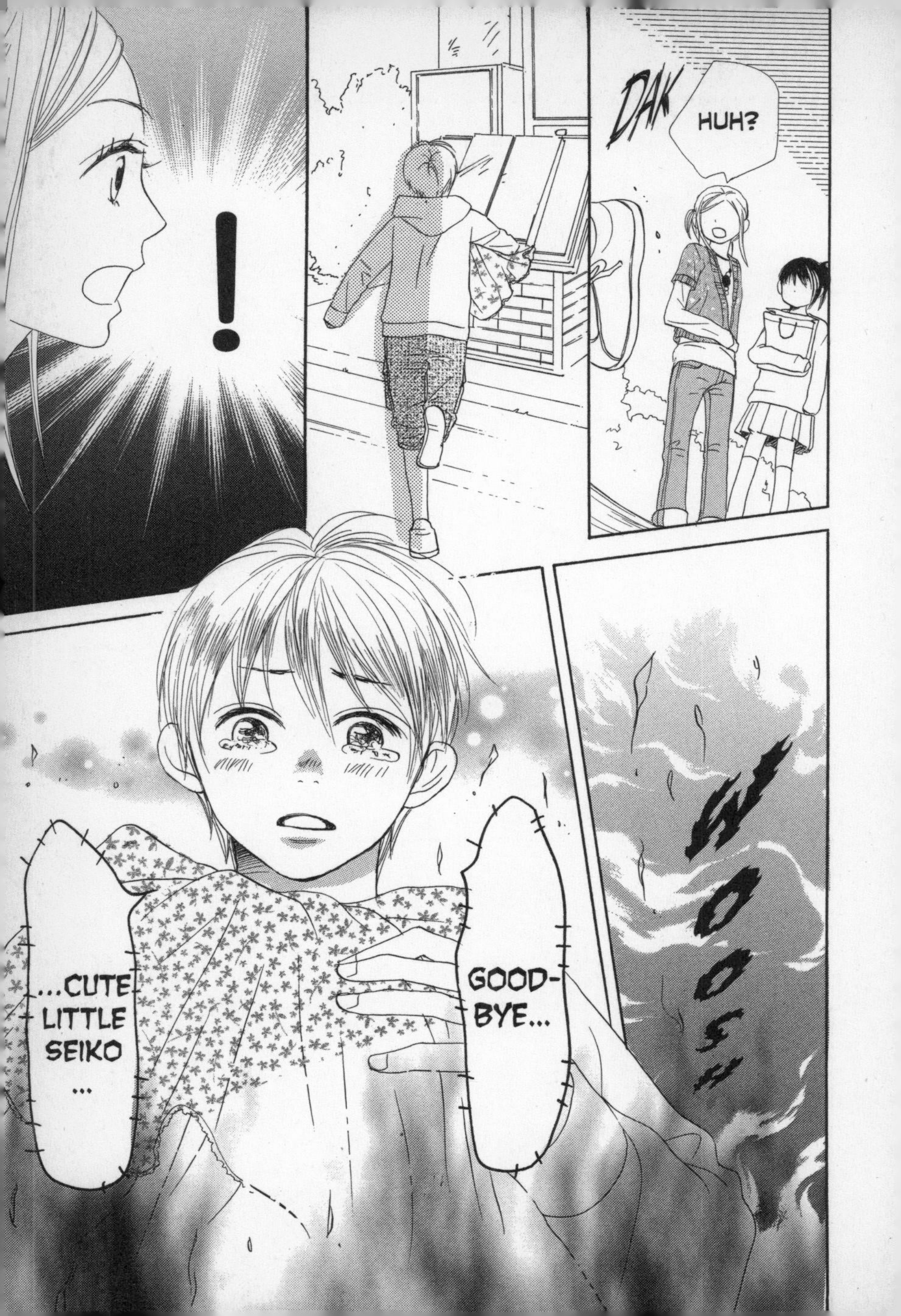
DAK
HUH?
!
WHOOSH
GOOD-BYE...
...CUTE LITTLE SEIKO...

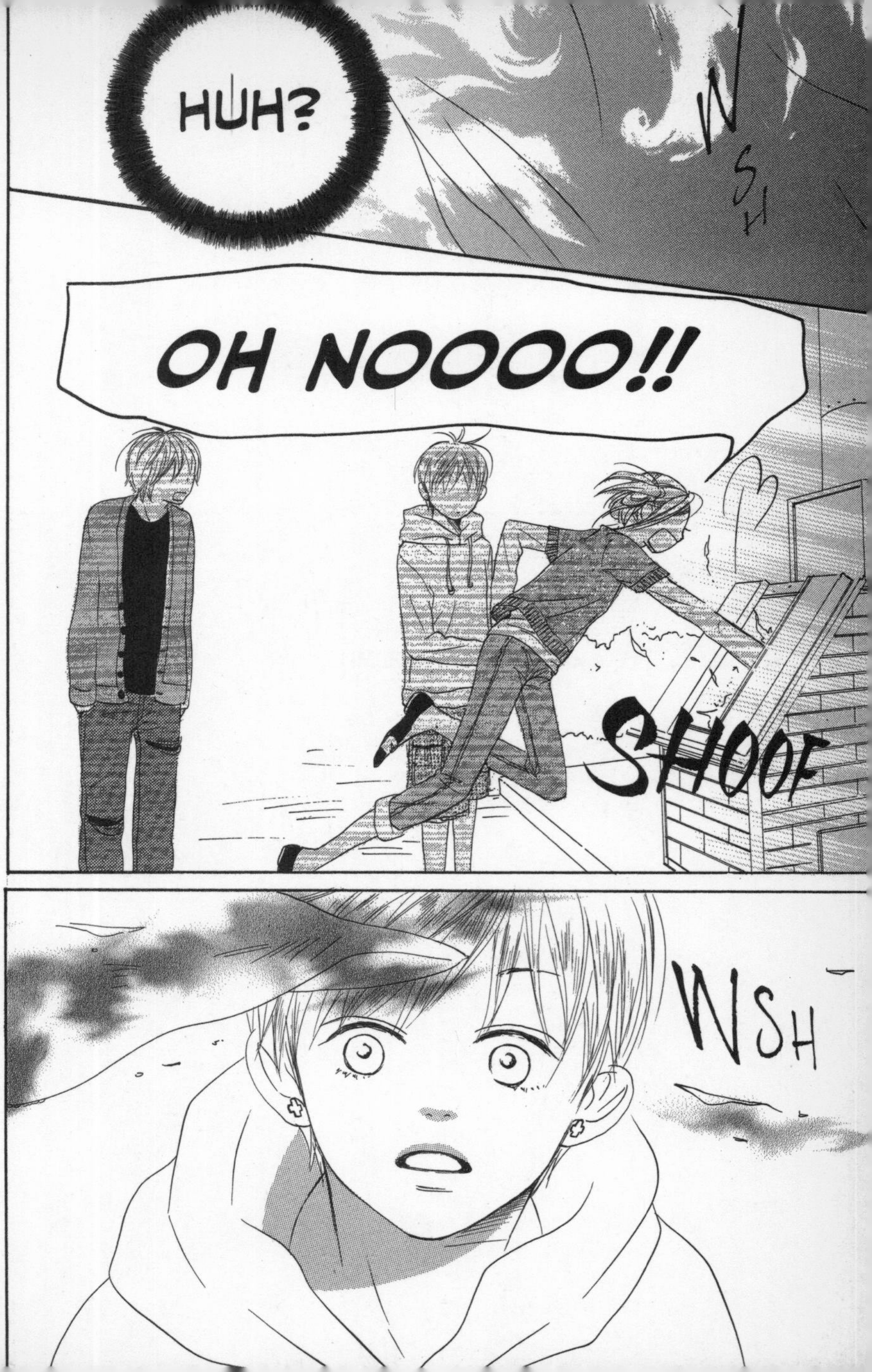
WSH
HUH?
OH NOOOO!!
SHOOF
WSH

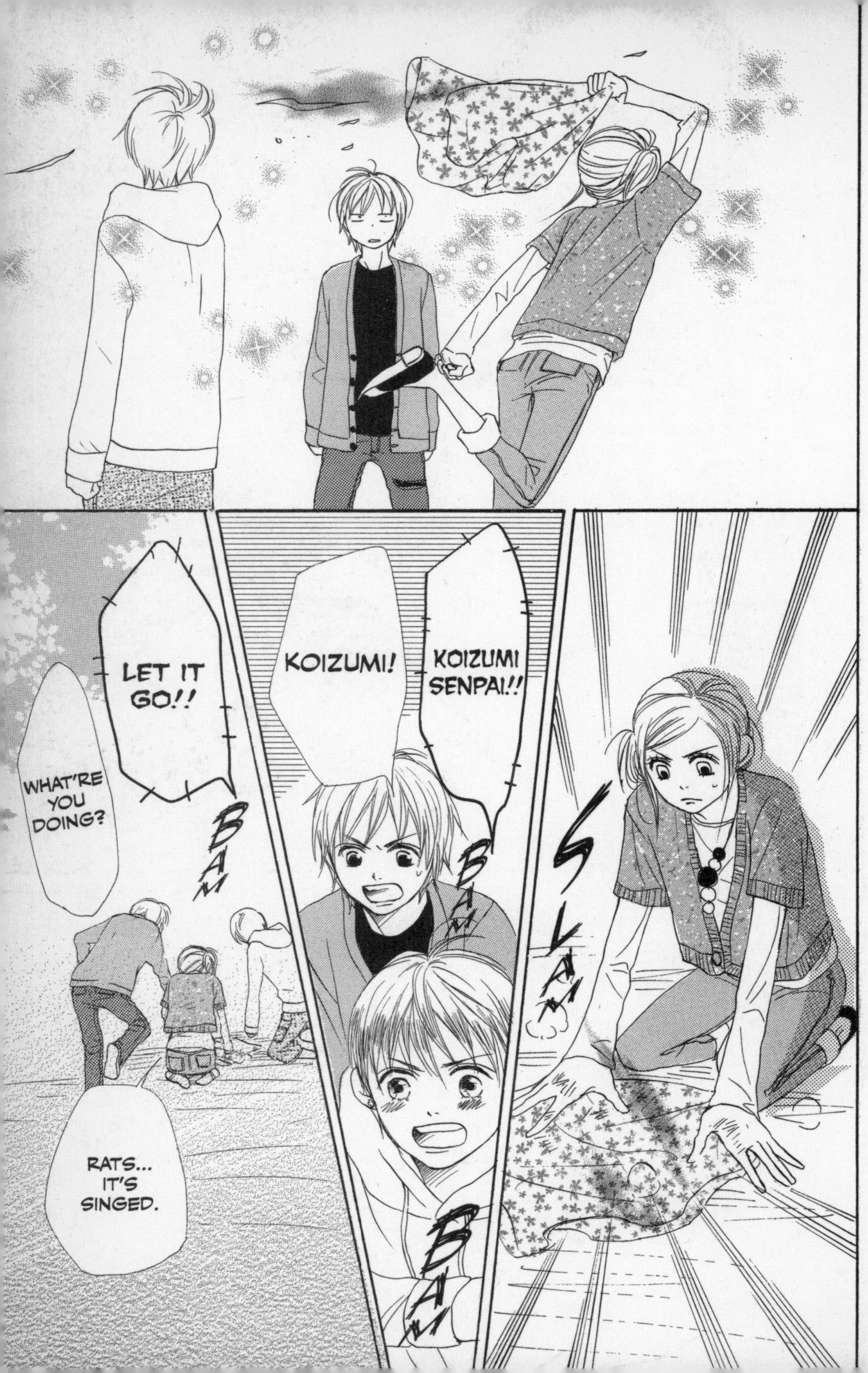
SLAM
KOIZUMI SENPAI!!
KOIZUMI!
BAM
BAM
LET IT GO!!
BAM
WHAT'RE YOU DOING?
RATS... IT'S SINGED.

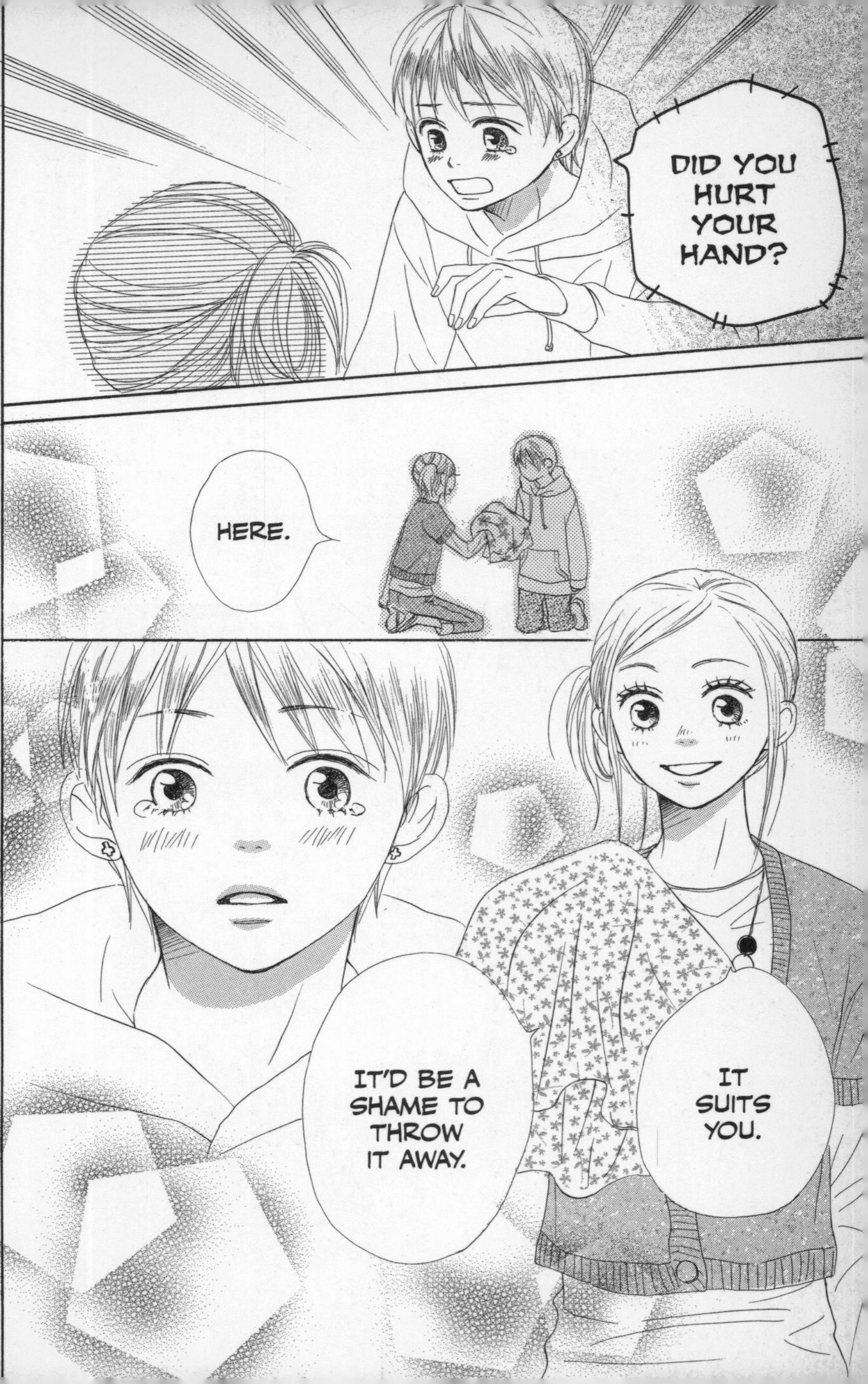
DID YOU HURT YOUR HAND?
HERE.
IT SUITS YOU.
IT'D BE A SHAME TO THROW IT AWAY.

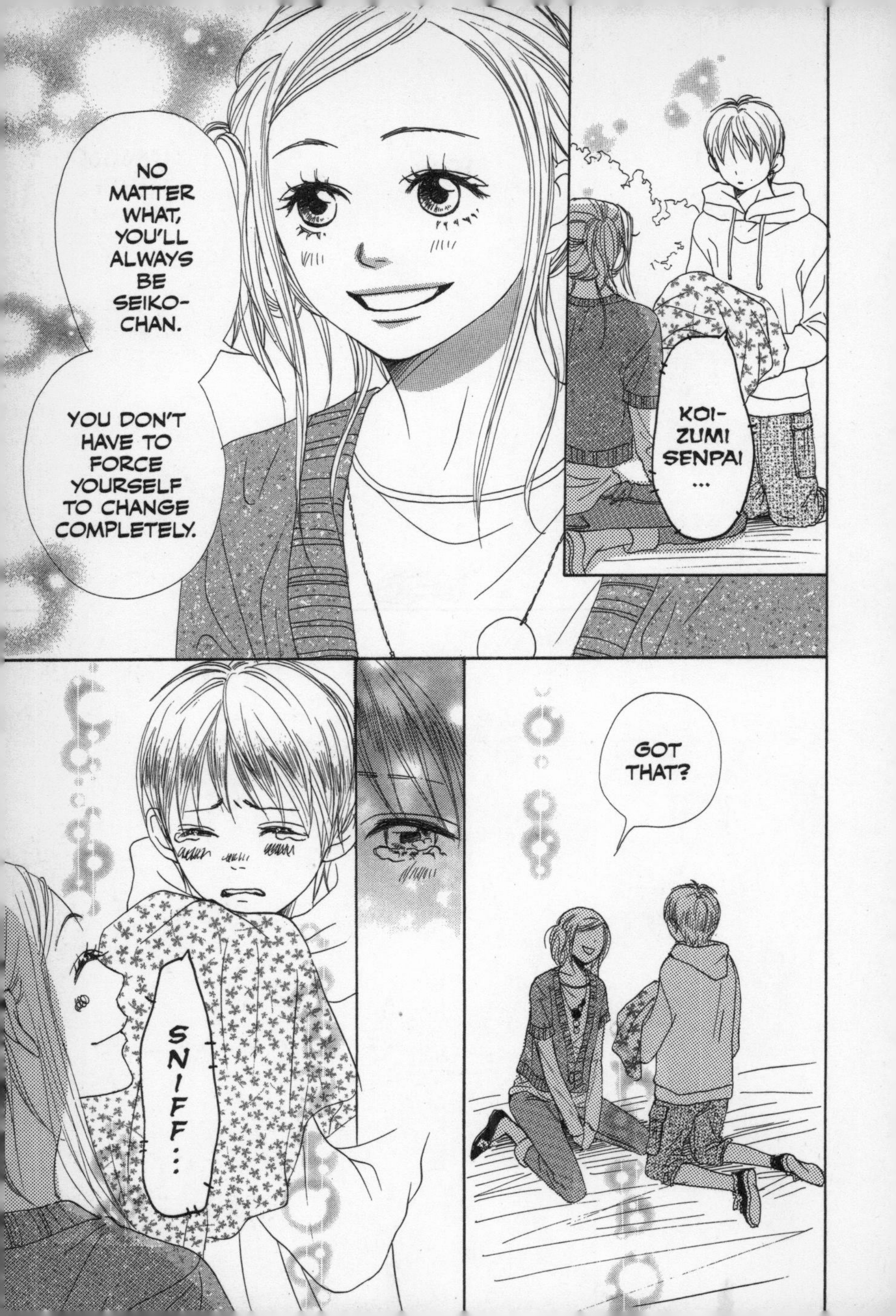
KOI-ZUMI SENPAI ...
NO MATTER WHAT, YOU'LL ALWAYS BE SEIKO-CHAN.
YOU DON'T HAVE TO FORCE YOURSELF TO CHANGE COMPLETELY.
GOT THAT?
SNIFF...

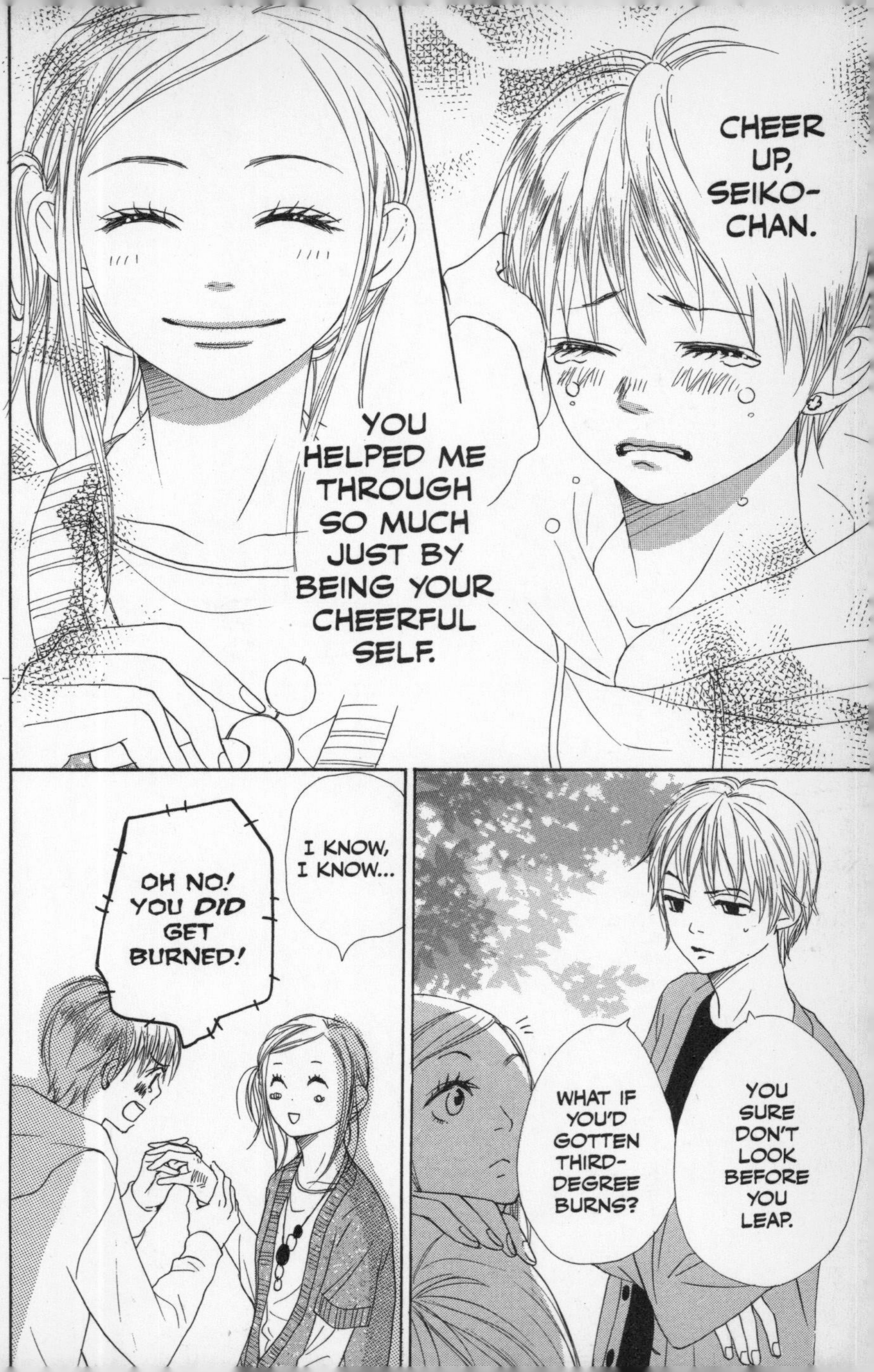
CHEER UP, SEIKO-CHAN.
YOU HELPED ME THROUGH SO MUCH JUST BY BEING YOUR CHEERFUL SELF.
YOU SURE DON'T LOOK BEFORE YOU LEAP.
WHAT IF YOU'D GOTTEN THIRD-DEGREE BURNS?
I KNOW, I KNOW...
OH NO! YOU *DID* GET BURNED!

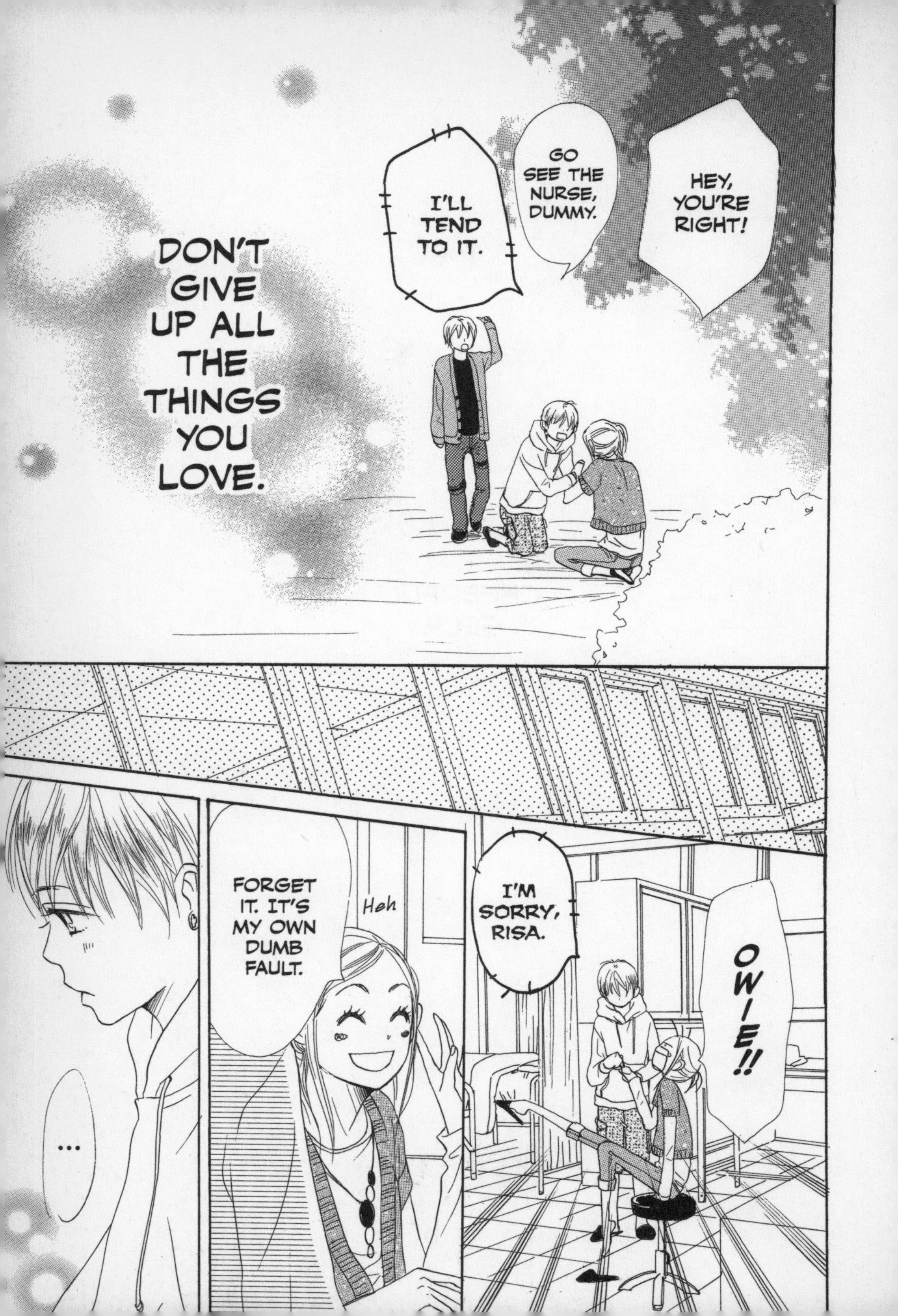
HEY, YOU'RE RIGHT!
GO SEE THE NURSE, DUMMY.
I'LL TEND TO IT.
DON'T GIVE UP ALL THE THINGS YOU LOVE.
OWIE!!
I'M SORRY, RISA.
FORGET IT. IT'S MY OWN DUMB FAULT.
Heh
...

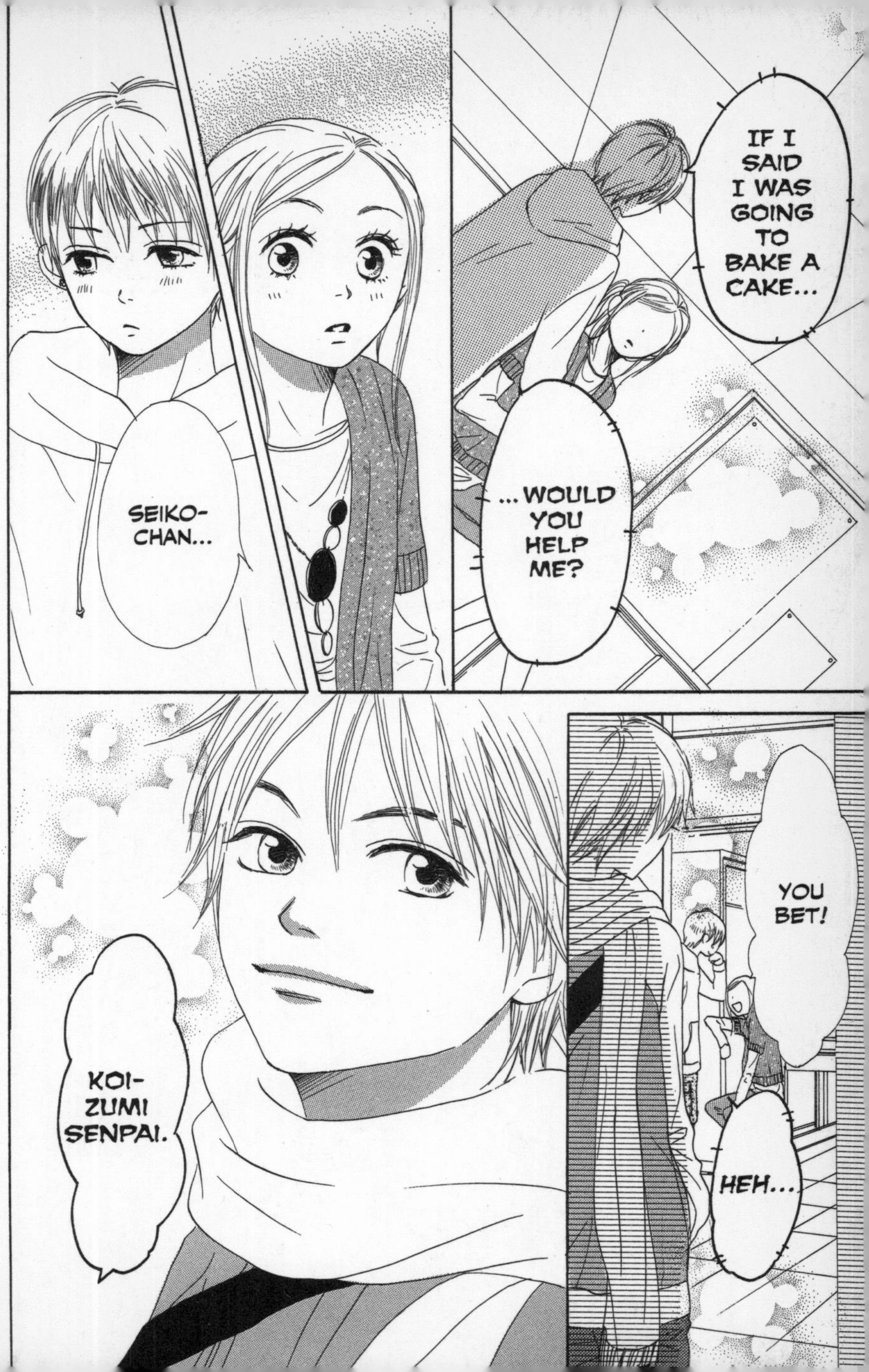
IF I SAID I WAS GOING TO BAKE A CAKE...
...WOULD YOU HELP ME?
SEIKO-CHAN...
YOU BET!
HEH...
KOI-ZUMI SENPAI.

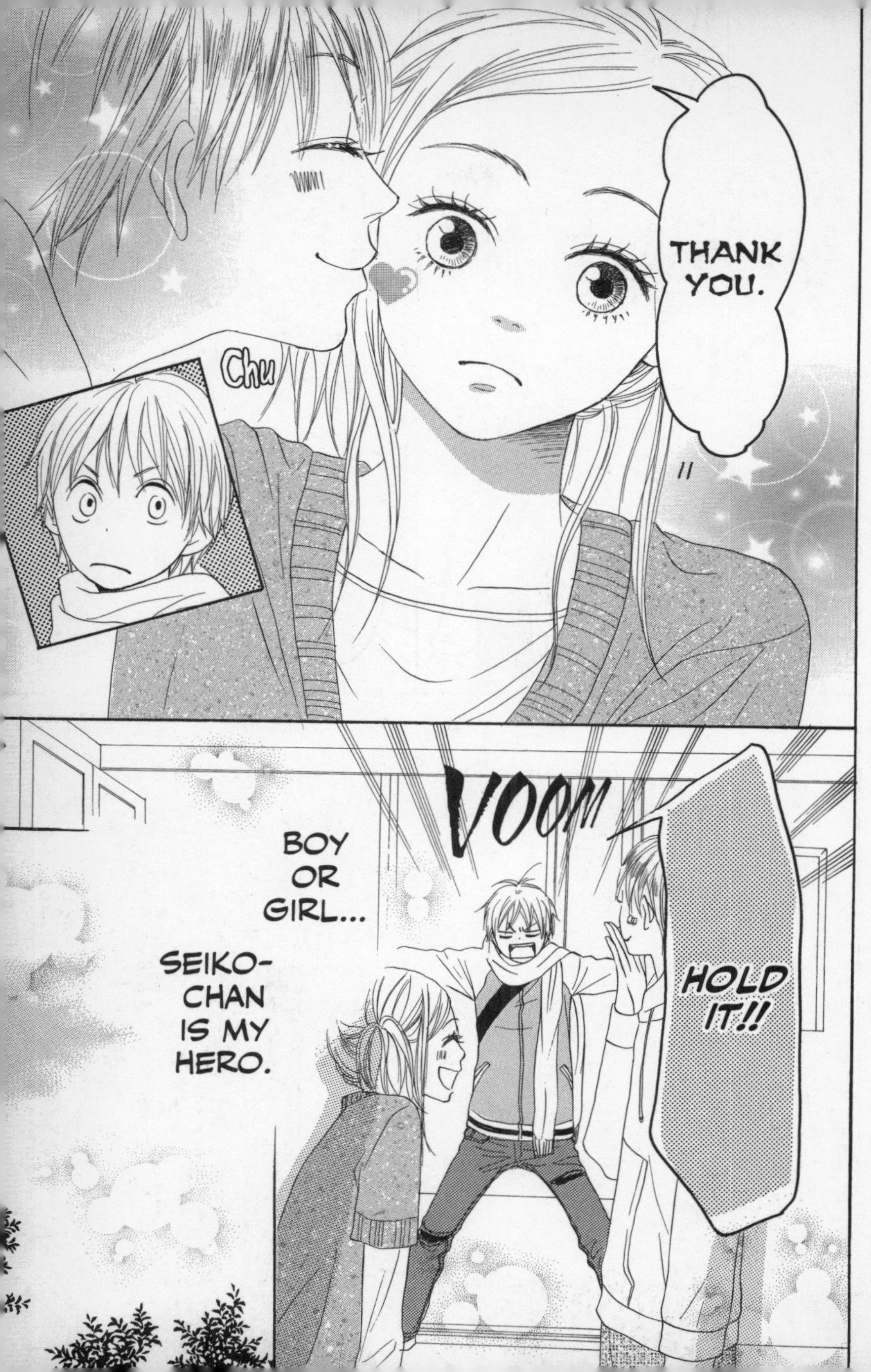
THANK YOU.
Chu
HOLD IT!!
VOOM
BOY OR GIRL...
SEIKO-CHAN IS MY HERO.

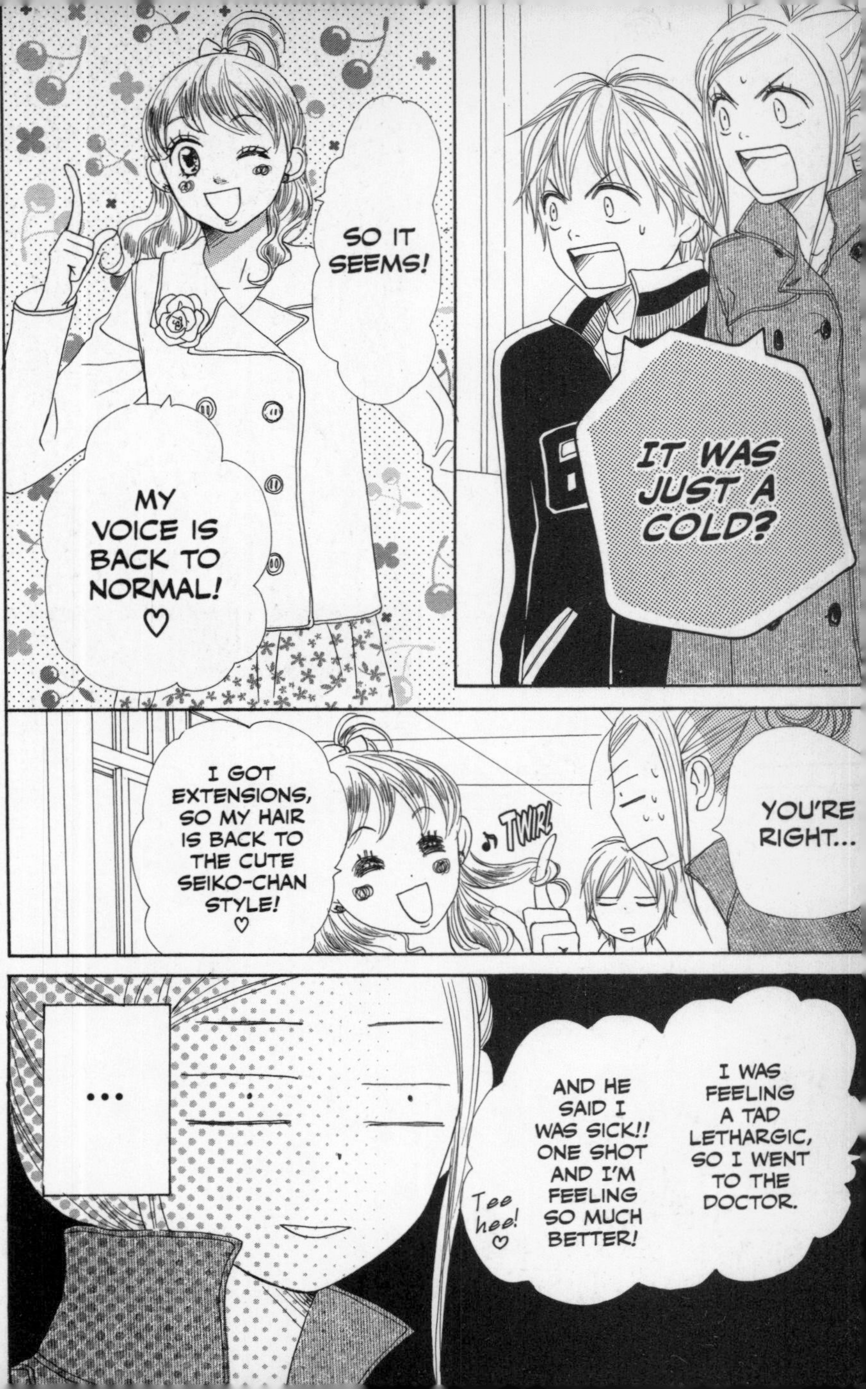
IT WAS JUST A COLD?
SO IT SEEMS!
MY VOICE IS BACK TO NORMAL! ♡
YOU'RE RIGHT...
I GOT EXTENSIONS, SO MY HAIR IS BACK TO THE CUTE SEIKO-CHAN STYLE! ♡
♪ TWIRL
I WAS FEELING A TAD LETHARGIC, SO I WENT TO THE DOCTOR.
AND HE SAID I WAS SICK!! ONE SHOT AND I'M FEELING SO MUCH BETTER!
Tee hee! ♡
...

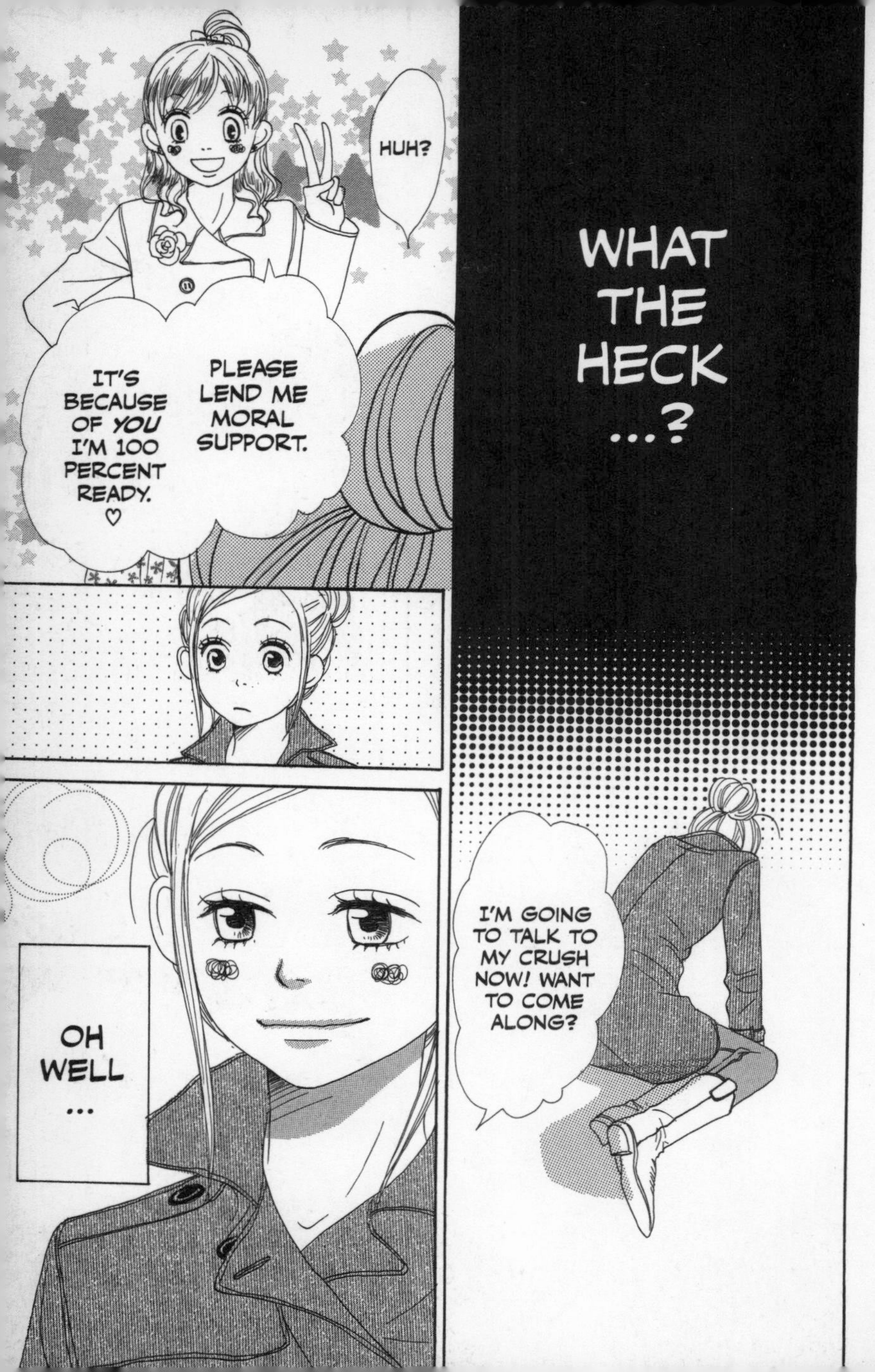
WHAT THE HECK ...?
I'M GOING TO TALK TO MY CRUSH NOW! WANT TO COME ALONG?
HUH?
PLEASE LEND ME MORAL SUPPORT.
IT'S BECAUSE OF *YOU* I'M 100 PERCENT READY. ♡
OH WELL ...

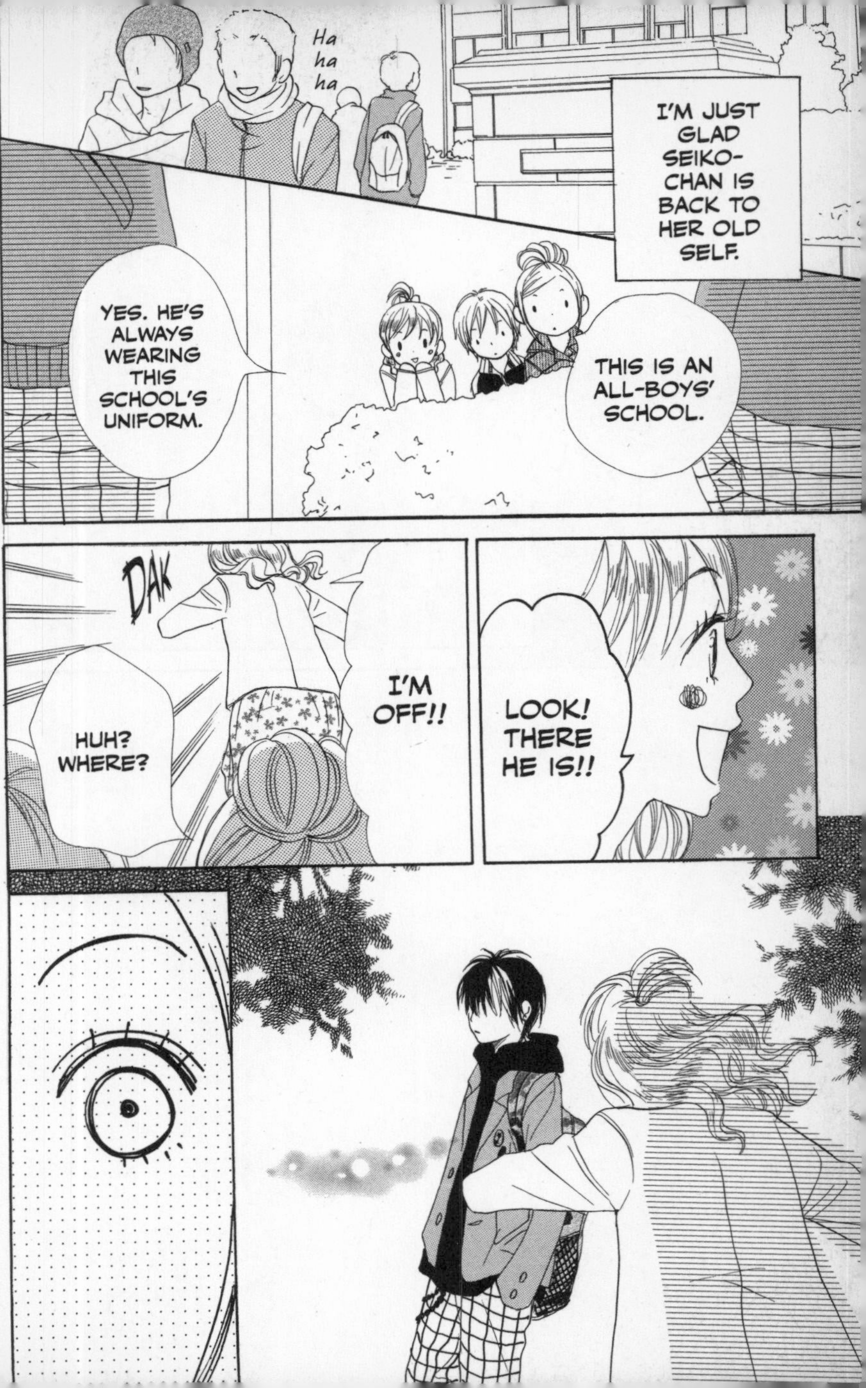
Ha ha ha
I'M JUST GLAD SEIKO-CHAN IS BACK TO HER OLD SELF.
THIS IS AN ALL-BOYS' SCHOOL.
YES. HE'S ALWAYS WEARING THIS SCHOOL'S UNIFORM.
LOOK! THERE HE IS!!
I'M OFF!!
DAK
HUH? WHERE?

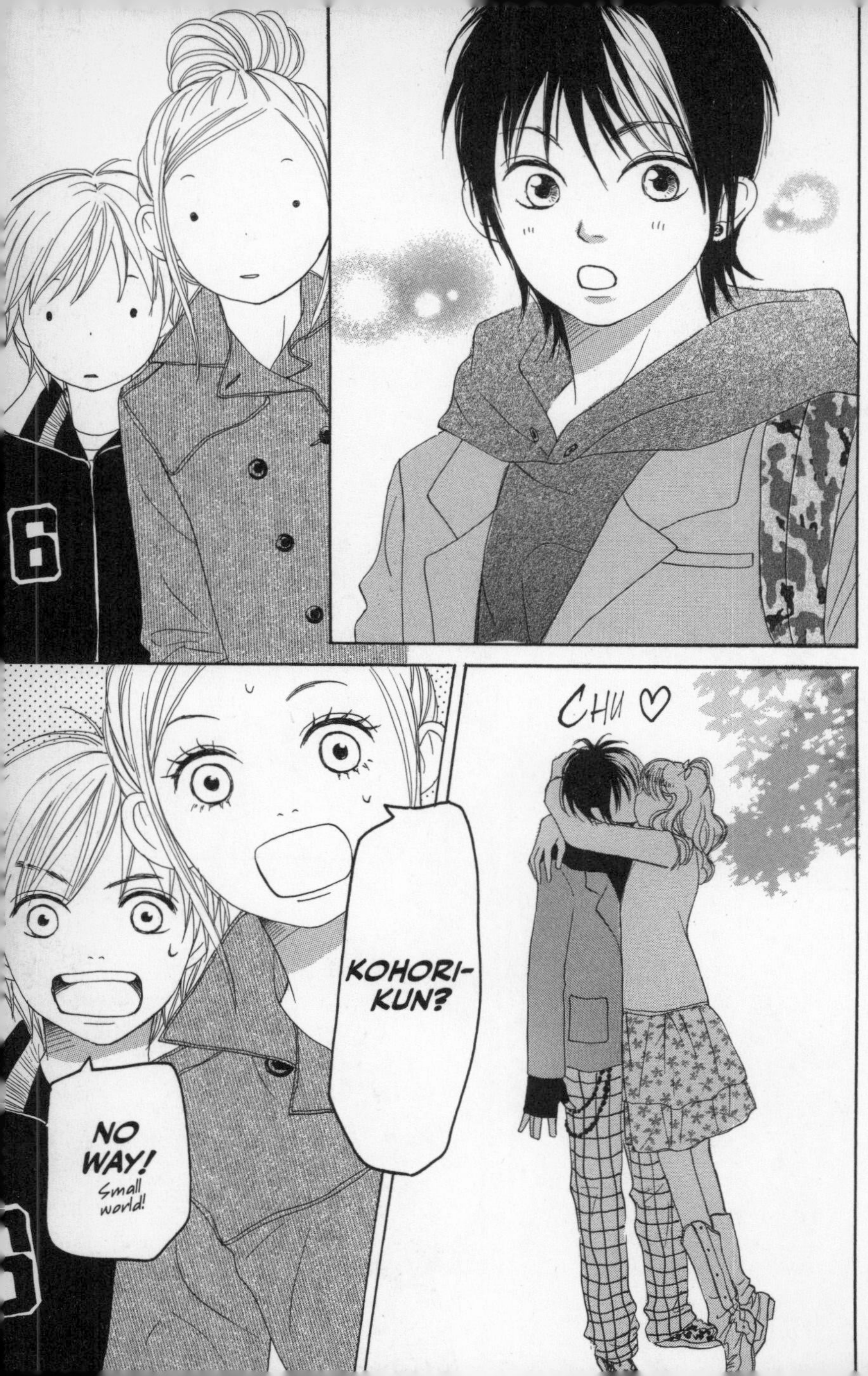
CHU ♡
KOHORI-KUN?
NO WAY! Small world!

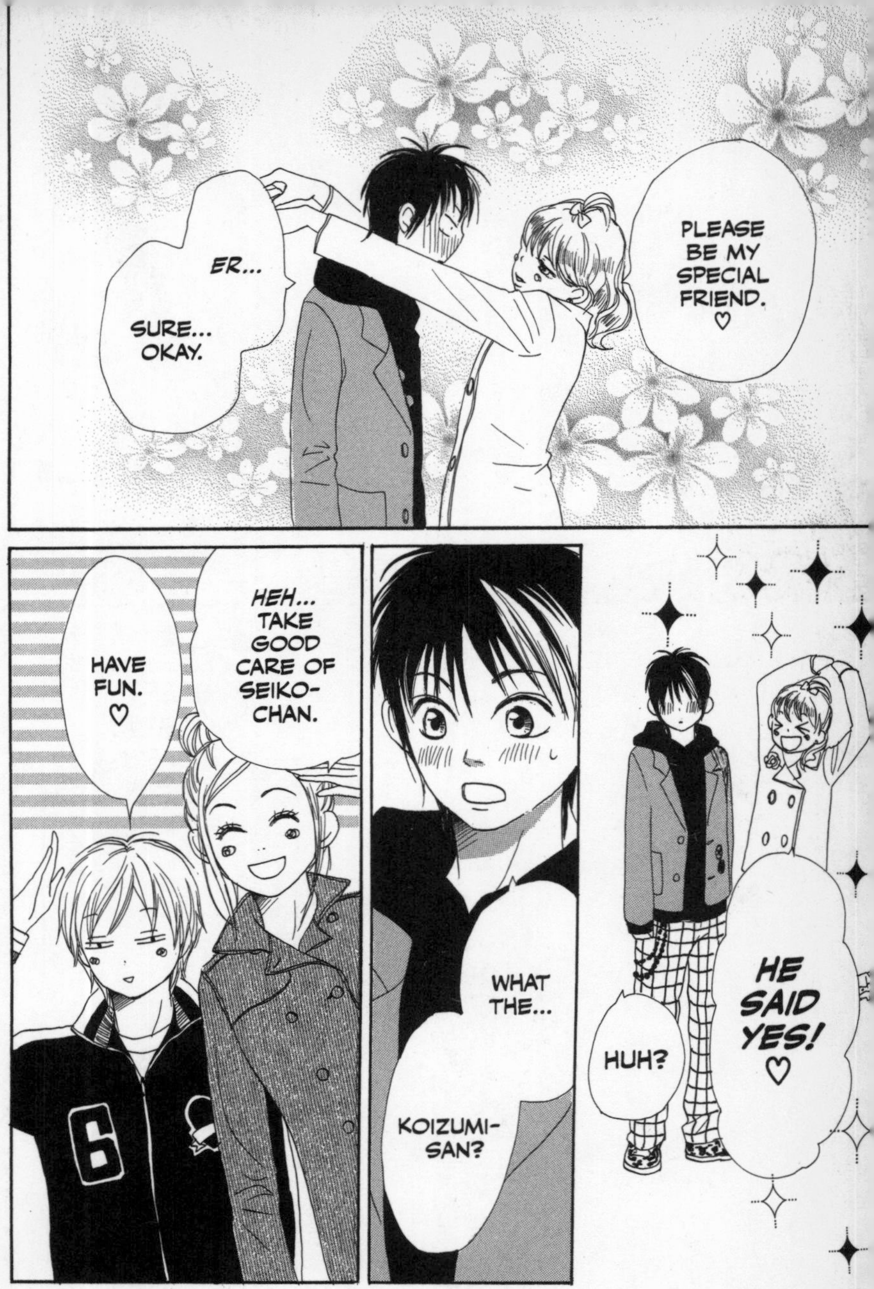
PLEASE BE MY SPECIAL FRIEND. ♡
ER... SURE... OKAY.
HE SAID YES! ♡
HUH?
WHAT THE... KOIZUMI-SAN?
HEH... TAKE GOOD CARE OF SEIKO-CHAN.
HAVE FUN. ♡

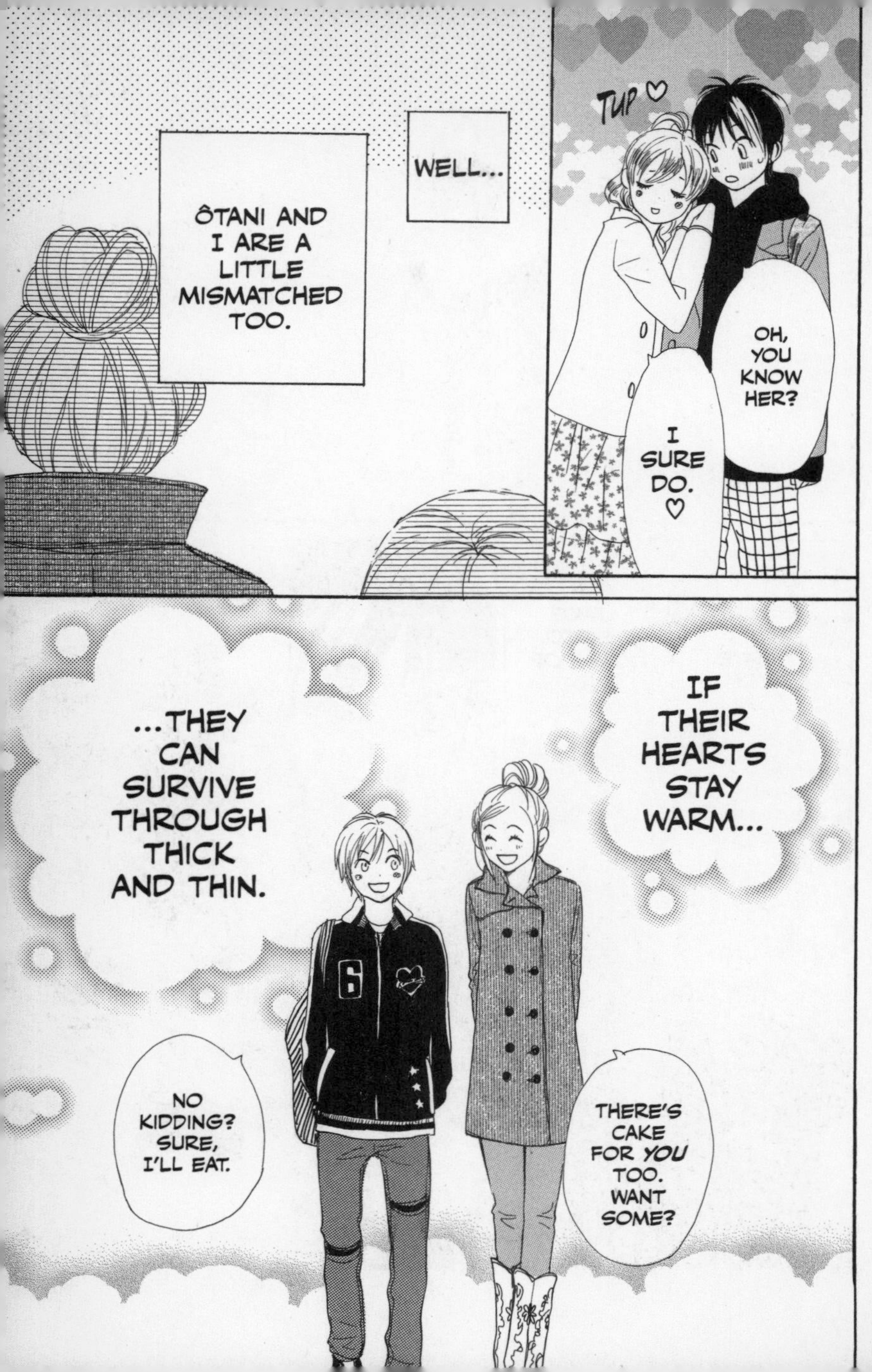
TUP ♡
OH, YOU KNOW HER?
I SURE DO. ♡
WELL...
ÔTANI AND I ARE A LITTLE MISMATCHED TOO.
IF THEIR HEARTS STAY WARM...
...THEY CAN SURVIVE THROUGH THICK AND THIN.
THERE'S CAKE FOR *YOU* TOO. WANT SOME?
NO KIDDING? SURE, I'LL EAT.

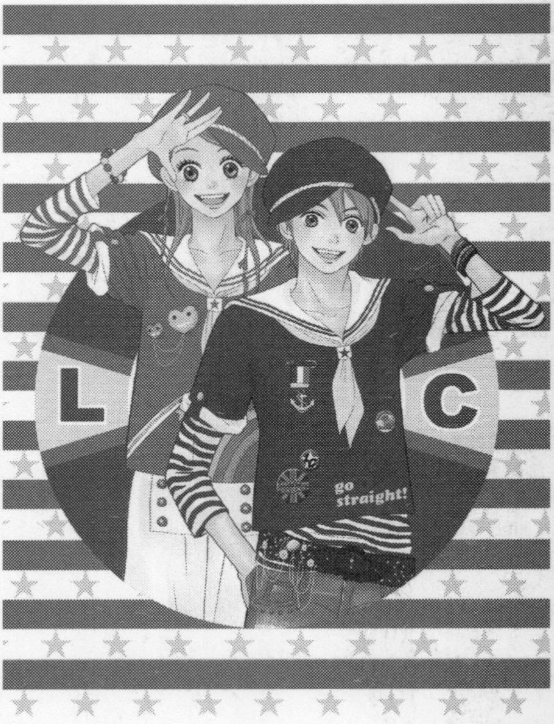
L
C
go straight!

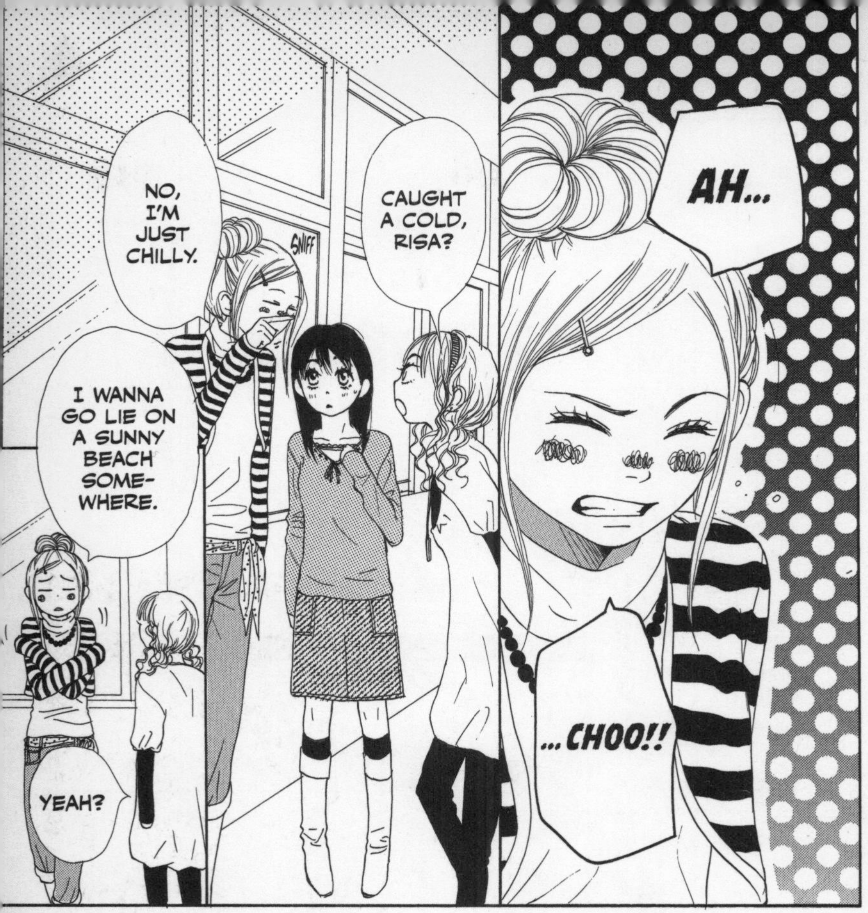
AH...
...CHOO!!
CAUGHT A COLD, RISA?
SNIFF
NO, I'M JUST CHILLY.
I WANNA GO LIE ON A SUNNY BEACH SOME-WHERE.
YEAH?

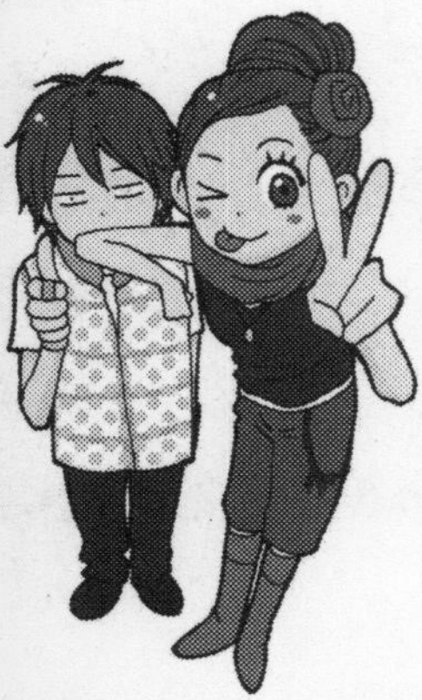

CHAPTER 57

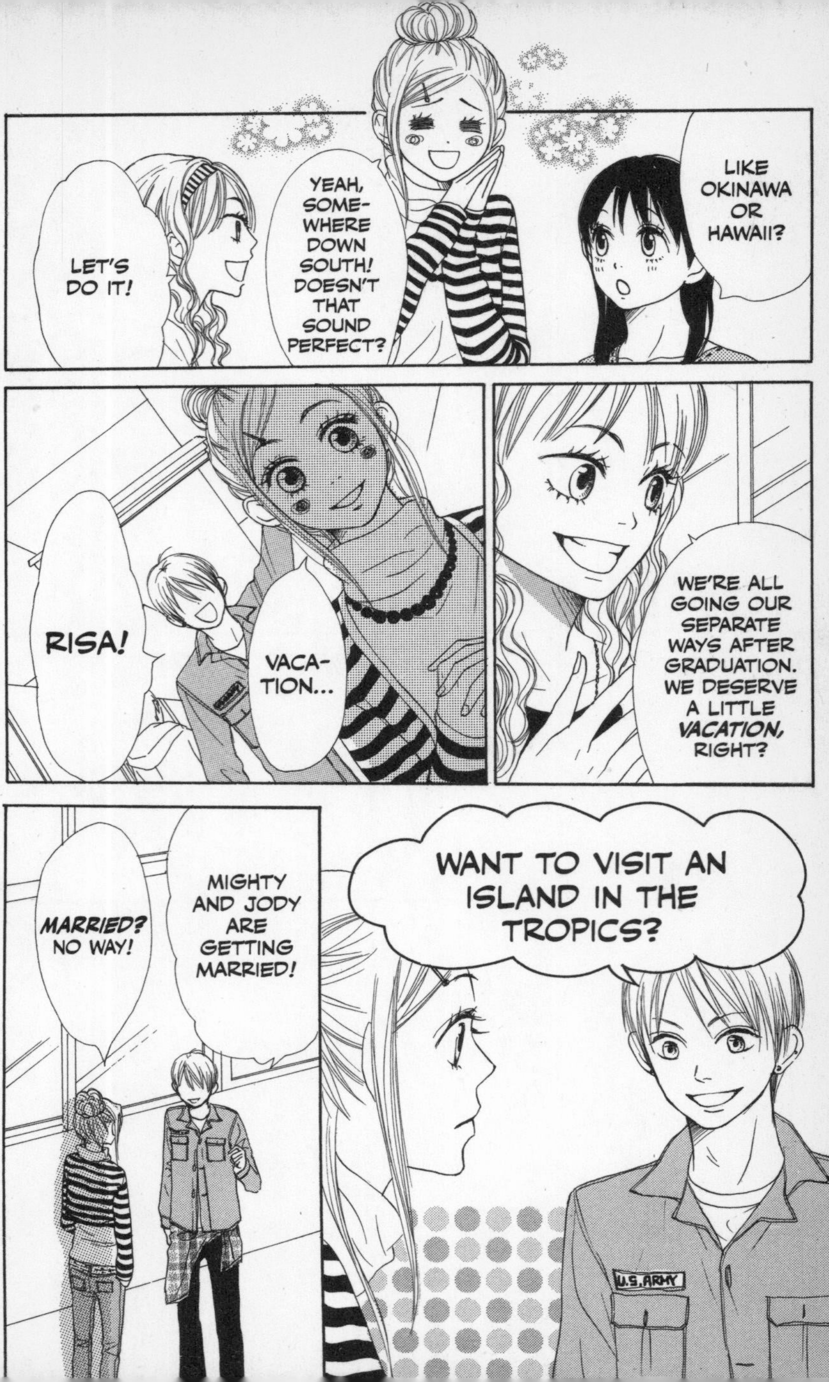
LIKE OKINAWA OR HAWAII?
YEAH, SOME-WHERE DOWN SOUTH! DOESN'T THAT SOUND PERFECT?
LET'S DO IT!
WE'RE ALL GOING OUR SEPARATE WAYS AFTER GRADUATION. WE DESERVE A LITTLE *VACATION*, RIGHT?
VACA-TION...
RISA!
WANT TO VISIT AN ISLAND IN THE TROPICS?
U.S.ARMY
MIGHTY AND JODY ARE GETTING MARRIED!
MARRIED? NO WAY!

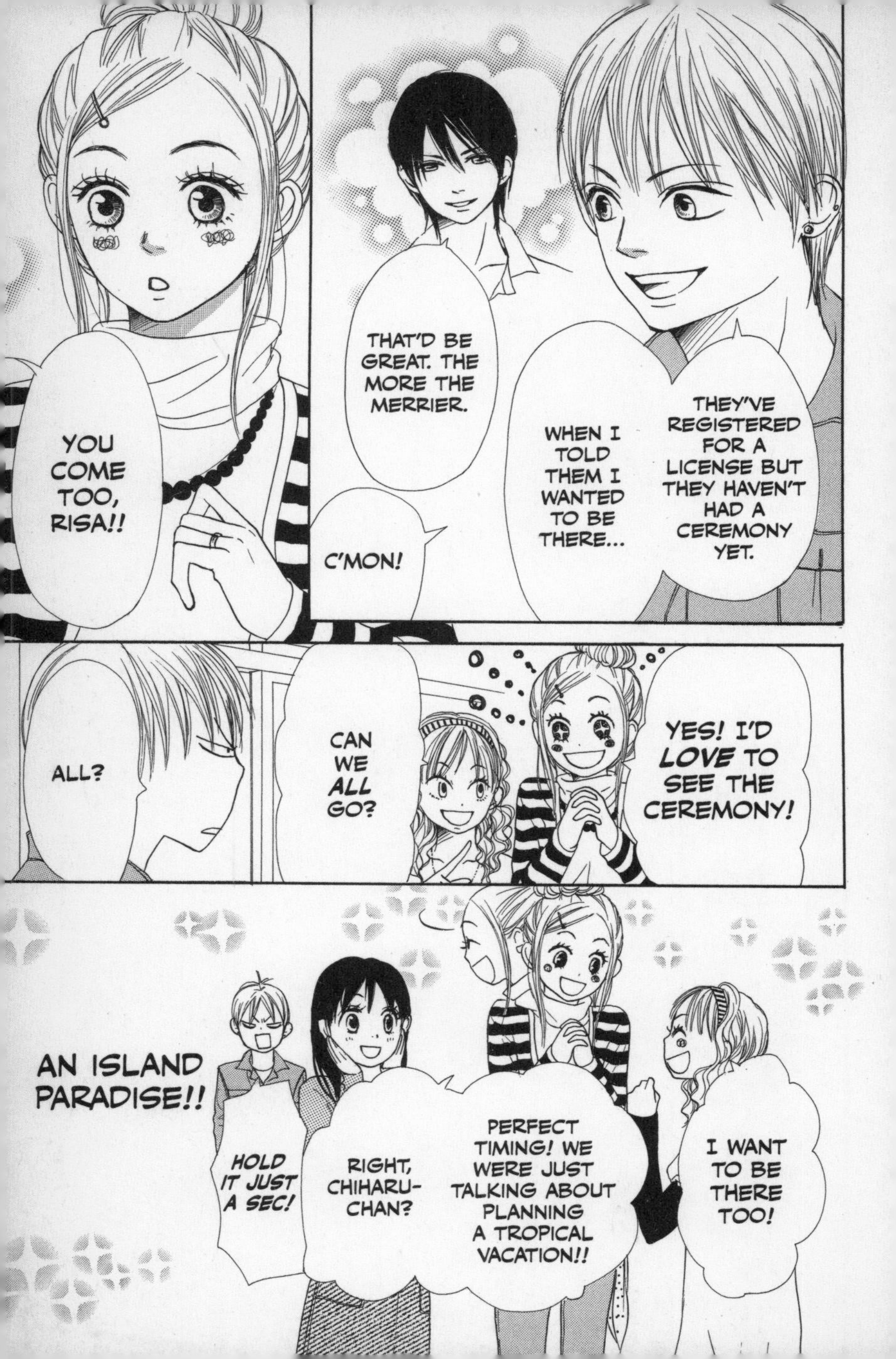
THEY'VE REGISTERED FOR A LICENSE BUT THEY HAVEN'T HAD A CEREMONY YET.
WHEN I TOLD THEM I WANTED TO BE THERE...
THAT'D BE GREAT. THE MORE THE MERRIER.
C'MON!
YOU COME TOO, RISA!!
YES! I'D LOVE TO SEE THE CEREMONY!
CAN WE ALL GO?
ALL?
I WANT TO BE THERE TOO!
PERFECT TIMING! WE WERE JUST TALKING ABOUT PLANNING A TROPICAL VACATION!!
RIGHT, CHIHARU-CHAN?
HOLD IT JUST A SEC!
AN ISLAND PARADISE!!

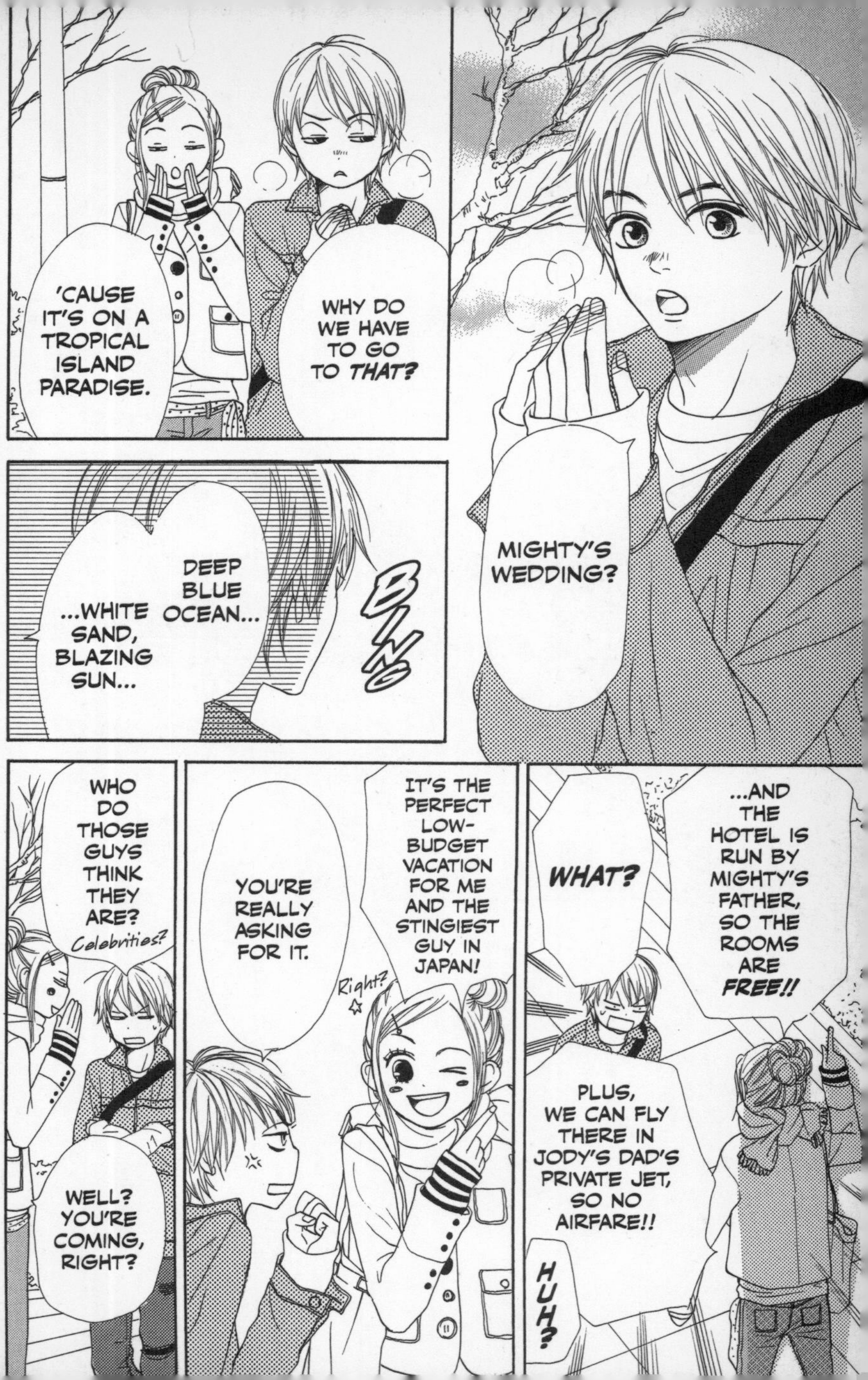
MIGHTY'S WEDDING?
WHY DO WE HAVE TO GO TO *THAT?*
'CAUSE IT'S ON A TROPICAL ISLAND PARADISE.
DEEP BLUE OCEAN...
...WHITE SAND, BLAZING SUN...
BING
...AND THE HOTEL IS RUN BY MIGHTY'S FATHER, SO THE ROOMS ARE *FREE!!*
WHAT?
PLUS, WE CAN FLY THERE IN JODY'S DAD'S PRIVATE JET, SO NO AIRFARE!!
HUH?
IT'S THE PERFECT LOW-BUDGET VACATION FOR ME AND THE STINGIEST GUY IN JAPAN!
Right?
YOU'RE REALLY ASKING FOR IT.
WHO DO THOSE GUYS THINK THEY ARE?
Celebrities?
WELL? YOU'RE COMING, RIGHT?

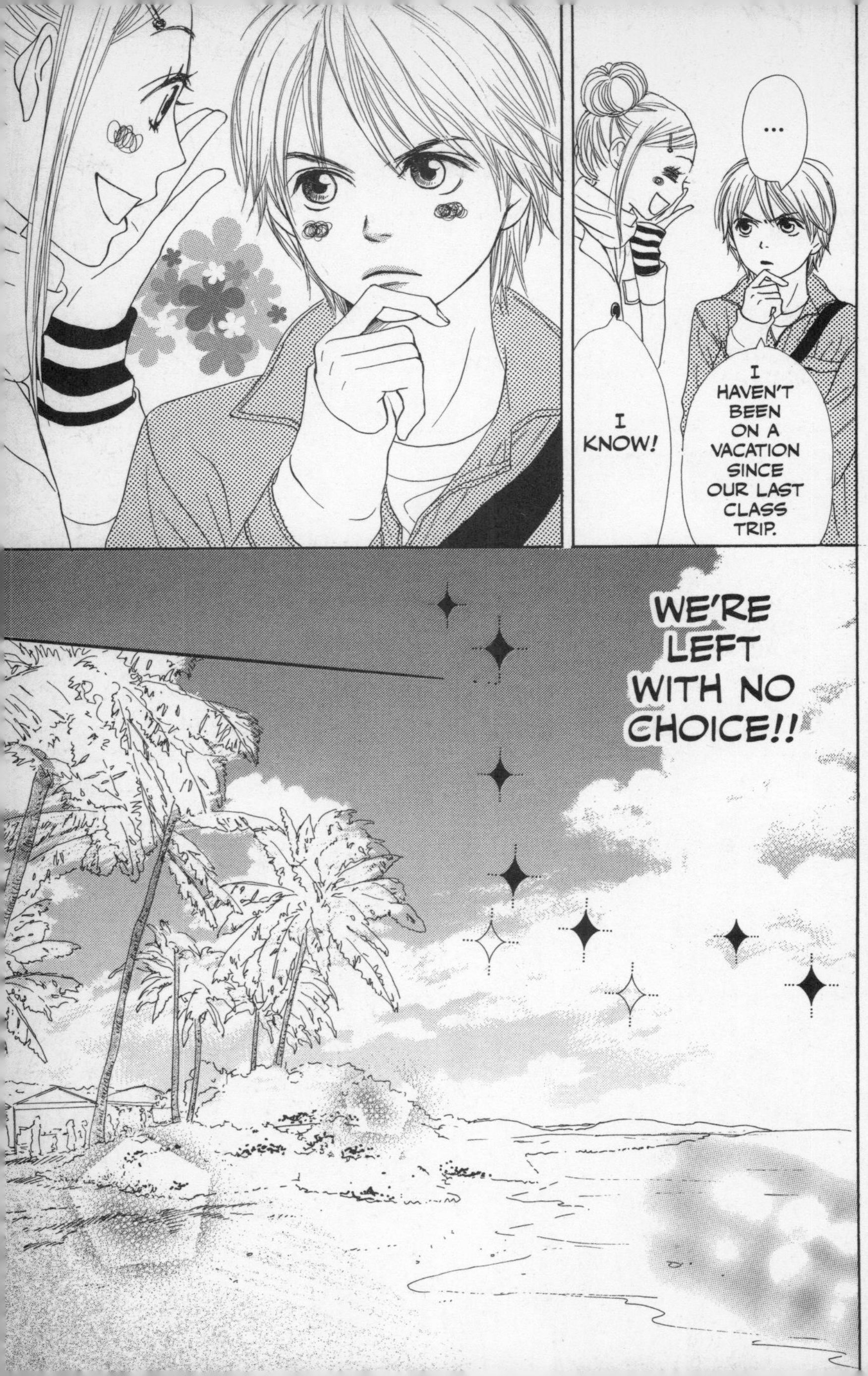
...
I HAVEN'T BEEN ON A VACATION SINCE OUR LAST CLASS TRIP.
I KNOW!
WE'RE LEFT WITH NO CHOICE!!

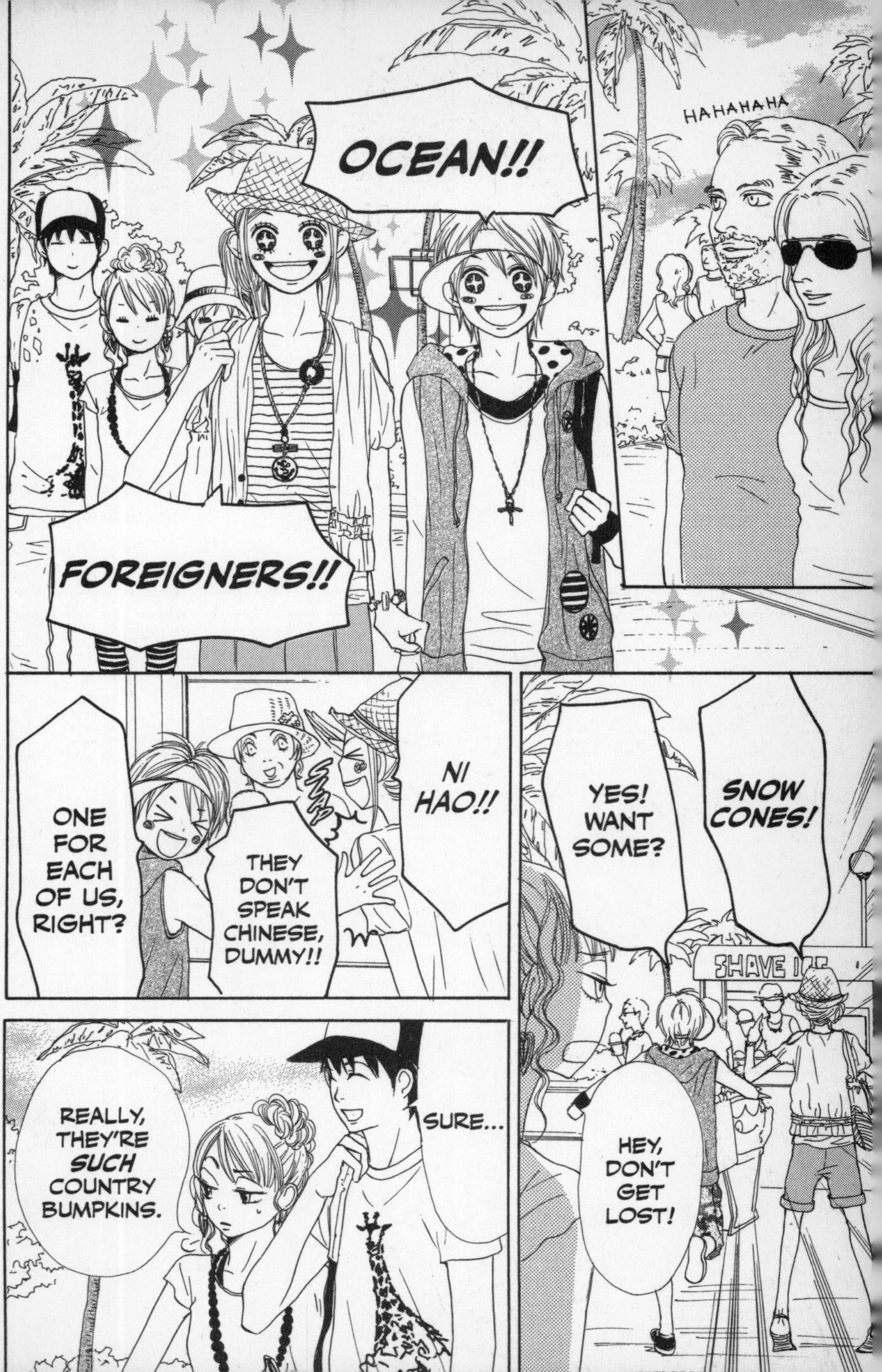
HAHAHAHA
OCEAN!!
FOREIGNERS!!
SNOW CONES!
YES! WANT SOME?
HEY, DON'T GET LOST!
NI HAO!!
THEY DON'T SPEAK CHINESE, DUMMY!!
ONE FOR EACH OF US, RIGHT?
SURE...
REALLY, THEY'RE *SUCH* COUNTRY BUMPKINS.

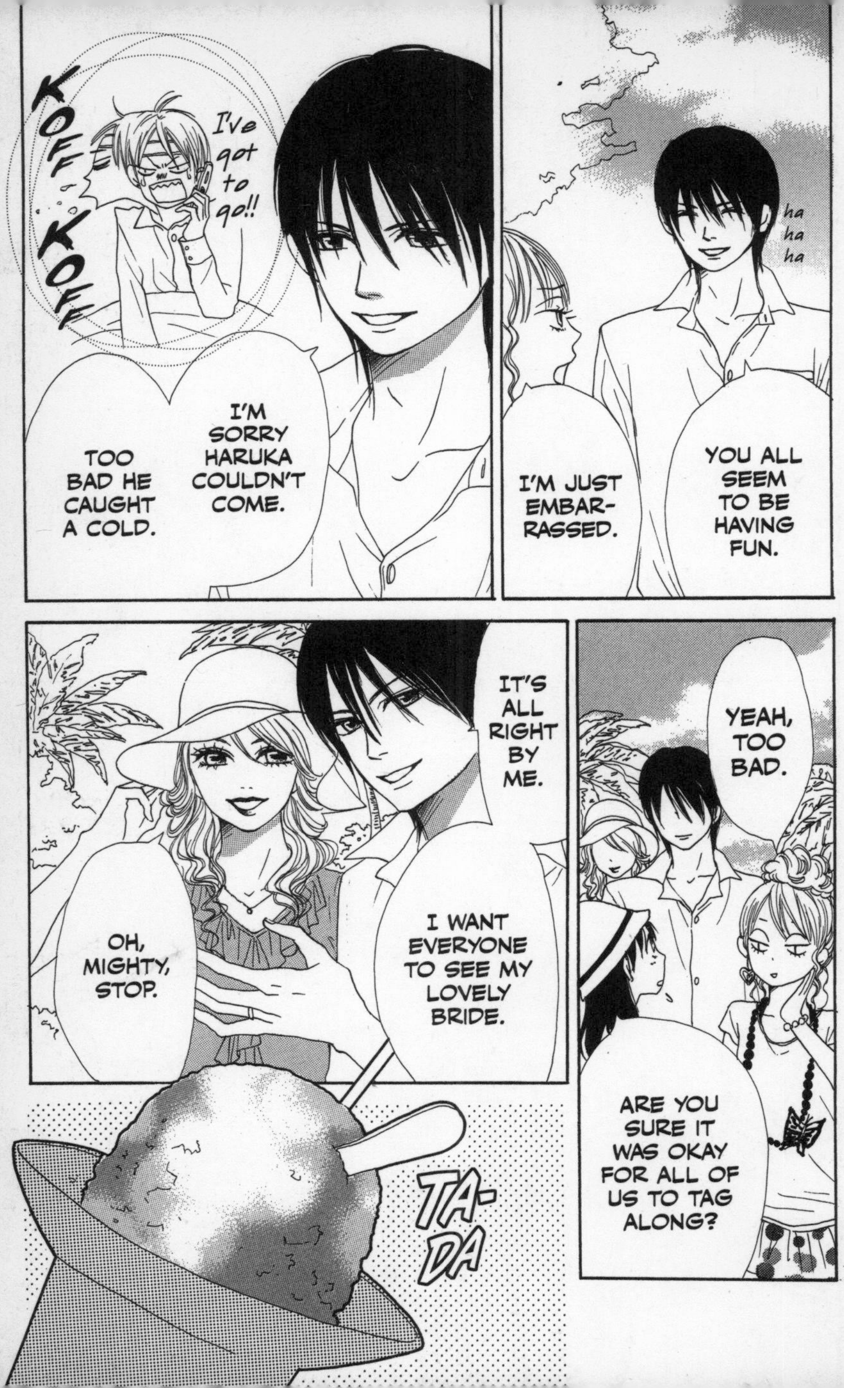
ha ha ha
YOU ALL SEEM TO BE HAVING FUN.
I'M JUST EMBAR-RASSED.
I've got to go!!
KOFF KOFF KOFF
I'M SORRY HARUKA COULDN'T COME.
TOO BAD HE CAUGHT A COLD.
YEAH, TOO BAD.
ARE YOU SURE IT WAS OKAY FOR ALL OF US TO TAG ALONG?
IT'S ALL RIGHT BY ME.
I WANT EVERYONE TO SEE MY LOVELY BRIDE.
OH, MIGHTY, STOP.
TA-DA

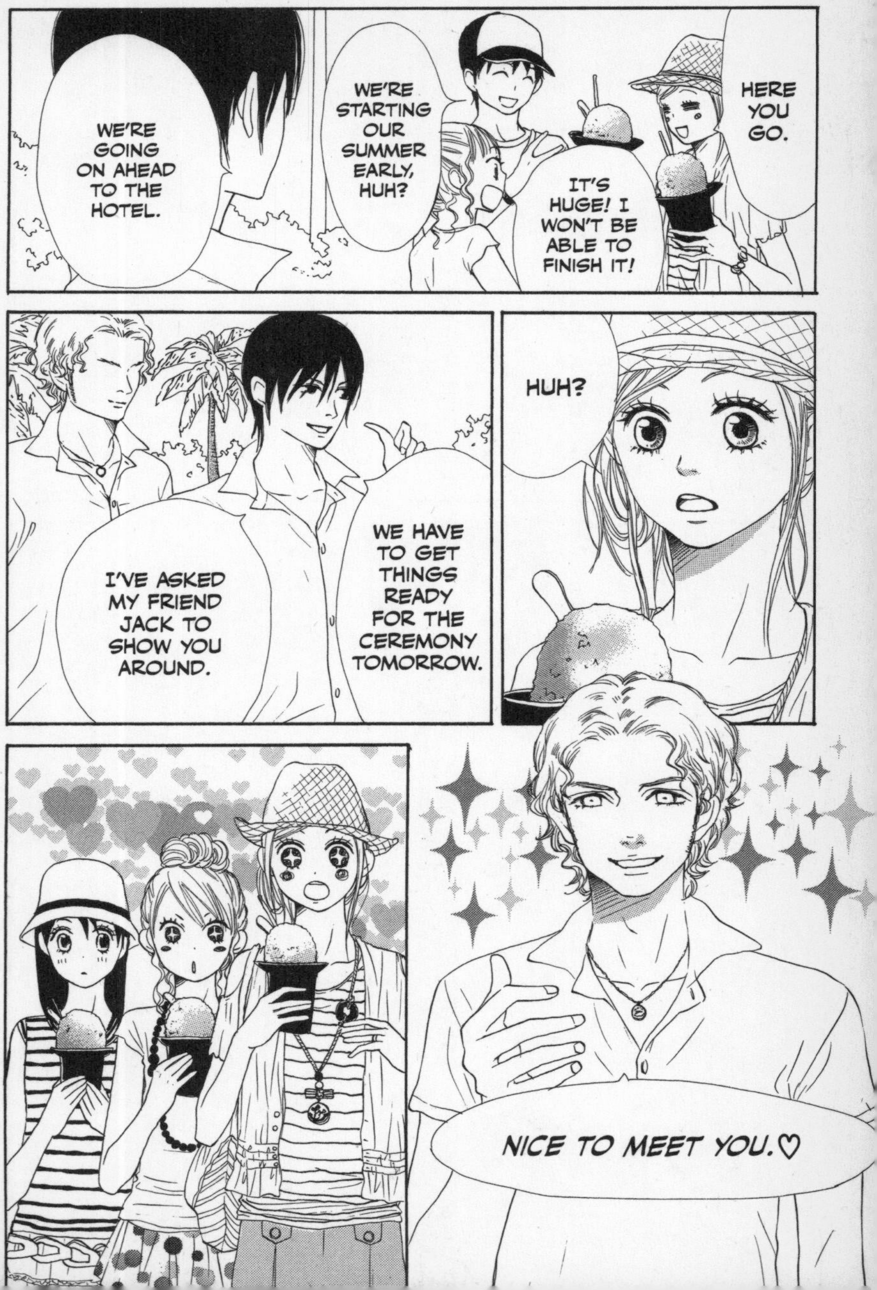
HERE YOU GO.
IT'S HUGE! I WON'T BE ABLE TO FINISH IT!
WE'RE STARTING OUR SUMMER EARLY, HUH?
WE'RE GOING ON AHEAD TO THE HOTEL.
HUH?
WE HAVE TO GET THINGS READY FOR THE CEREMONY TOMORROW.
I'VE ASKED MY FRIEND JACK TO SHOW YOU AROUND.
NICE TO MEET YOU.♡

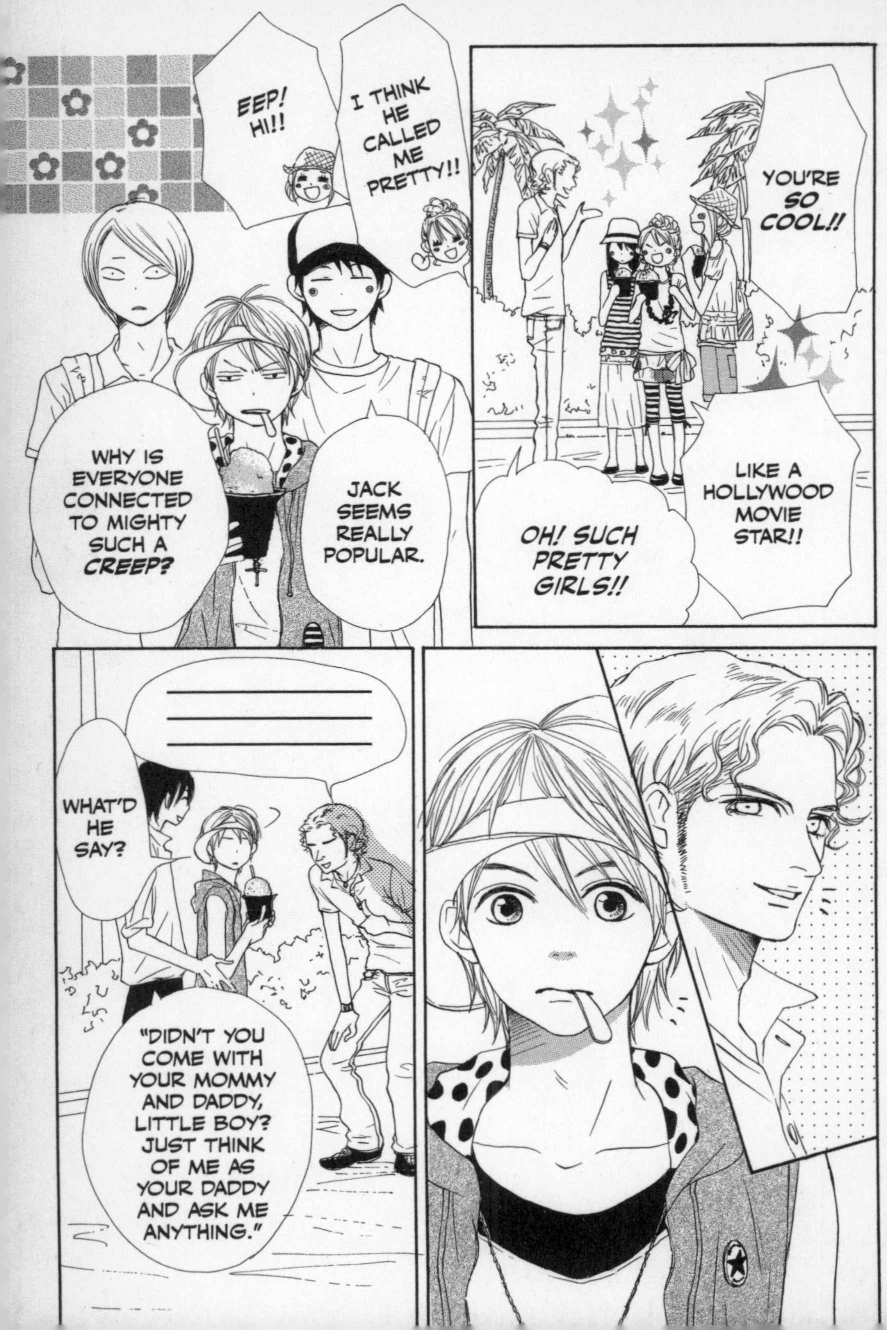
YOU'RE SO COOL!!
LIKE A HOLLYWOOD MOVIE STAR!!
OH! SUCH PRETTY GIRLS!!
I THINK HE CALLED ME PRETTY!!
EEP! HI!!
JACK SEEMS REALLY POPULAR.
WHY IS EVERYONE CONNECTED TO MIGHTY SUCH A *CREEP?*
WHAT'D HE SAY?
"DIDN'T YOU COME WITH YOUR MOMMY AND DADDY, LITTLE BOY? JUST THINK OF ME AS YOUR DADDY AND ASK ME ANYTHING."

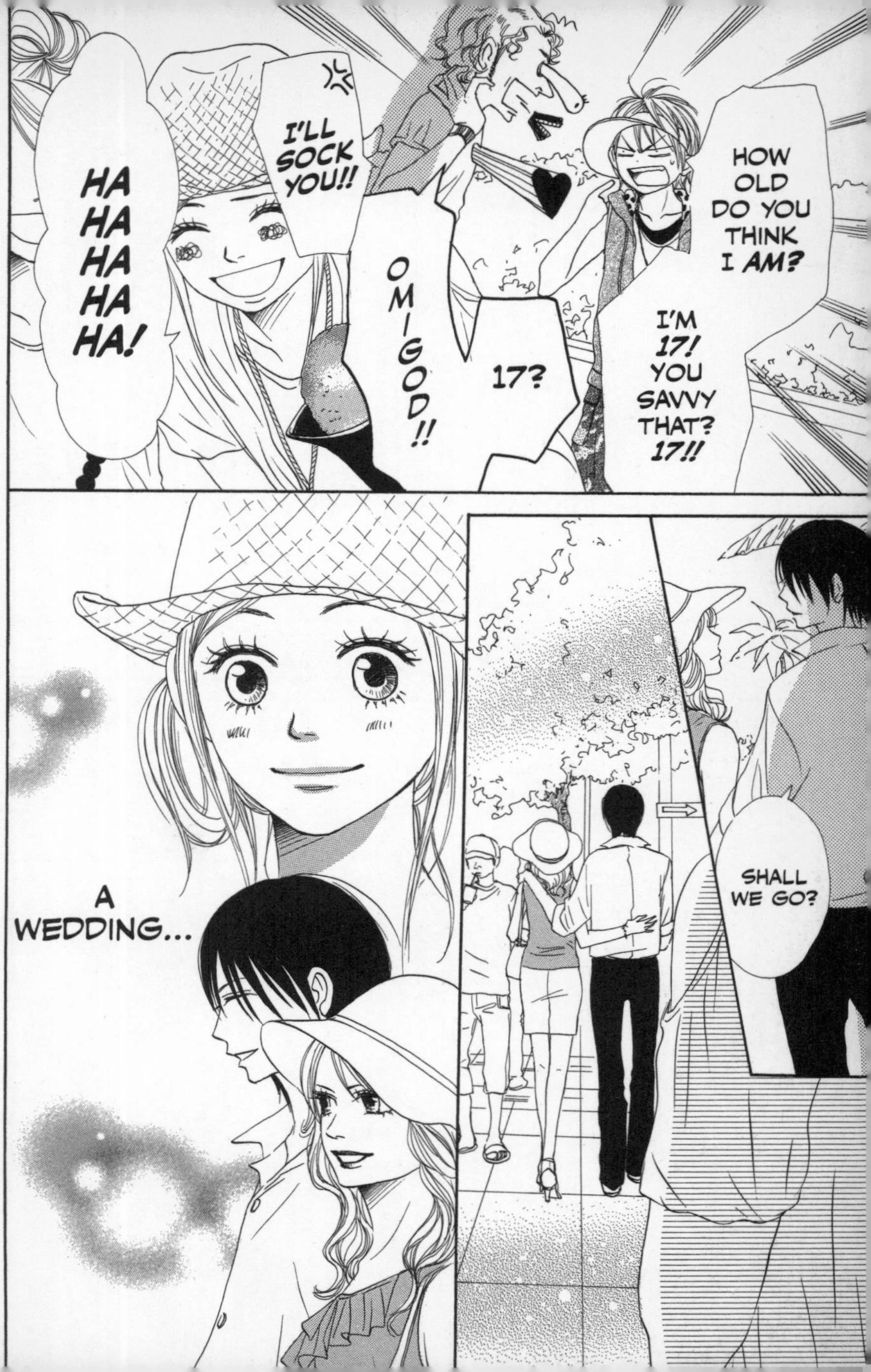
HOW OLD DO YOU THINK I AM?
I'M 17! YOU SAVVY THAT? 17!!
17?
OMIGOD!!
I'LL SOCK YOU!!
HA HA HA HA HA!
SHALL WE GO?
A WEDDING...

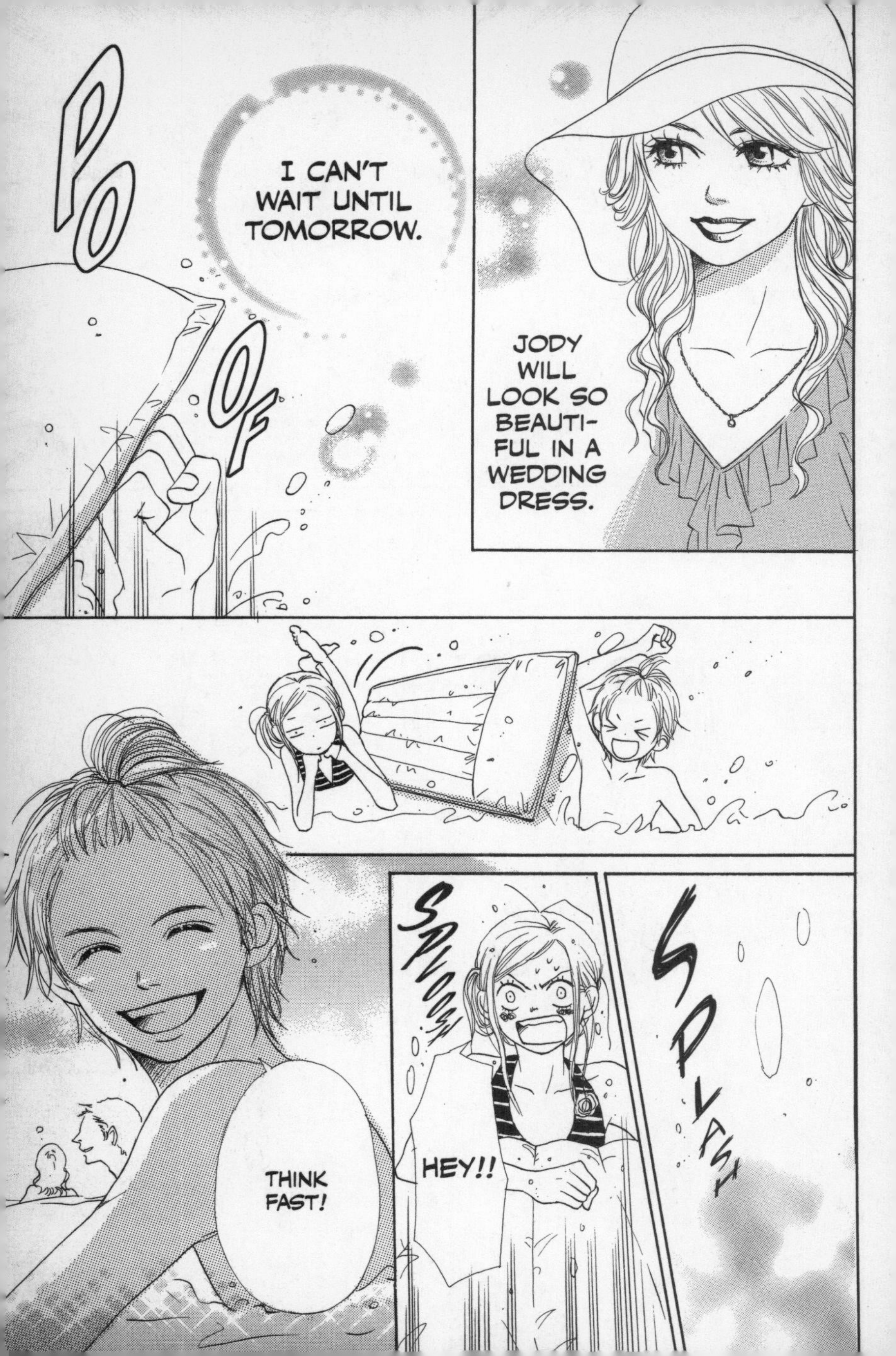
JODY WILL LOOK SO BEAUTIFUL IN A WEDDING DRESS.
I CAN'T WAIT UNTIL TOMORROW.
POOF
HEY!!
THINK FAST!

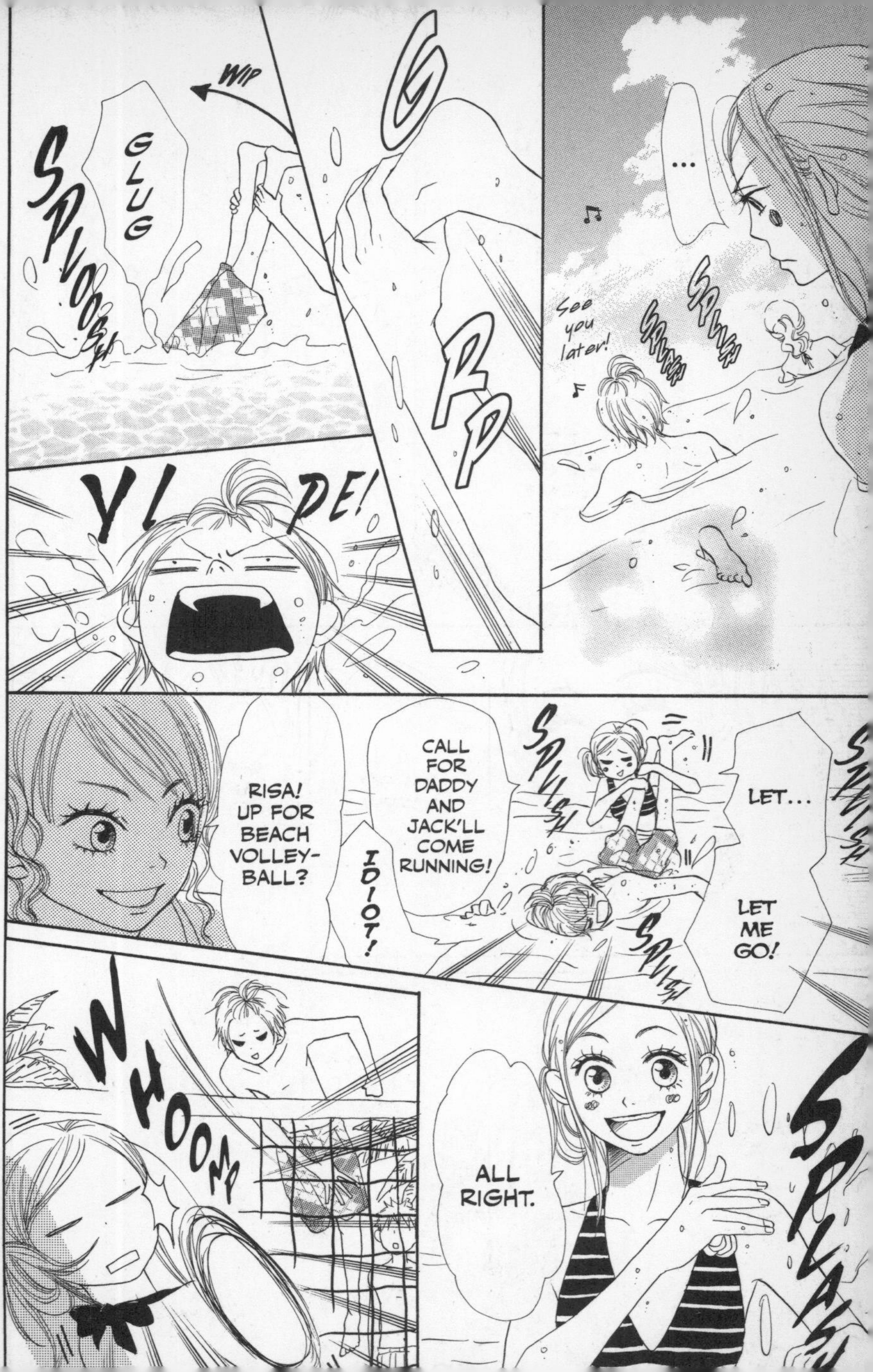
...
See you later!
GRP
SPLOOSH
GLUG
WIP
YI
DE!
LET...
CALL FOR DADDY AND JACK'LL COME RUNNING!
IDIOT!
LET ME GO!
RISA! UP FOR BEACH VOLLEY-BALL?
SPLASH
ALL RIGHT.
WHOOSH

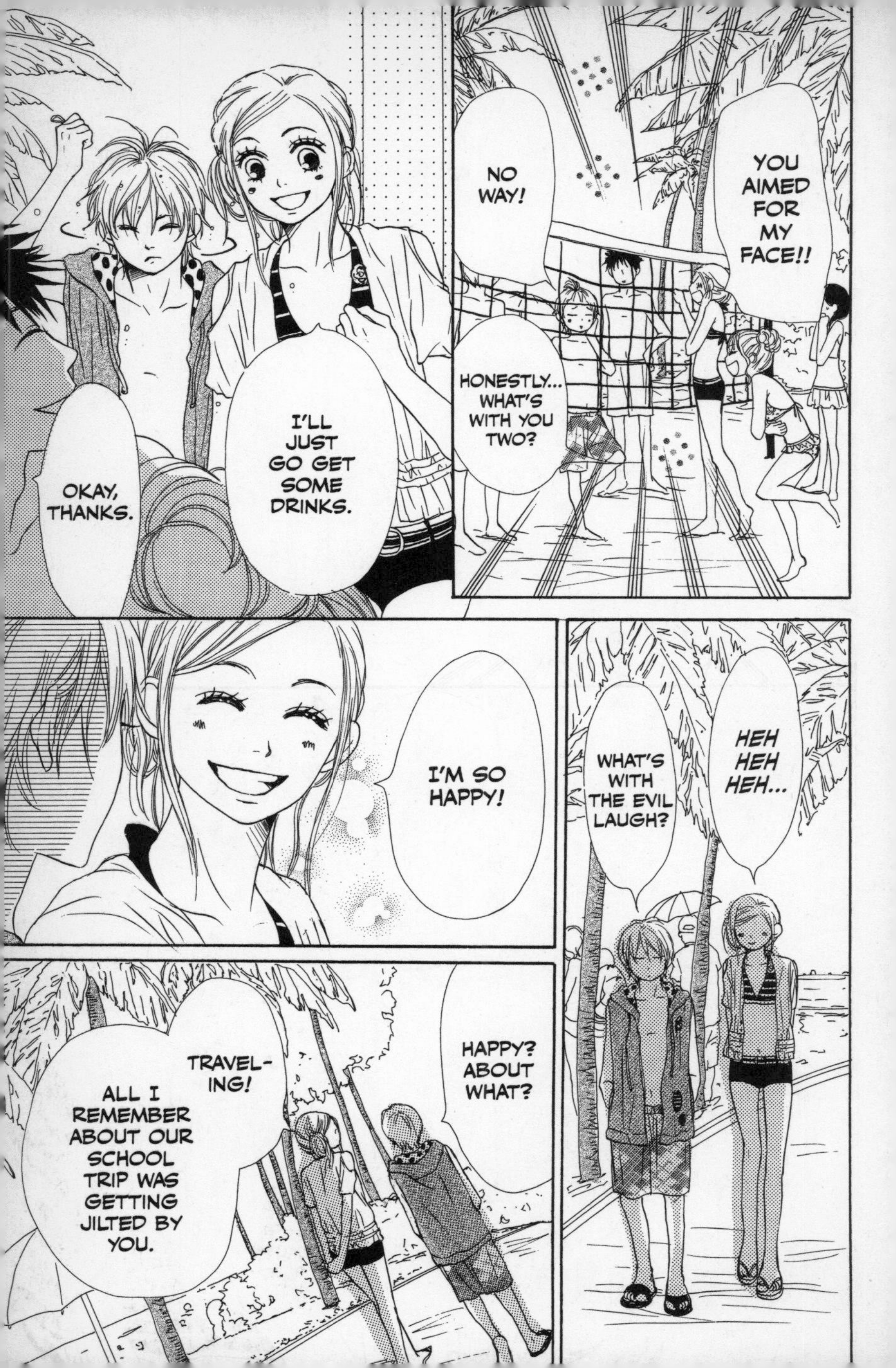
YOU AIMED FOR MY FACE!!
NO WAY!
HONESTLY... WHAT'S WITH YOU TWO?
I'LL JUST GO GET SOME DRINKS.
OKAY, THANKS.
HEH HEH HEH...
WHAT'S WITH THE EVIL LAUGH?
I'M SO HAPPY!
HAPPY? ABOUT WHAT?
TRAVEL-ING!
ALL I REMEMBER ABOUT OUR SCHOOL TRIP WAS GETTING JILTED BY YOU.

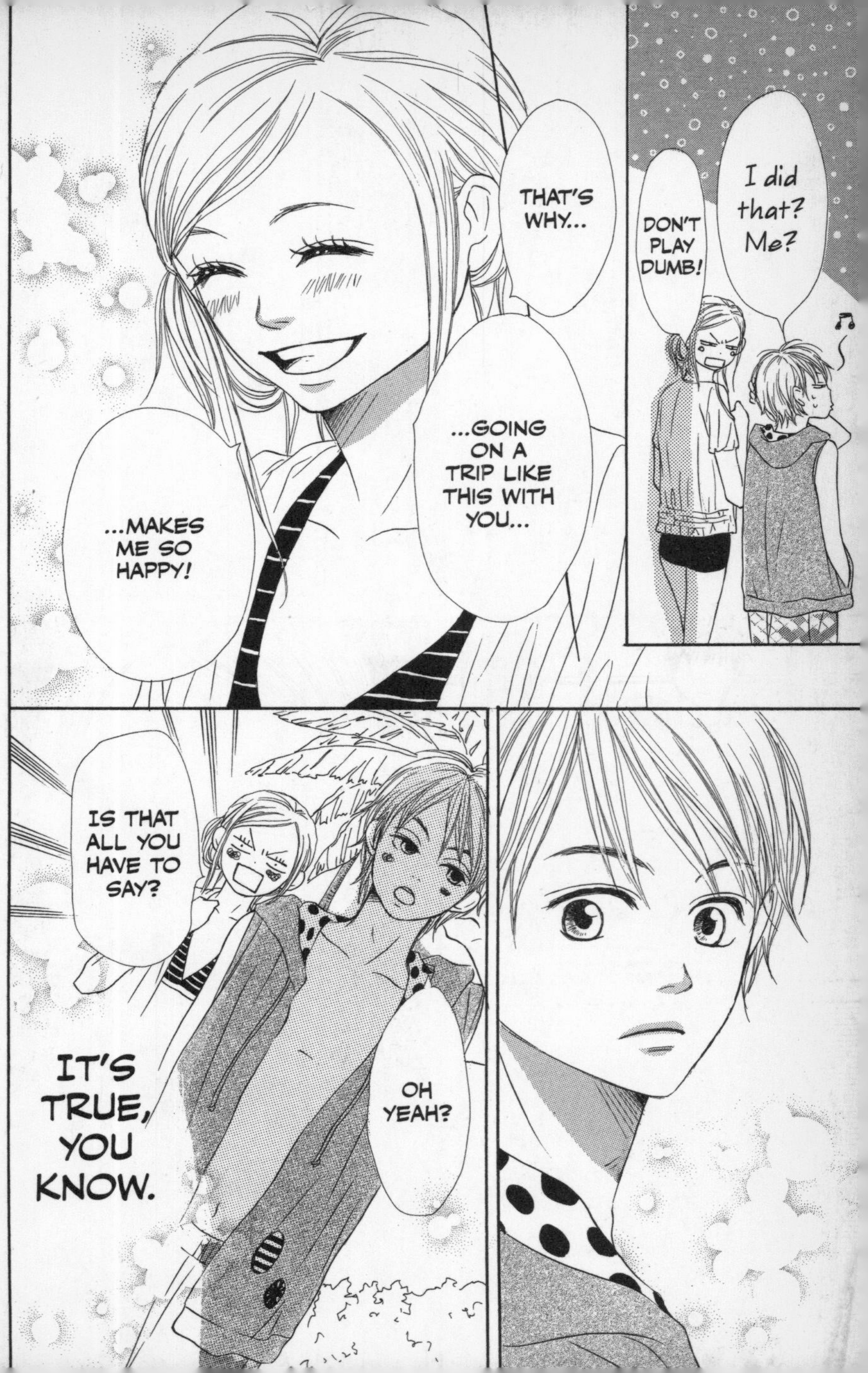
I did that? Me?
DON'T PLAY DUMB!
THAT'S WHY...
...GOING ON A TRIP LIKE THIS WITH YOU...
...MAKES ME SO HAPPY!
IT'S TRUE, YOU KNOW.
OH YEAH?
IS THAT ALL YOU HAVE TO SAY?

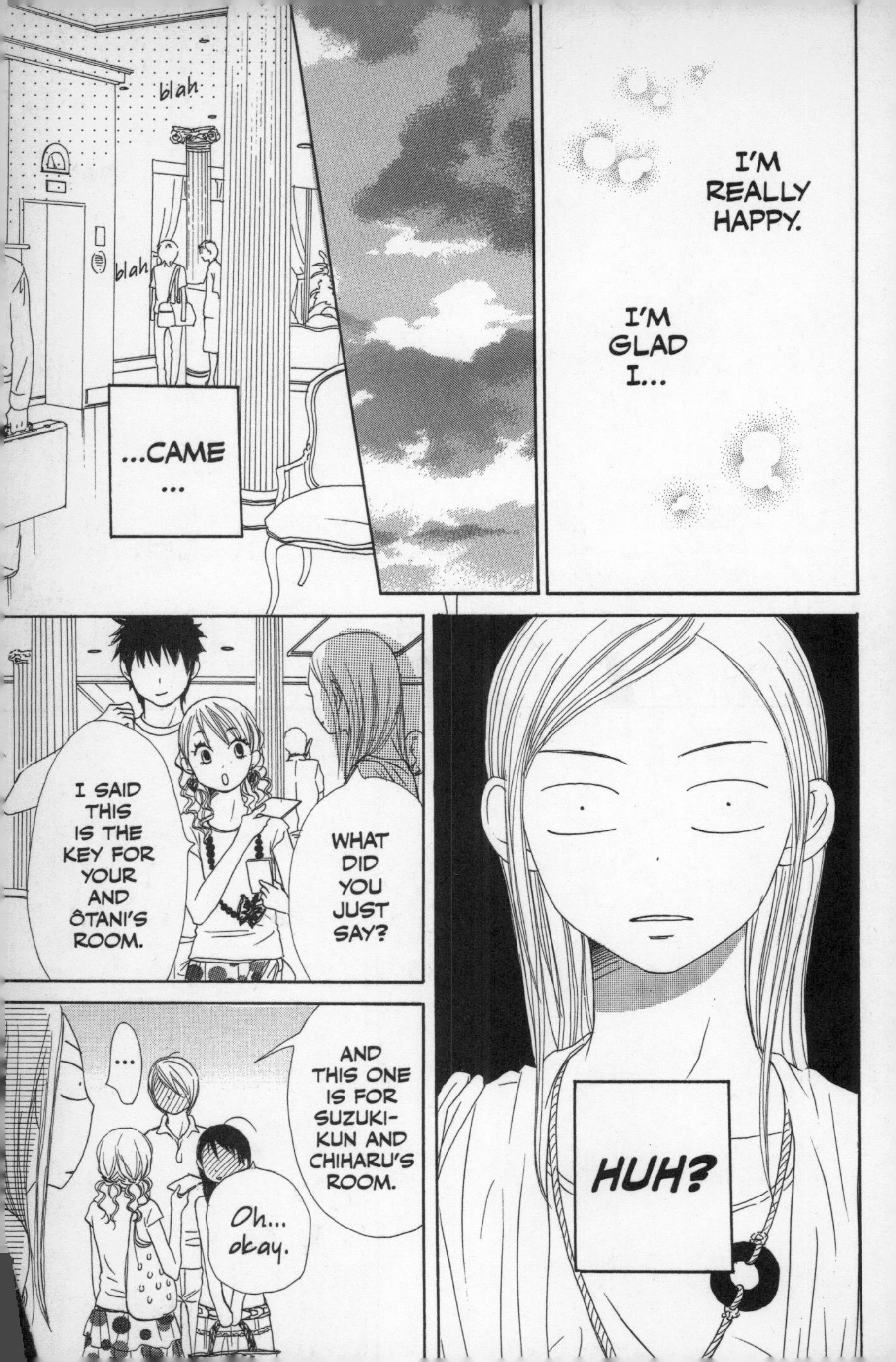

I'M REALLY HAPPY.
I'M GLAD I...
blah
blah
...CAME ...
HUH?
WHAT DID YOU JUST SAY?
I SAID THIS IS THE KEY FOR YOUR AND ÔTANI'S ROOM.
AND THIS ONE IS FOR SUZUKI-KUN AND CHIHARU'S ROOM.
...
Oh... okay.

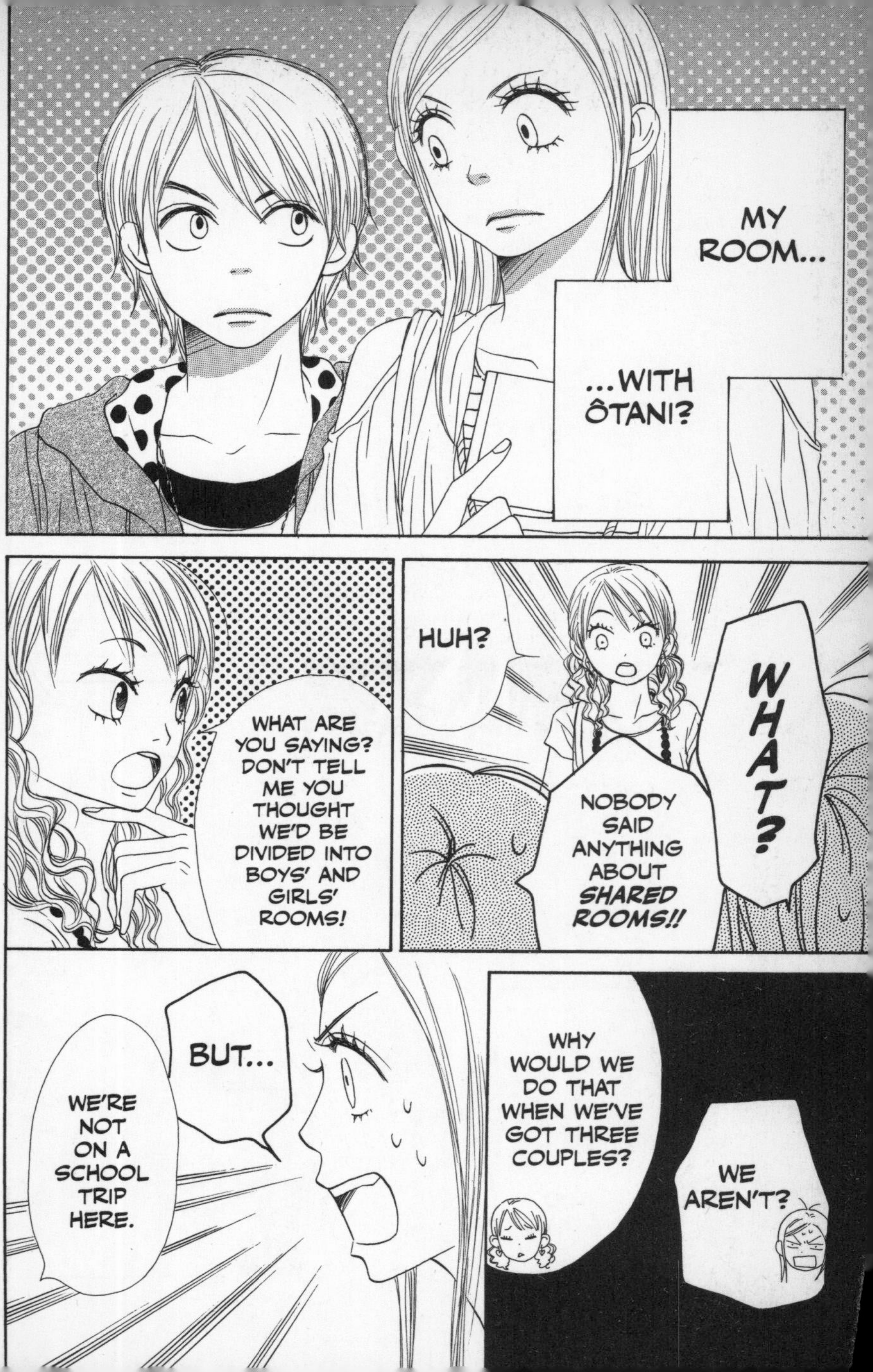
MY ROOM...
...WITH ÔTANI?
WHAT?
HUH?
NOBODY SAID ANYTHING ABOUT *SHARED ROOMS!!*
WHAT ARE YOU SAYING? DON'T TELL ME YOU THOUGHT WE'D BE DIVIDED INTO BOYS' AND GIRLS' ROOMS!
WHY WOULD WE DO THAT WHEN WE'VE GOT THREE COUPLES?
WE AREN'T?
BUT...
WE'RE NOT ON A SCHOOL TRIP HERE.

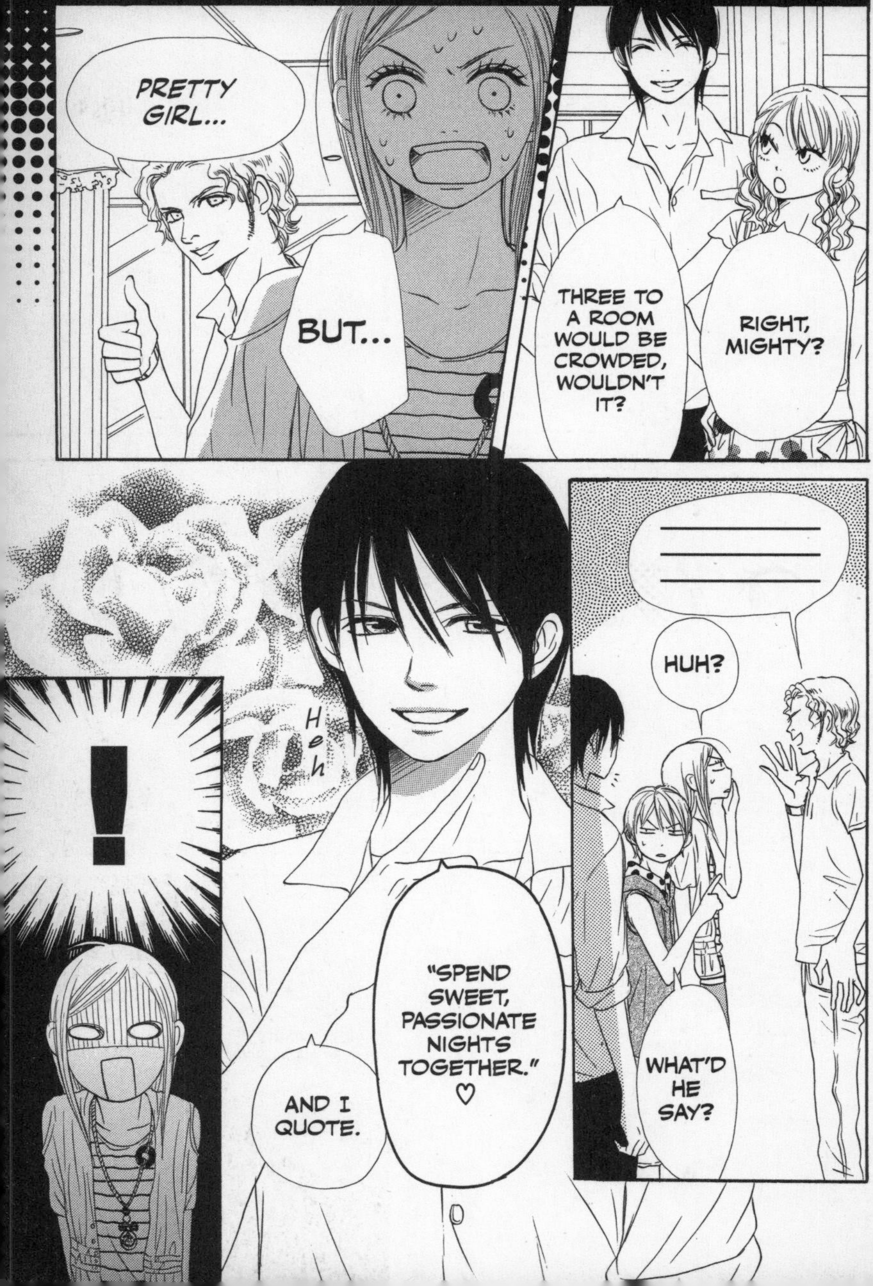
RIGHT, MIGHTY?
THREE TO A ROOM WOULD BE CROWDED, WOULDN'T IT?
BUT...
PRETTY GIRL...
———
HUH?
WHAT'D HE SAY?
Heh
"SPEND SWEET, PASSIONATE NIGHTS TOGETHER." ♡
AND I QUOTE.
!

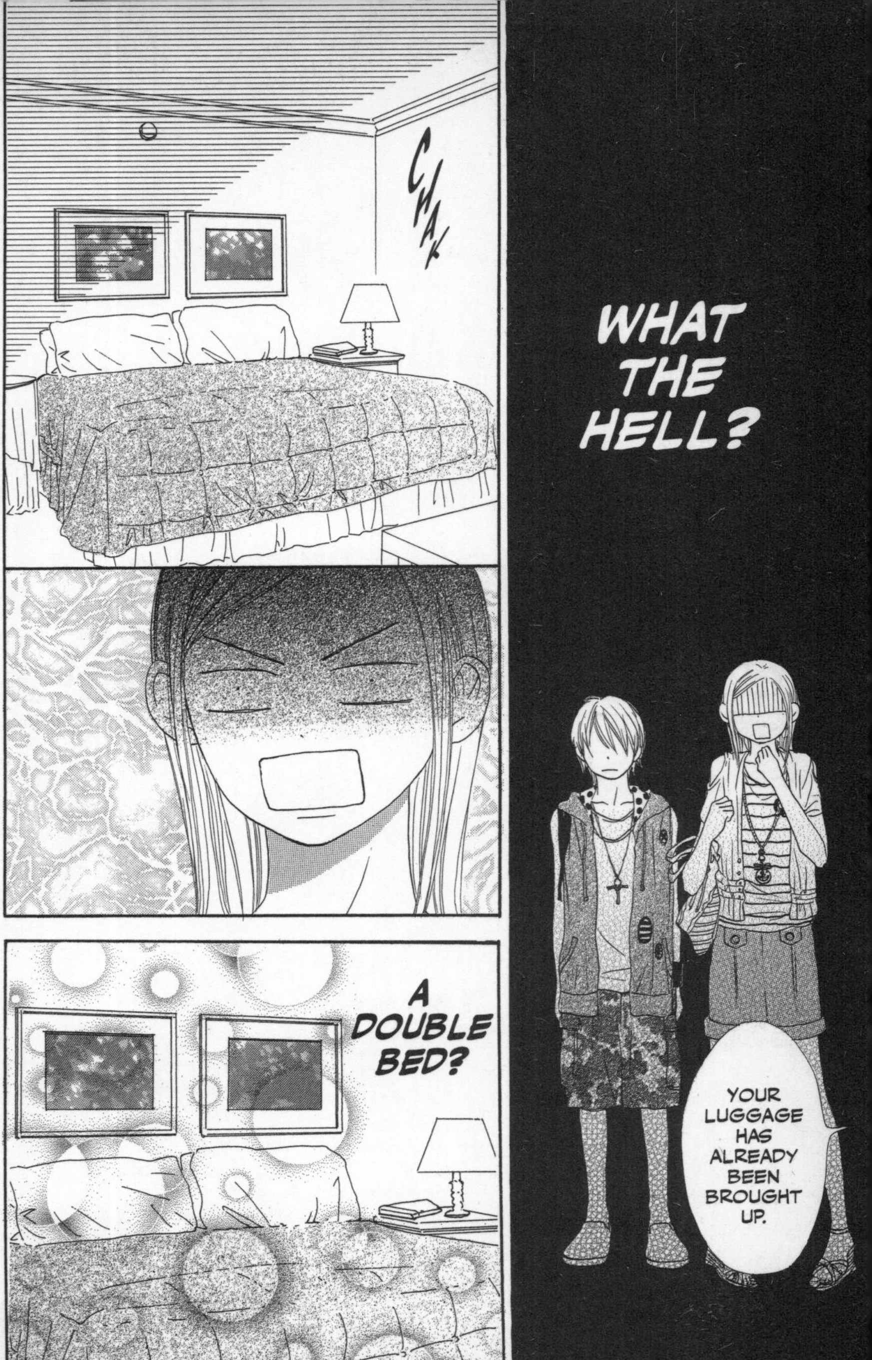
WHAT THE HELL?
YOUR LUGGAGE HAS ALREADY BEEN BROUGHT UP.
CHAK
A DOUBLE BED?

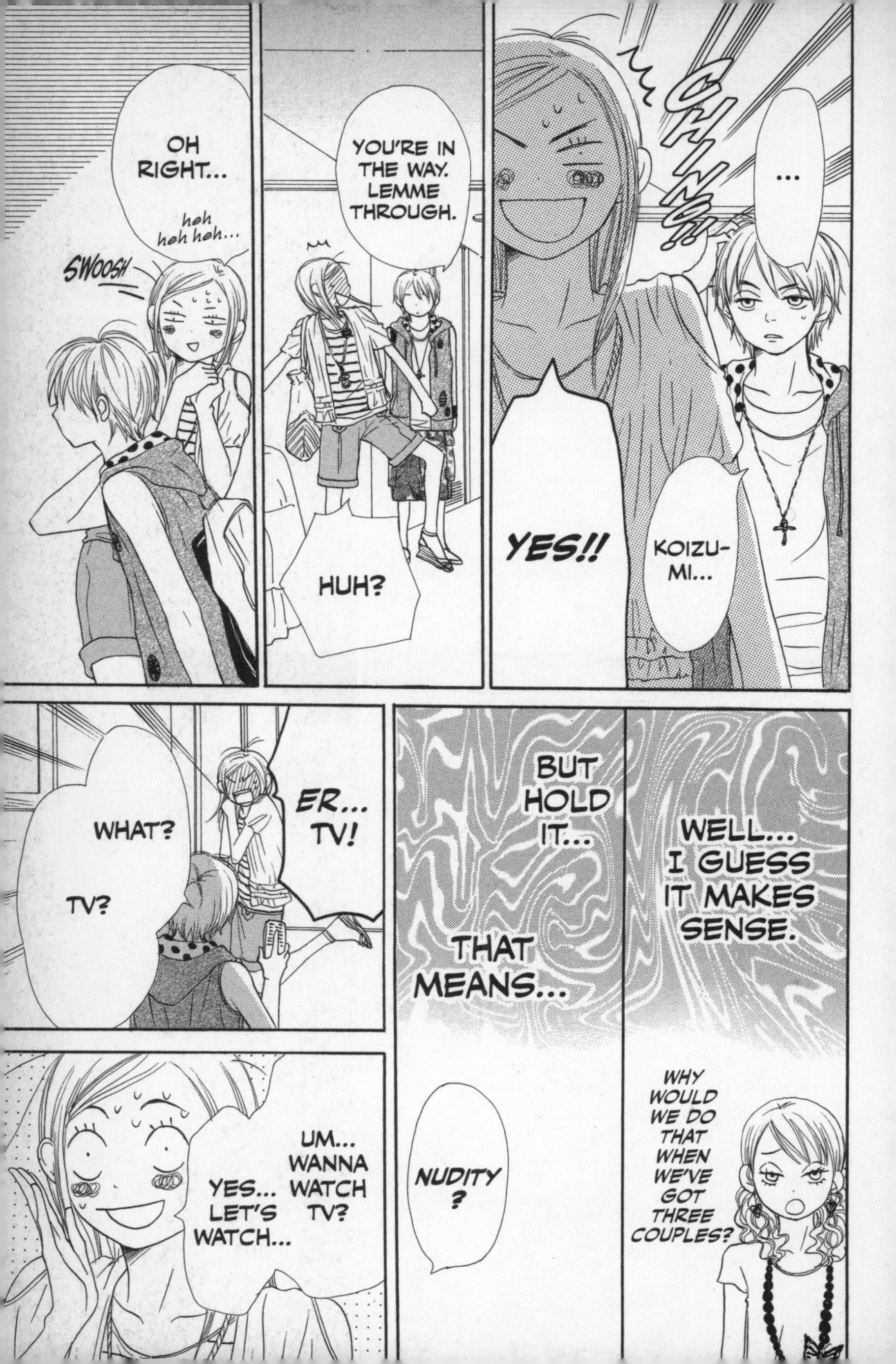
...
KOIZUMI...
YES!!
YOU'RE IN THE WAY. LEMME THROUGH.
HUH?
OH RIGHT...
heh heh heh...
SWOOSH
WELL... I GUESS IT MAKES SENSE.
BUT HOLD IT...
THAT MEANS...
WHY WOULD WE DO THAT WHEN WE'VE GOT THREE COUPLES?
NUDITY?
ER... TV!
WHAT?
TV?
UM... WANNA WATCH TV?
YES... LET'S WATCH...

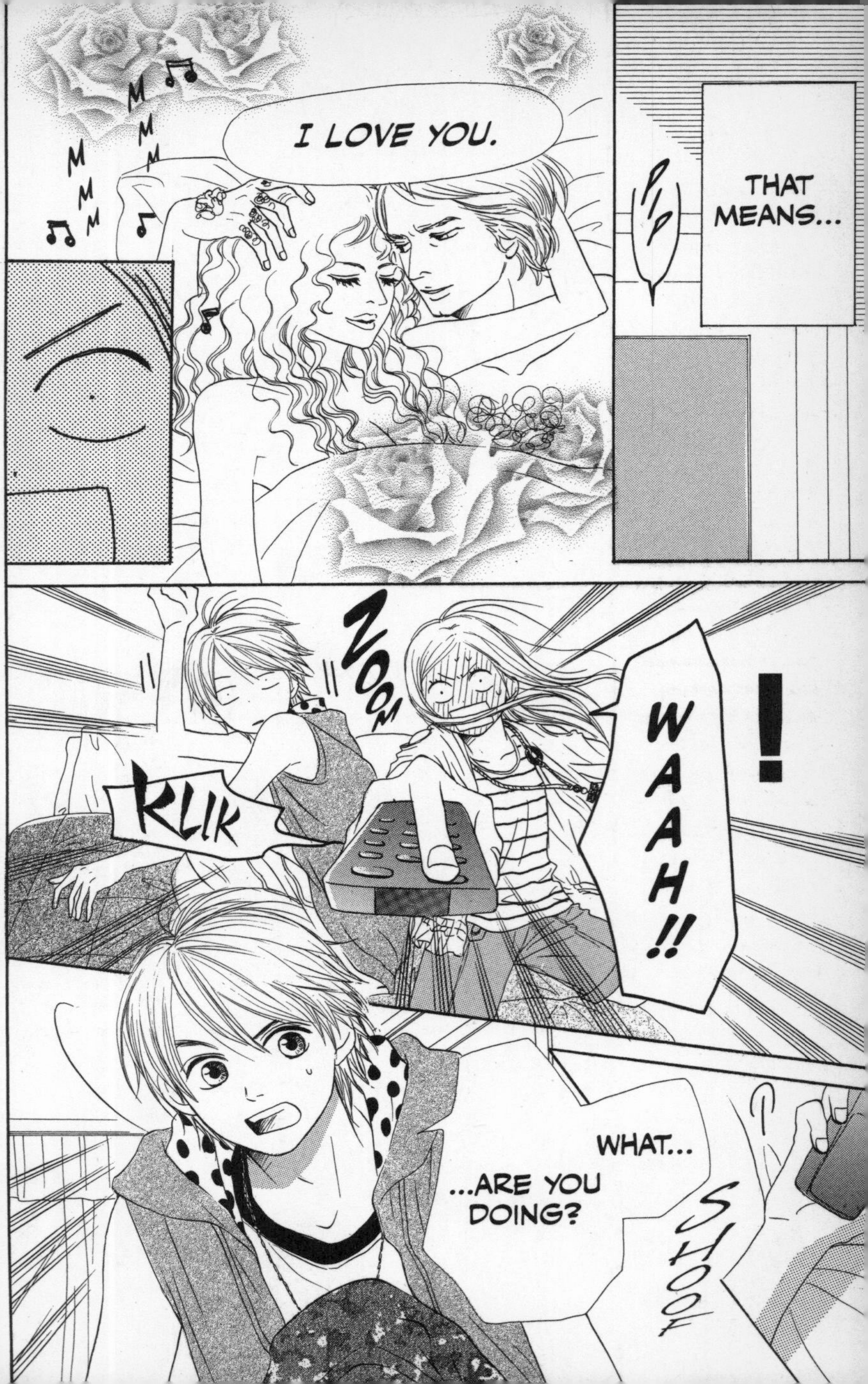
PIP
THAT MEANS...
I LOVE YOU.
MMM
MMM
!
WAAH!!
ZOOM
KLIK
SHOOF
WHAT...
...ARE YOU DOING?

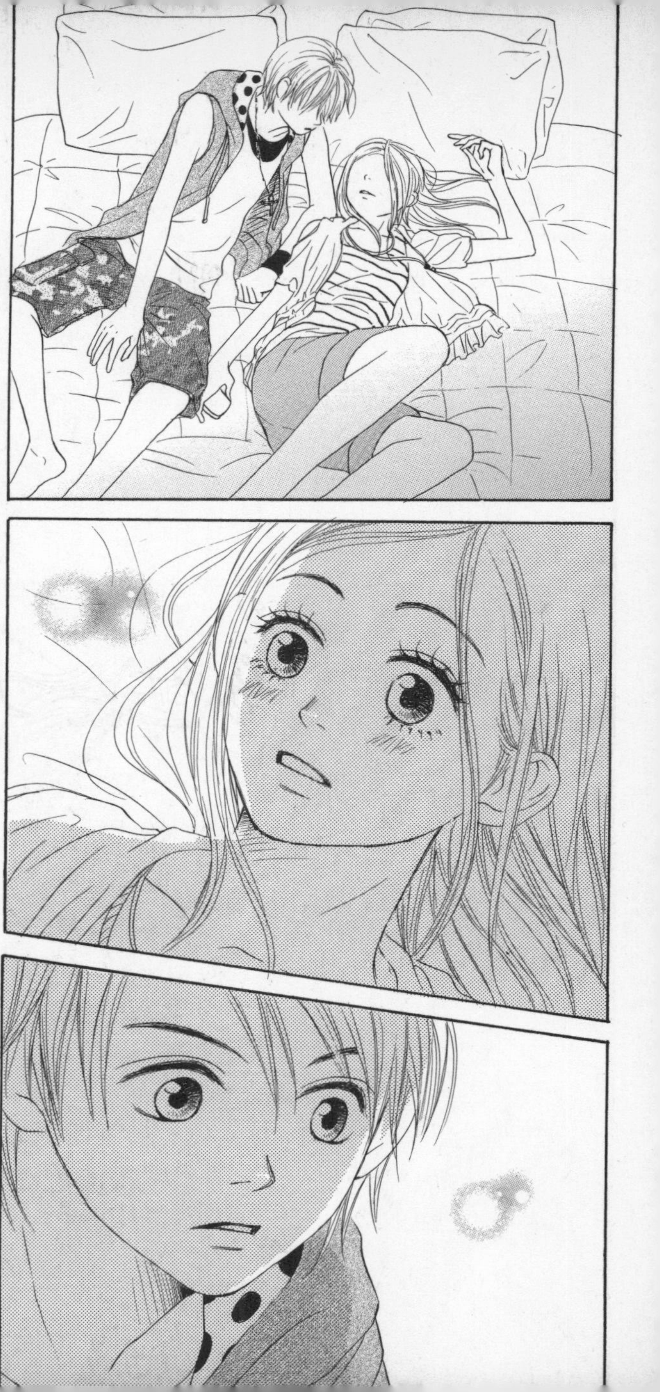

2

Well, summer is over!

Summer came and went like a whirlwind, what with all the meetings and preparations for the movie premiere. We collaborated on a lot of things that appear in both the comic and the live-action movie, like the costumes and plotlines. It was a new experience and it was lots of fun. It also seemed like I was working on color illustrations at a fever pitch all summer. Then the deadline for the manga kept looming. So every day was really busy. I have nothing left in me. I'm just a shell of my former self.

It's always this way.

Ha ha ha...

Hang in there!!

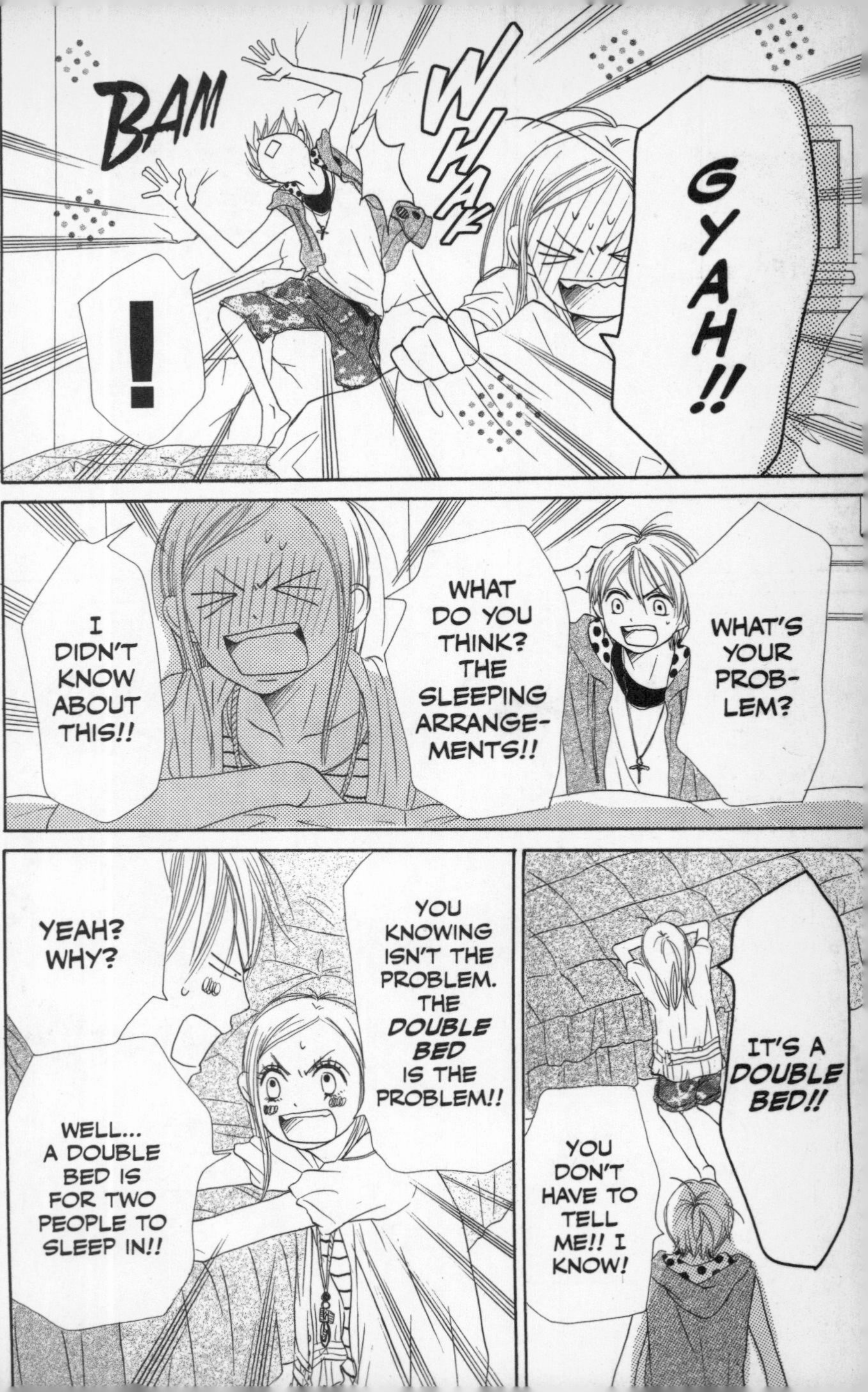
GYAH!!
WHAP
BAM
!
WHAT'S YOUR PROB-LEM?
WHAT DO YOU THINK? THE SLEEPING ARRANGE-MENTS!!
I DIDN'T KNOW ABOUT THIS!!
IT'S A *DOUBLE BED!!*
YOU DON'T HAVE TO TELL ME!! I KNOW!
YOU KNOWING ISN'T THE PROBLEM. THE *DOUBLE BED* IS THE PROBLEM!!
YEAH? WHY?
WELL... A DOUBLE BED IS FOR TWO PEOPLE TO SLEEP IN!!

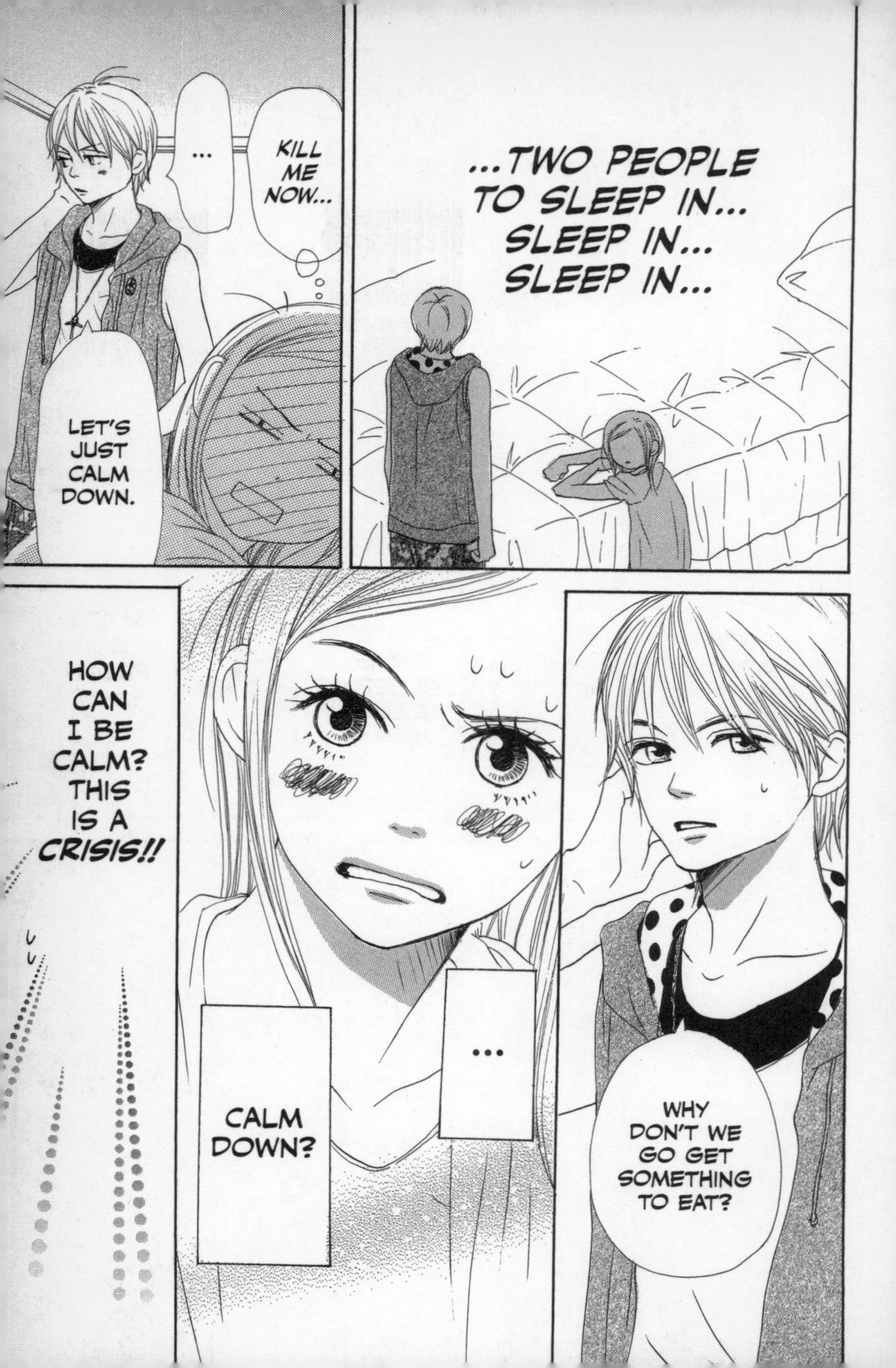
...TWO PEOPLE TO SLEEP IN... SLEEP IN... SLEEP IN...
KILL ME NOW...
...
LET'S JUST CALM DOWN.
WHY DON'T WE GO GET SOMETHING TO EAT?
...
CALM DOWN?
HOW CAN I BE CALM? THIS IS A CRISIS!!

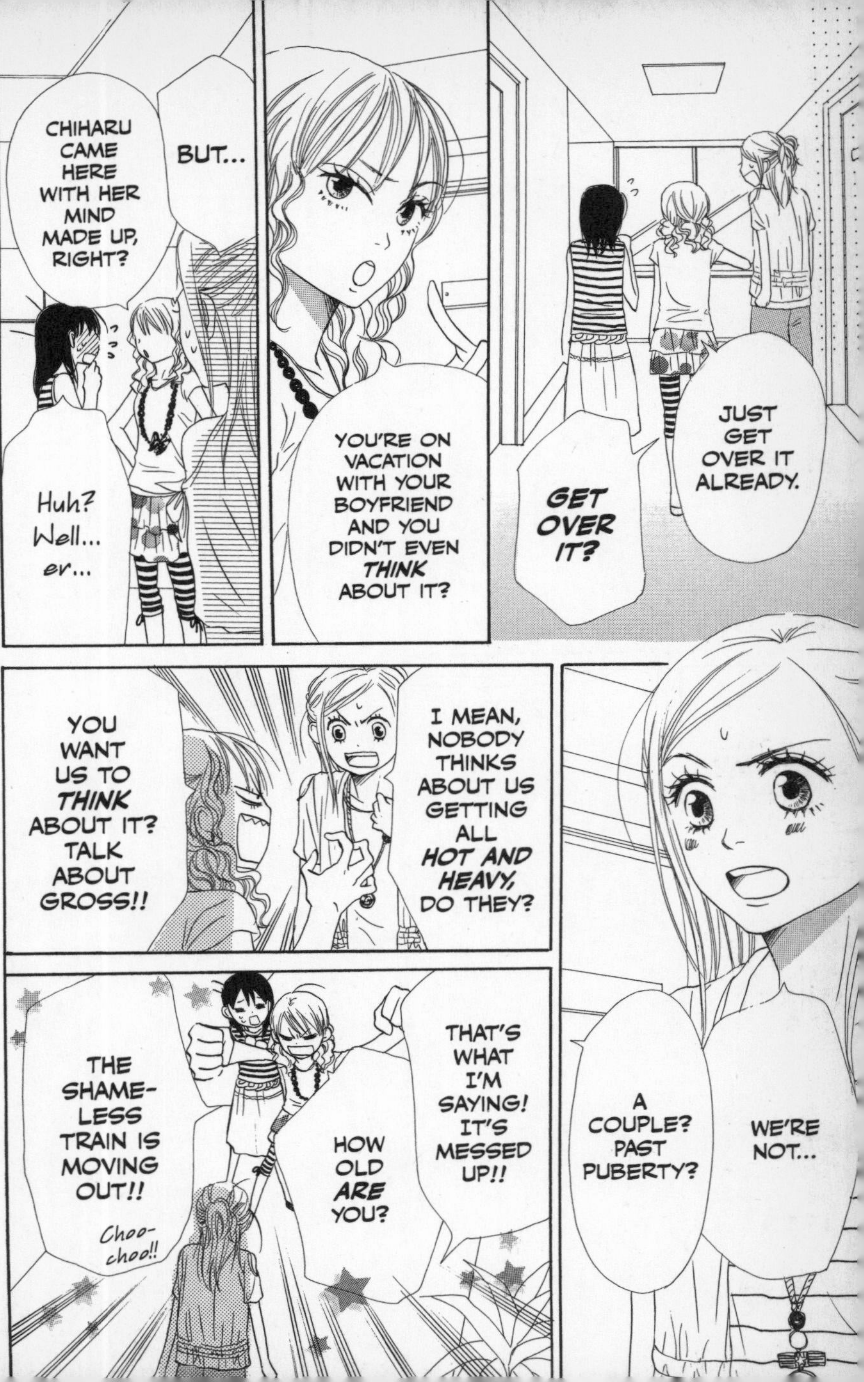
JUST GET OVER IT ALREADY.
GET OVER IT?
YOU'RE ON VACATION WITH YOUR BOYFRIEND AND YOU DIDN'T EVEN THINK ABOUT IT?
BUT...
CHIHARU CAME HERE WITH HER MIND MADE UP, RIGHT?
Huh? Well... er...
WE'RE NOT...
A COUPLE? PAST PUBERTY?
I MEAN, NOBODY THINKS ABOUT US GETTING ALL HOT AND HEAVY, DO THEY?
YOU WANT US TO THINK ABOUT IT? TALK ABOUT GROSS!!
THAT'S WHAT I'M SAYING! IT'S MESSED UP!!
HOW OLD ARE YOU?
THE SHAME-LESS TRAIN IS MOVING OUT!!
Choo-choo!!

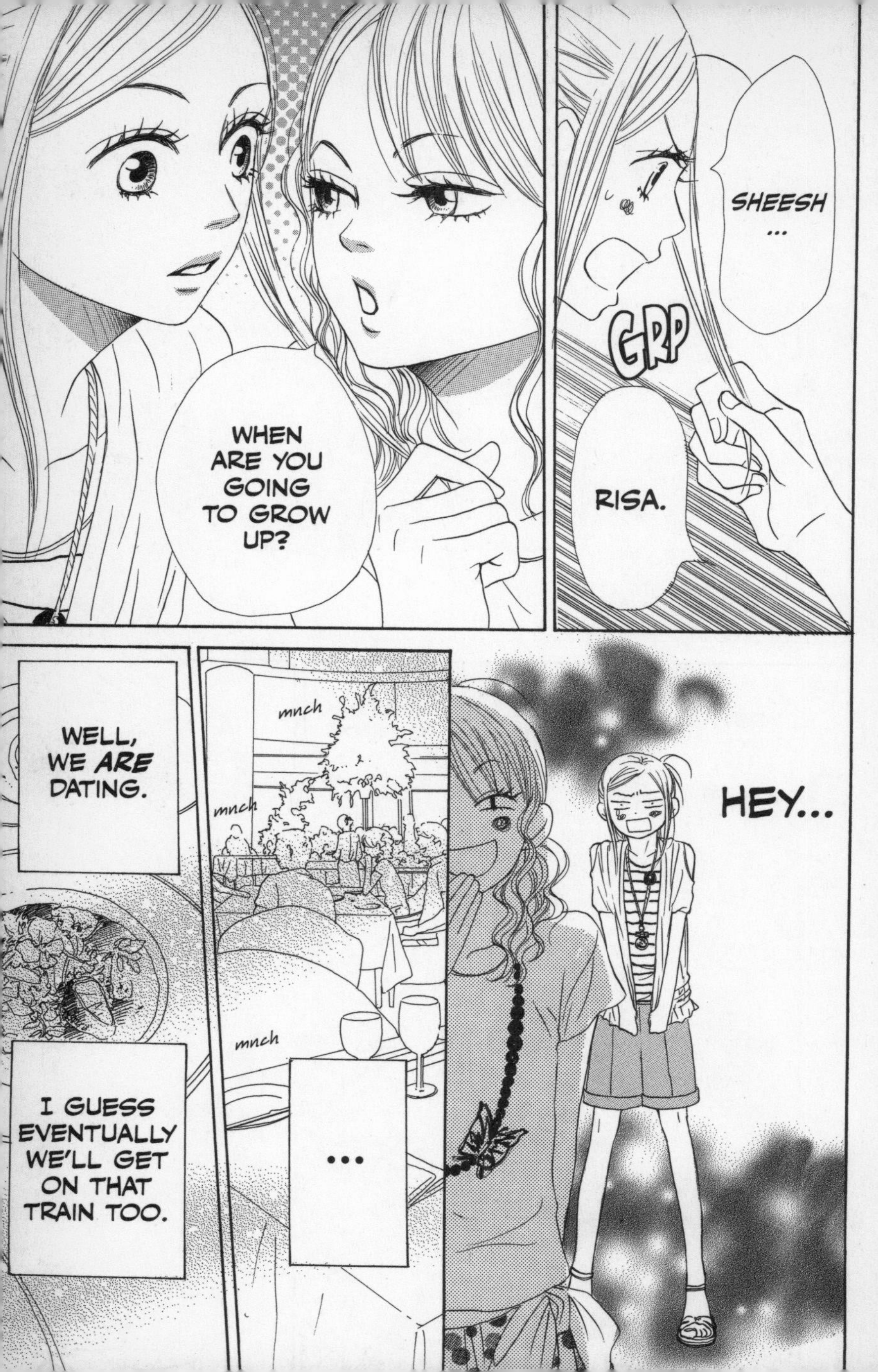
SHEESH ...
GRP
RISA.
WHEN ARE YOU GOING TO GROW UP?
HEY...
mnch
mnch
mnch
...
WELL, WE *ARE* DATING.
I GUESS EVENTUALLY WE'LL GET ON THAT TRAIN TOO.

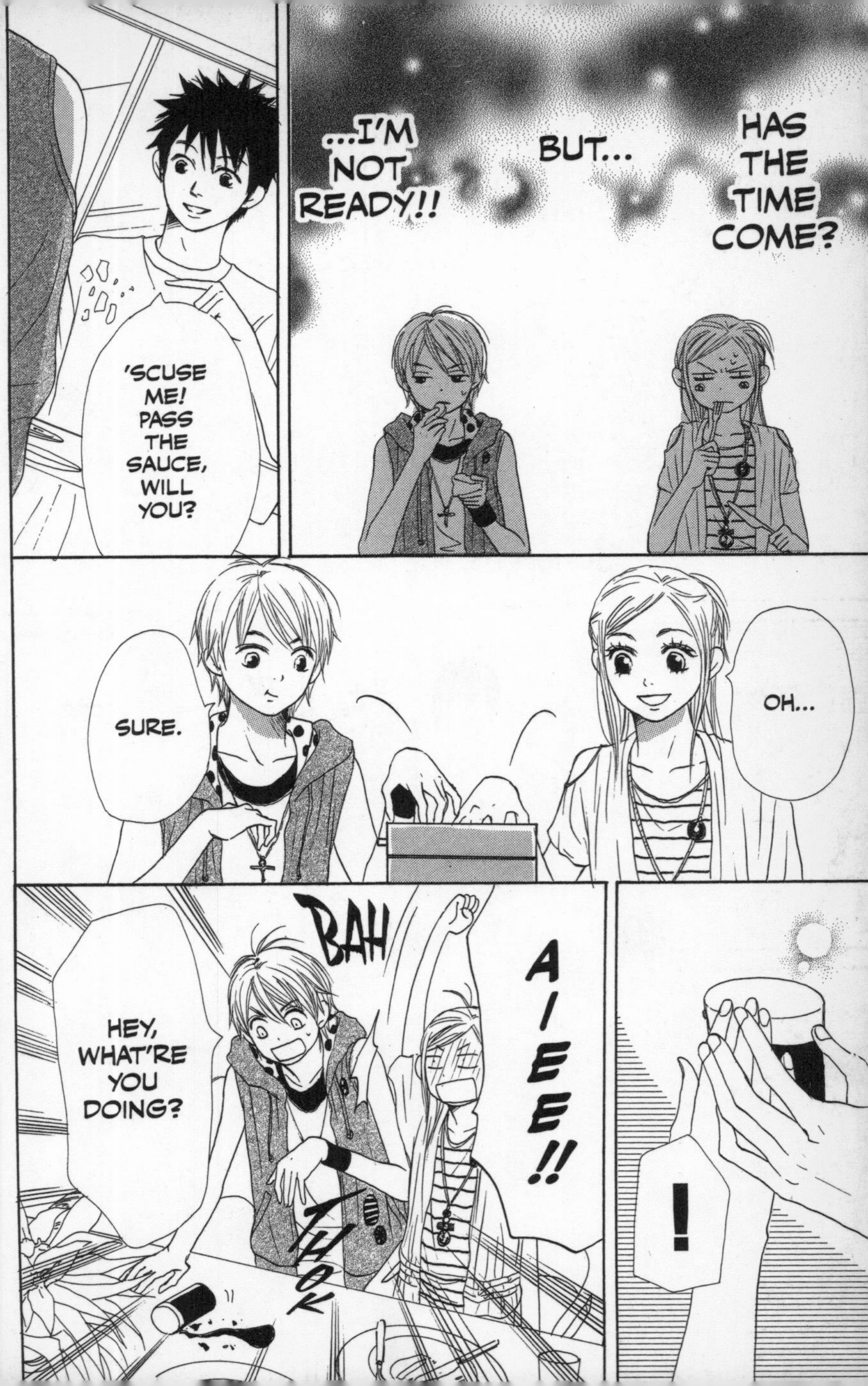
HAS THE TIME COME?
BUT...
...I'M NOT READY!!
'SCUSE ME! PASS THE SAUCE, WILL YOU?
OH...
SURE.
!
AIEE!!
BAH
HEY, WHAT'RE YOU DOING?
THOK

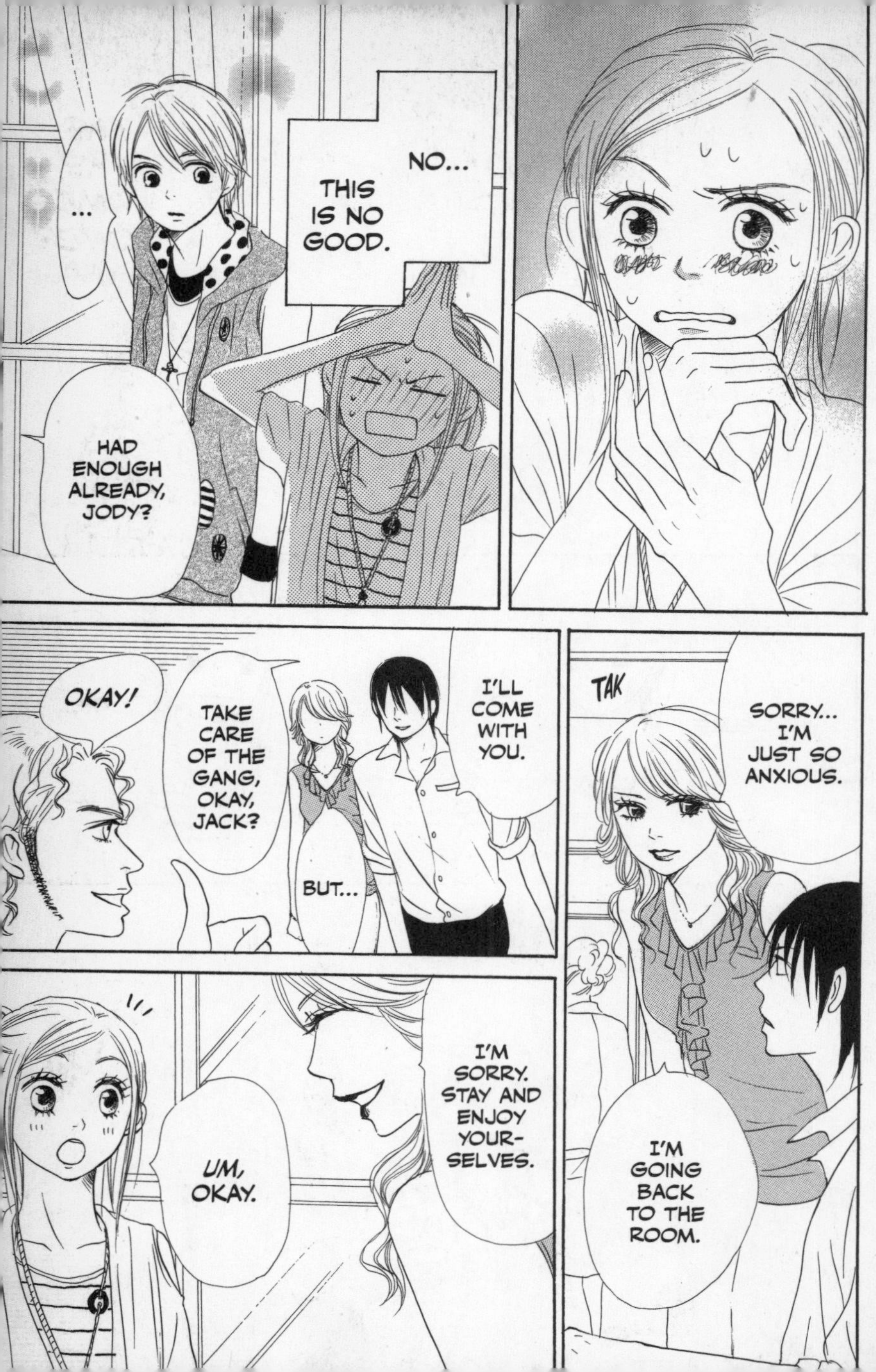
NO...
THIS IS NO GOOD.
...
HAD ENOUGH ALREADY, JODY?
TAK
SORRY... I'M JUST SO ANXIOUS.
I'M GOING BACK TO THE ROOM.
I'LL COME WITH YOU.
TAKE CARE OF THE GANG, OKAY, JACK?
BUT...
OKAY!
I'M SORRY. STAY AND ENJOY YOUR-SELVES.
UM, OKAY.

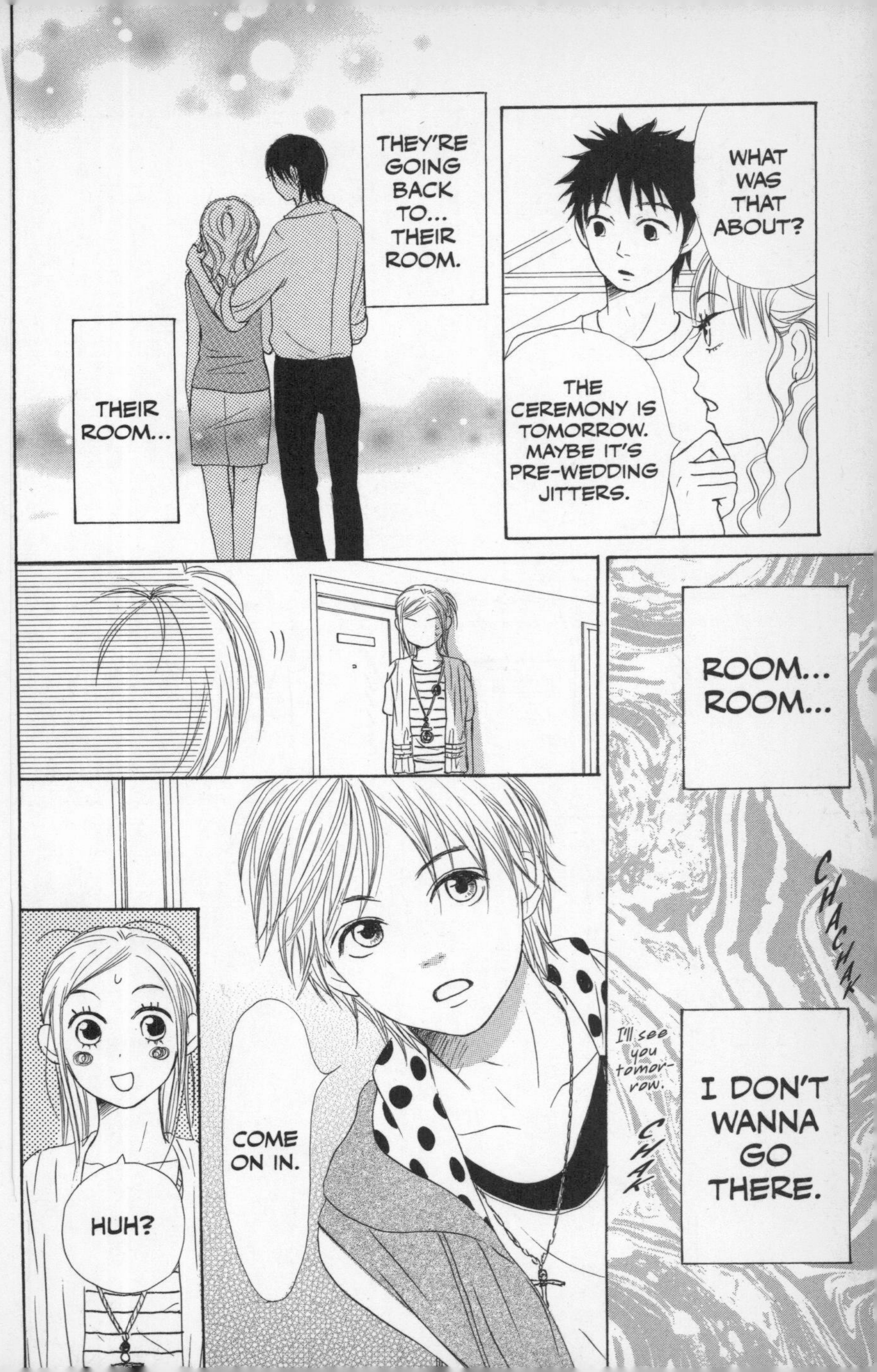
WHAT WAS THAT ABOUT?
THE CEREMONY IS TOMORROW. MAYBE IT'S PRE-WEDDING JITTERS.
THEY'RE GOING BACK TO... THEIR ROOM.
THEIR ROOM...
ROOM... ROOM...
CHACHAK
I DON'T WANNA GO THERE.
I'll see you tomorrow.
CHAK
COME ON IN.
HUH?

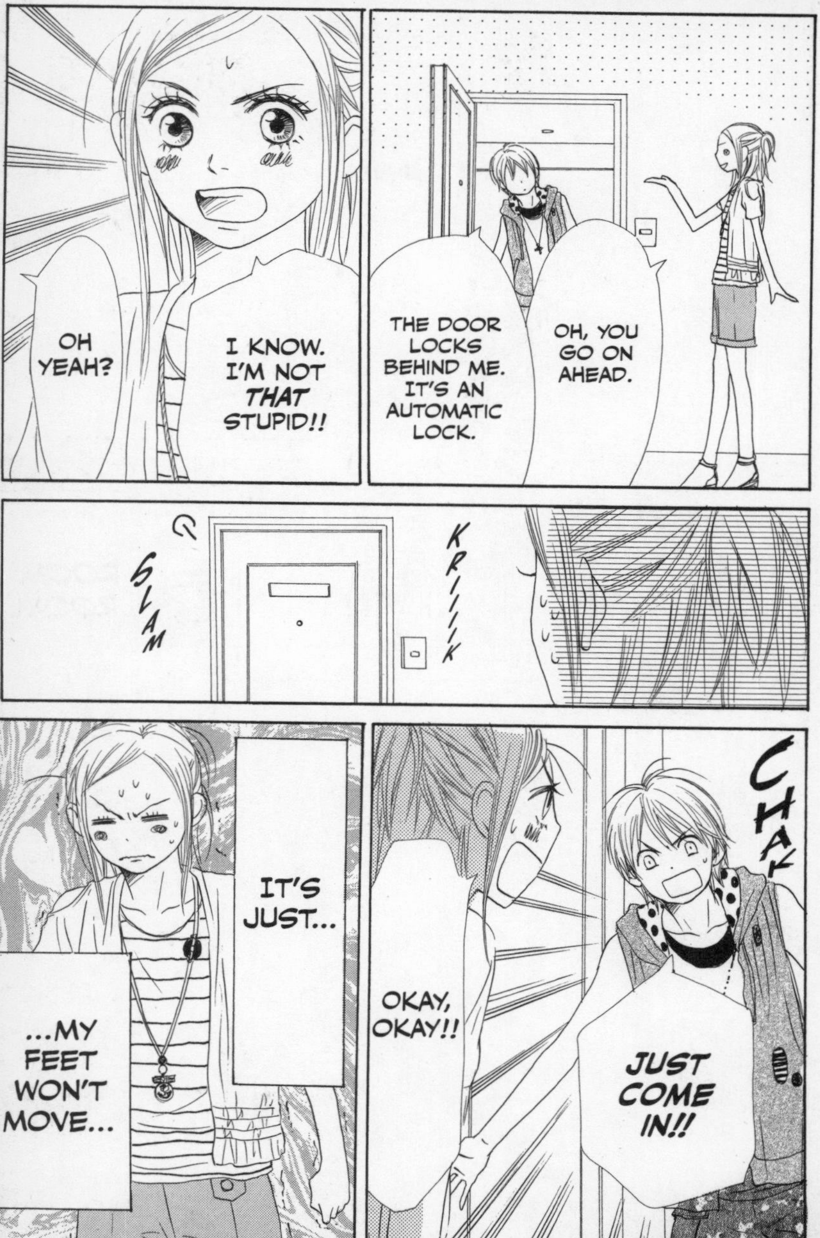
OH, YOU GO ON AHEAD.
THE DOOR LOCKS BEHIND ME. IT'S AN AUTOMATIC LOCK.
I KNOW. I'M NOT *THAT* STUPID!!
OH YEAH?
KRIIIIK
SLAM
CHAK
JUST COME IN!!
OKAY, OKAY!!
IT'S JUST...
...MY FEET WON'T MOVE...

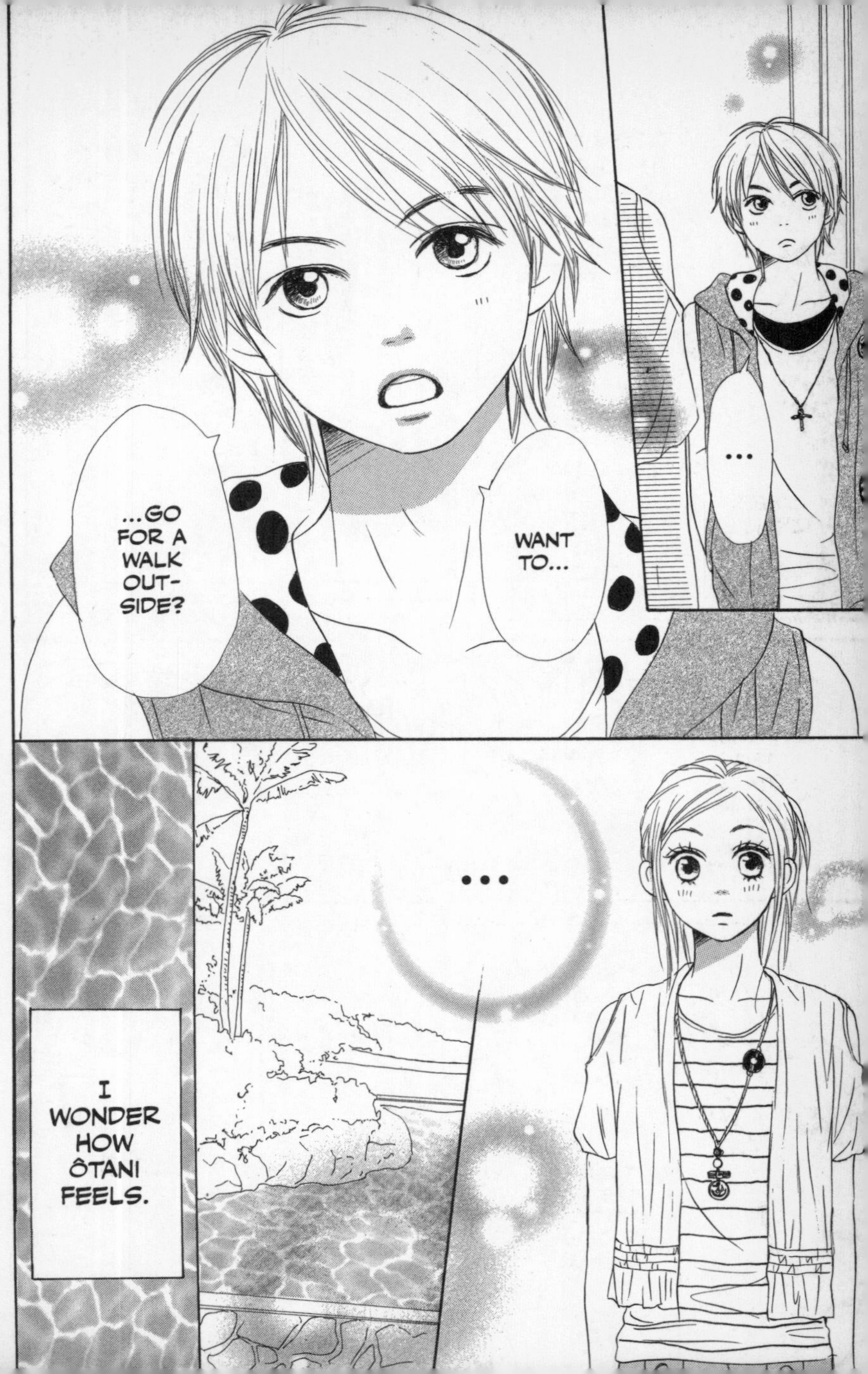
...
WANT TO...
...GO FOR A WALK OUT-SIDE?
...
I WONDER HOW ÔTANI FEELS.

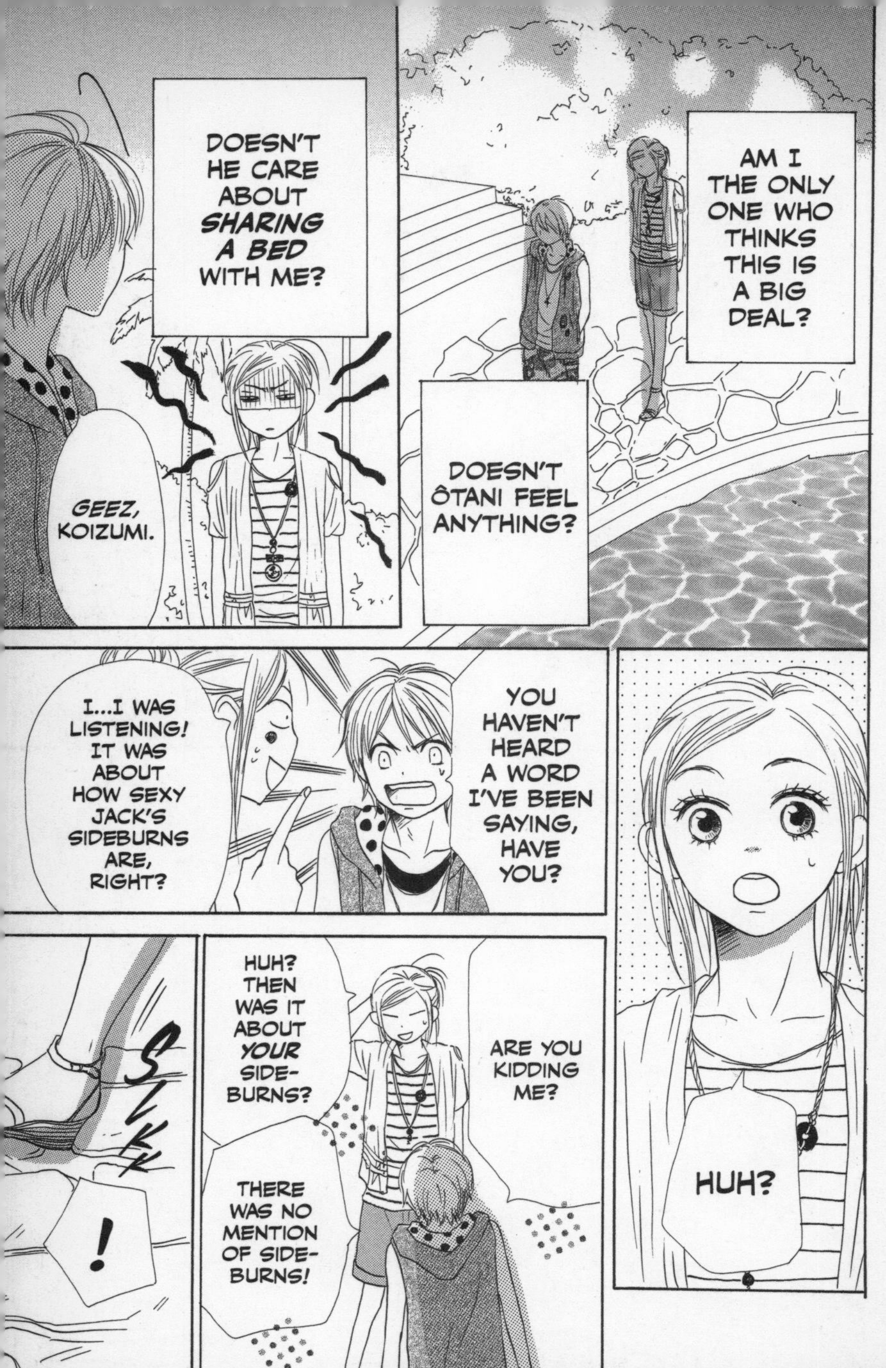
AM I THE ONLY ONE WHO THINKS THIS IS A BIG DEAL?
DOESN'T ÔTANI FEEL ANYTHING?
DOESN'T HE CARE ABOUT *SHARING A BED* WITH ME?
GEEZ, KOIZUMI.
HUH?
YOU HAVEN'T HEARD A WORD I'VE BEEN SAYING, HAVE YOU?
I...I WAS LISTENING! IT WAS ABOUT HOW SEXY JACK'S SIDEBURNS ARE, RIGHT?
ARE YOU KIDDING ME?
HUH? THEN WAS IT ABOUT *YOUR* SIDE-BURNS?
THERE WAS NO MENTION OF SIDE-BURNS!
SLIKK
!

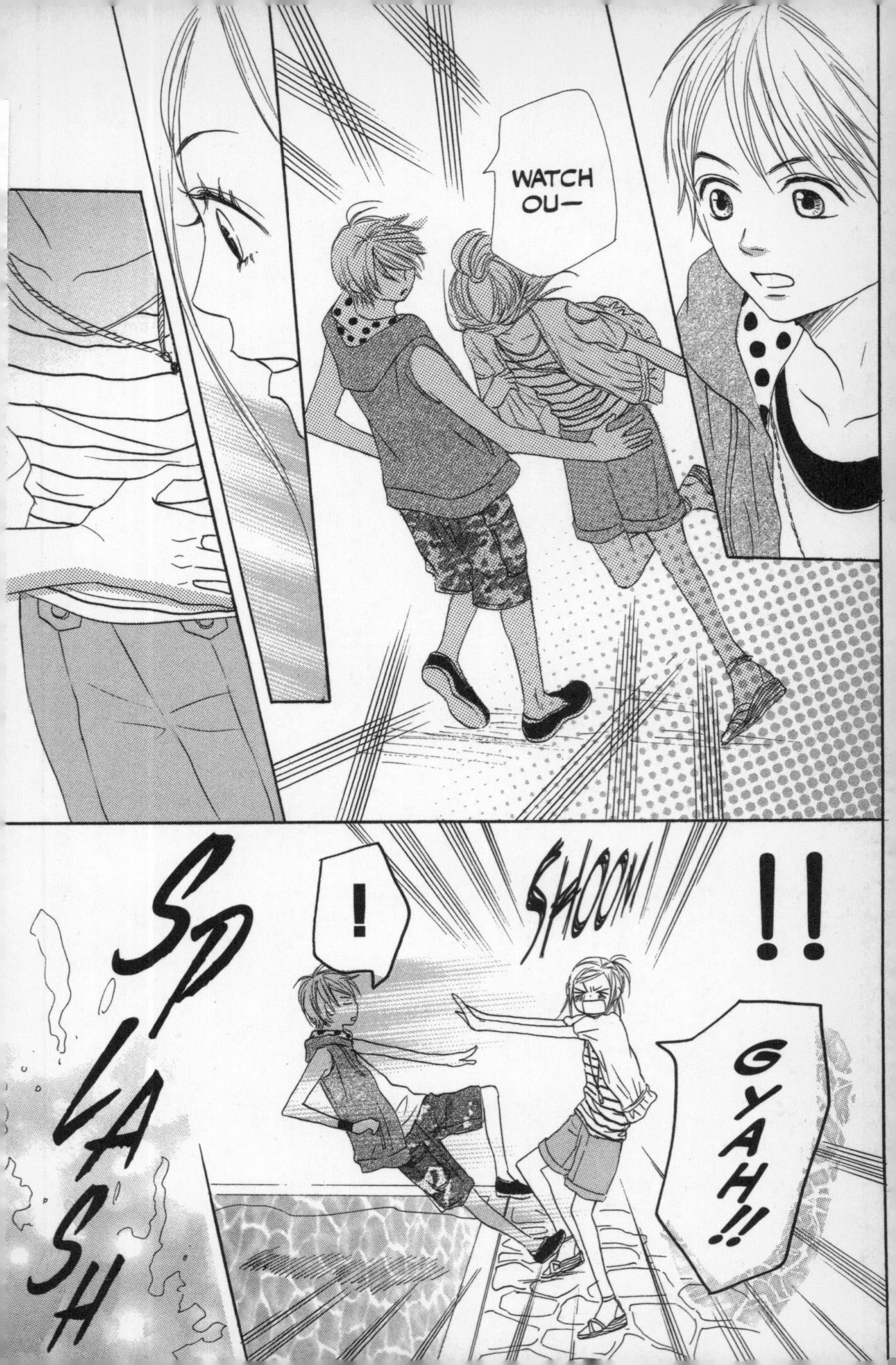
WATCH OU—
!!
GYAH!!
SHOOM
!
SPLASH

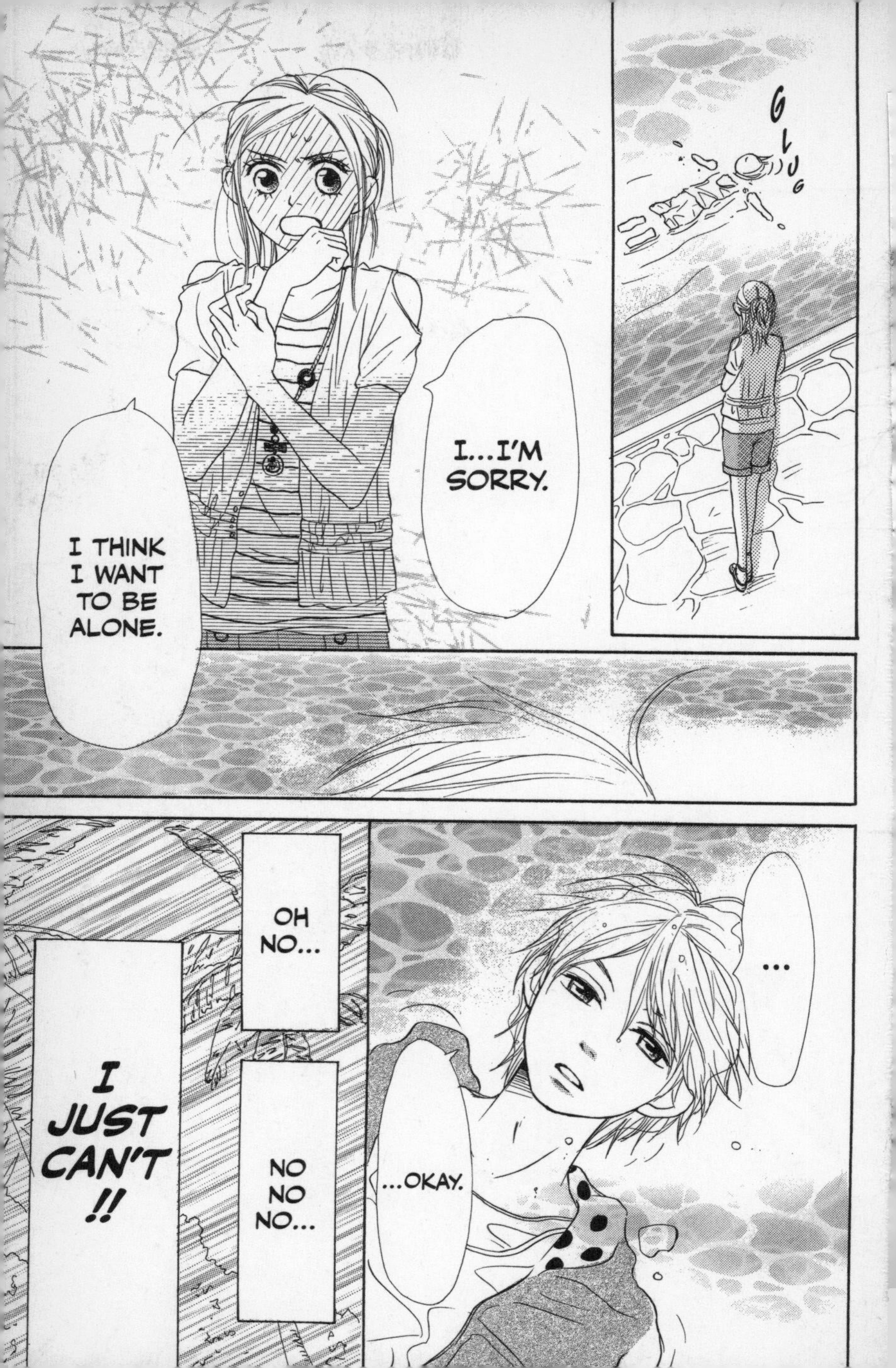
GLUG
I...I'M SORRY.
I THINK I WANT TO BE ALONE.
...
...OKAY.
OH NO...
NO NO NO...
I JUST CAN'T!!

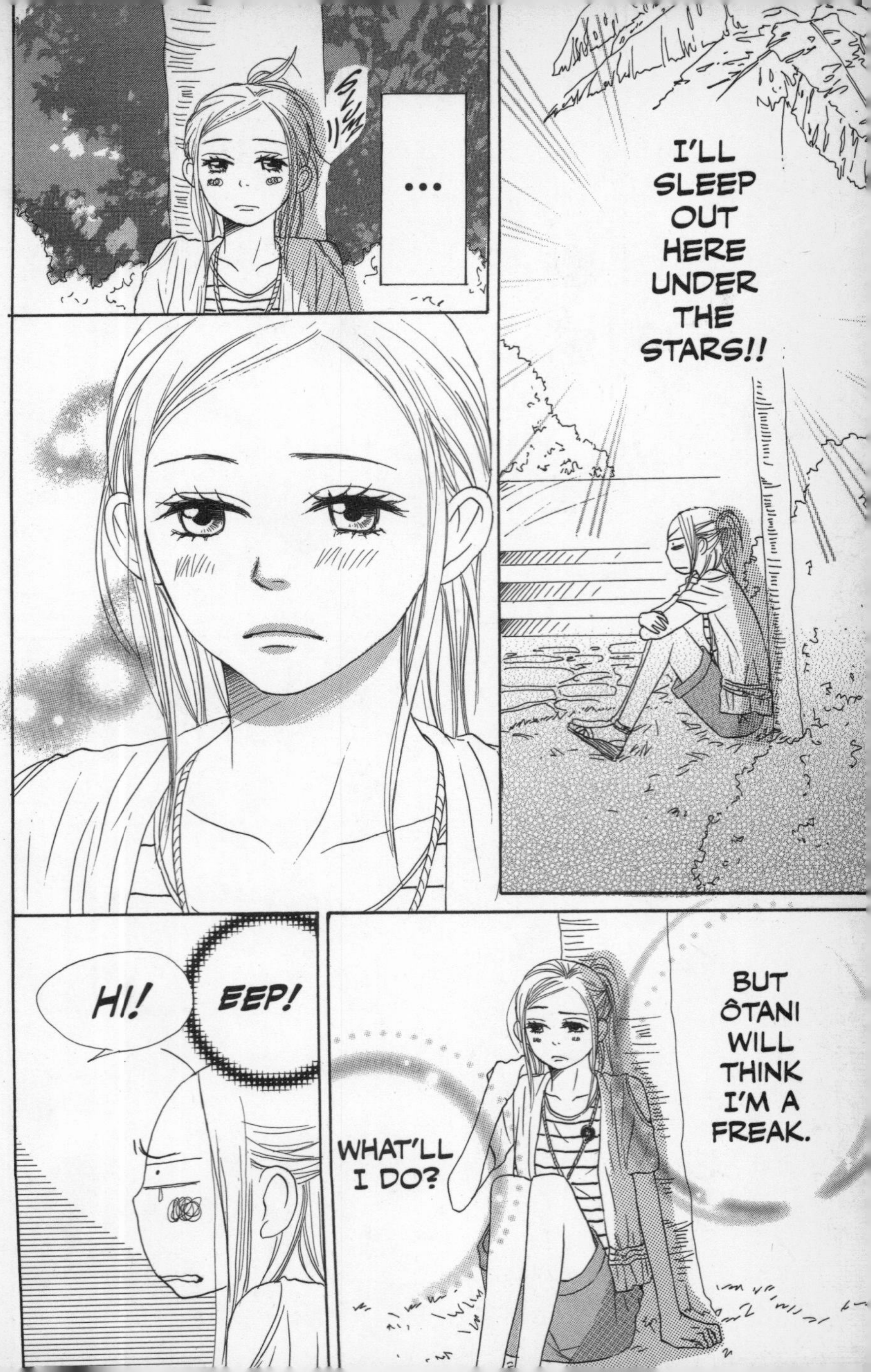
I'LL SLEEP OUT HERE UNDER THE STARS!!
...
BUT ŌTANI WILL THINK I'M A FREAK.
WHAT'LL I DO?
EEP!
HI!

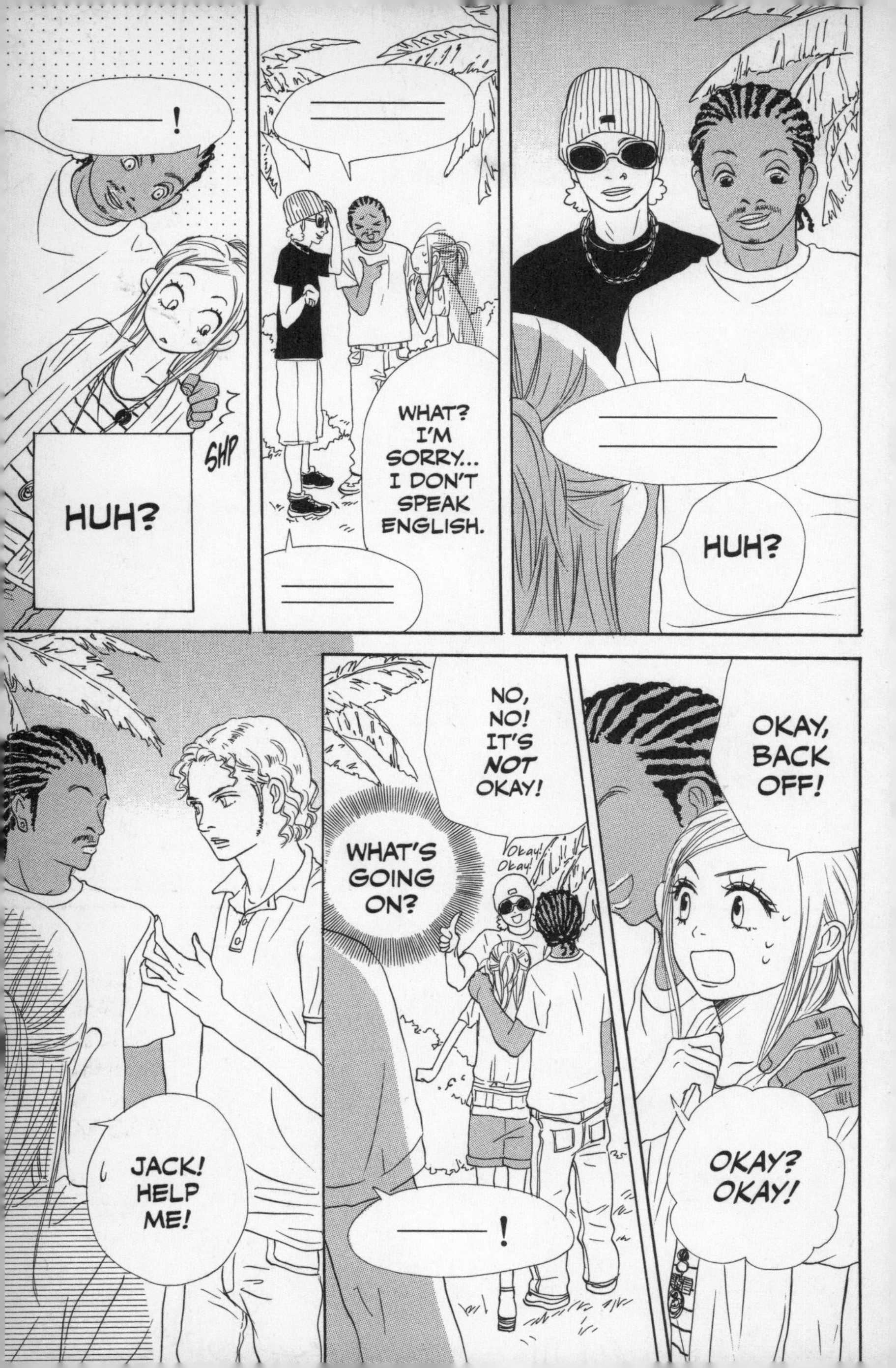
HUH?
WHAT? I'M SORRY... I DON'T SPEAK ENGLISH.
SHP
HUH?
OKAY, BACK OFF!
OKAY? OKAY!
NO, NO! IT'S *NOT* OKAY!
WHAT'S GOING ON?
Okay! Okay!
JACK! HELP ME!

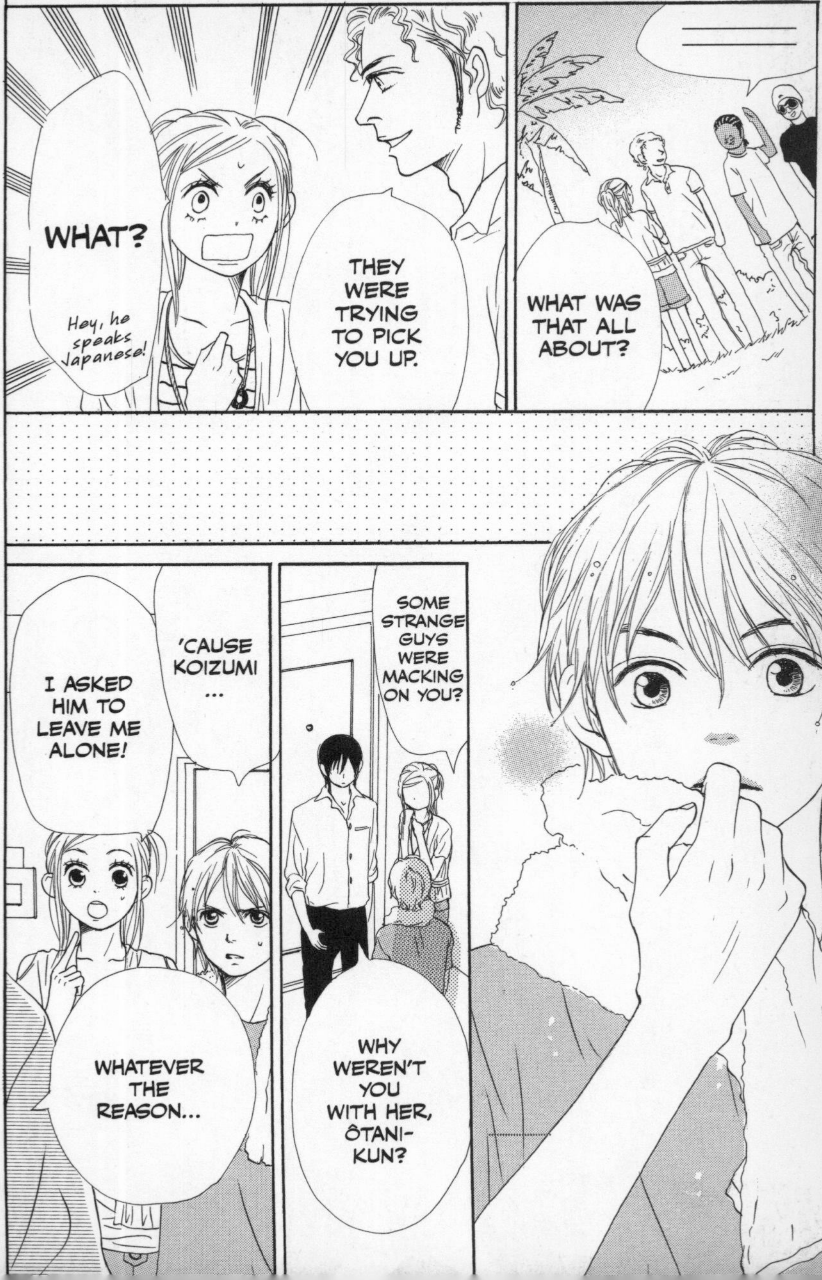
WHAT WAS THAT ALL ABOUT?
THEY WERE TRYING TO PICK YOU UP.
WHAT?
Hey, he speaks Japanese!
SOME STRANGE GUYS WERE MACKING ON YOU?
WHY WEREN'T YOU WITH HER, ÔTANI-KUN?
'CAUSE KOIZUMI ...
I ASKED HIM TO LEAVE ME ALONE!
WHATEVER THE REASON...

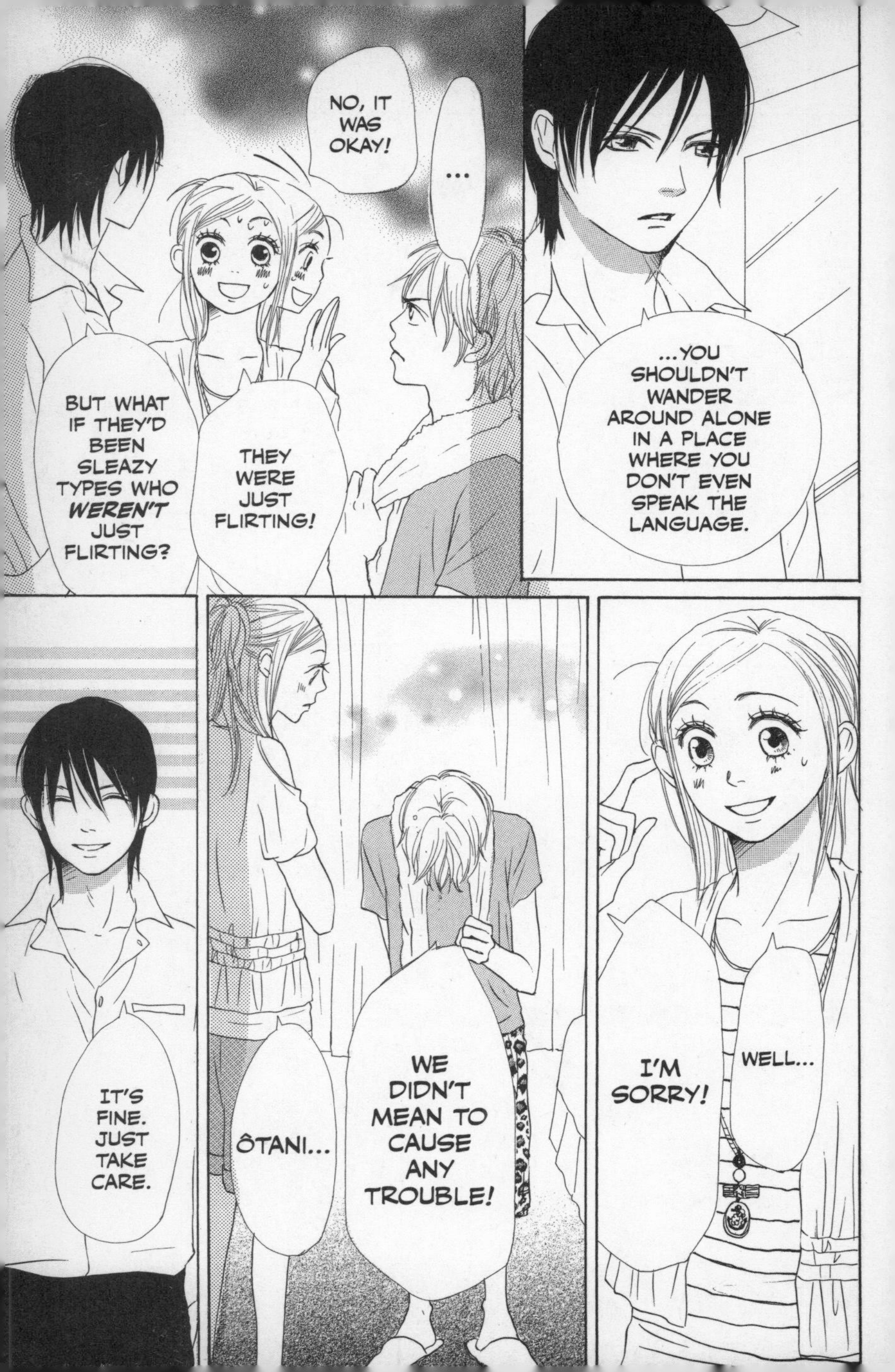
...YOU SHOULDN'T WANDER AROUND ALONE IN A PLACE WHERE YOU DON'T EVEN SPEAK THE LANGUAGE.
...
NO, IT WAS OKAY!
THEY WERE JUST FLIRTING!
BUT WHAT IF THEY'D BEEN SLEAZY TYPES WHO *WEREN'T* JUST FLIRTING?
WELL...
I'M SORRY!
WE DIDN'T MEAN TO CAUSE ANY TROUBLE!
ÔTANI...
IT'S FINE. JUST TAKE CARE.

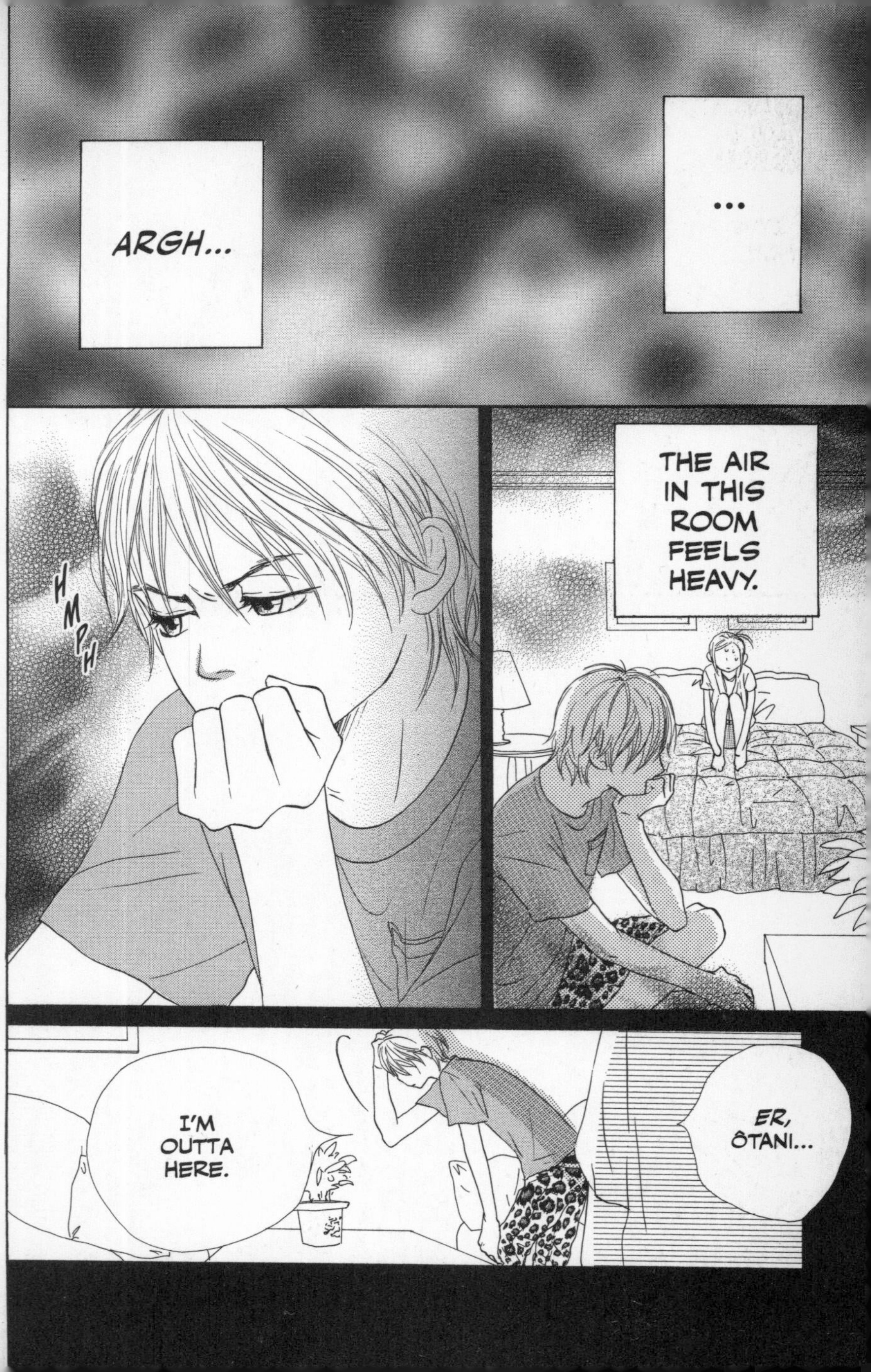
...
ARGH...
THE AIR IN THIS ROOM FEELS HEAVY.
HMPH
ER, ŌTANI...
I'M OUTTA HERE.

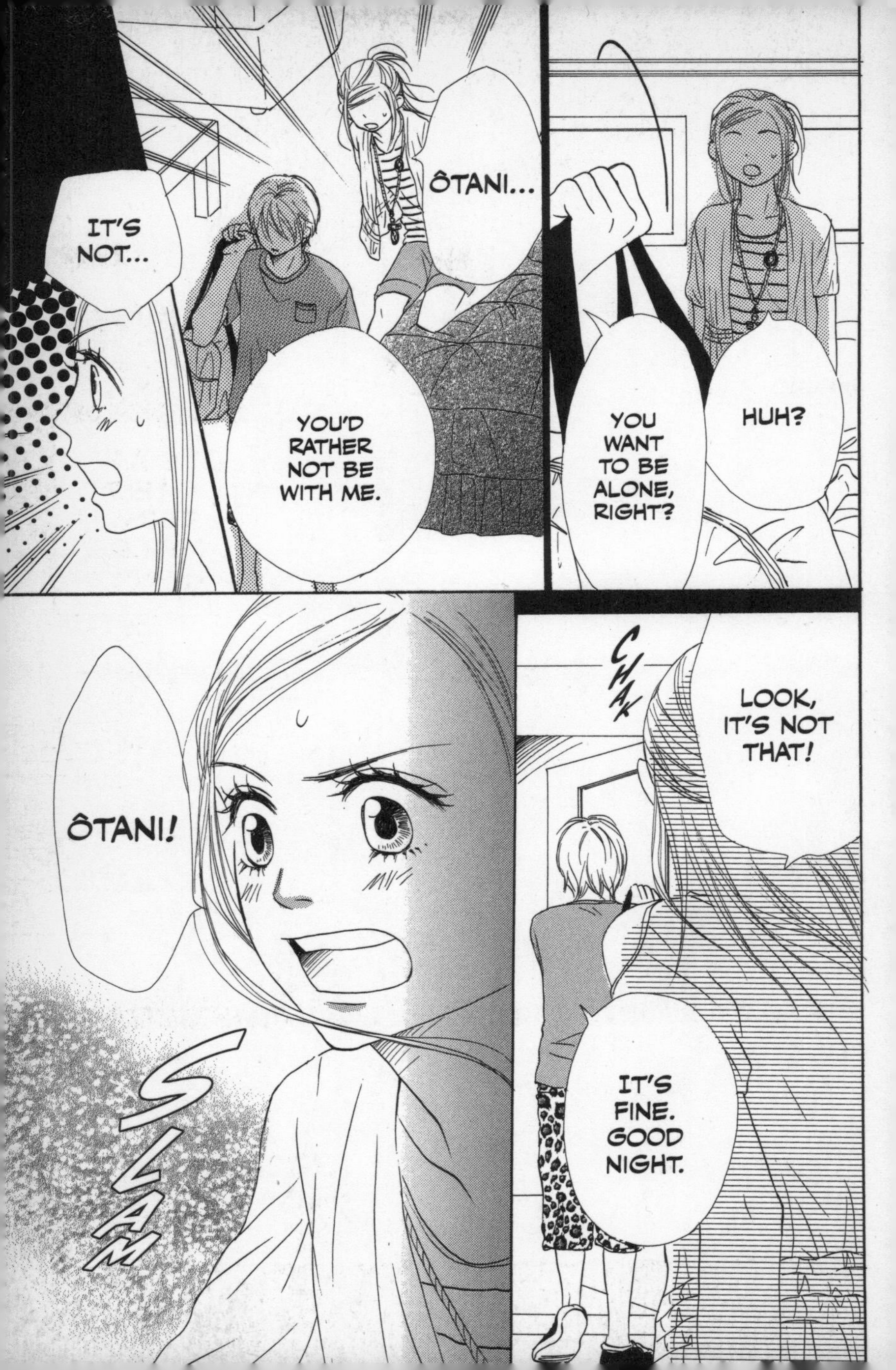
HUH?
YOU WANT TO BE ALONE, RIGHT?
ÔTANI...
YOU'D RATHER NOT BE WITH ME.
IT'S NOT...
CHAK
LOOK, IT'S NOT THAT!
IT'S FINE. GOOD NIGHT.
ÔTANI!
SLAM

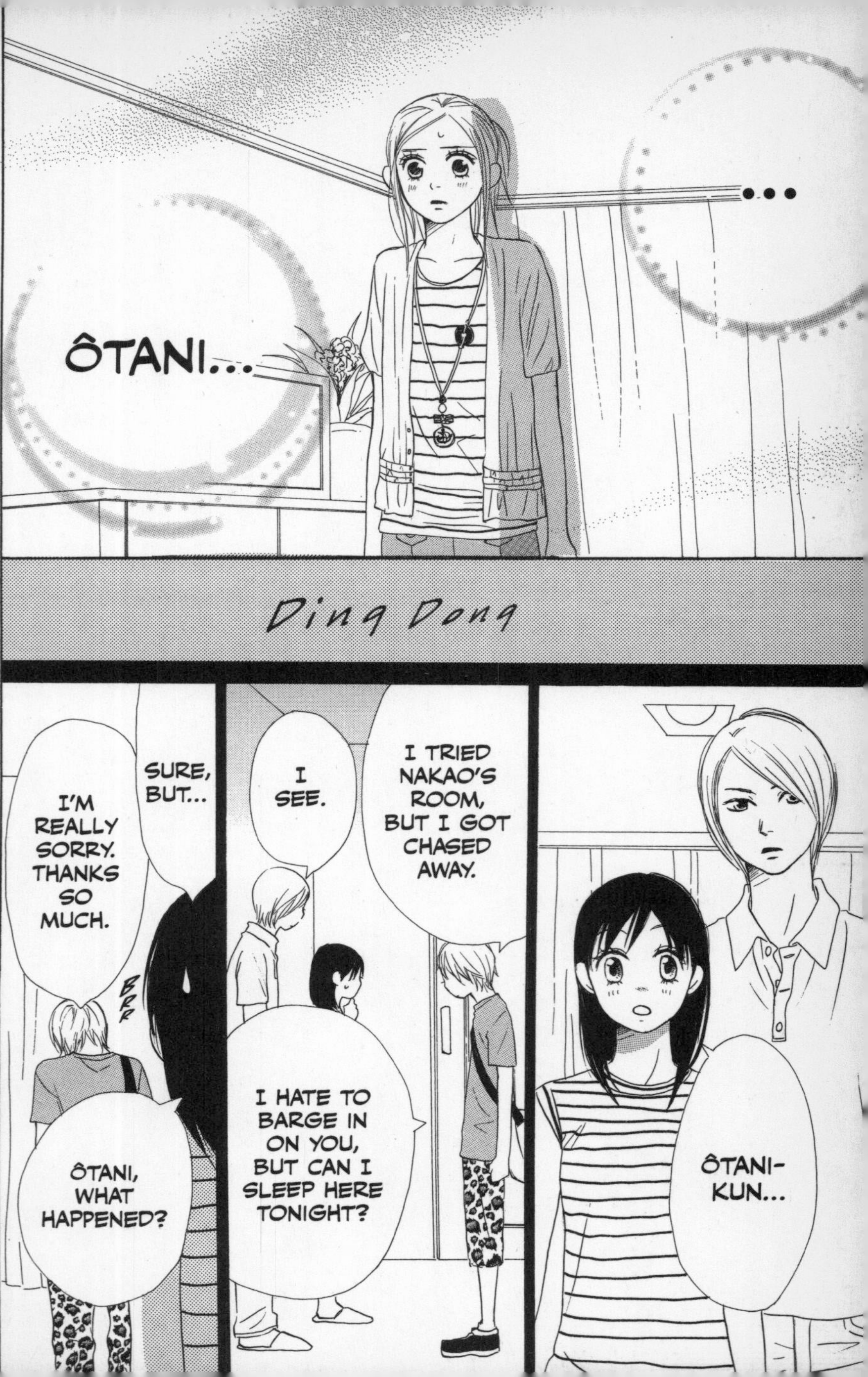
...
ÔTANI...
Ding Dong
ÔTANI-KUN...
I TRIED NAKAO'S ROOM, BUT I GOT CHASED AWAY.
I SEE.
I HATE TO BARGE IN ON YOU, BUT CAN I SLEEP HERE TONIGHT?
SURE, BUT...
I'M REALLY SORRY. THANKS SO MUCH.
BRR
ÔTANI, WHAT HAPPENED?

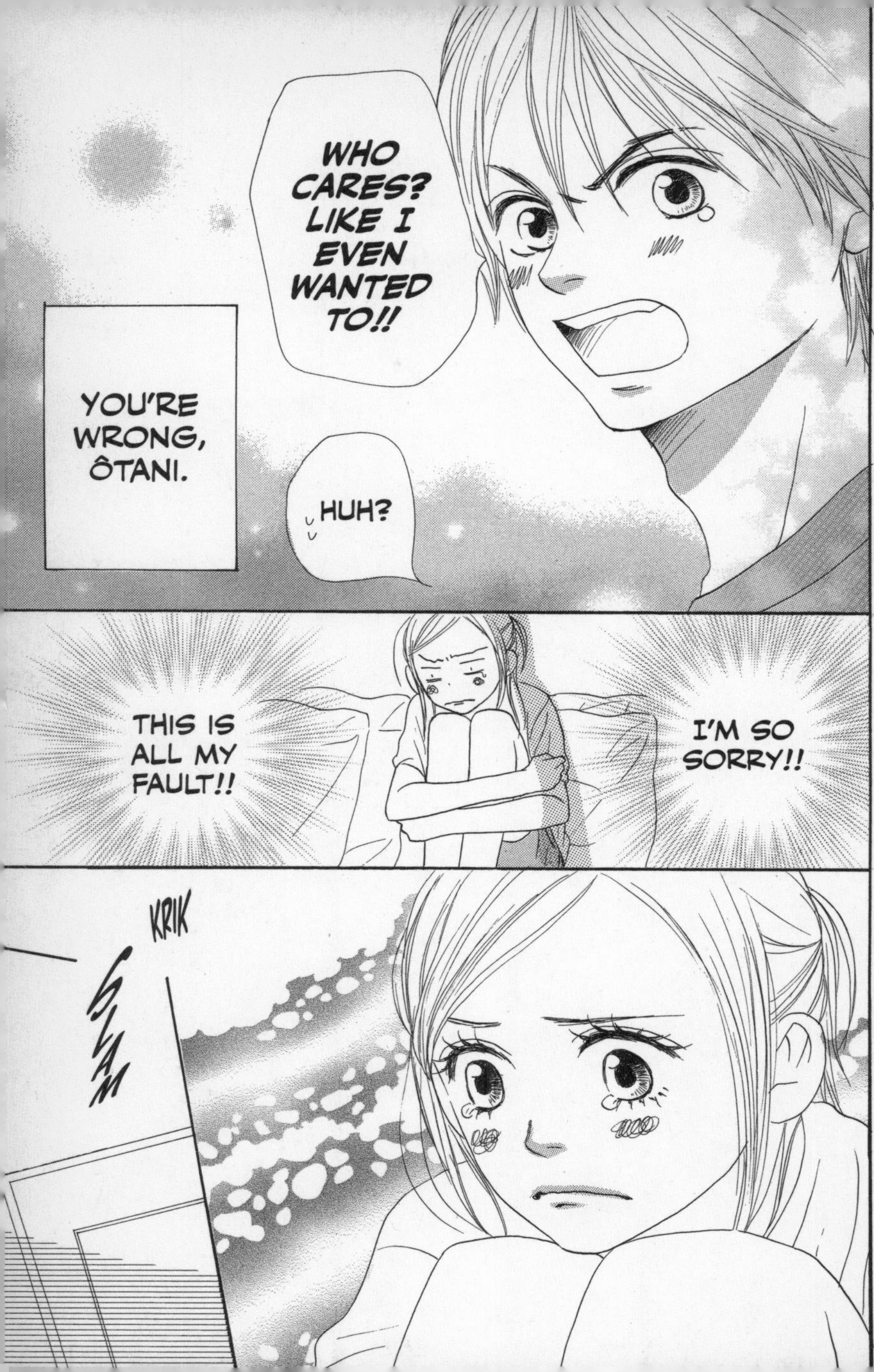
WHO CARES? LIKE I EVEN WANTED TO!!
HUH?
YOU'RE WRONG, ÔTANI.
I'M SO SORRY!!
THIS IS ALL MY FAULT!!
KRIK
SLAM

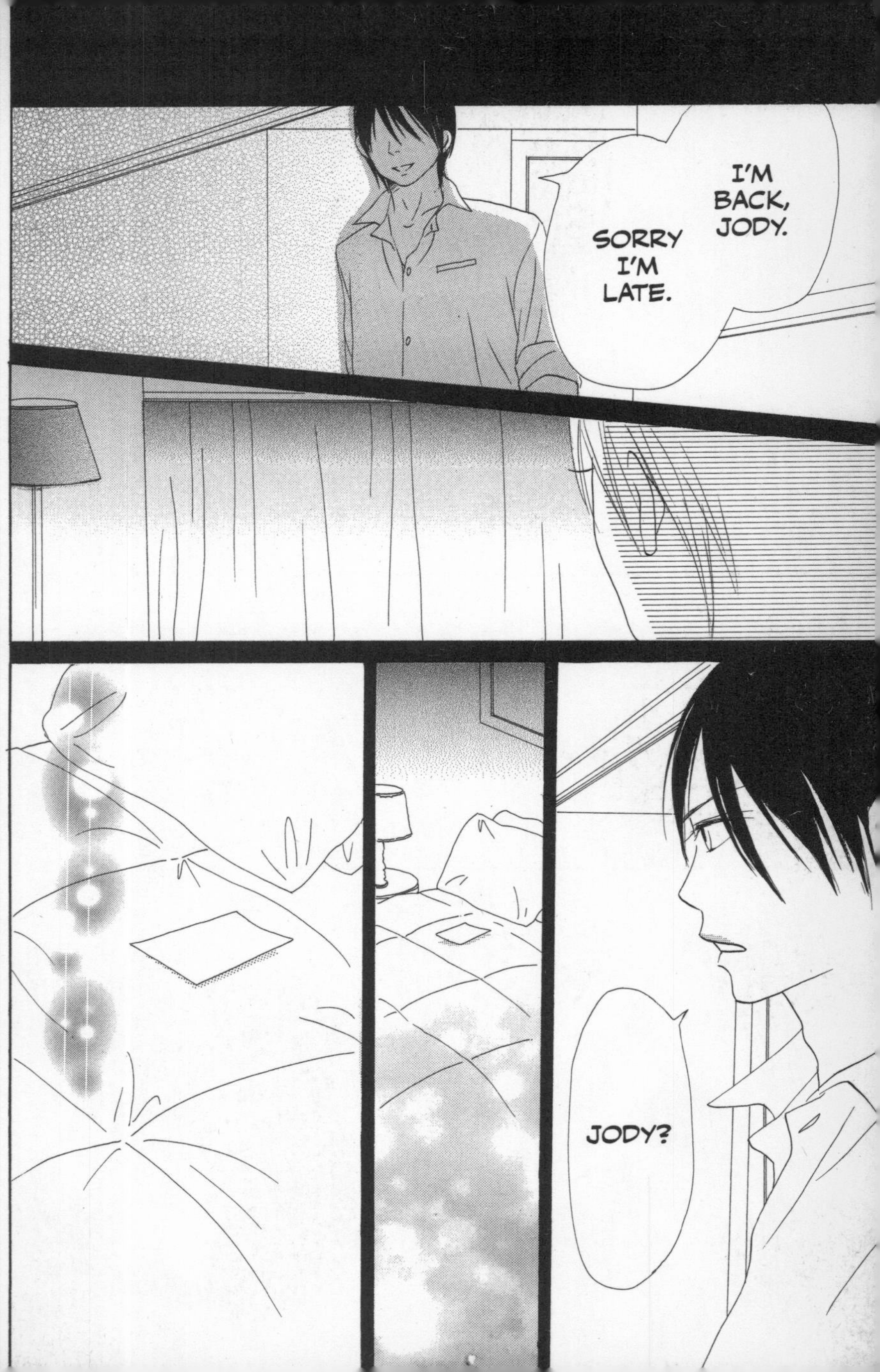
I'M BACK, JODY.
SORRY I'M LATE.
JODY?

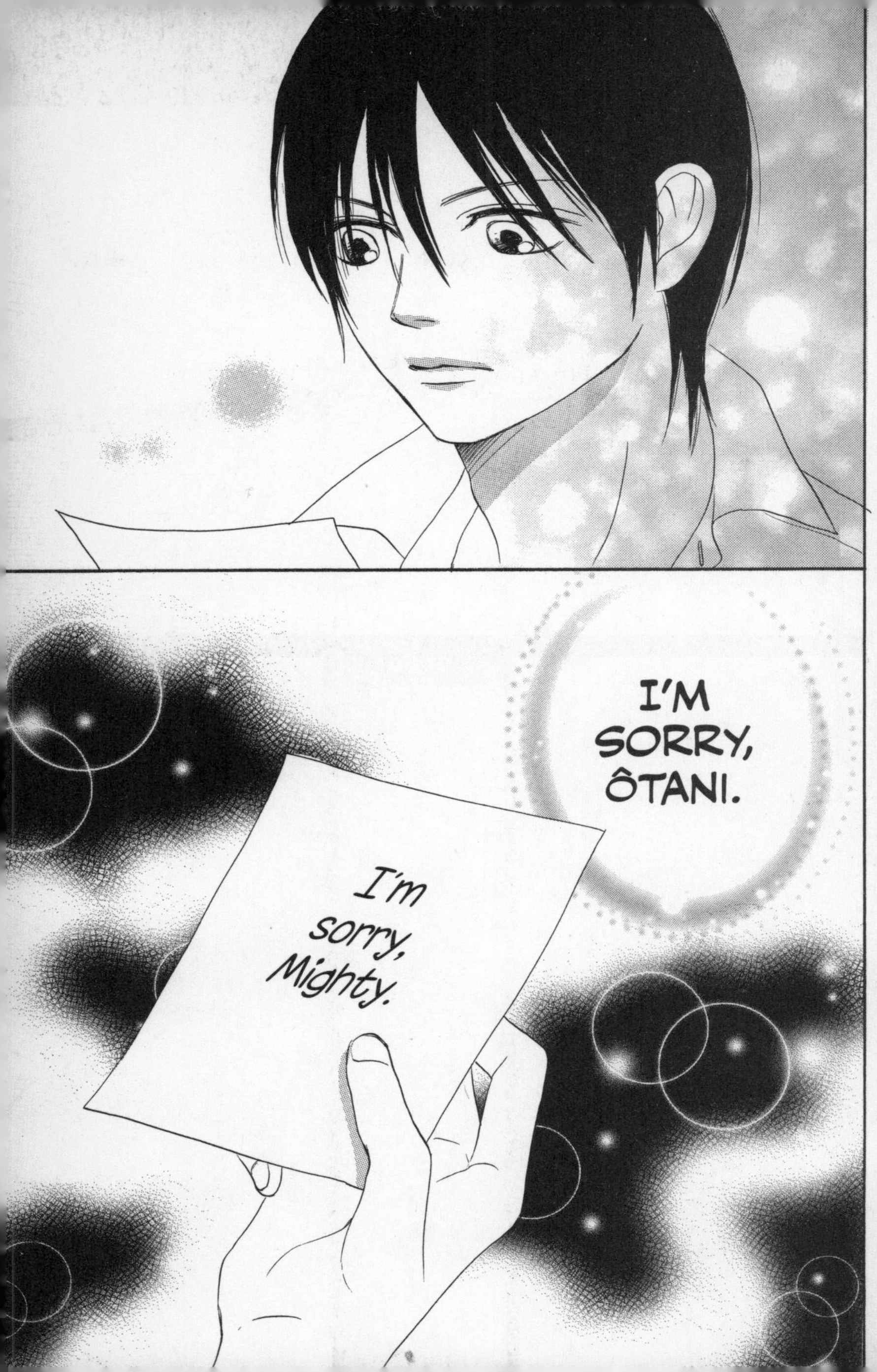
I'M SORRY, ÔTANI.
I'm sorry, Mighty.

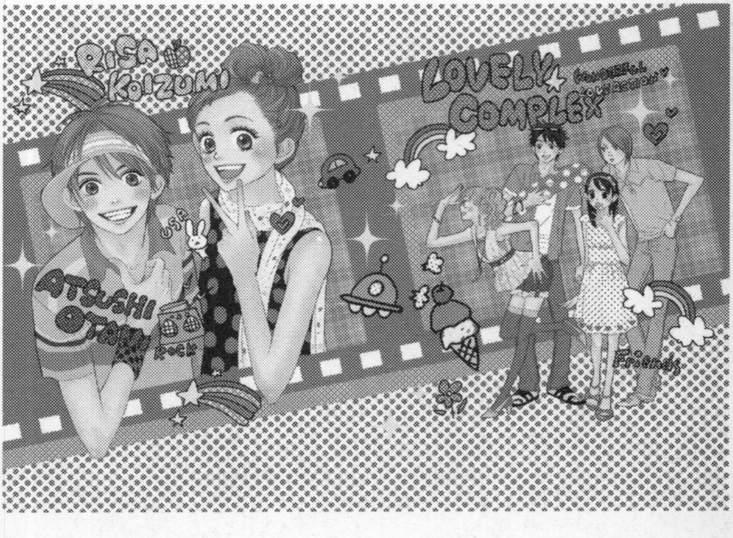
RISA KOIZUMI
LOVELY★COMPLEX
USA
ATSUSHI
rock
Friends

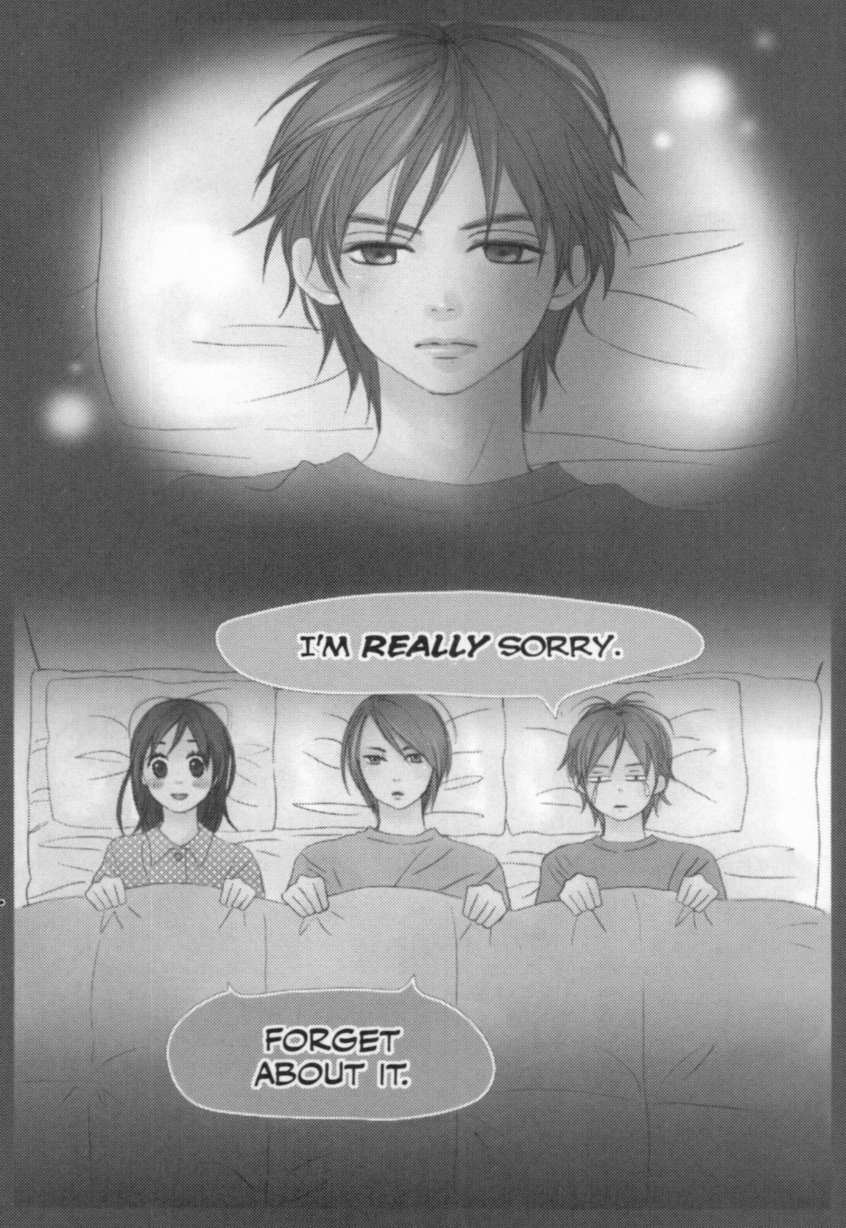
I'M **REALLY** SORRY.
FORGET ABOUT IT.

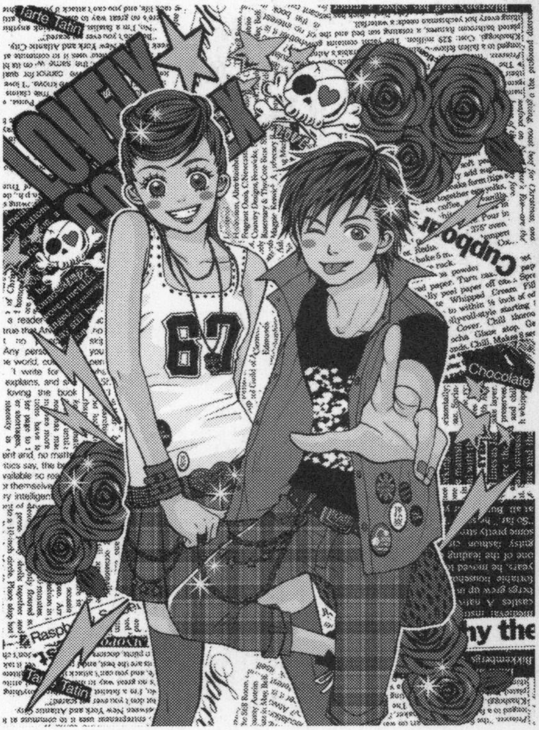
Tarte Tatin
67
Chocolate
Tarte Tatin

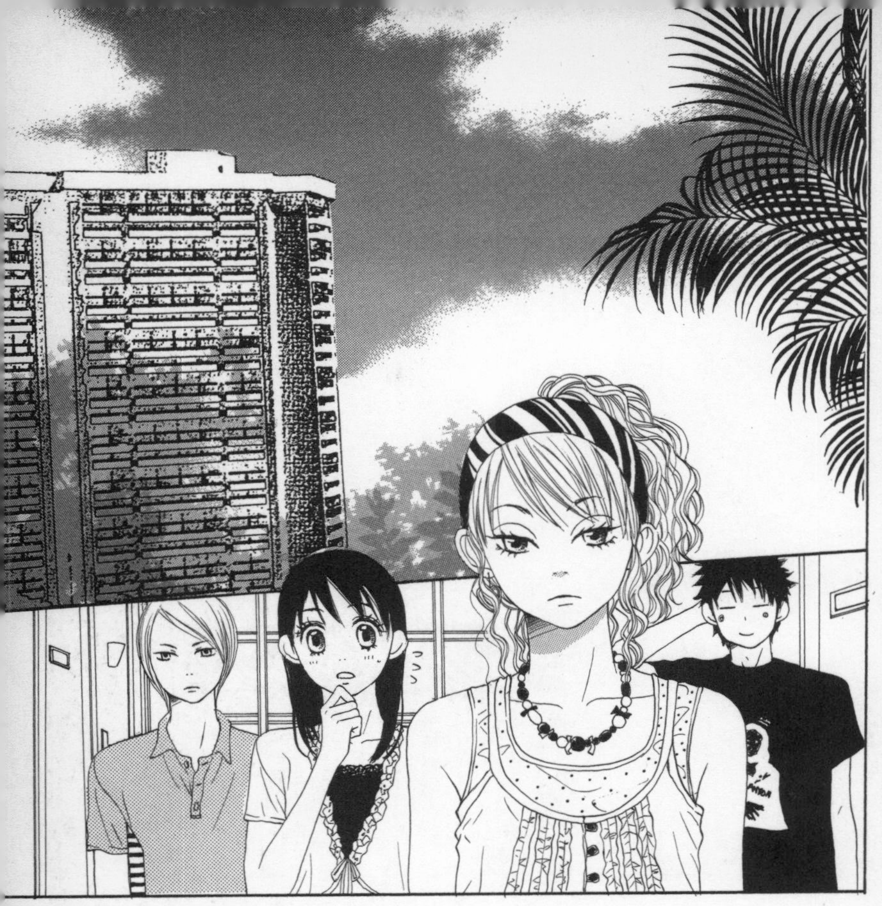

CHAPTER 58

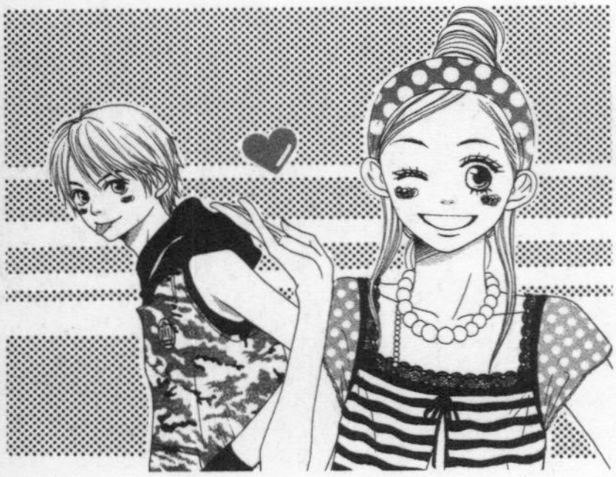

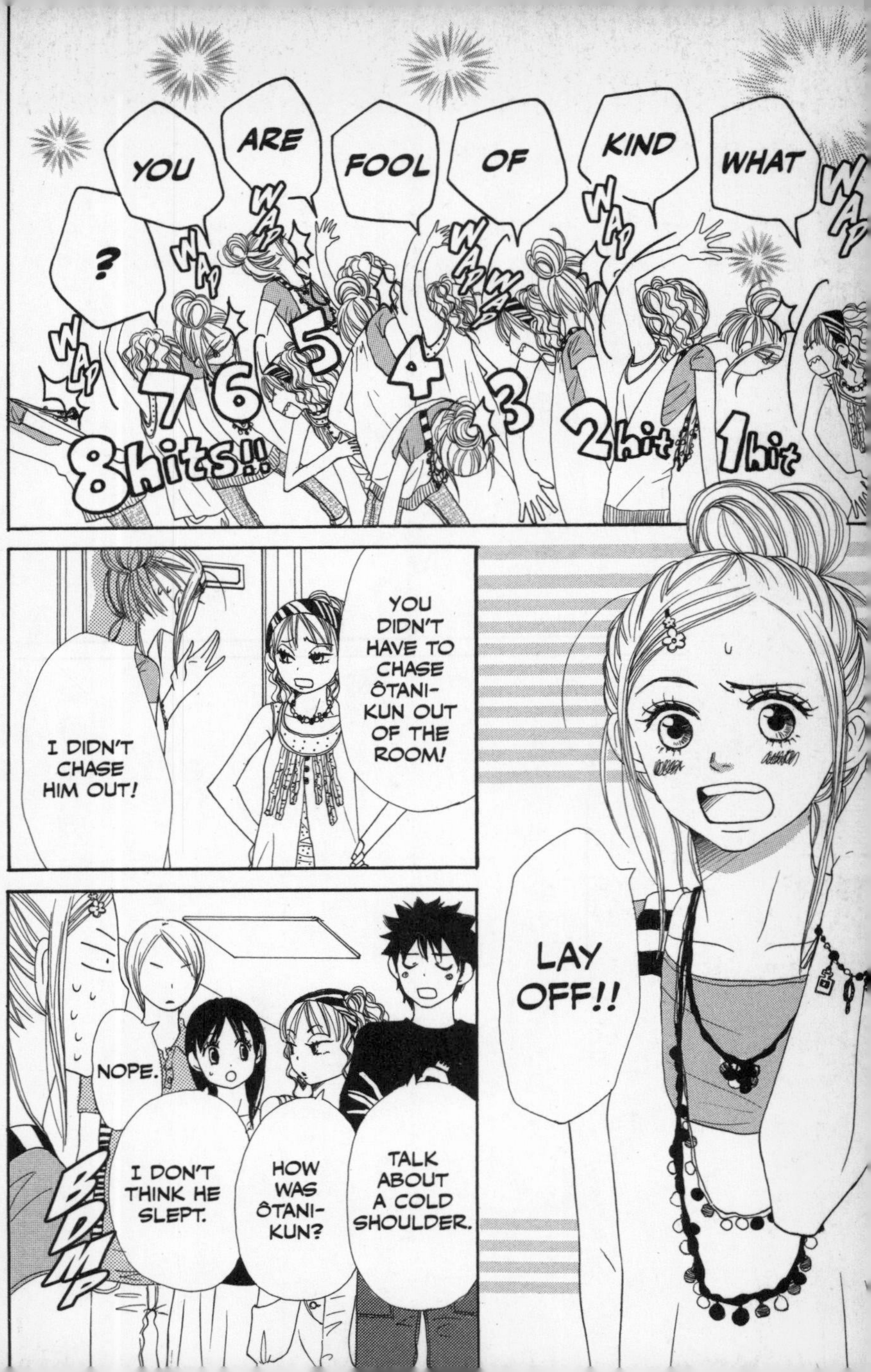
WHAT
KIND
OF
FOOL
ARE
YOU
?
WAP
WAP
WAP
WAP
WAP
WAP
WAP
WAP
1 hit
2 hit
3
4
5
6
7
8 hits!!
LAY OFF!!
YOU DIDN'T HAVE TO CHASE ŌTANI-KUN OUT OF THE ROOM!
I DIDN'T CHASE HIM OUT!
TALK ABOUT A COLD SHOULDER.
HOW WAS ŌTANI-KUN?
I DON'T THINK HE SLEPT.
NOPE.
BDMP

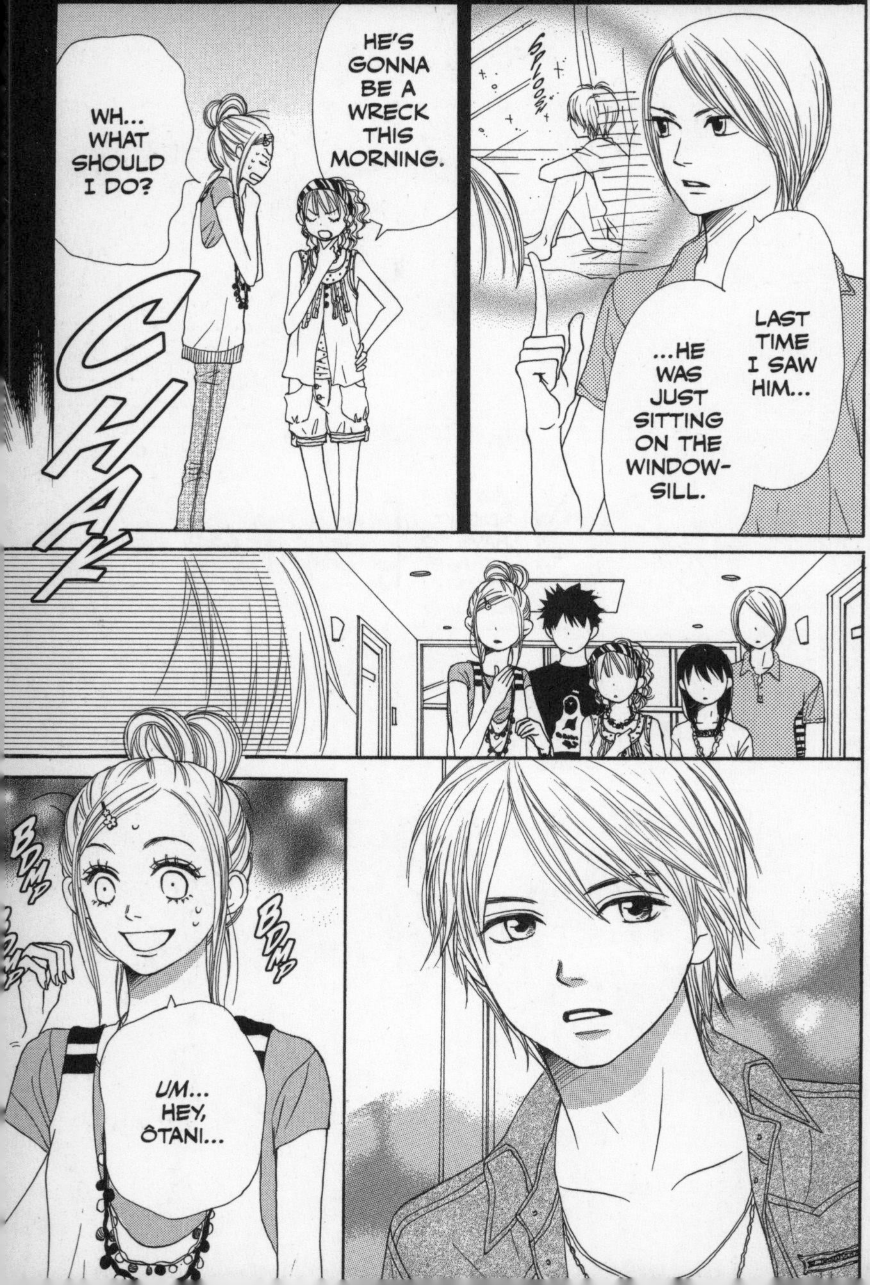
SPLOOSH
LAST TIME I SAW HIM...
...HE WAS JUST SITTING ON THE WINDOW-SILL.
HE'S GONNA BE A WRECK THIS MORNING.
WH... WHAT SHOULD I DO?
CHAK
UM... HEY, ÔTANI...
BDMP
BDMP

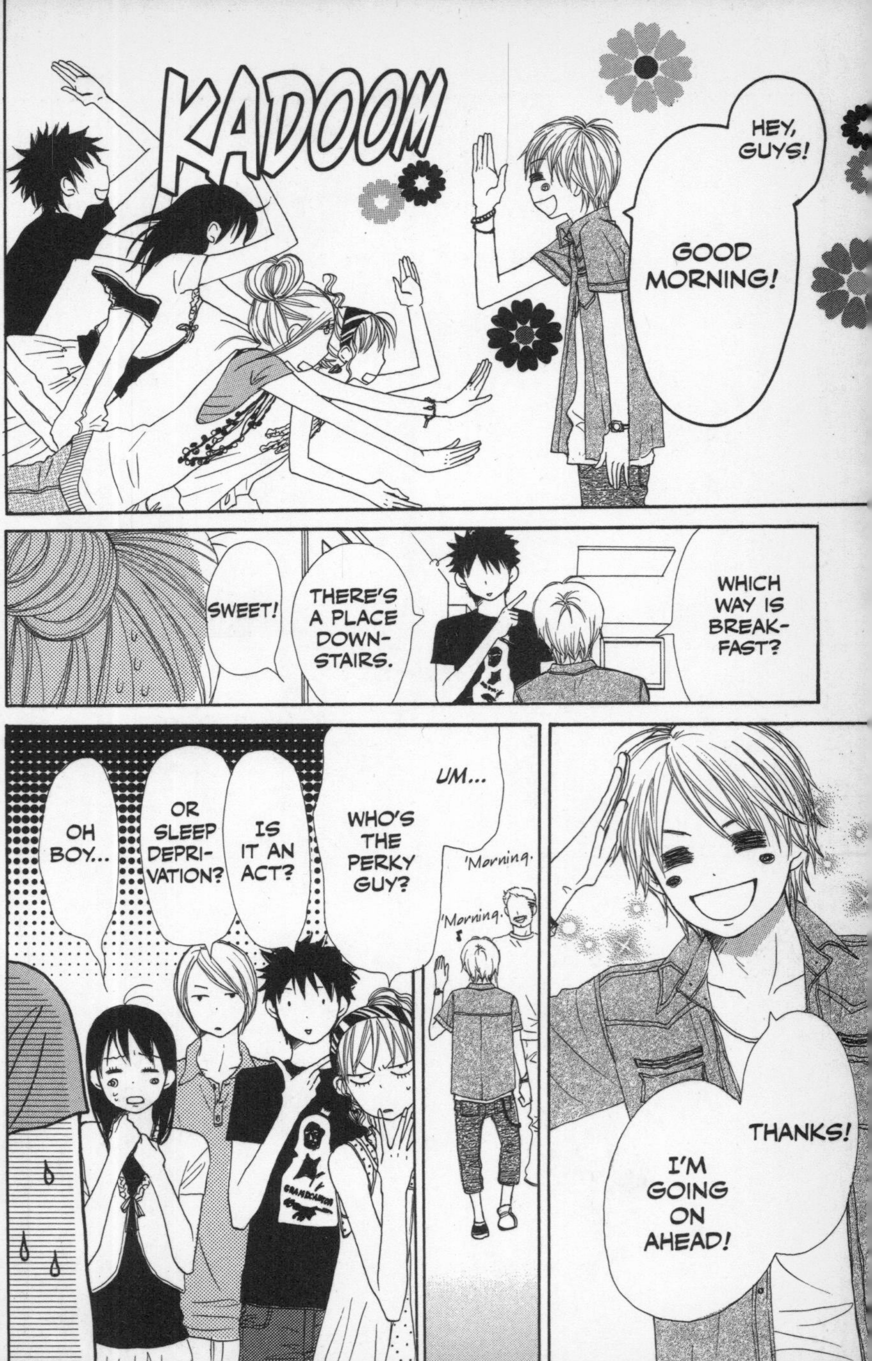
HEY, GUYS!
GOOD MORNING!
KADOOM
WHICH WAY IS BREAK-FAST?
THERE'S A PLACE DOWN-STAIRS.
SWEET!
THANKS!
I'M GOING ON AHEAD!
UM...
WHO'S THE PERKY GUY?
'Morning.
'Morning.
IS IT AN ACT?
OR SLEEP DEPRI-VATION?
OH BOY...

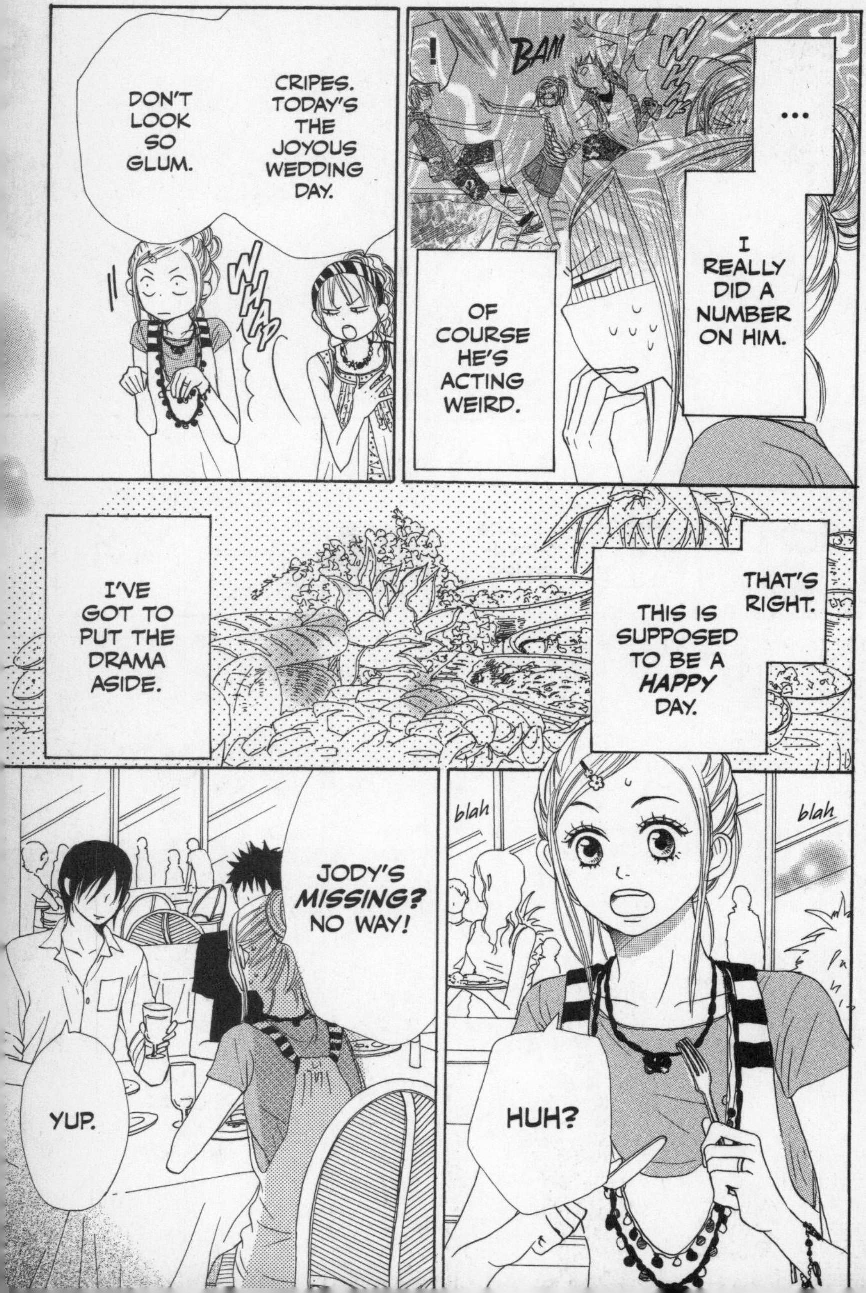

...
BAM
!
I REALLY DID A NUMBER ON HIM.
OF COURSE HE'S ACTING WEIRD.
CRIPES. TODAY'S THE JOYOUS WEDDING DAY.
DON'T LOOK SO GLUM.
WHAP
THAT'S RIGHT.
THIS IS SUPPOSED TO BE A *HAPPY* DAY.
I'VE GOT TO PUT THE DRAMA ASIDE.
blah
blah
HUH?
JODY'S *MISSING?* NO WAY!
YUP.

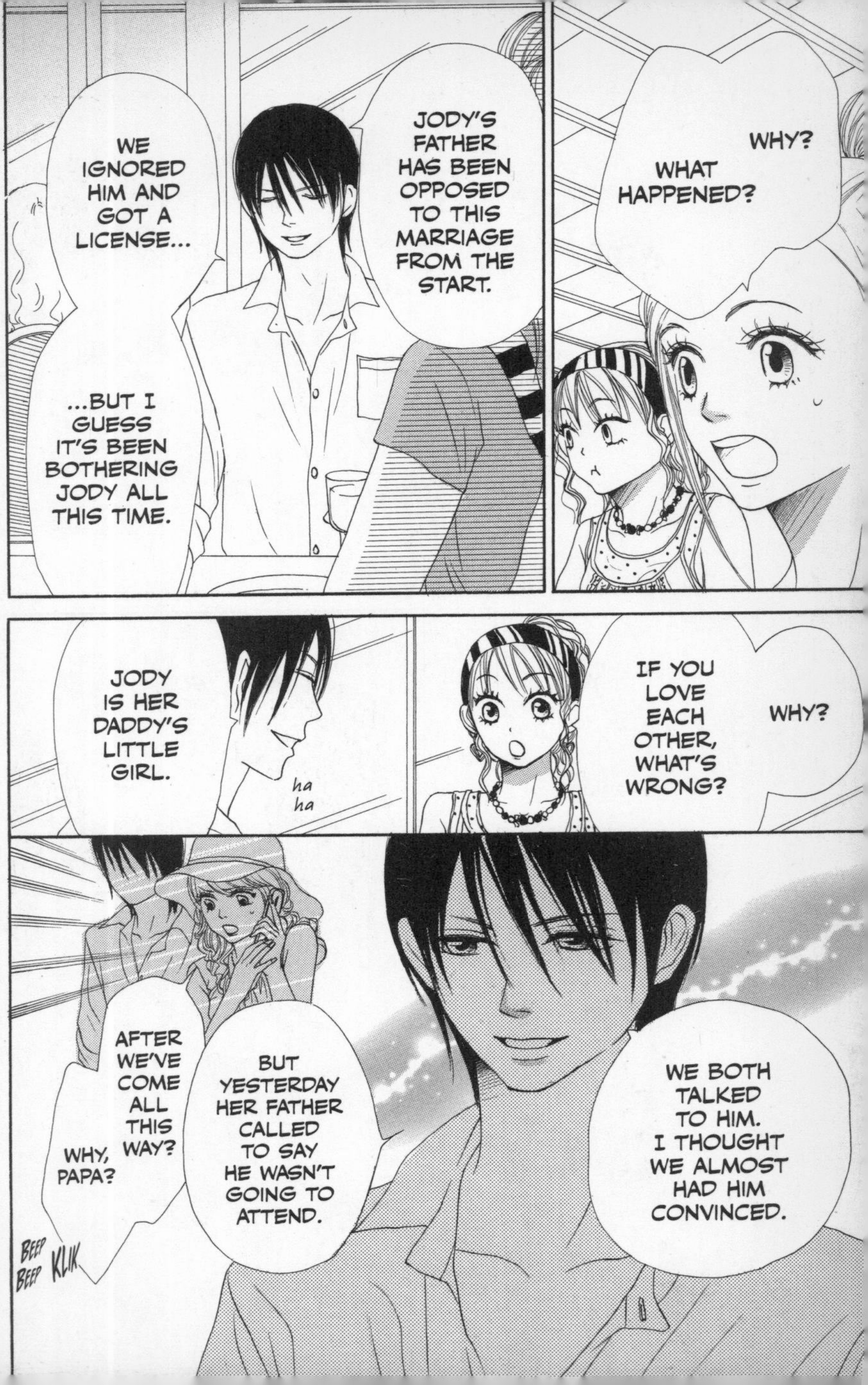
WHY?
WHAT HAPPENED?
JODY'S FATHER HAS BEEN OPPOSED TO THIS MARRIAGE FROM THE START.
WE IGNORED HIM AND GOT A LICENSE...
...BUT I GUESS IT'S BEEN BOTHERING JODY ALL THIS TIME.
WHY?
IF YOU LOVE EACH OTHER, WHAT'S WRONG?
JODY IS HER DADDY'S LITTLE GIRL.
ha ha
WE BOTH TALKED TO HIM. I THOUGHT WE ALMOST HAD HIM CONVINCED.
BUT YESTERDAY HER FATHER CALLED TO SAY HE WASN'T GOING TO ATTEND.
AFTER WE'VE COME ALL THIS WAY?
WHY, PAPA?
BEEP BEEP
KLIK

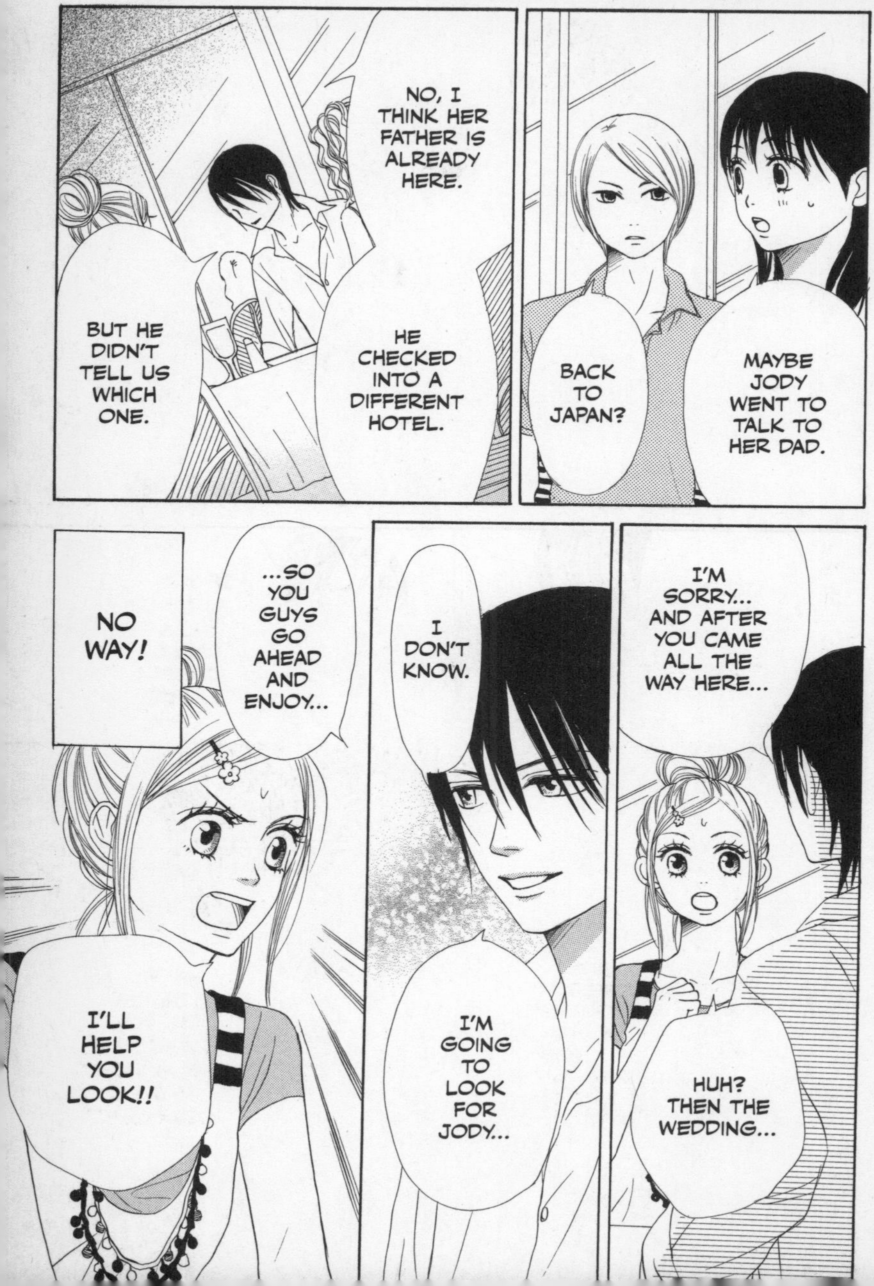
MAYBE JODY WENT TO TALK TO HER DAD.
BACK TO JAPAN?
NO, I THINK HER FATHER IS ALREADY HERE.
HE CHECKED INTO A DIFFERENT HOTEL.
BUT HE DIDN'T TELL US WHICH ONE.
I'M SORRY... AND AFTER YOU CAME ALL THE WAY HERE...
HUH? THEN THE WEDDING...
I DON'T KNOW.
I'M GOING TO LOOK FOR JODY...
...SO YOU GUYS GO AHEAD AND ENJOY...
NO WAY!
I'LL HELP YOU LOOK!!

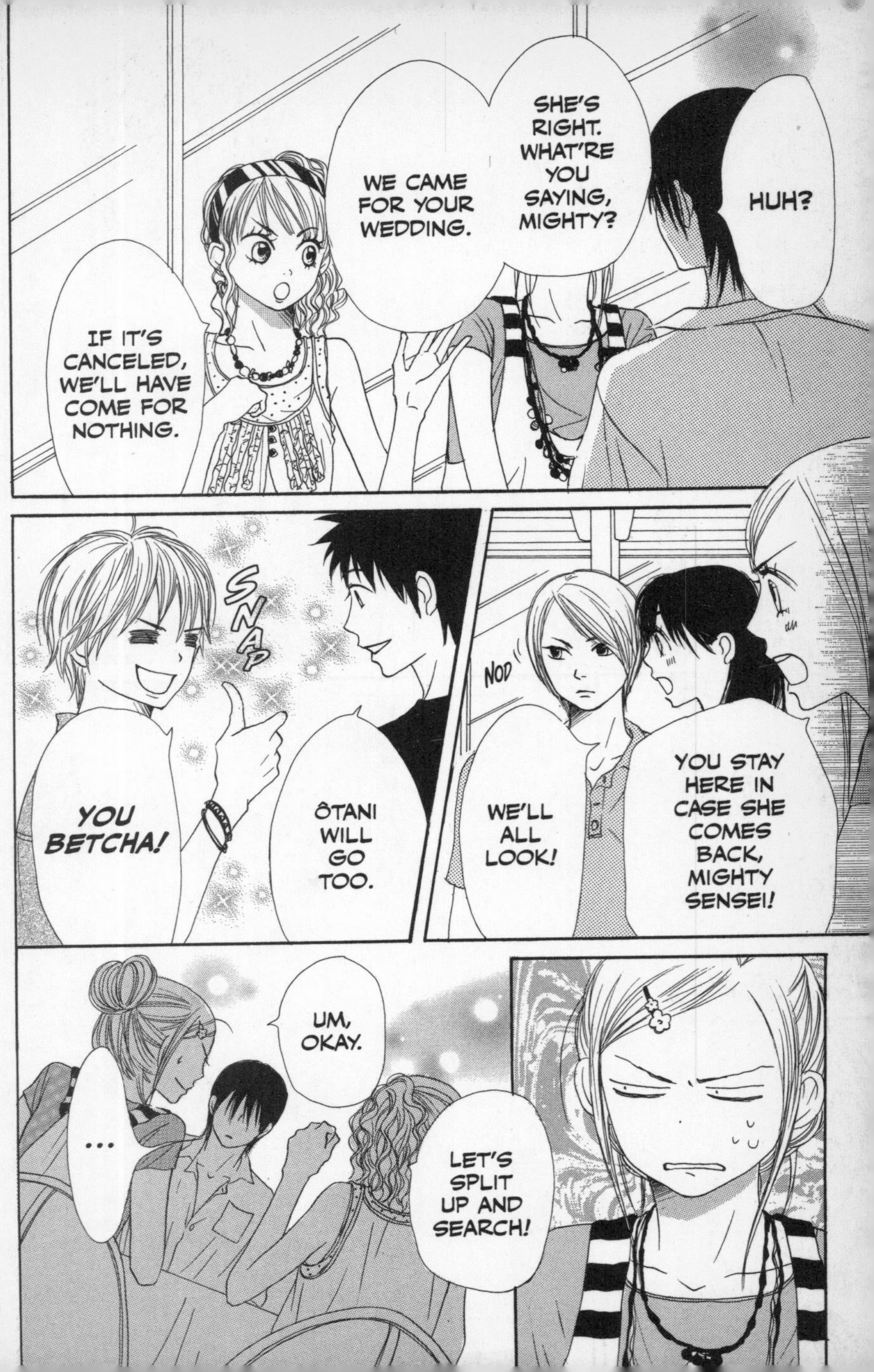
HUH?
SHE'S RIGHT. WHAT'RE YOU SAYING, MIGHTY?
WE CAME FOR YOUR WEDDING.
IF IT'S CANCELED, WE'LL HAVE COME FOR NOTHING.
YOU STAY HERE IN CASE SHE COMES BACK, MIGHTY SENSEI!
NOD
WE'LL ALL LOOK!
ŌTANI WILL GO TOO.
SNAP
YOU BETCHA!
LET'S SPLIT UP AND SEARCH!
UM, OKAY.
...

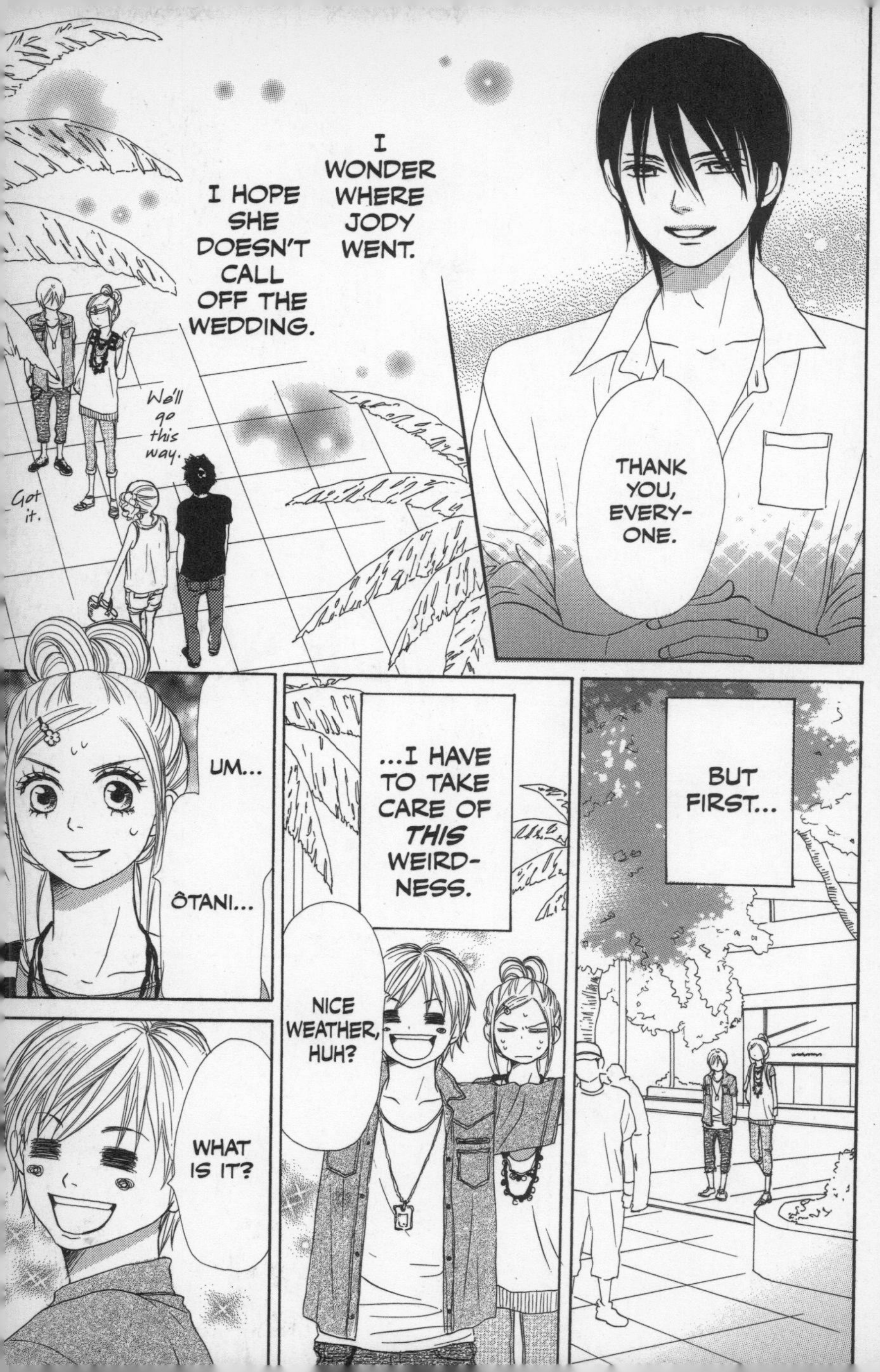
THANK YOU, EVERY-ONE.
I WONDER WHERE JODY WENT.
I HOPE SHE DOESN'T CALL OFF THE WEDDING.
We'll go this way.
Got it.
BUT FIRST...
...I HAVE TO TAKE CARE OF *THIS* WEIRD-NESS.
NICE WEATHER, HUH?
UM...
ÔTANI...
WHAT IS IT?

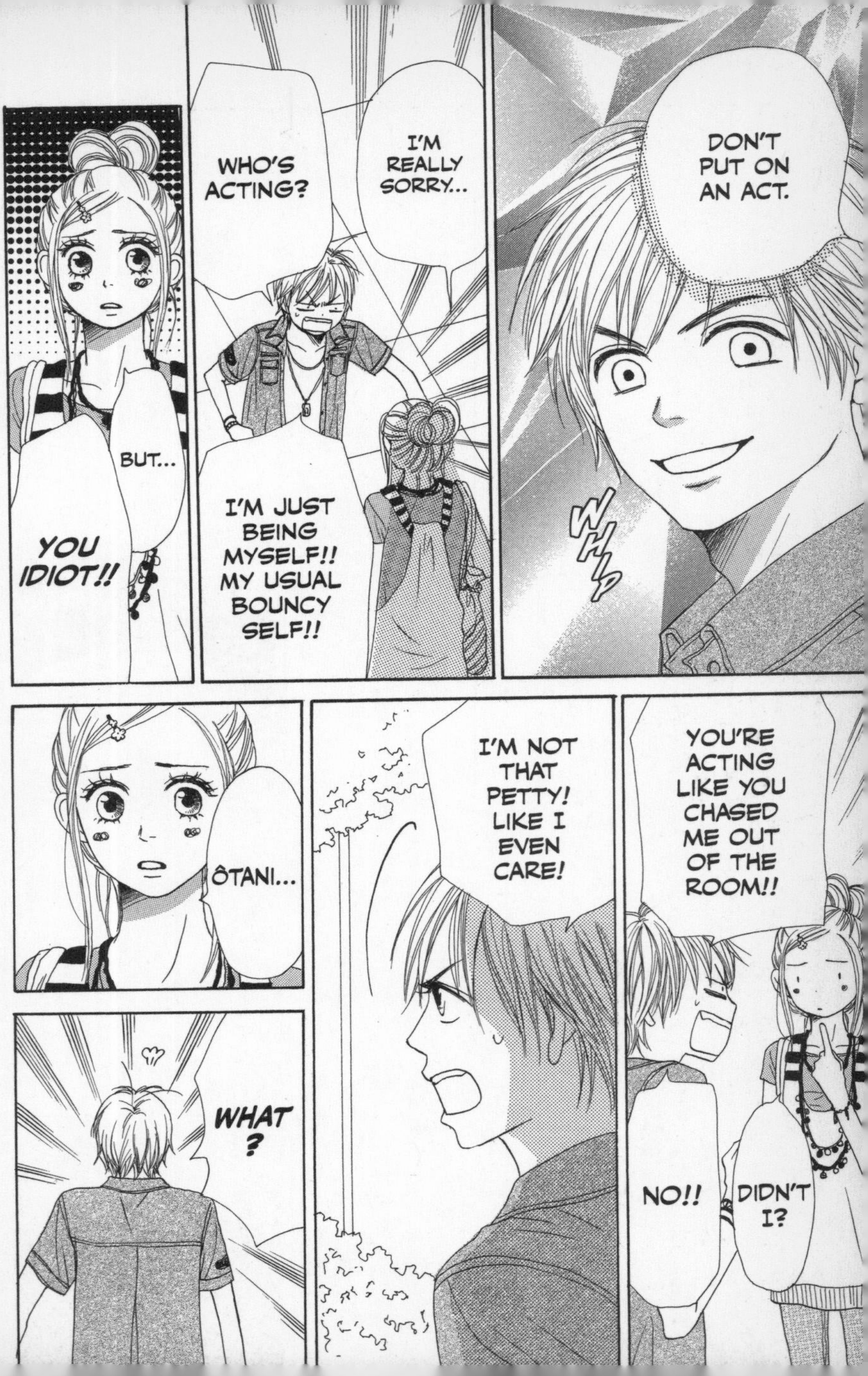
DON'T PUT ON AN ACT.
WHIP
I'M REALLY SORRY...
WHO'S ACTING?
I'M JUST BEING MYSELF!! MY USUAL BOUNCY SELF!!
BUT...
YOU IDIOT!!
YOU'RE ACTING LIKE YOU CHASED ME OUT OF THE ROOM!!
DIDN'T I?
NO!!
I'M NOT THAT PETTY! LIKE I EVEN CARE!
ÔTANI...
WHAT?

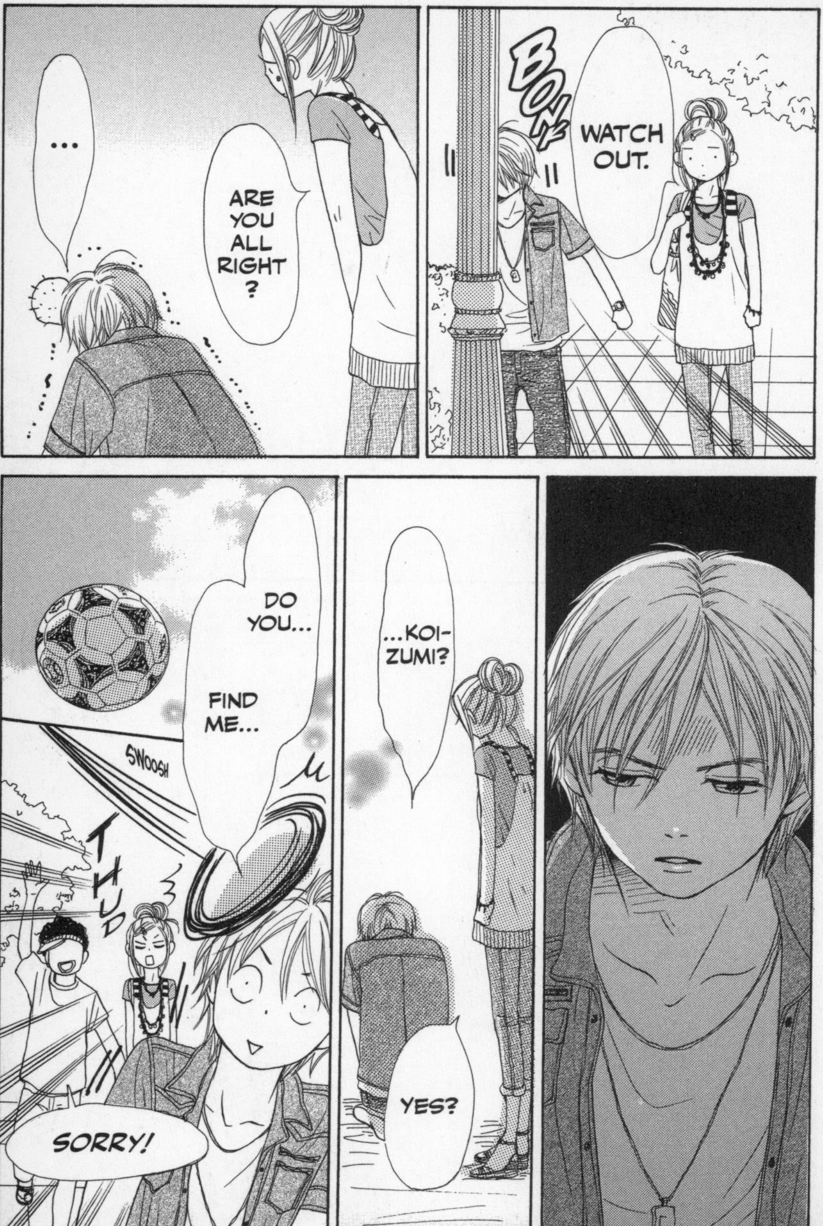
WATCH OUT.
BONK
ARE YOU ALL RIGHT?
...
...KOI-ZUMI?
YES?
DO YOU... FIND ME...
SWOOSH
THUD
SORRY!

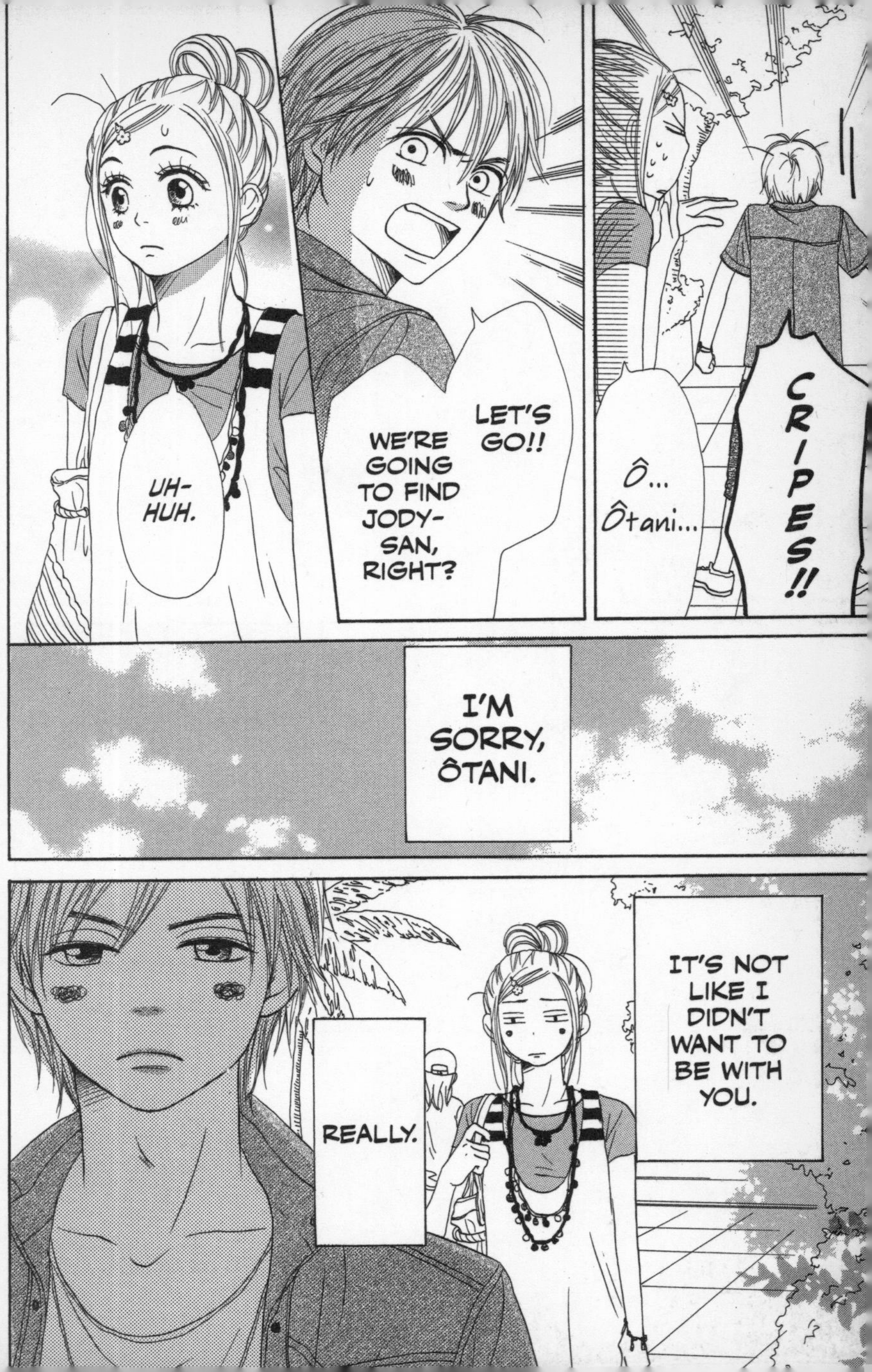
CRIPES!!
Ô... Ôtani...
LET'S GO!!
WE'RE GOING TO FIND JODY-SAN, RIGHT?
UH-HUH.
I'M SORRY, ÔTANI.
IT'S NOT LIKE I DIDN'T WANT TO BE WITH YOU.
REALLY.

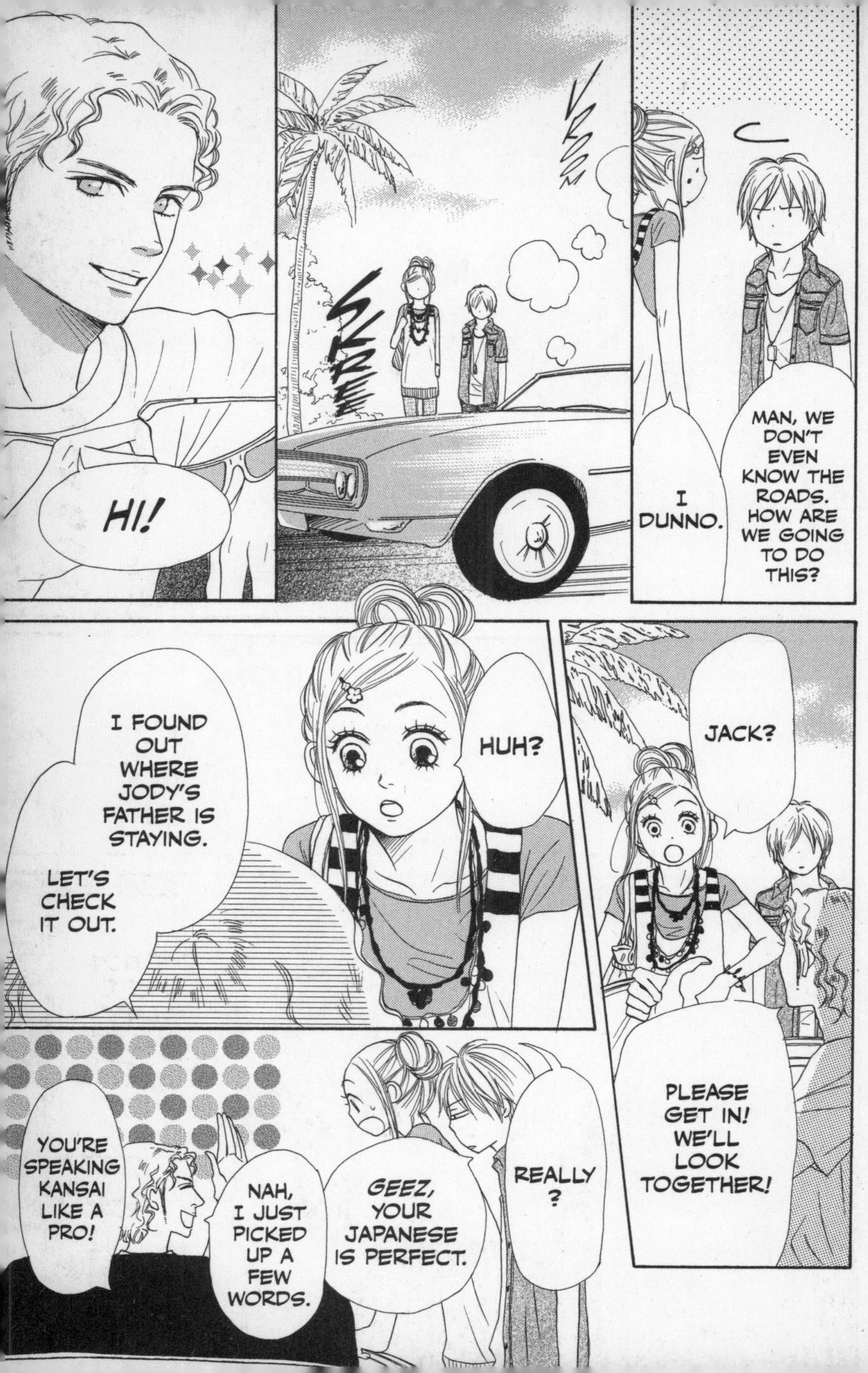
MAN, WE DON'T EVEN KNOW THE ROADS. HOW ARE WE GOING TO DO THIS?
I DUNNO.
VROOM
SKREE
HI!
JACK?
PLEASE GET IN! WE'LL LOOK TOGETHER!
HUH?
I FOUND OUT WHERE JODY'S FATHER IS STAYING.
LET'S CHECK IT OUT.
REALLY?
GEEZ, YOUR JAPANESE IS PERFECT.
NAH, I JUST PICKED UP A FEW WORDS.
YOU'RE SPEAKING KANSAI LIKE A PRO!

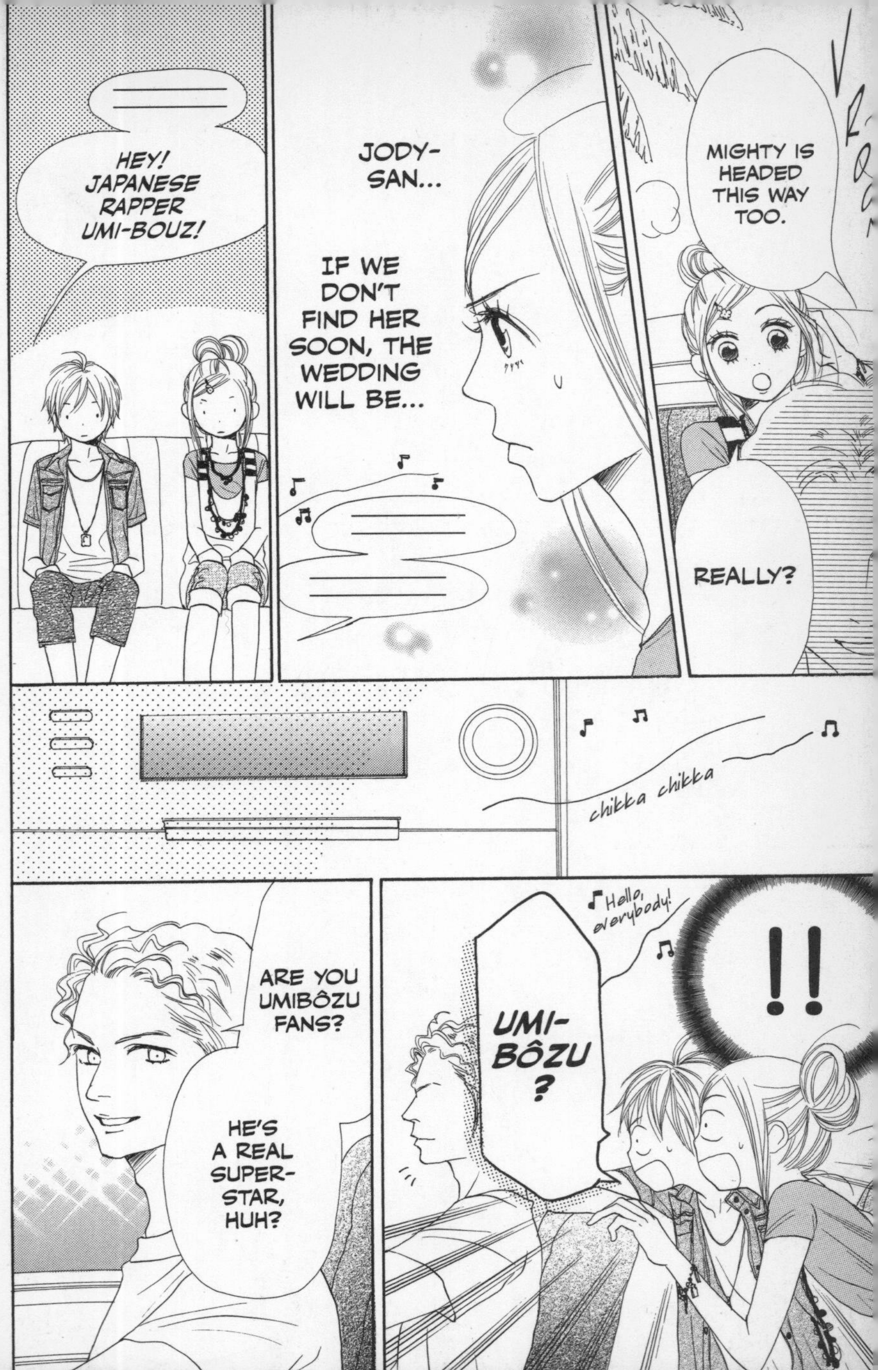
MIGHTY IS HEADED THIS WAY TOO.
REALLY?
JODY-SAN...
IF WE DON'T FIND HER SOON, THE WEDDING WILL BE...
HEY! JAPANESE RAPPER UMI-BOUZ!
chikka chikka
!!
Hello, everybody!
UMI-BÔZU?
ARE YOU UMIBÔZU FANS?
HE'S A REAL SUPER-STAR, HUH?

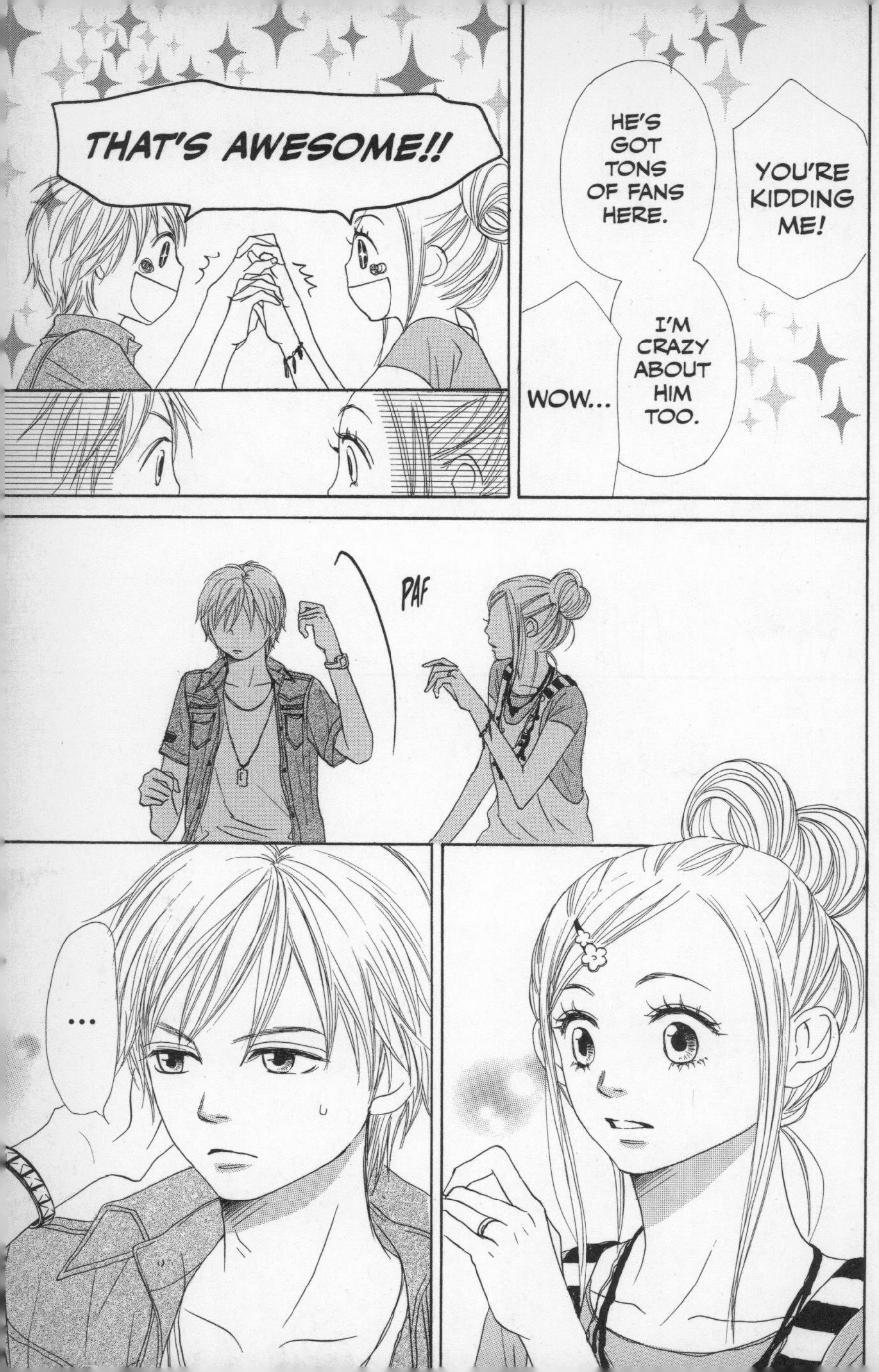
YOU'RE KIDDING ME!
HE'S GOT TONS OF FANS HERE.
I'M CRAZY ABOUT HIM TOO.
WOW...
THAT'S AWESOME!!
PAF
...

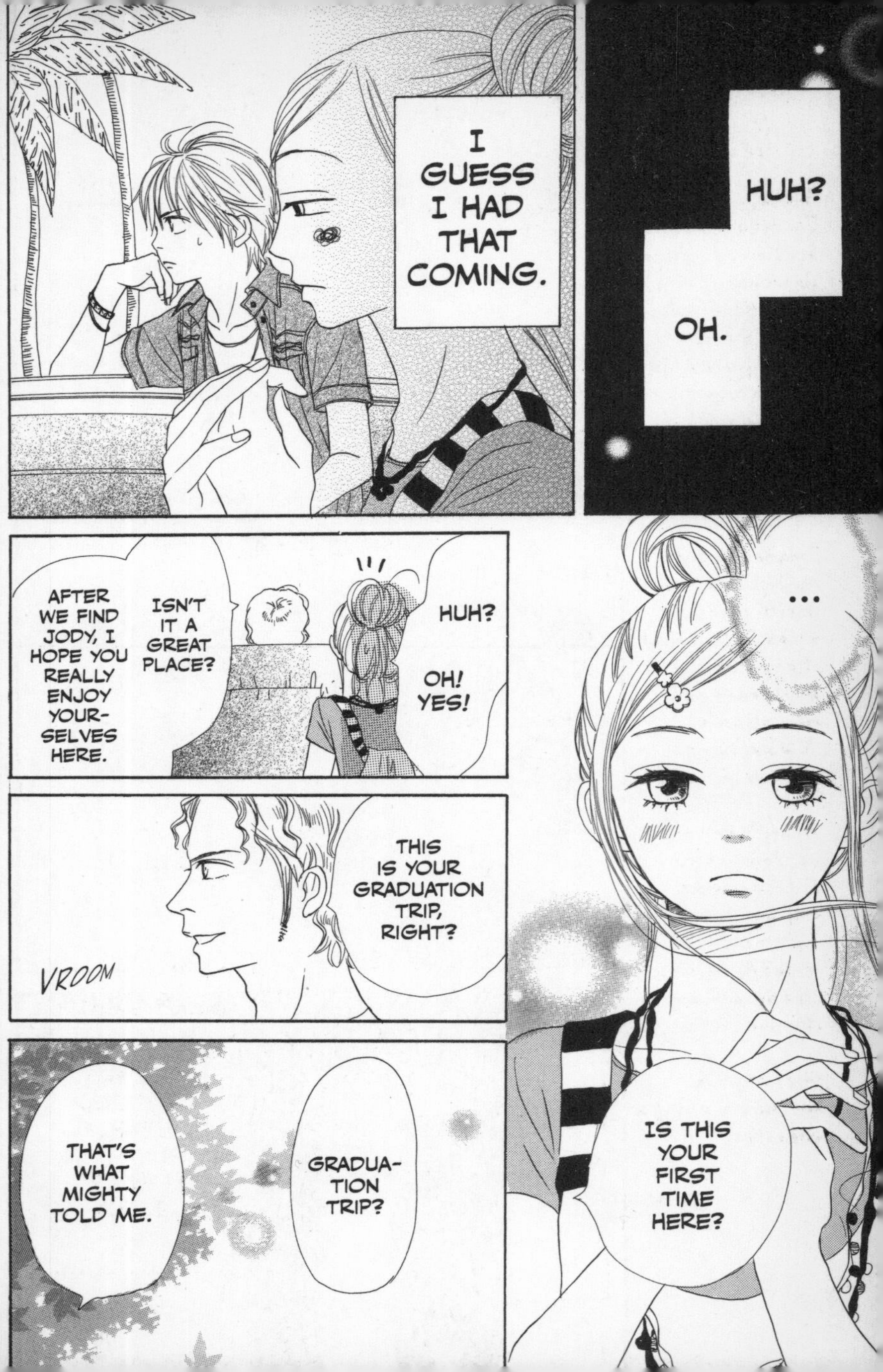
HUH?
OH.
I GUESS I HAD THAT COMING.
...
IS THIS YOUR FIRST TIME HERE?
HUH?
OH! YES!
ISN'T IT A GREAT PLACE?
AFTER WE FIND JODY, I HOPE YOU REALLY ENJOY YOURSELVES HERE.
THIS IS YOUR GRADUATION TRIP, RIGHT?
VROOM
GRADUATION TRIP?
THAT'S WHAT MIGHTY TOLD ME.

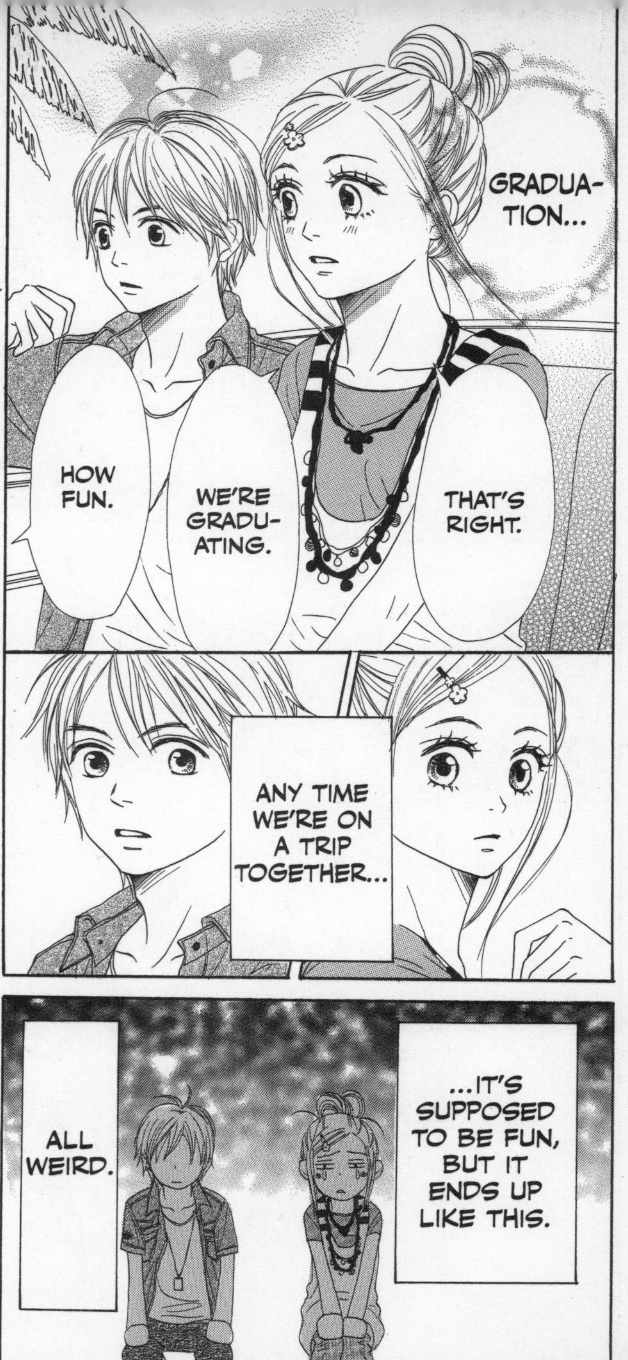
GRADUA-TION...
THAT'S RIGHT.
WE'RE GRADU-ATING.
HOW FUN.
ANY TIME WE'RE ON A TRIP TOGETHER...
...IT'S SUPPOSED TO BE FUN, BUT IT ENDS UP LIKE THIS.
ALL WEIRD.

3

Anyway... I've returned to my usual work schedule. Things were so hectic during the summer that it all seems leisurely now. I went out and bought some cookbooks and stuff and started cooking seriously! ♥ Well, sort of.

I made chopped burdock and frozen yogurt, then I got bored. I'm not much of an eater, so I guess it was a bad idea for a hobby. I'll leave the cooking to my mom.

Tonight's dinner was oden hot pot, chop suey, miso soup and tempura!! Isn't that way too much? And what a strange combination of dishes!

She serves miso soup with everything, even stew.

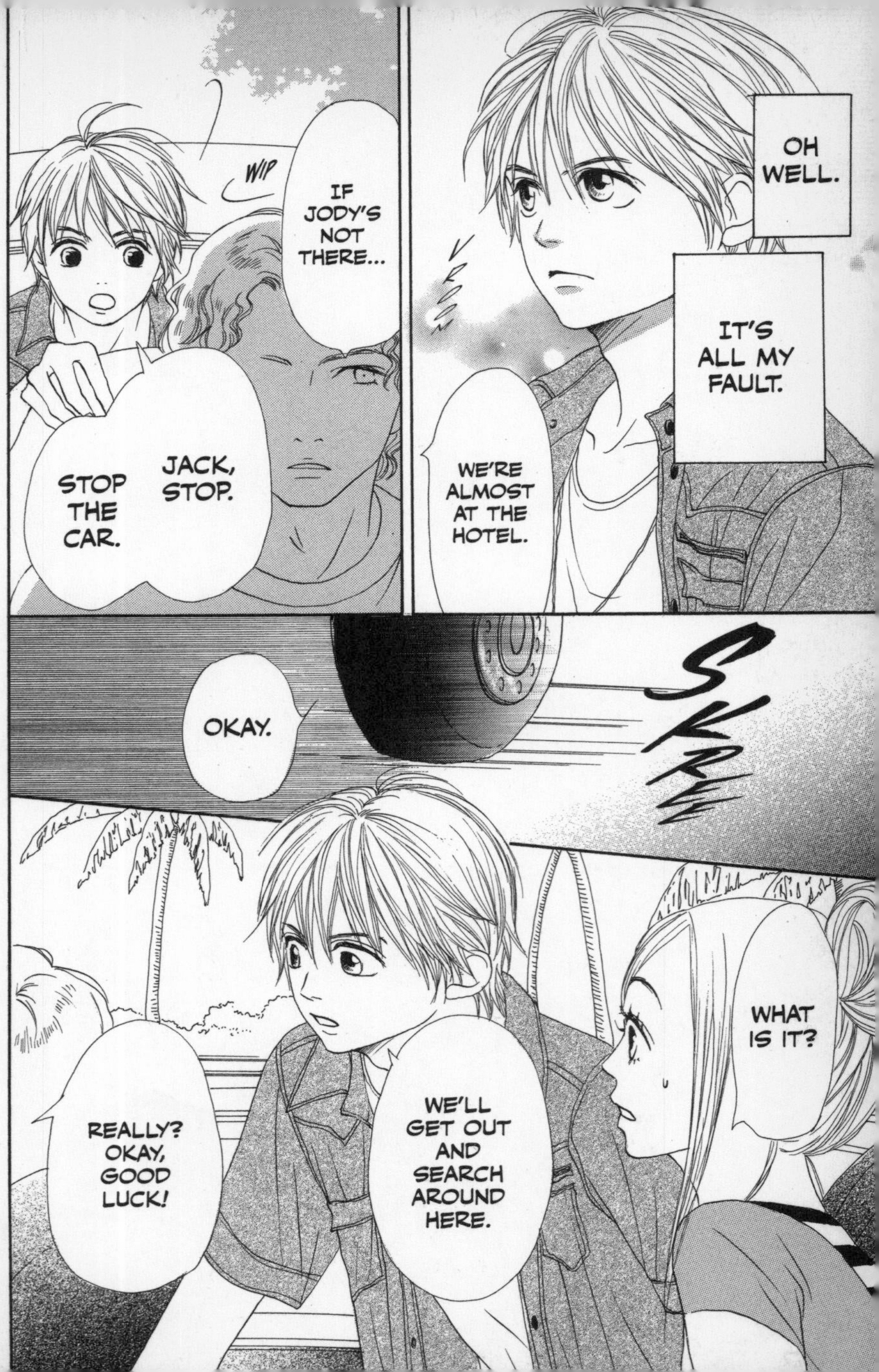
OH WELL.
IT'S ALL MY FAULT.
WE'RE ALMOST AT THE HOTEL.
WIP
IF JODY'S NOT THERE...
JACK, STOP.
STOP THE CAR.
OKAY.
WHAT IS IT?
WE'LL GET OUT AND SEARCH AROUND HERE.
REALLY? OKAY, GOOD LUCK!

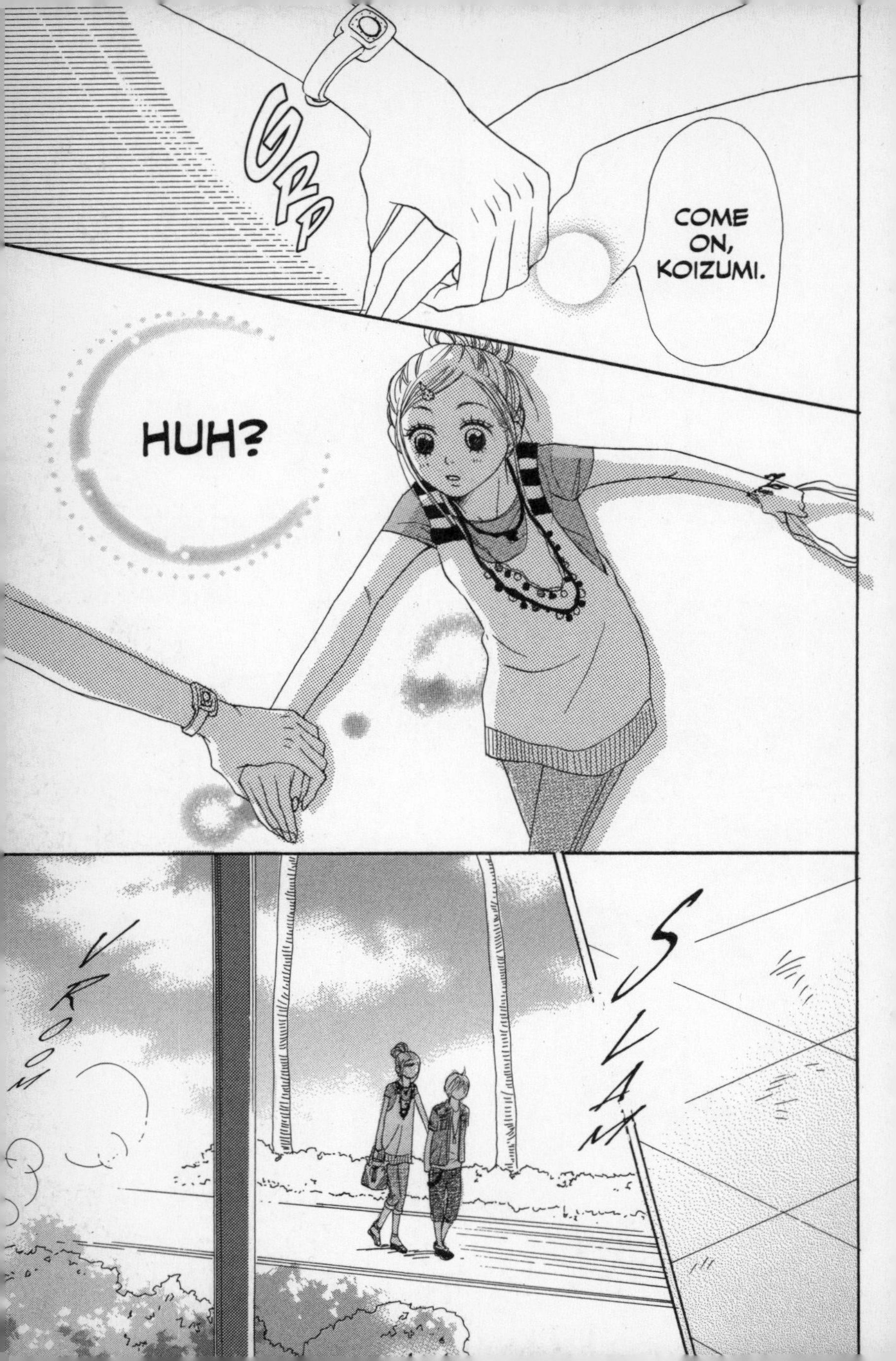
COME ON, KOIZUMI.
GRP
HUH?
SVAH
VROOM

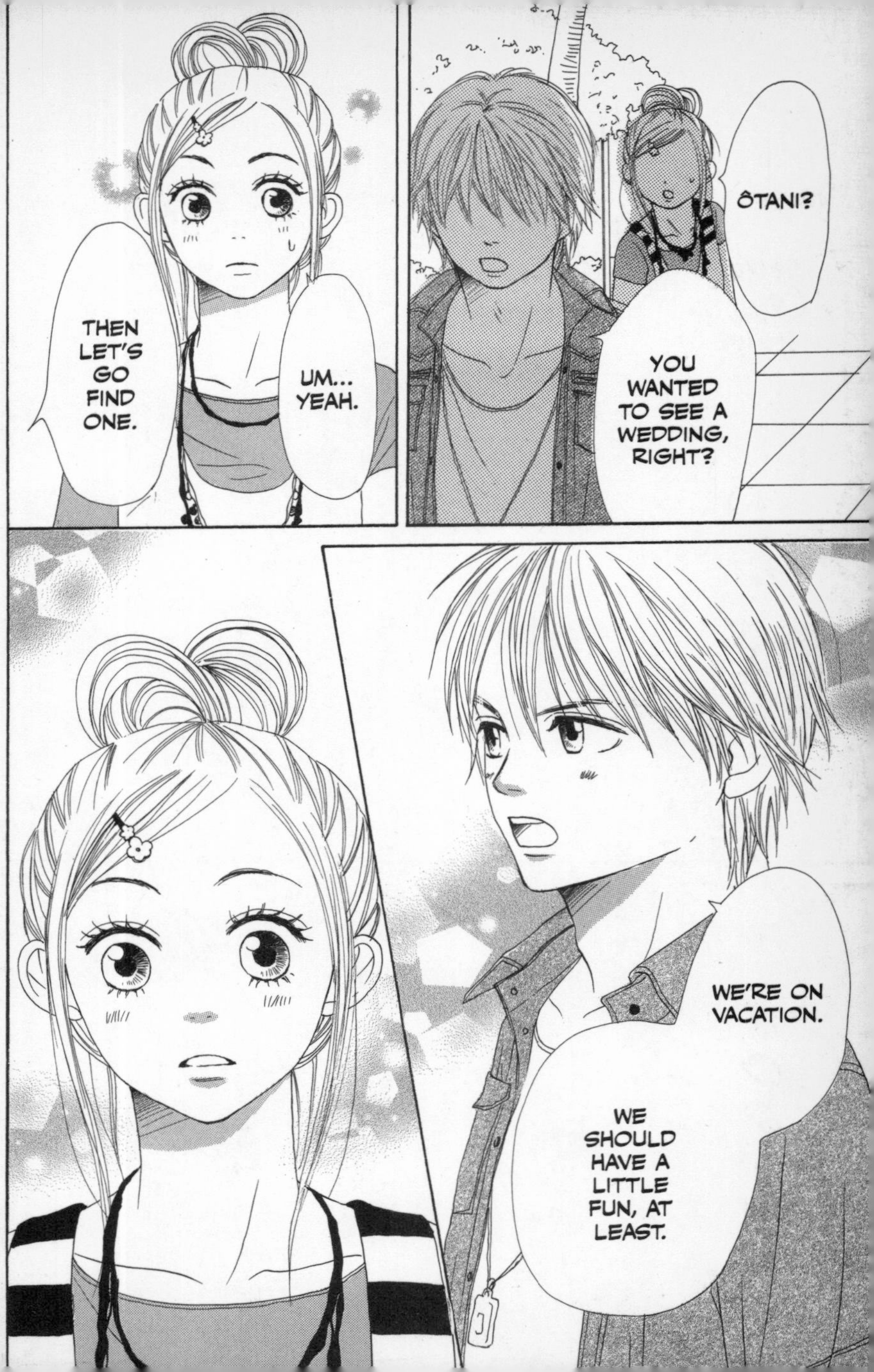

ÔTANI?
YOU WANTED TO SEE A WEDDING, RIGHT?
UM... YEAH.
THEN LET'S GO FIND ONE.
WE'RE ON VACATION.
WE SHOULD HAVE A LITTLE FUN, AT LEAST.

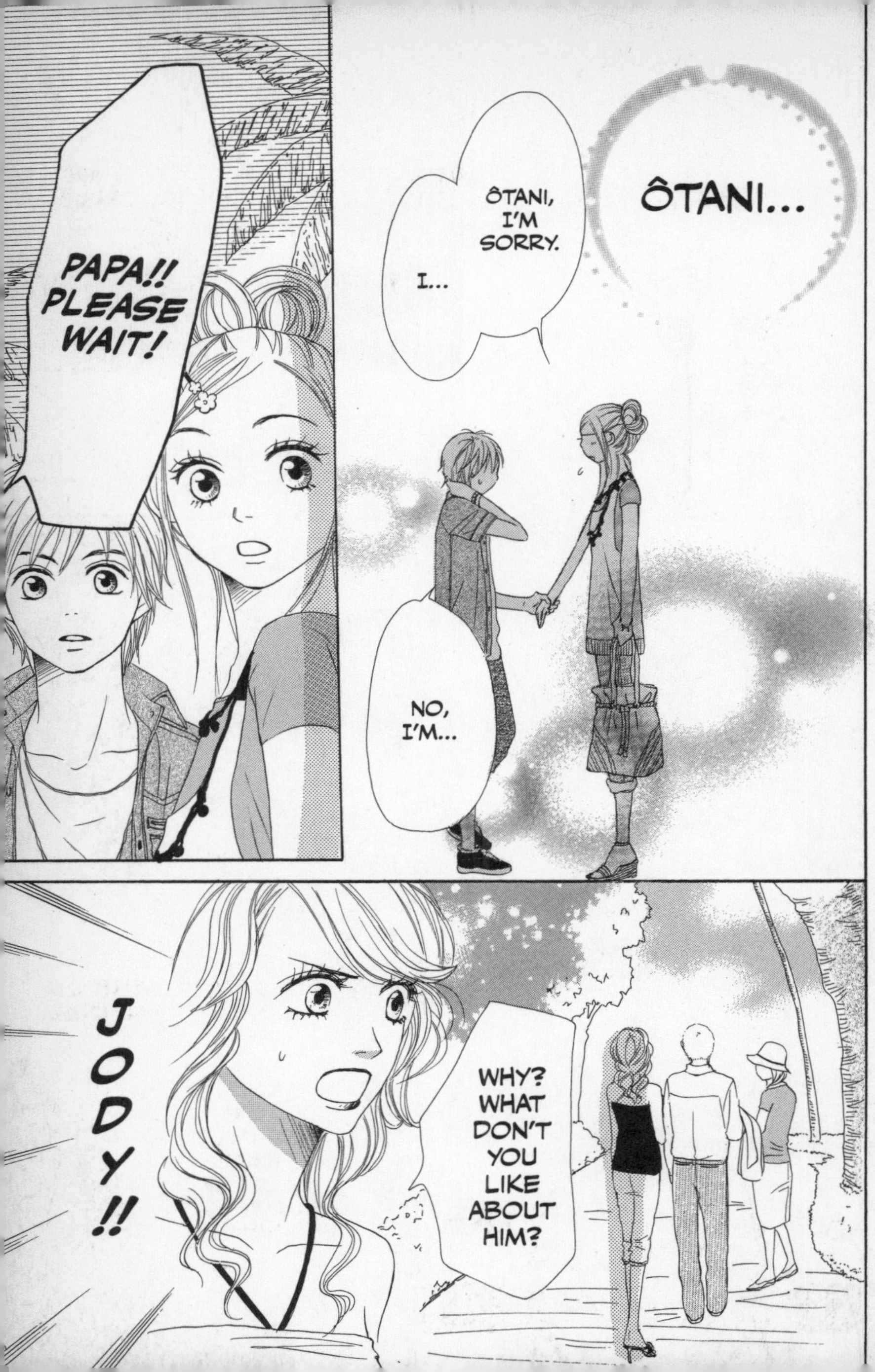
ÔTANI...
ÔTANI, I'M SORRY.
I...
NO, I'M...
PAPA!! PLEASE WAIT!
WHY? WHAT DON'T YOU LIKE ABOUT HIM?
JODY!!

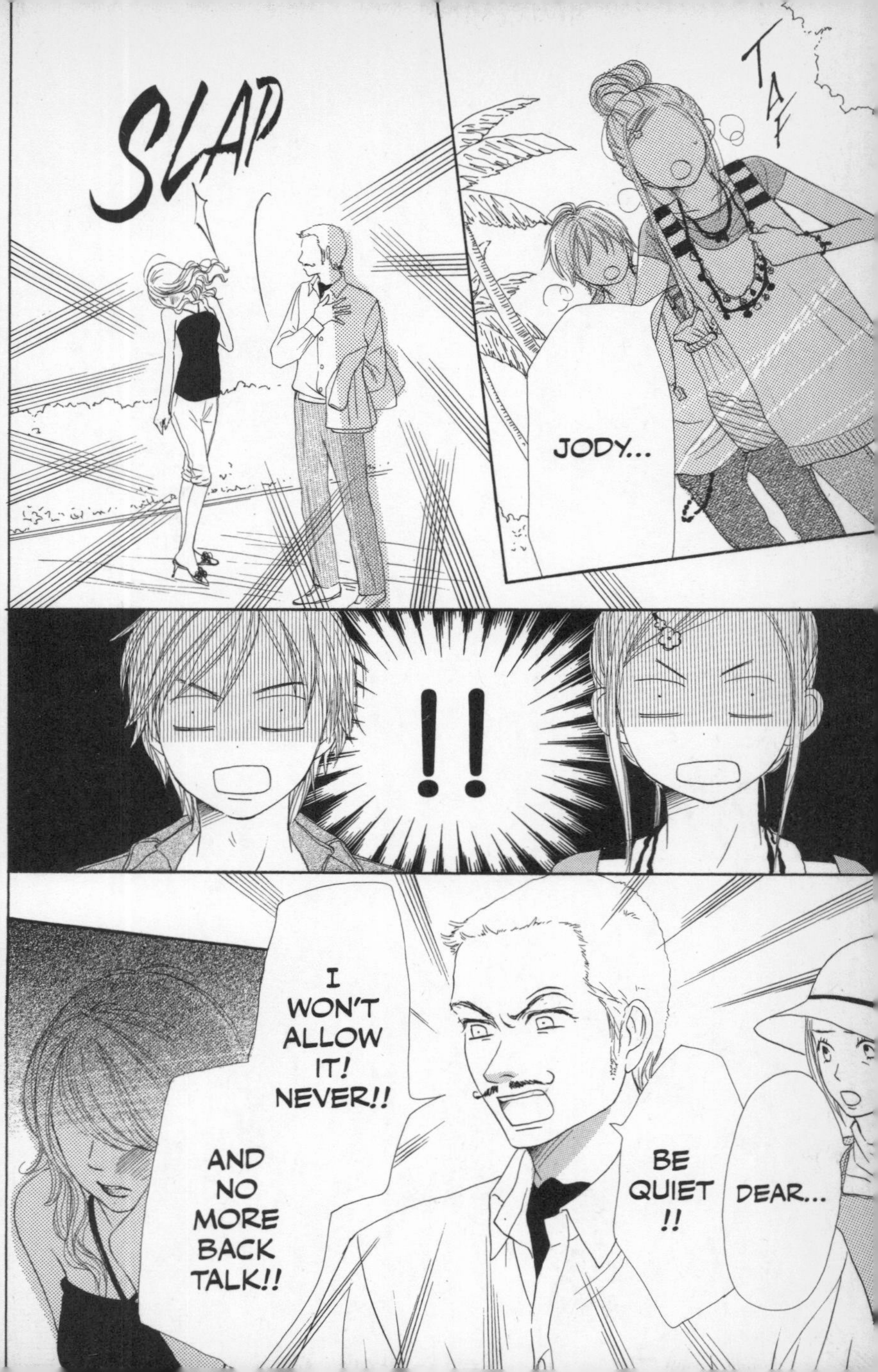
JODY...
SLAP
!!
DEAR...
BE QUIET!!
I WON'T ALLOW IT! NEVER!!
AND NO MORE BACK TALK!!

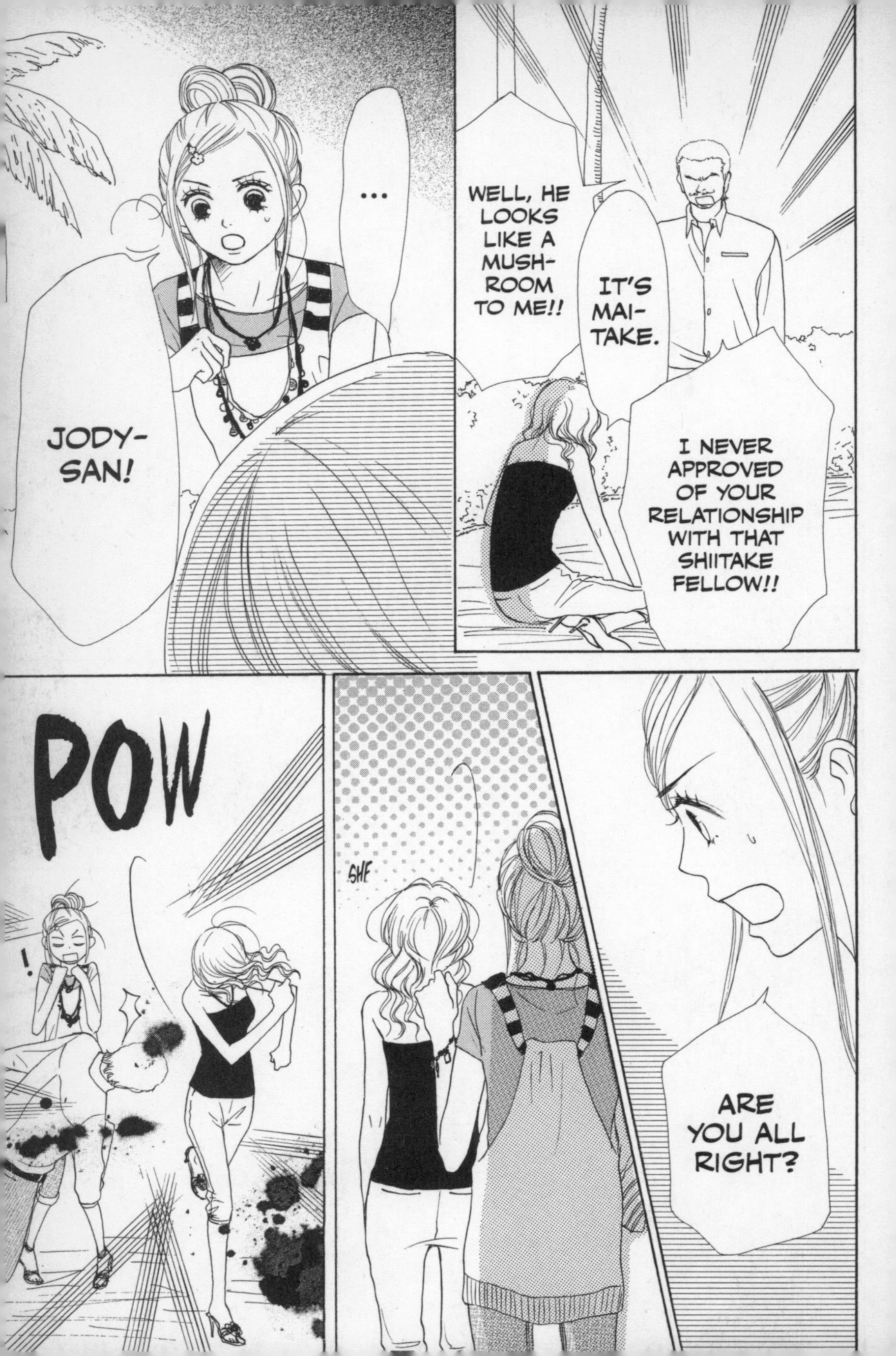
I NEVER APPROVED OF YOUR RELATIONSHIP WITH THAT SHIITAKE FELLOW!!
IT'S MAI-TAKE.
WELL, HE LOOKS LIKE A MUSH-ROOM TO ME!!
...
JODY-SAN!
ARE YOU ALL RIGHT?
SHF
POW
!

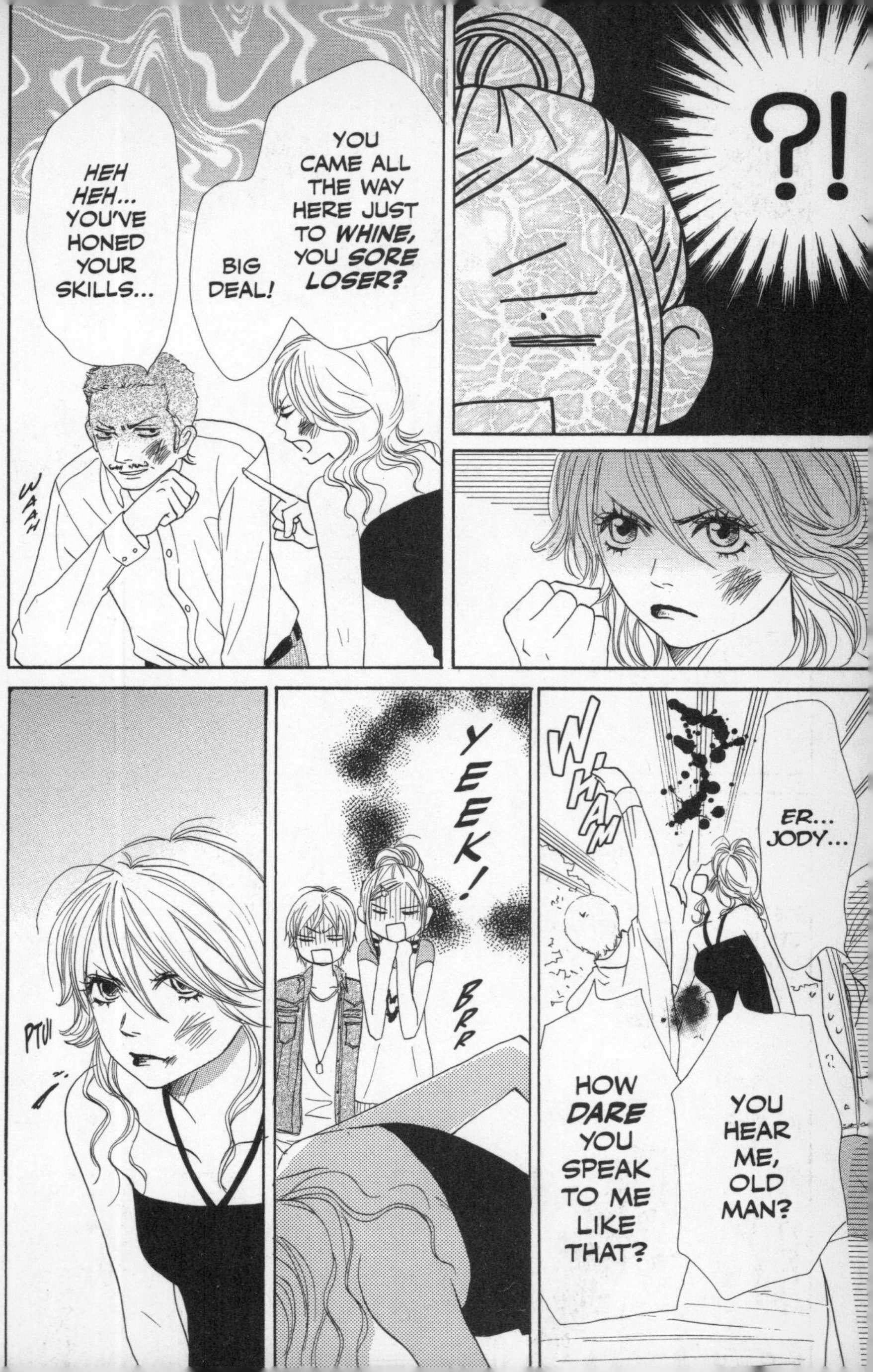
?!
YOU CAME ALL THE WAY HERE JUST TO WHINE, YOU SORE LOSER?
BIG DEAL!
HEH HEH... YOU'VE HONED YOUR SKILLS...
WAAH
WHAM
ER... JODY...
YOU HEAR ME, OLD MAN?
HOW DARE YOU SPEAK TO ME LIKE THAT?
YEEK!
BRR
PTUI

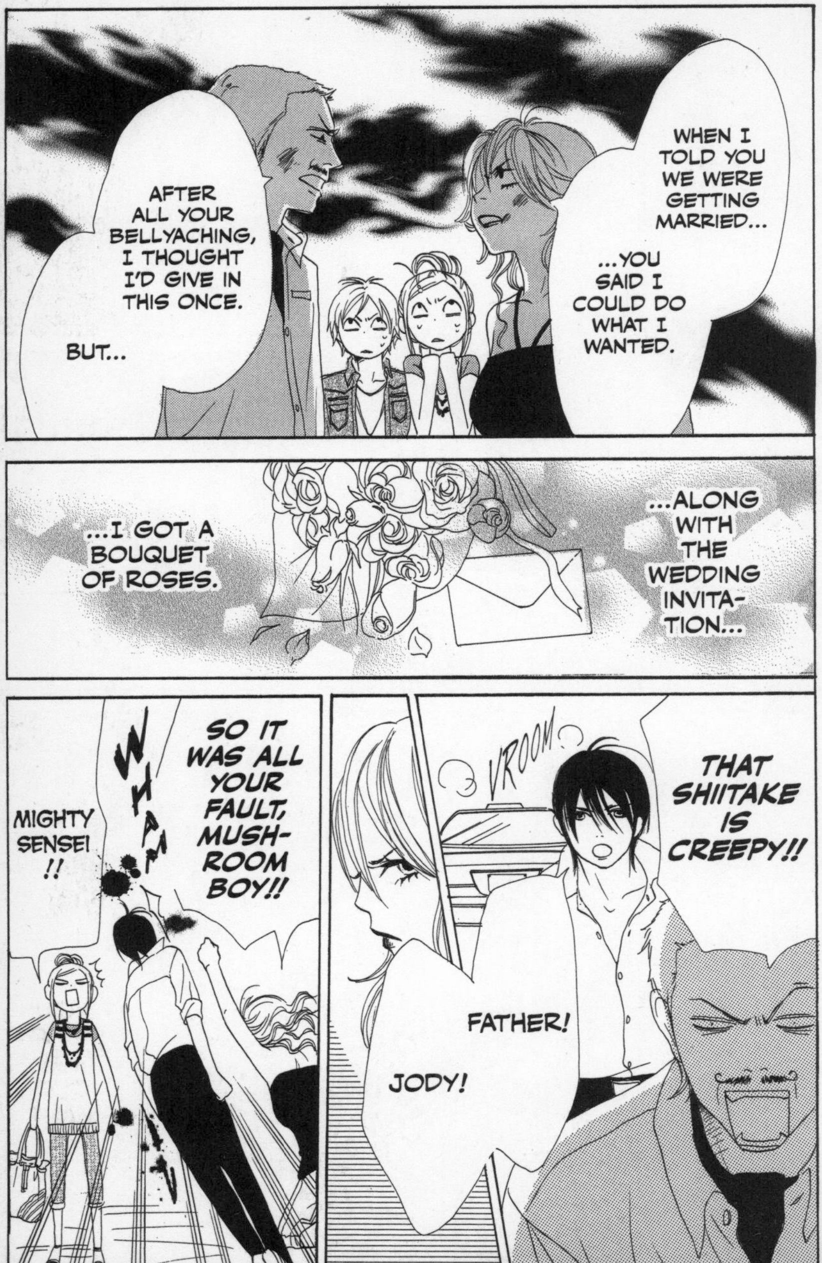
WHEN I TOLD YOU WE WERE GETTING MARRIED...
...YOU SAID I COULD DO WHAT I WANTED.
AFTER ALL YOUR BELLYACHING, I THOUGHT I'D GIVE IN THIS ONCE.
BUT...
...ALONG WITH THE WEDDING INVITA-TION...
...I GOT A BOUQUET OF ROSES.
THAT SHIITAKE IS CREEPY!!
VROOM
FATHER!
JODY!
SO IT WAS ALL YOUR FAULT, MUSH-ROOM BOY!!
WHAM
MIGHTY SENSEI !!

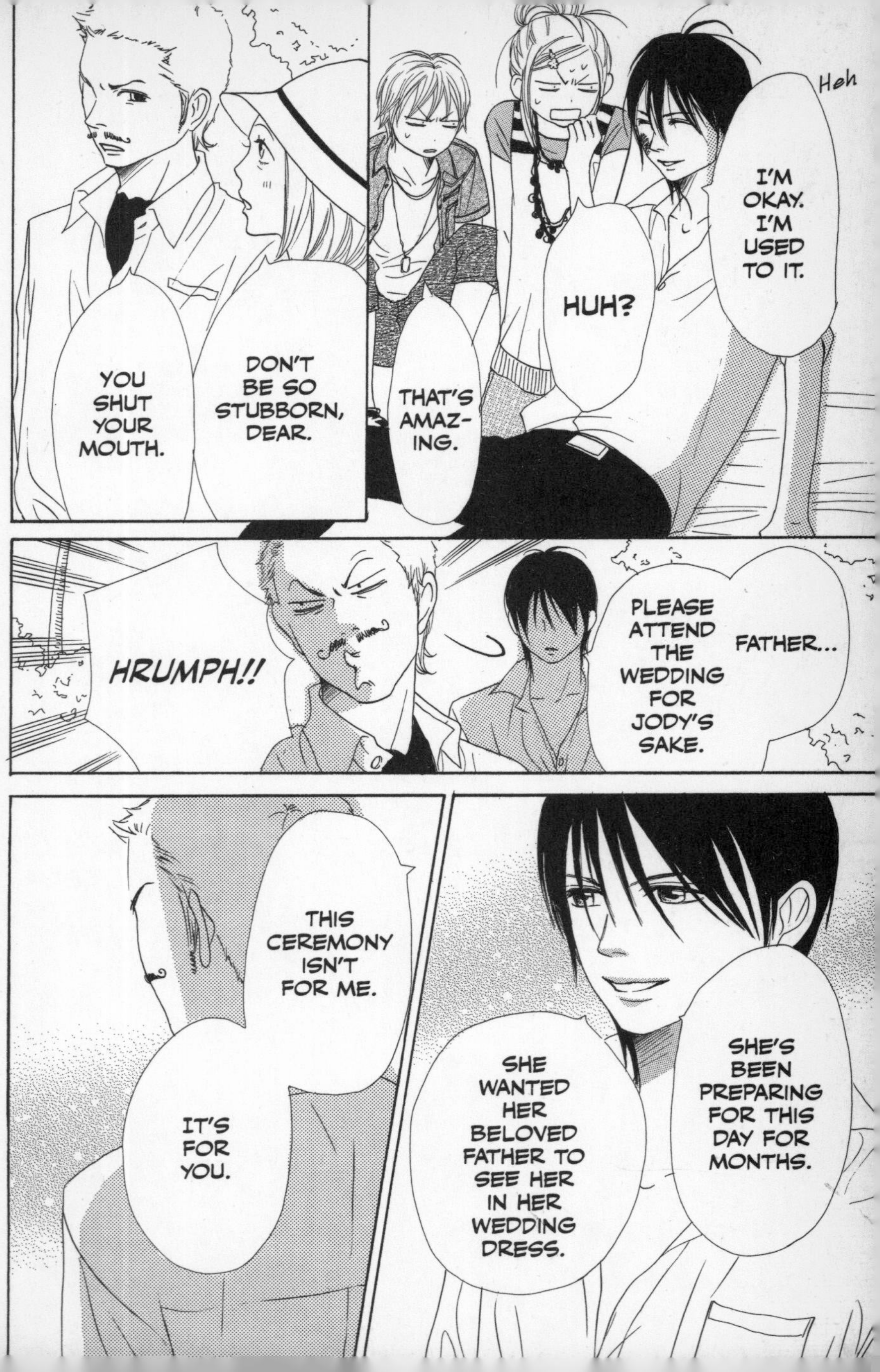
Heh
I'M OKAY. I'M USED TO IT.
HUH?
THAT'S AMAZ-ING.
DON'T BE SO STUBBORN, DEAR.
YOU SHUT YOUR MOUTH.
FATHER...
PLEASE ATTEND THE WEDDING FOR JODY'S SAKE.
HRUMPH!!
SHE'S BEEN PREPARING FOR THIS DAY FOR MONTHS.
SHE WANTED HER BELOVED FATHER TO SEE HER IN HER WEDDING DRESS.
THIS CEREMONY ISN'T FOR ME.
IT'S FOR YOU.

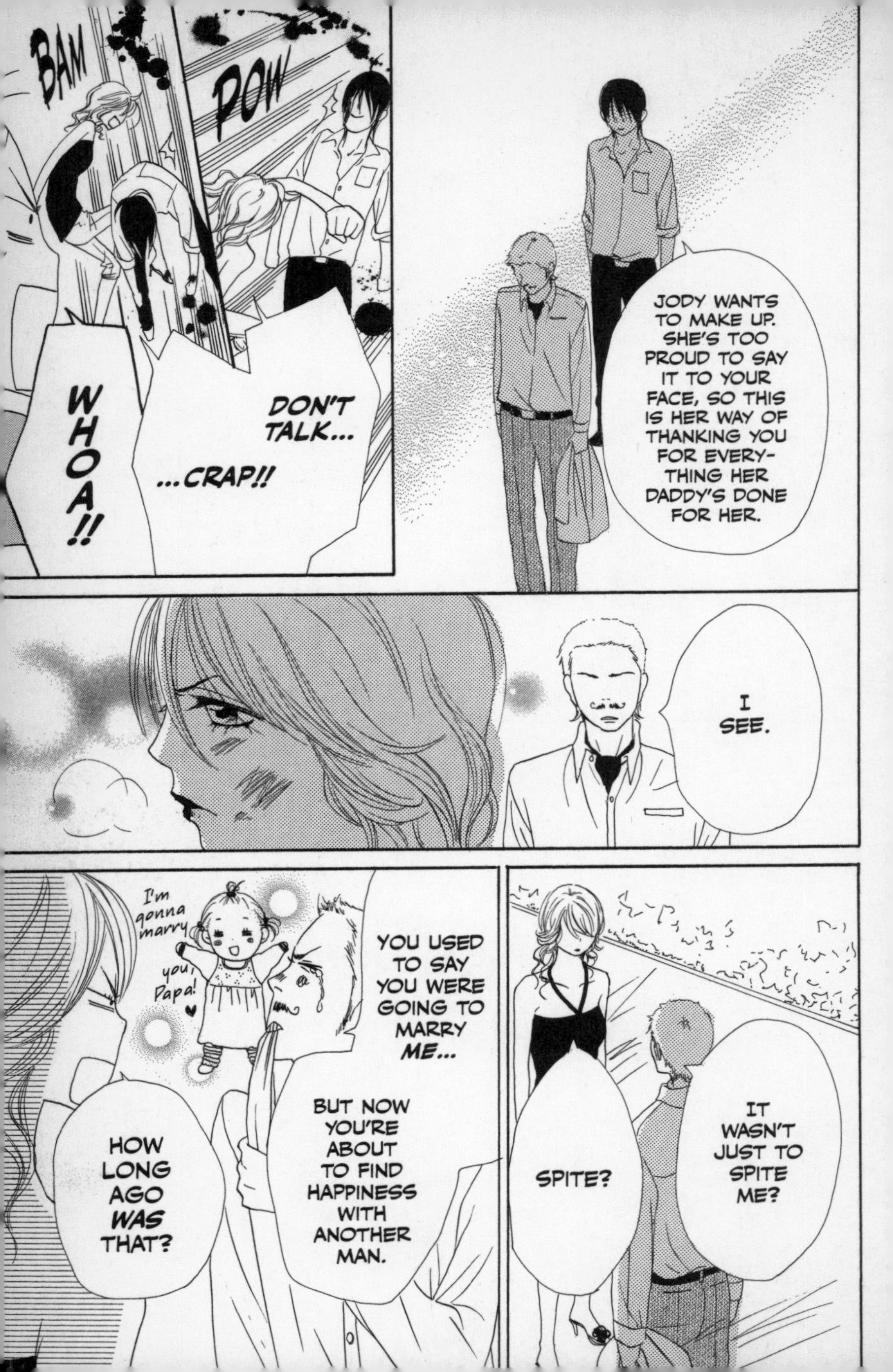
JODY WANTS TO MAKE UP. SHE'S TOO PROUD TO SAY IT TO YOUR FACE, SO THIS IS HER WAY OF THANKING YOU FOR EVERY-THING HER DADDY'S DONE FOR HER.
BAM
POW
DON'T TALK...
...CRAP!!
WHOA!!
I SEE.
IT WASN'T JUST TO SPITE ME?
SPITE?
YOU USED TO SAY YOU WERE GOING TO MARRY *ME*...
I'm gonna marry you, Papa!
BUT NOW YOU'RE ABOUT TO FIND HAPPINESS WITH ANOTHER MAN.
HOW LONG AGO *WAS* THAT?

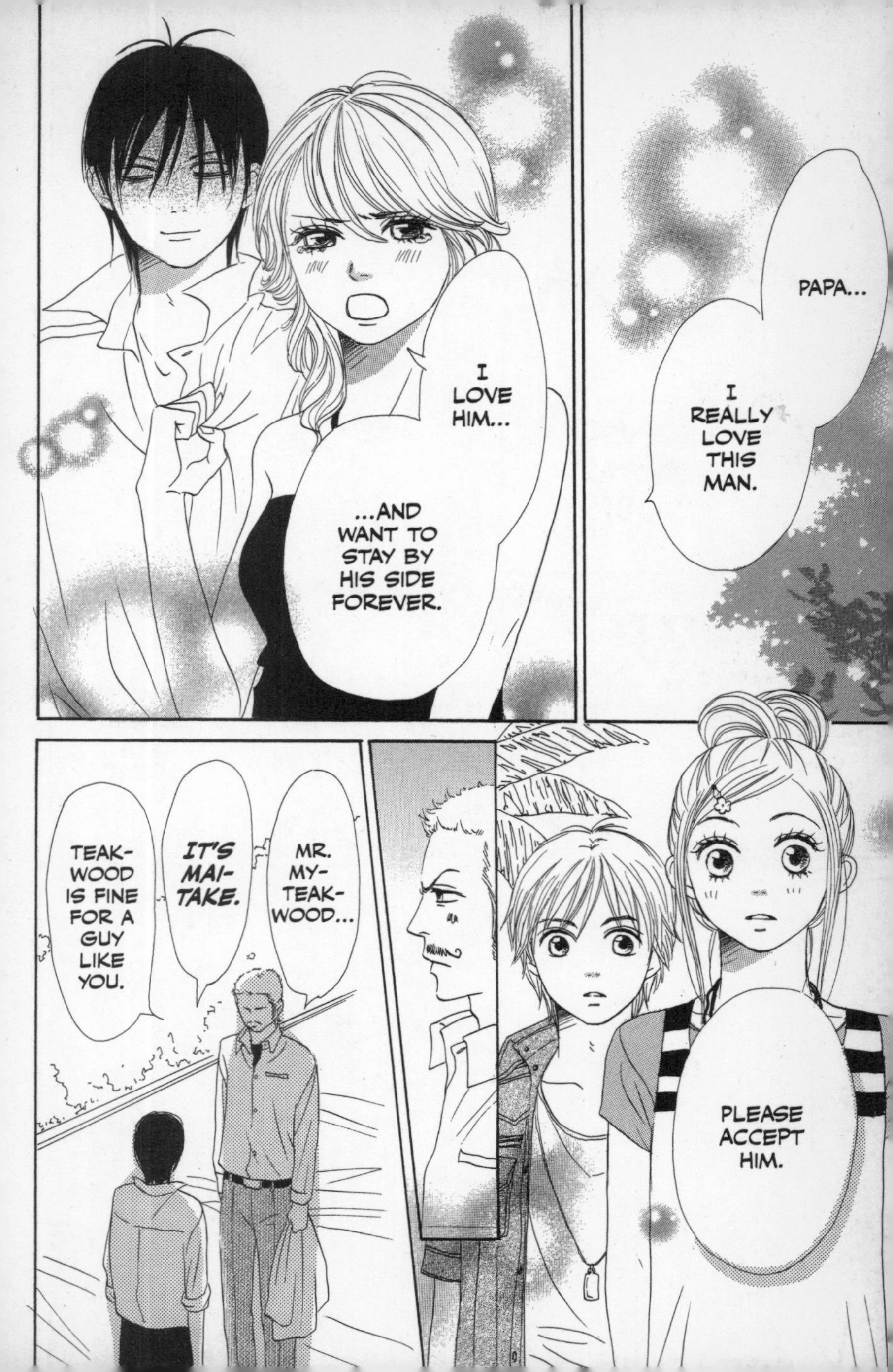
PAPA...
I REALLY LOVE THIS MAN.
I LOVE HIM...
...AND WANT TO STAY BY HIS SIDE FOREVER.
PLEASE ACCEPT HIM.
MR. MY-TEAK-WOOD...
IT'S MAI-TAKE.
TEAK-WOOD IS FINE FOR A GUY LIKE YOU.

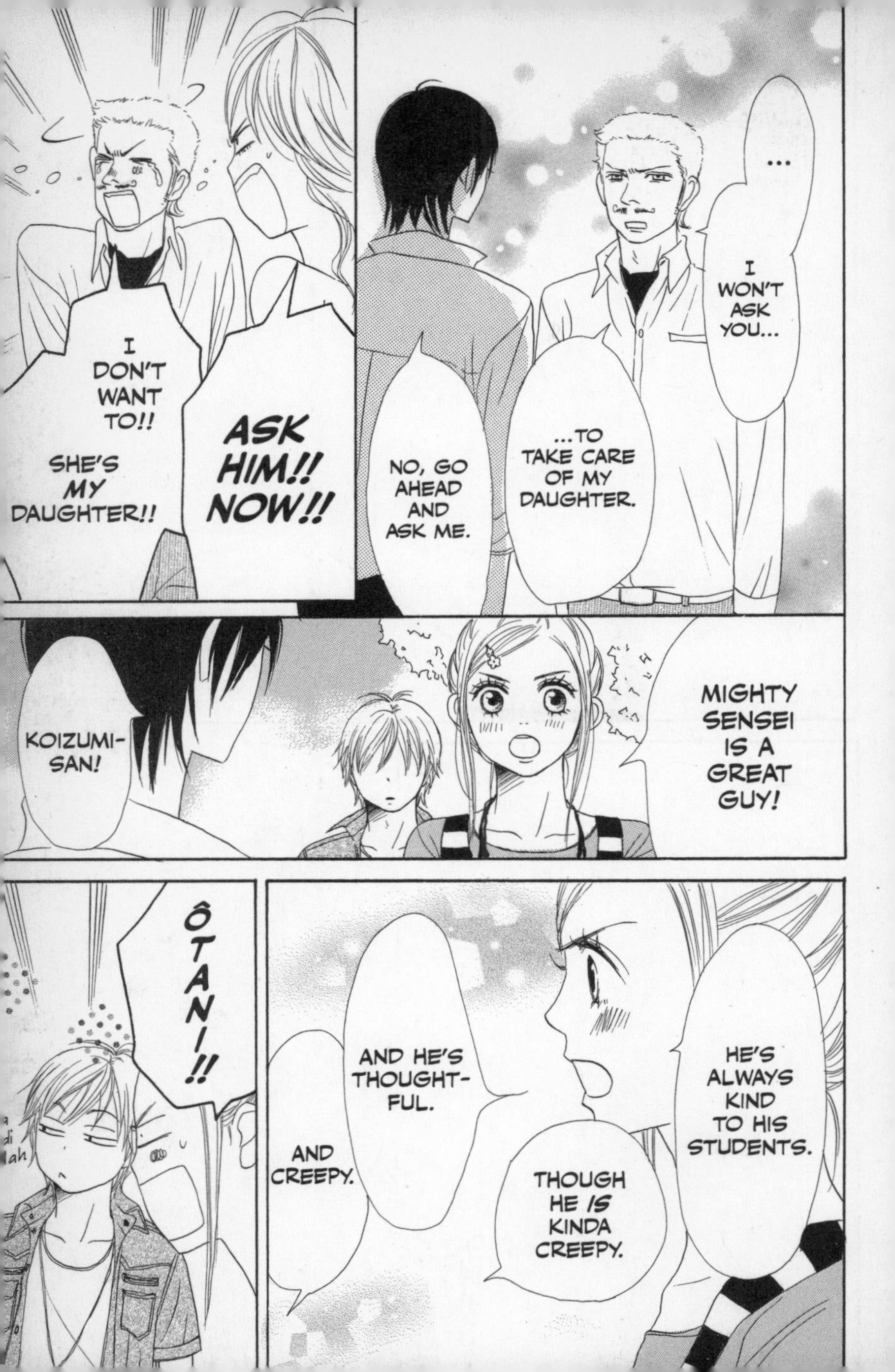
...
I WON'T ASK YOU...
...TO TAKE CARE OF MY DAUGHTER.
NO, GO AHEAD AND ASK ME.
ASK HIM!! NOW!!
I DON'T WANT TO!!
SHE'S MY DAUGHTER!!
MIGHTY SENSEI IS A GREAT GUY!
KOIZUMI-SAN!
HE'S ALWAYS KIND TO HIS STUDENTS.
AND HE'S THOUGHTFUL.
THOUGH HE IS KINDA CREEPY.
AND CREEPY.
ÔTANI!!

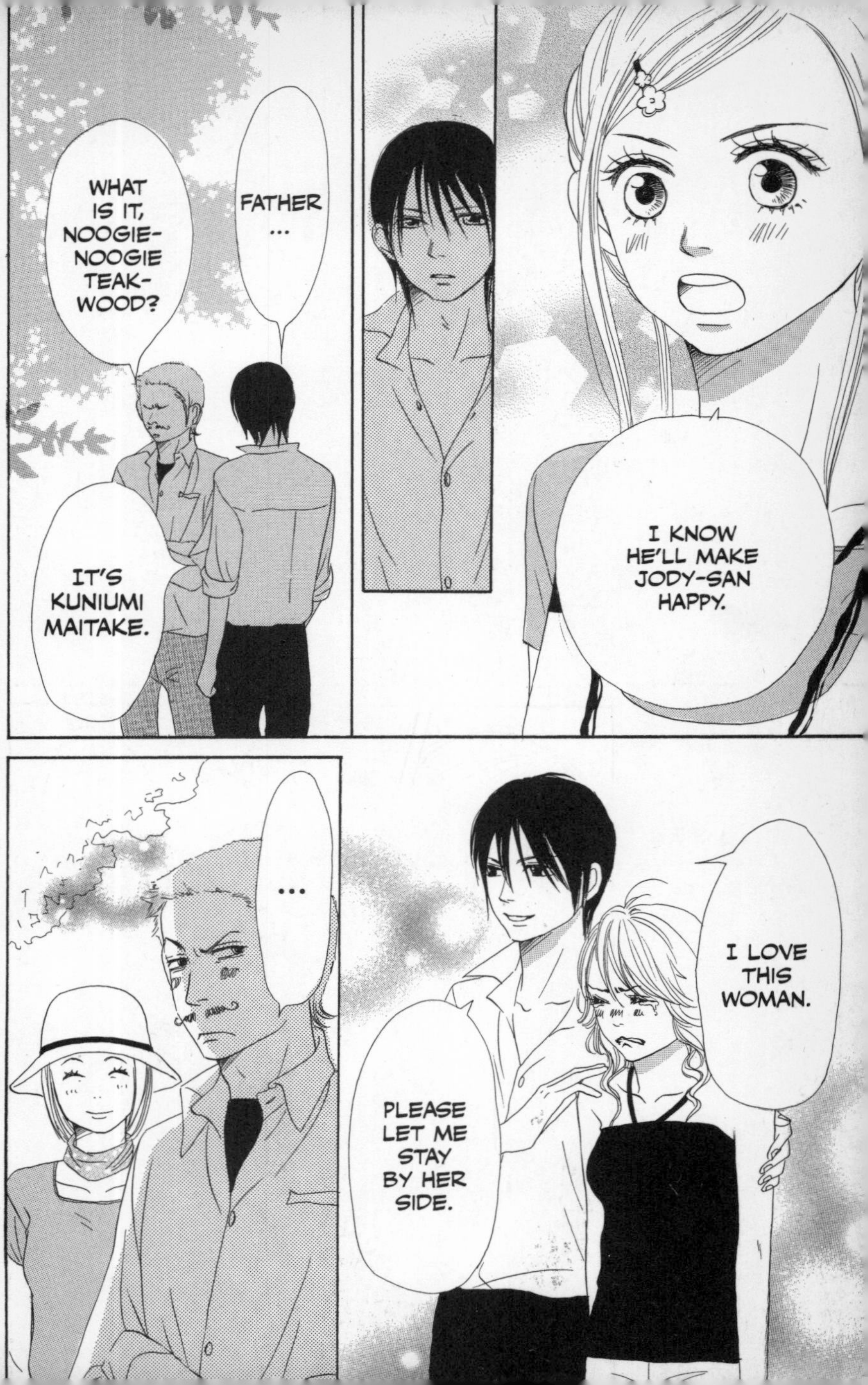
I KNOW HE'LL MAKE JODY-SAN HAPPY.
FATHER ...
WHAT IS IT, NOOGIE-NOOGIE TEAKWOOD?
IT'S KUNIUMI MAITAKE.
I LOVE THIS WOMAN.
PLEASE LET ME STAY BY HER SIDE.
...

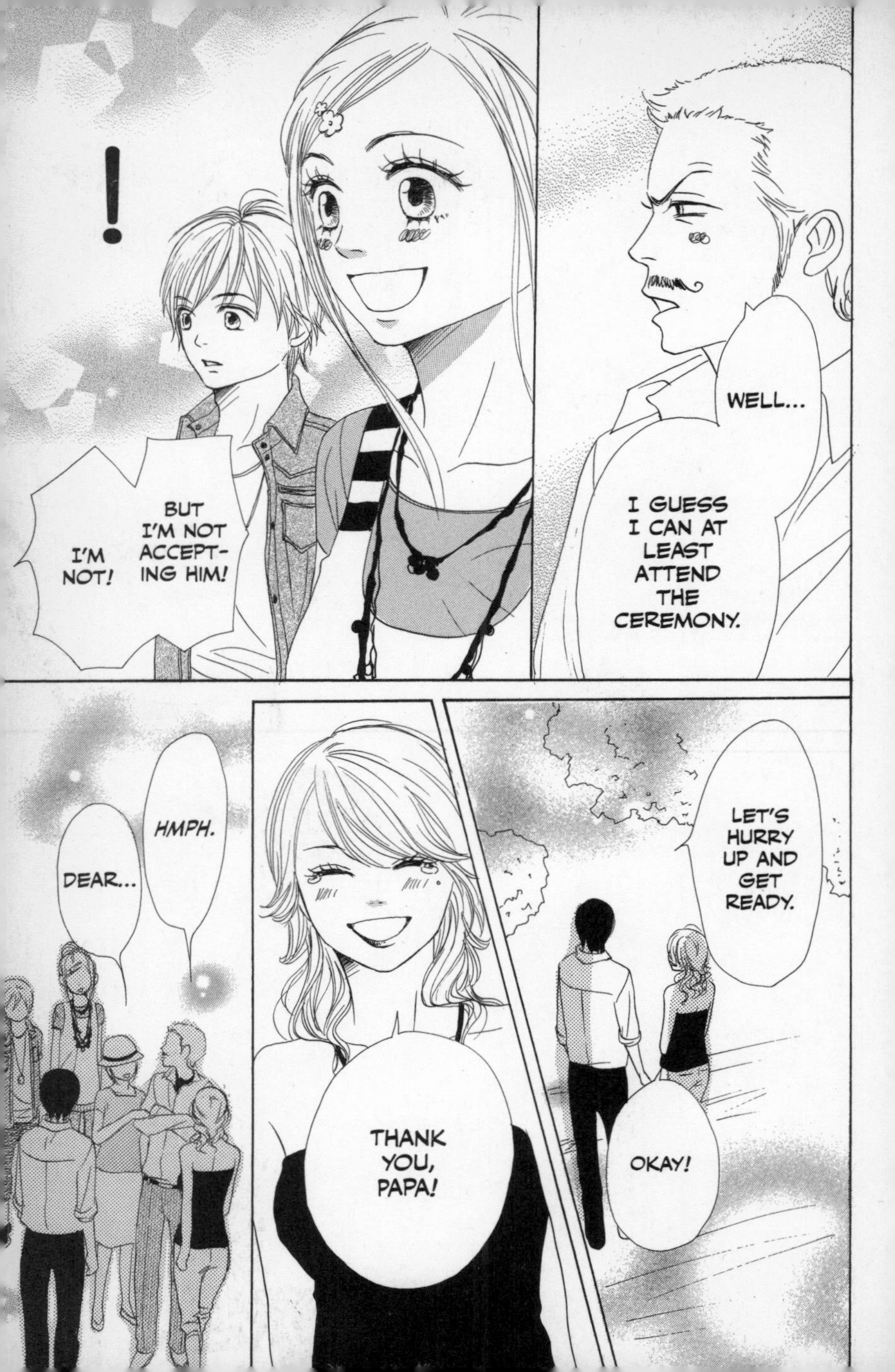
WELL...
I GUESS I CAN AT LEAST ATTEND THE CEREMONY.
!
BUT I'M NOT ACCEPT-ING HIM!
I'M NOT!
LET'S HURRY UP AND GET READY.
OKAY!
THANK YOU, PAPA!
HMPH.
DEAR...

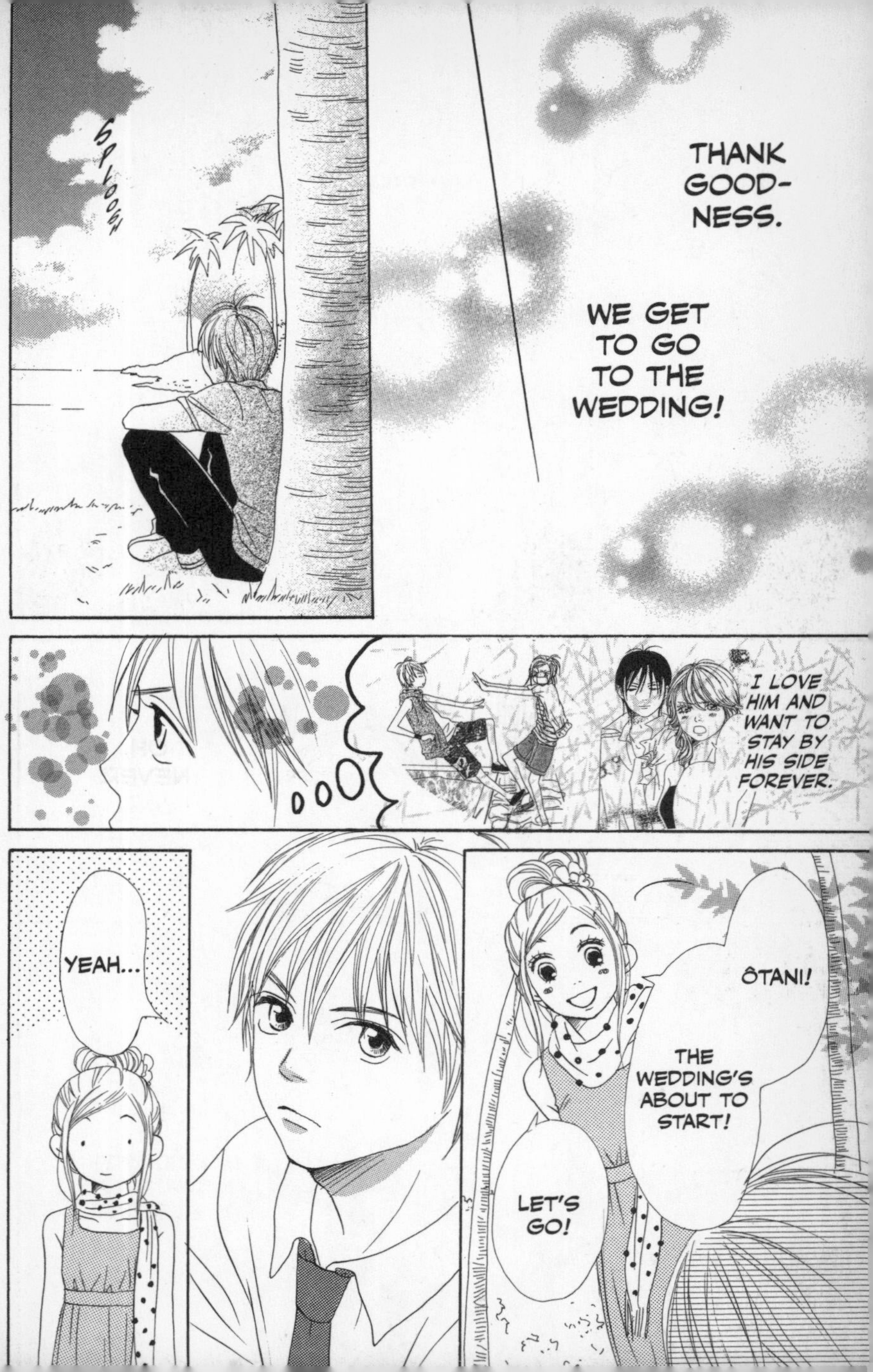
THANK GOODNESS.
WE GET TO GO TO THE WEDDING!
SPLOOSH
I LOVE HIM AND WANT TO STAY BY HIS SIDE FOREVER.
ŌTANI!
THE WEDDING'S ABOUT TO START!
LET'S GO!
YEAH...

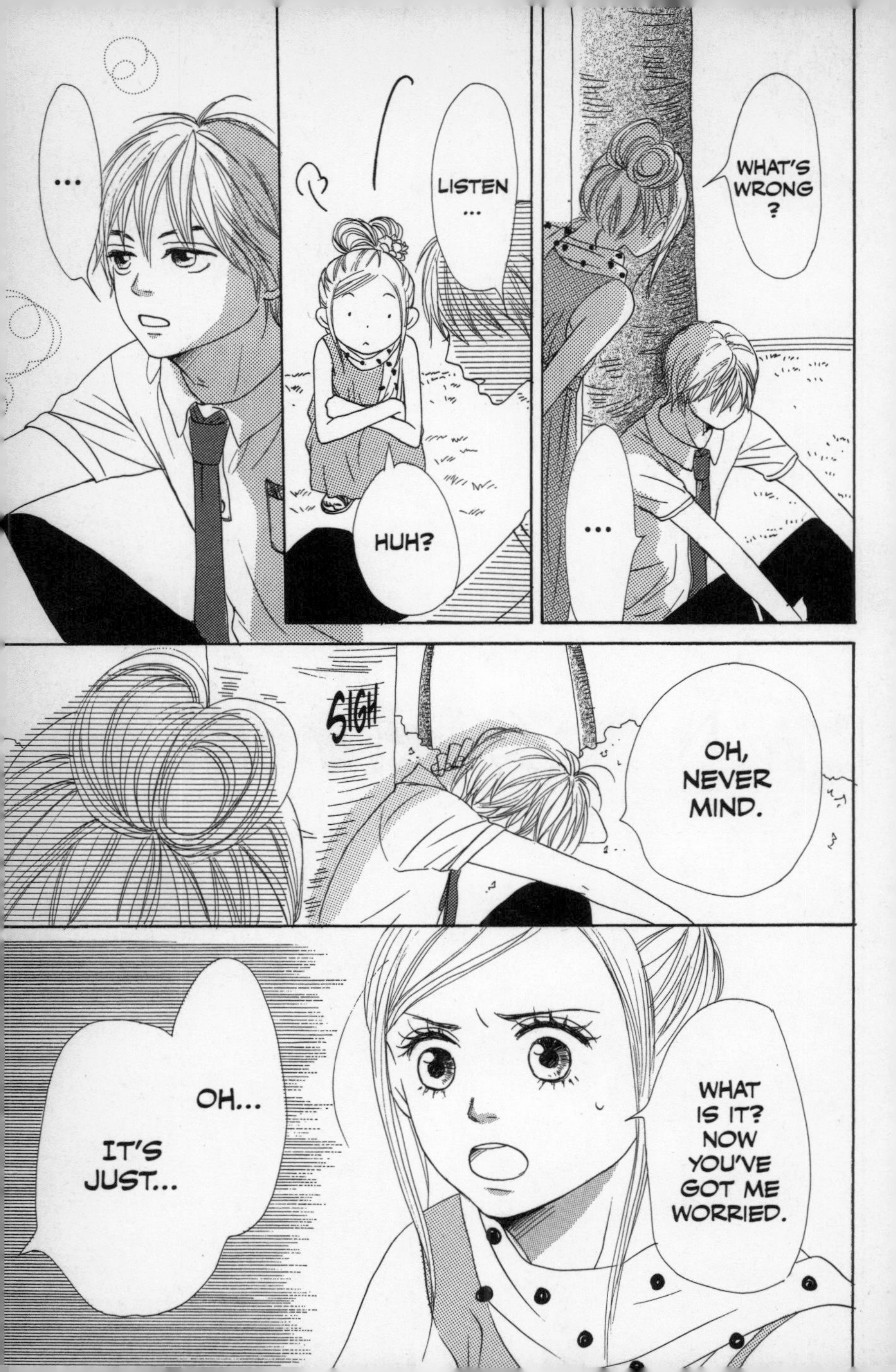
WHAT'S WRONG?
...
LISTEN...
HUH?
...
OH, NEVER MIND.
SIGH
WHAT IS IT? NOW YOU'VE GOT ME WORRIED.
OH... IT'S JUST...

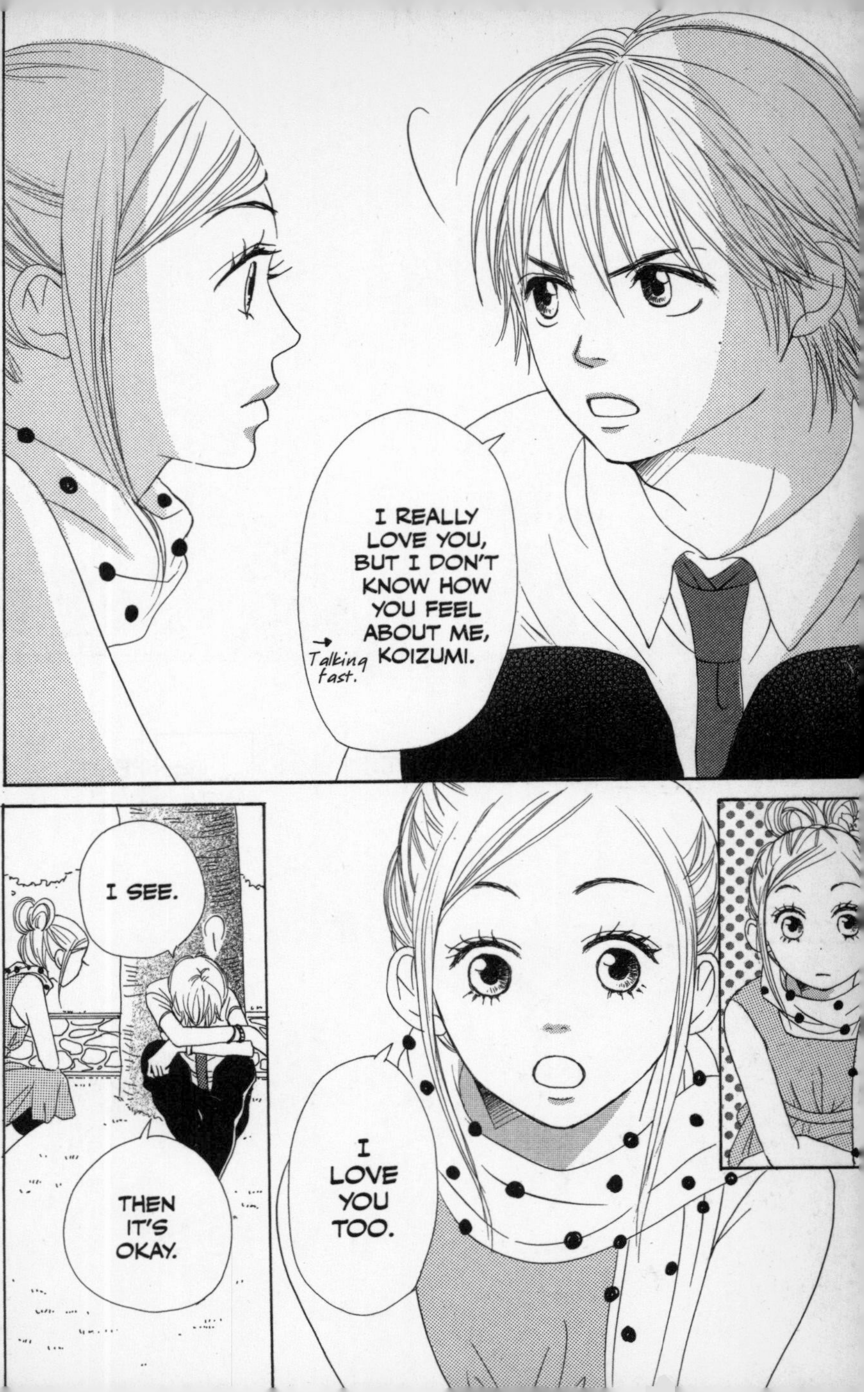
I REALLY LOVE YOU, BUT I DON'T KNOW HOW YOU FEEL ABOUT ME, KOIZUMI.
Talking fast.
I LOVE YOU TOO.
I SEE.
THEN IT'S OKAY.

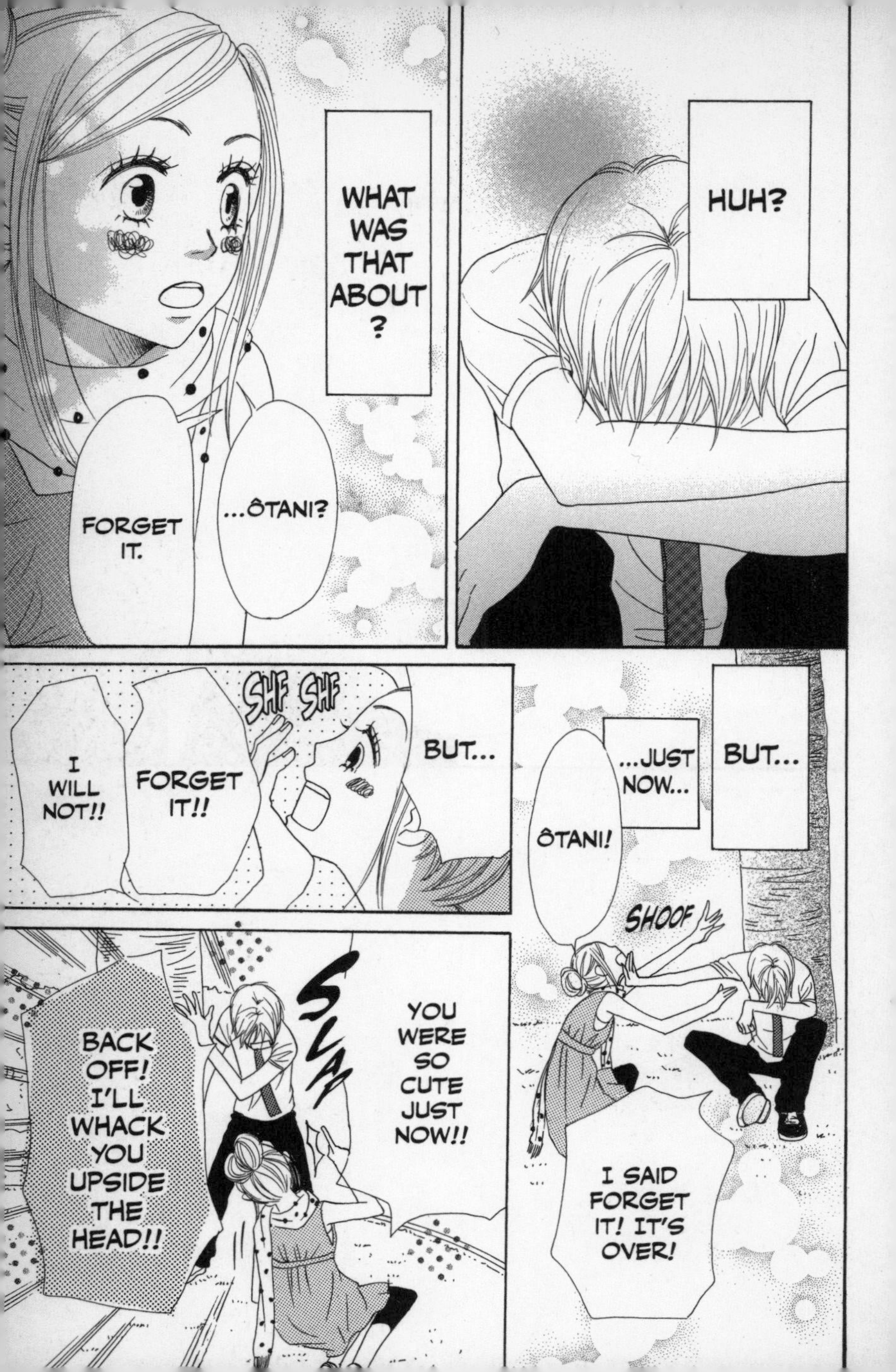
HUH?
WHAT WAS THAT ABOUT?
...ÔTANI?
FORGET IT.
BUT...
...JUST NOW...
ÔTANI!
SHOOF
I SAID FORGET IT! IT'S OVER!
SHF SHF
BUT...
FORGET IT!!
I WILL NOT!!
YOU WERE SO CUTE JUST NOW!!
SLAM
BACK OFF! I'LL WHACK YOU UPSIDE THE HEAD!!

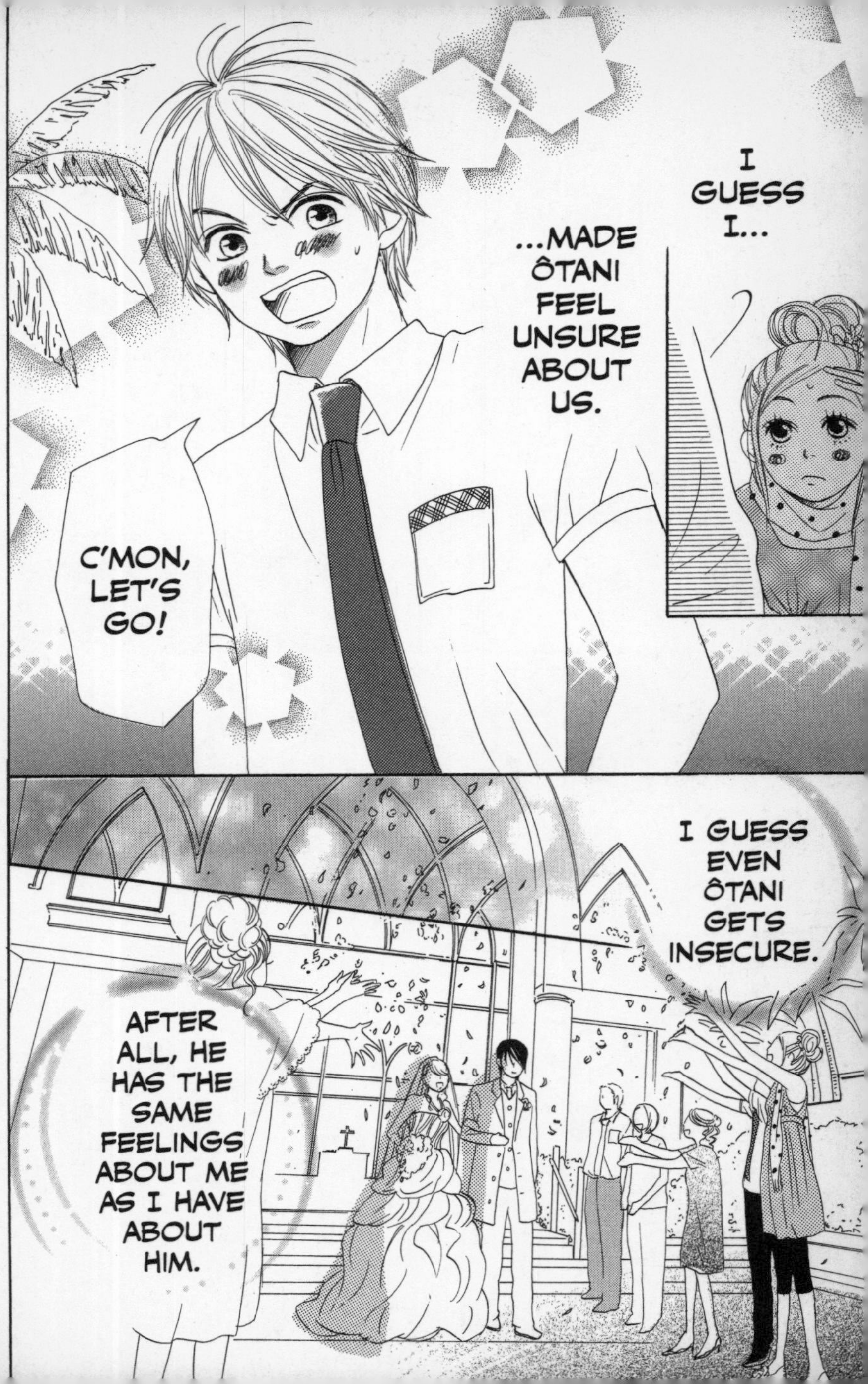
I GUESS I...
...MADE ÔTANI FEEL UNSURE ABOUT US.
C'MON, LET'S GO!
I GUESS EVEN ÔTANI GETS INSECURE.
AFTER ALL, HE HAS THE SAME FEELINGS ABOUT ME AS I HAVE ABOUT HIM.

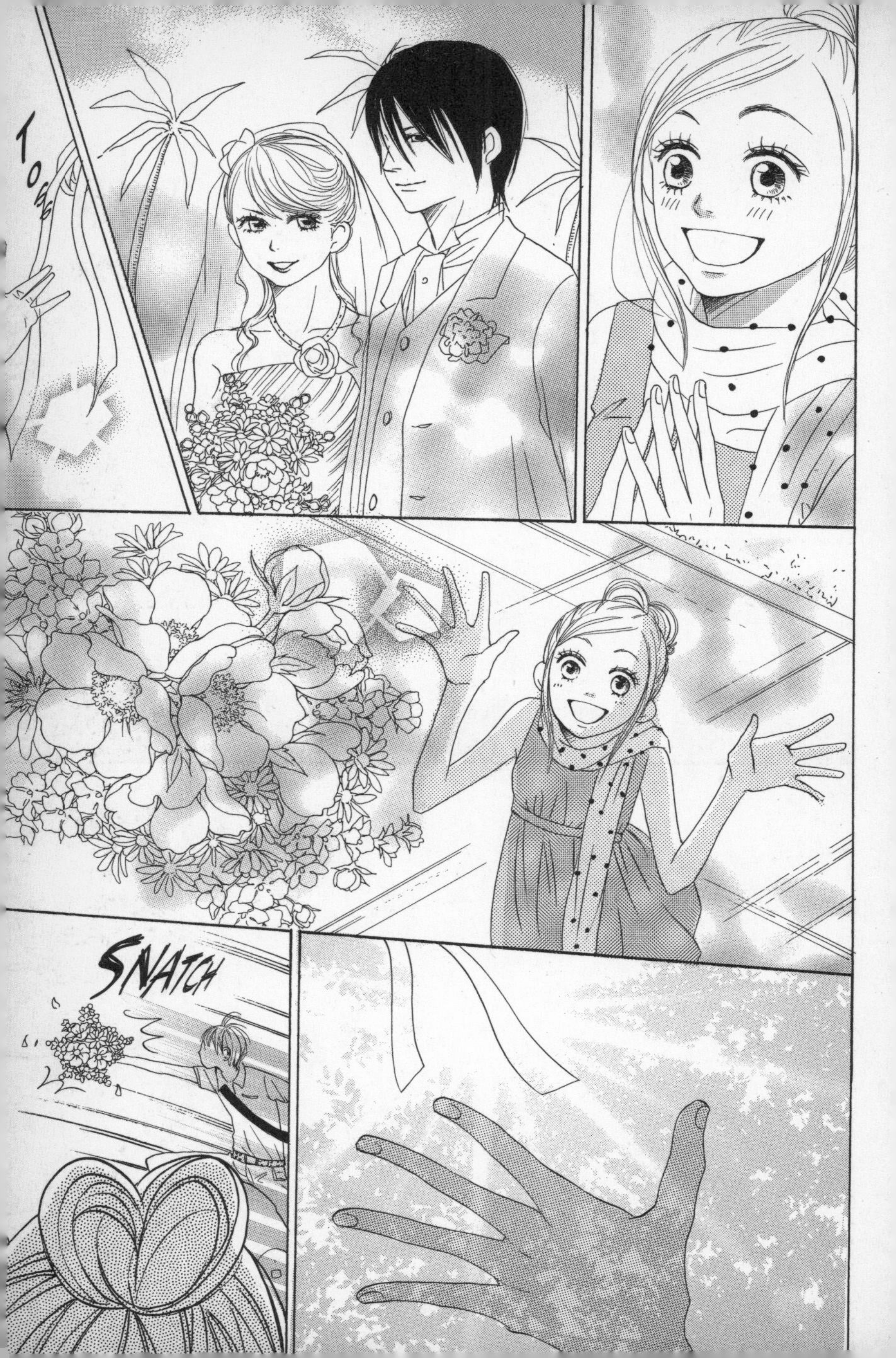
TOSS
SNATCH

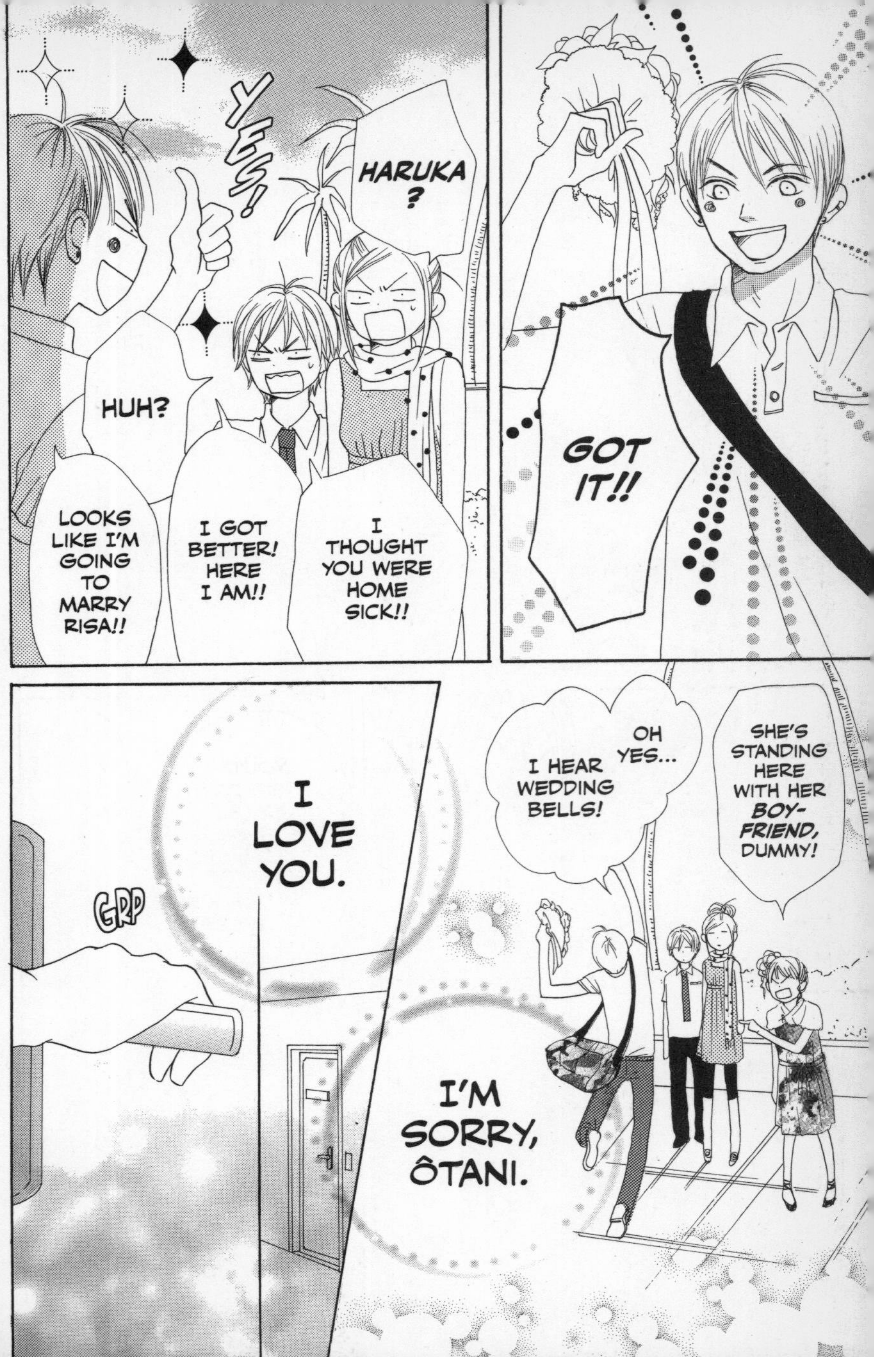
GOT IT!!
HARUKA ?
YES!
HUH?
I THOUGHT YOU WERE HOME SICK!!
I GOT BETTER! HERE I AM!!
LOOKS LIKE I'M GOING TO MARRY RISA!!
SHE'S STANDING HERE WITH HER *BOY-FRIEND*, DUMMY!
OH YES...
I HEAR WEDDING BELLS!
I'M SORRY, ÔTANI.
I LOVE YOU.
GRP

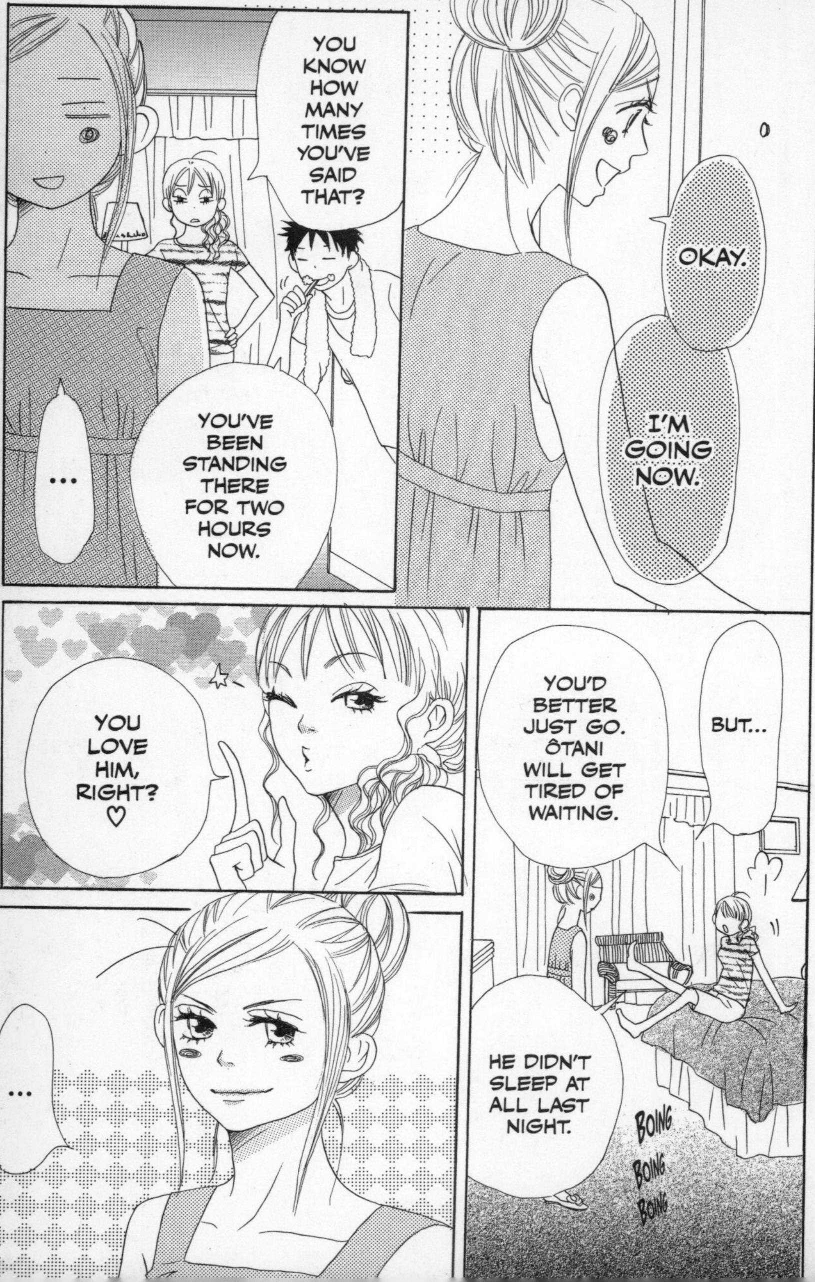
OKAY.
I'M GOING NOW.
YOU KNOW HOW MANY TIMES YOU'VE SAID THAT?
YOU'VE BEEN STANDING THERE FOR TWO HOURS NOW.
...
BUT...
YOU'D BETTER JUST GO. ÔTANI WILL GET TIRED OF WAITING.
HE DIDN'T SLEEP AT ALL LAST NIGHT.
BOING
BOING
BOING
YOU LOVE HIM, RIGHT? ♡
...

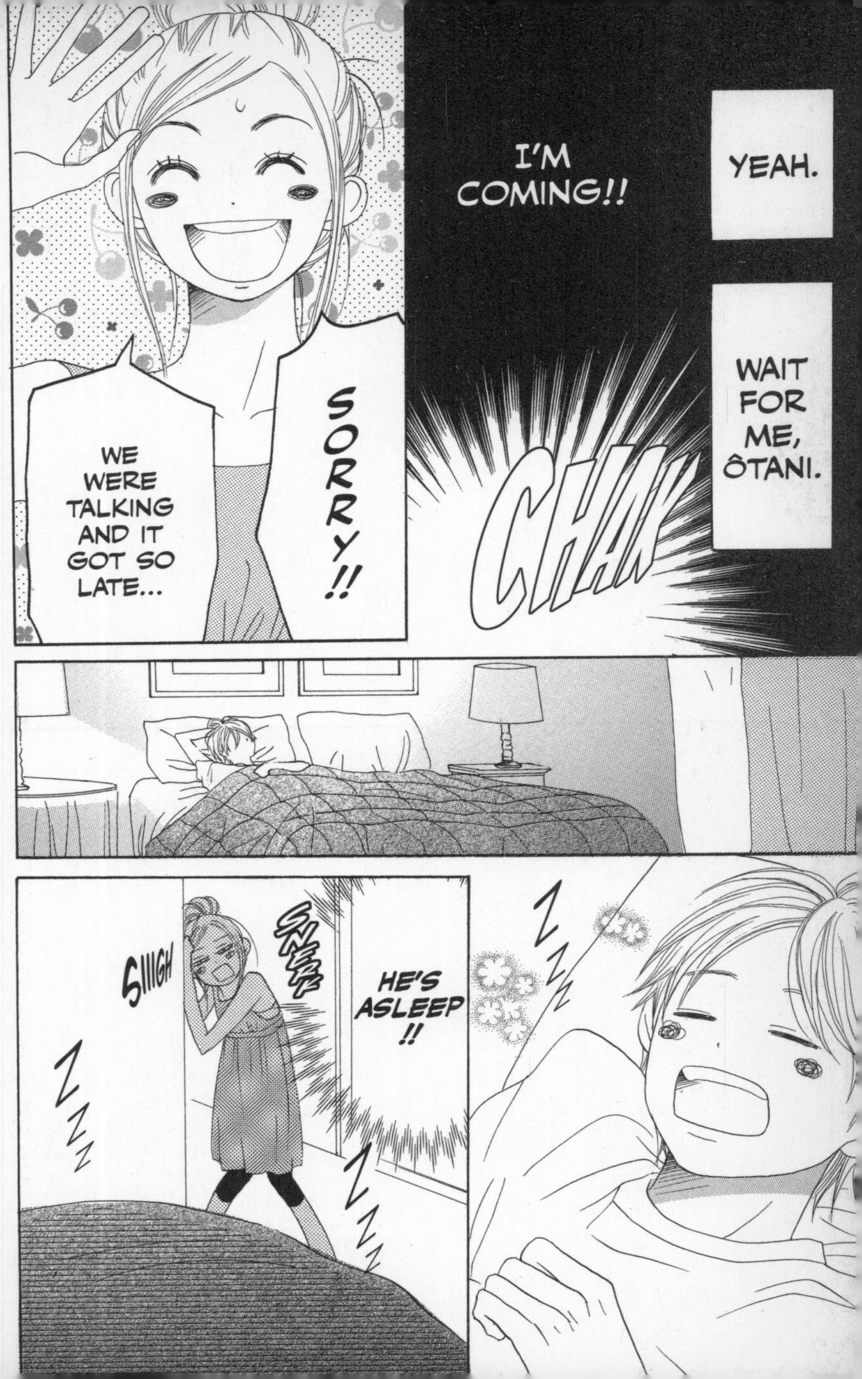
YEAH.
WAIT FOR ME, ÔTANI.
I'M COMING!!
CHAN
SORRY!!
WE WERE TALKING AND IT GOT SO LATE...
ZZZ
HE'S ASLEEP!!
SIIIGH
ZZZ
ZZZ

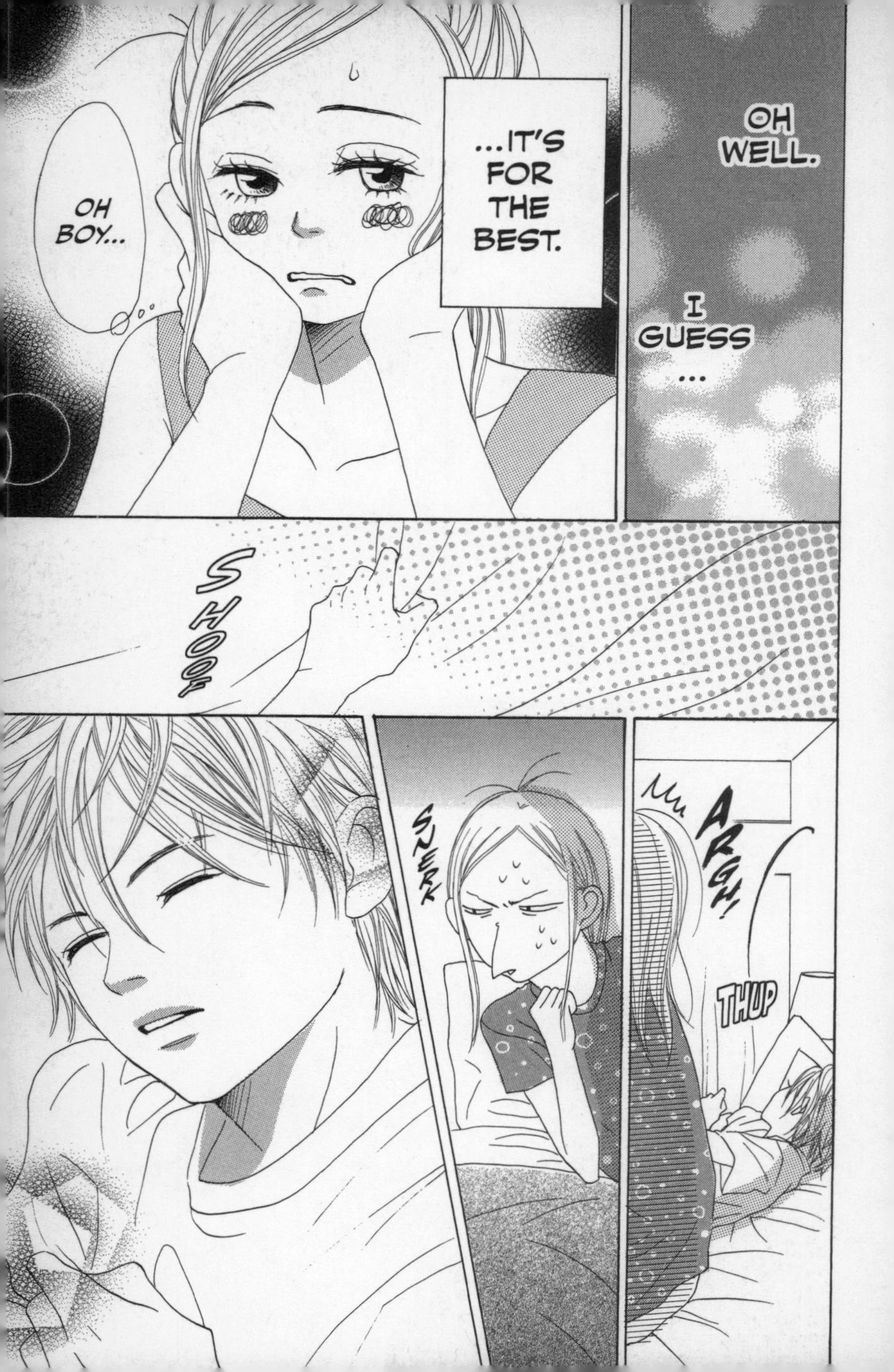
OH WELL.
I GUESS...
...IT'S FOR THE BEST.
OH BOY...
SHOOF
Mu
ARGH!
THUP
SNERK

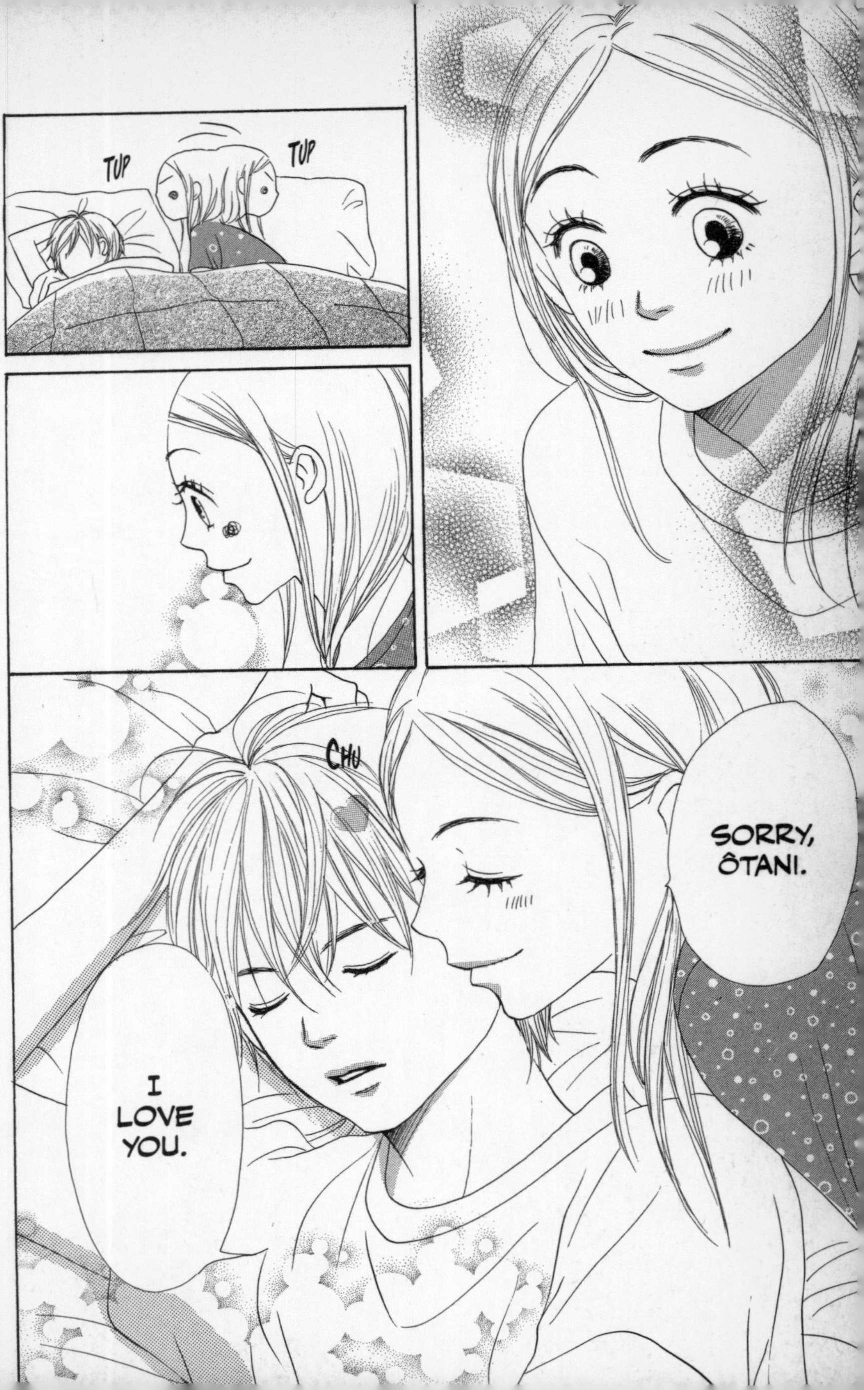
TUP
TUP
CHU
SORRY, ÔTANI.
I LOVE YOU.

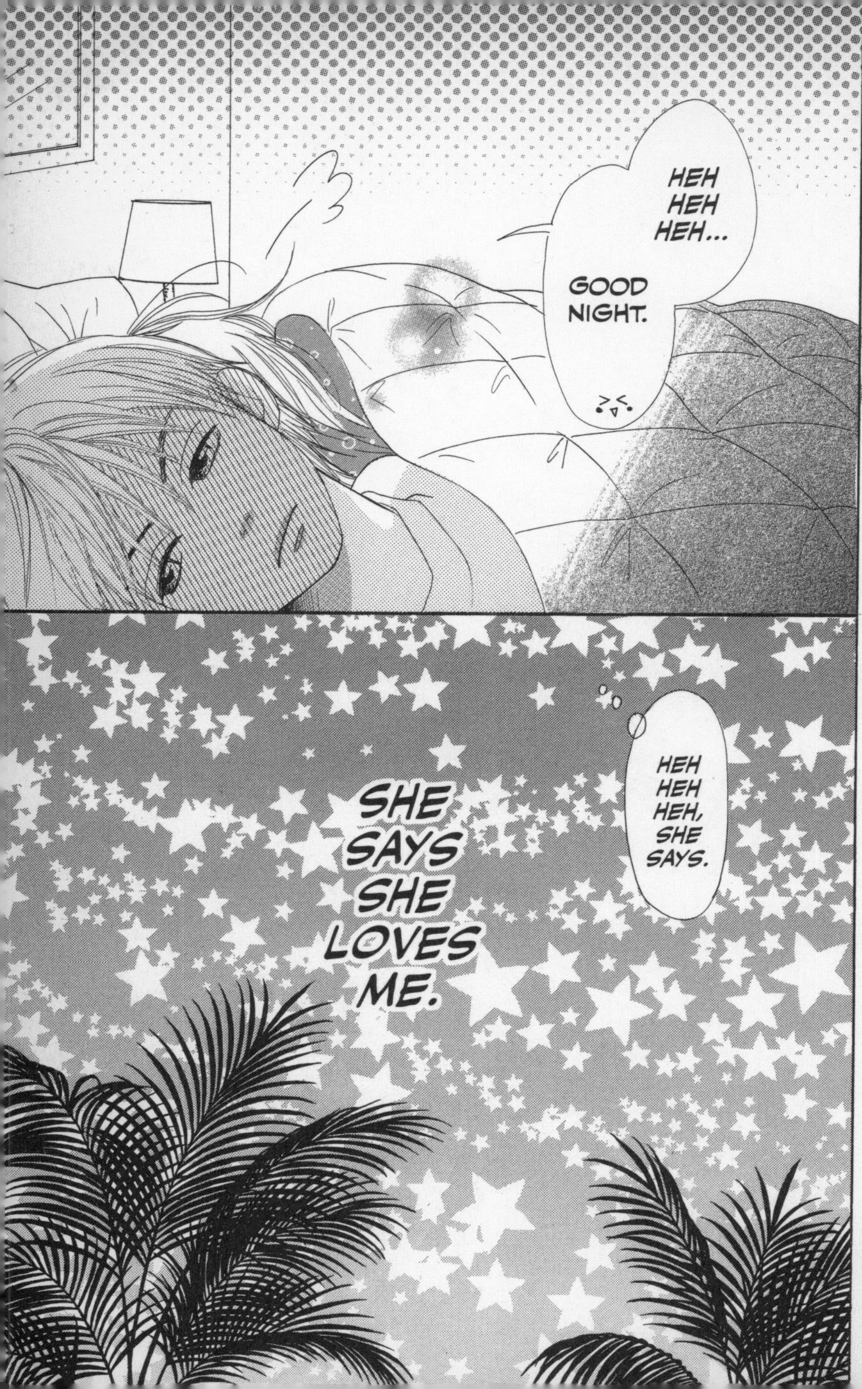
HEH HEH HEH...
GOOD NIGHT.
HEH HEH HEH, SHE SAYS.
SHE SAYS SHE LOVES ME.

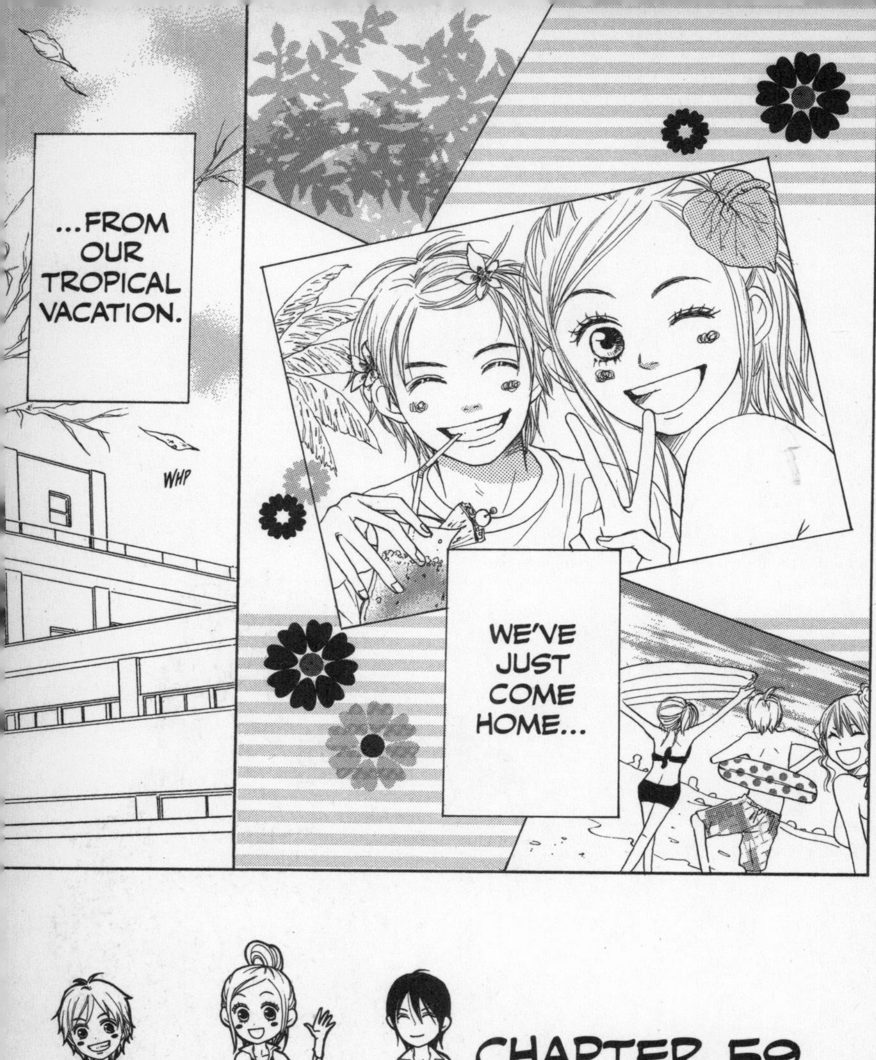
WE'VE JUST COME HOME...
...FROM OUR TROPICAL VACATION.
WHP

CHAPTER 59

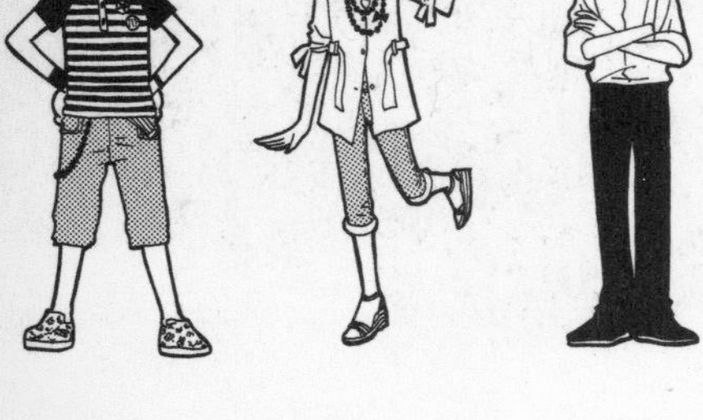

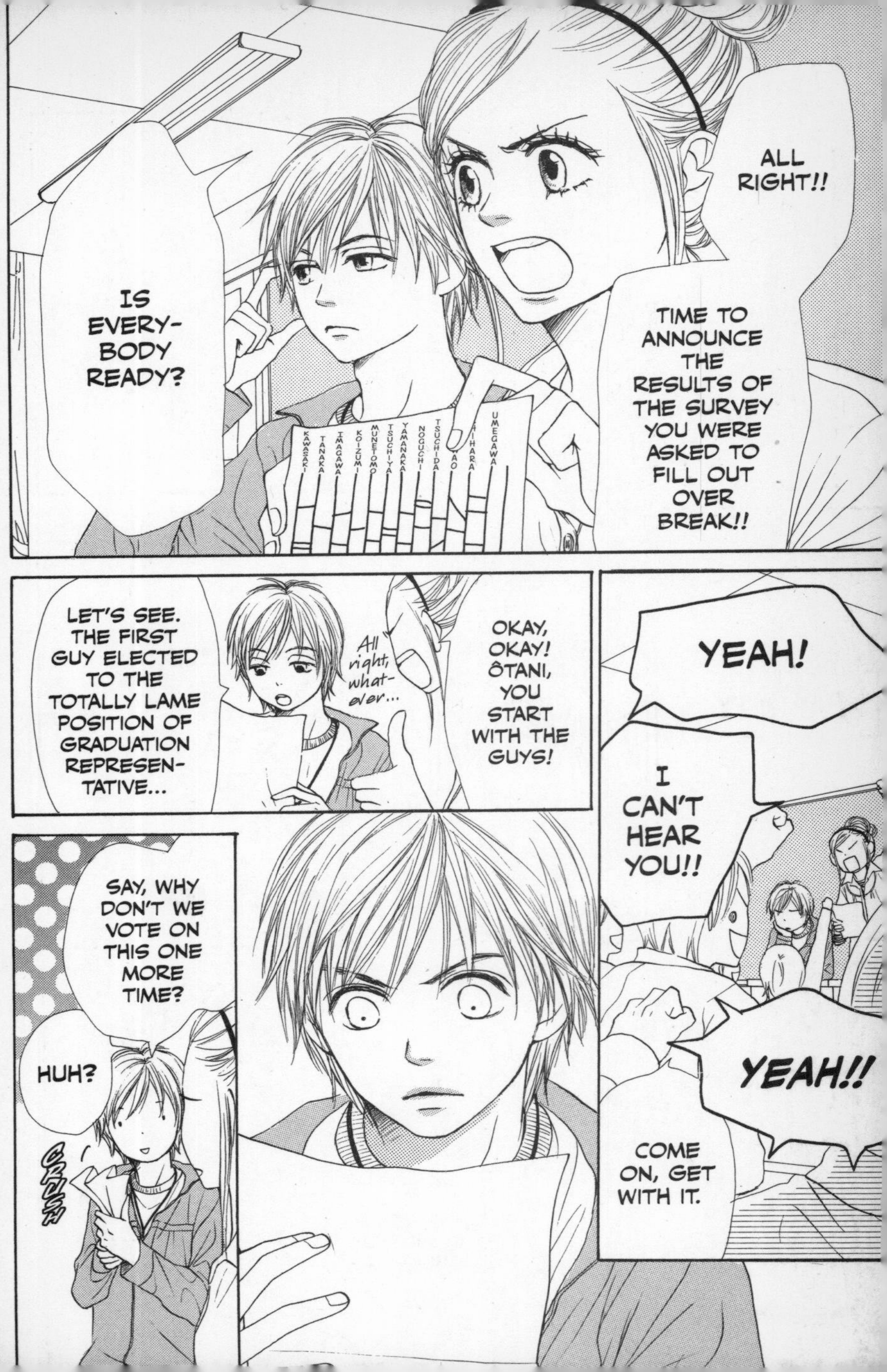
ALL RIGHT!!
TIME TO ANNOUNCE THE RESULTS OF THE SURVEY YOU WERE ASKED TO FILL OUT OVER BREAK!!
UMEGAWA
TSUCHIDA
NOGUCHI
YAMANAKA
TSUCHIYA
MUNETOMO
KOIZUMI
IMAGAWA
TANAKA
KAWASAKI
IS EVERY-BODY READY?
YEAH!
I CAN'T HEAR YOU!!
YEAH!!
COME ON, GET WITH IT.
OKAY, OKAY! ŌTANI, YOU START WITH THE GUYS!
All right, whatever...
LET'S SEE. THE FIRST GUY ELECTED TO THE TOTALLY LAME POSITION OF GRADUATION REPRESEN-TATIVE...
SAY, WHY DON'T WE VOTE ON THIS ONE MORE TIME?
HUH?
CRUSH

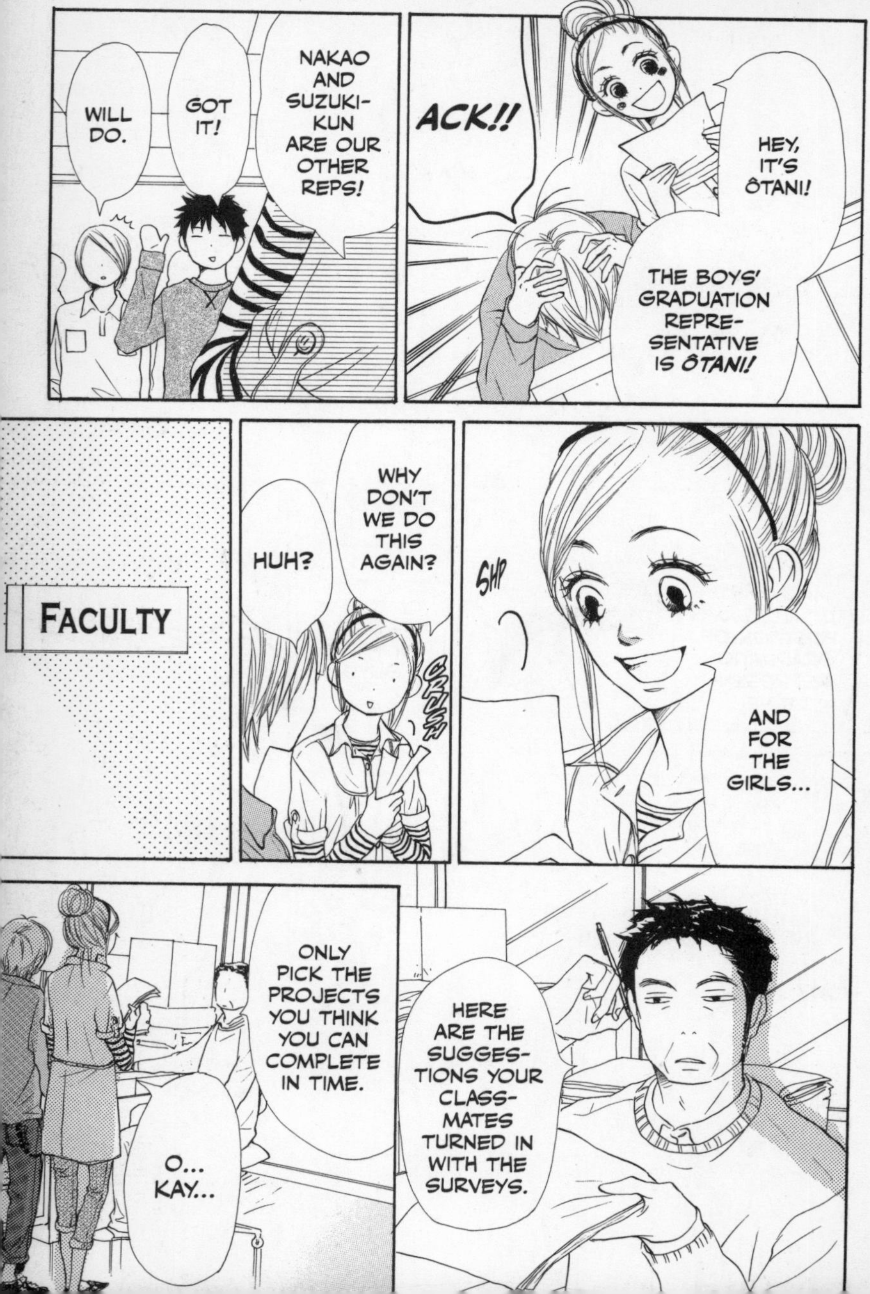
HEY, IT'S ŌTANI!
THE BOYS' GRADUATION REPRESENTATIVE IS ŌTANI!
ACK!!
NAKAO AND SUZUKI-KUN ARE OUR OTHER REPS!
GOT IT!
WILL DO.
SHP
AND FOR THE GIRLS...
WHY DON'T WE DO THIS AGAIN?
HUH?
FACULTY
HERE ARE THE SUGGESTIONS YOUR CLASSMATES TURNED IN WITH THE SURVEYS.
ONLY PICK THE PROJECTS YOU THINK YOU CAN COMPLETE IN TIME.
O... KAY...

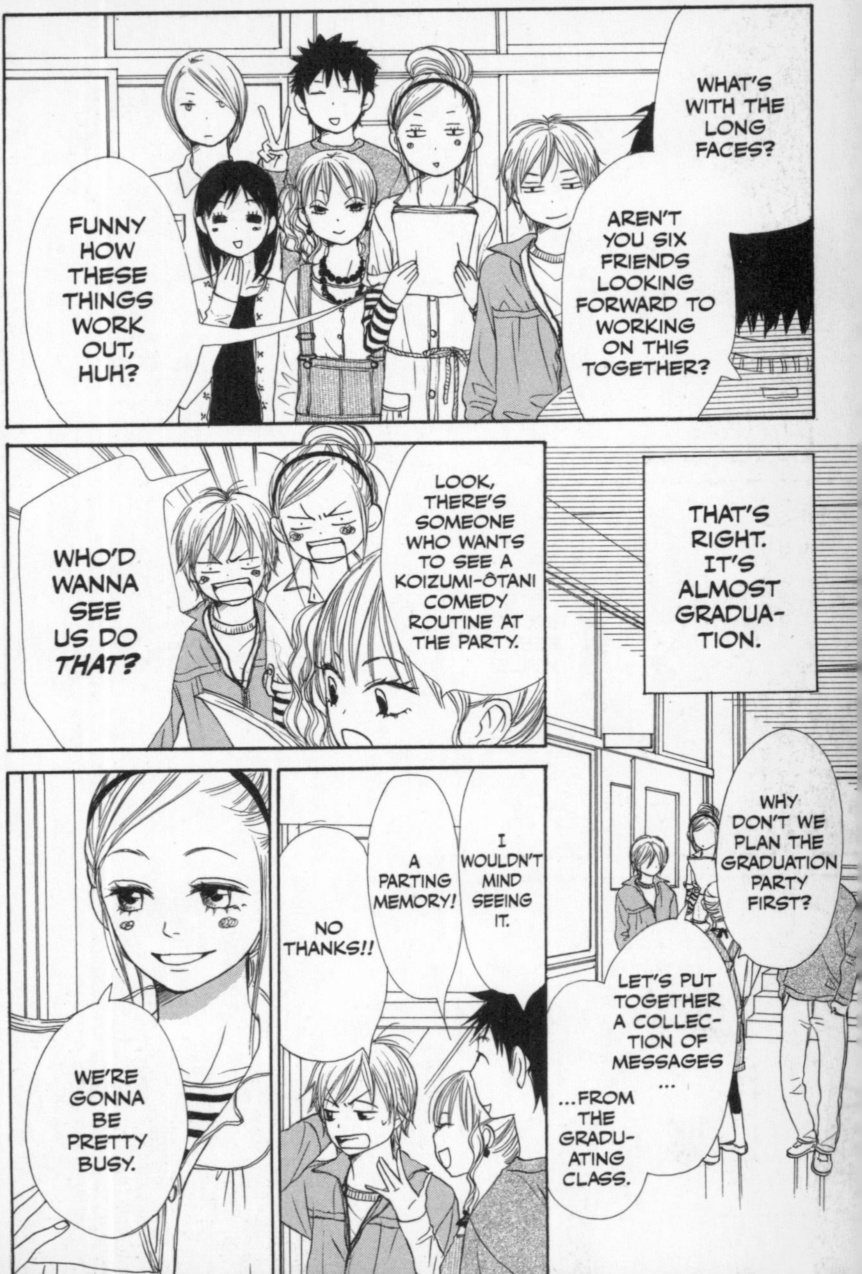
WHAT'S WITH THE LONG FACES?
AREN'T YOU SIX FRIENDS LOOKING FORWARD TO WORKING ON THIS TOGETHER?
FUNNY HOW THESE THINGS WORK OUT, HUH?
THAT'S RIGHT. IT'S ALMOST GRADUATION.
WHY DON'T WE PLAN THE GRADUATION PARTY FIRST?
LET'S PUT TOGETHER A COLLECTION OF MESSAGES ...
...FROM THE GRADUATING CLASS.
LOOK, THERE'S SOMEONE WHO WANTS TO SEE A KOIZUMI-ÔTANI COMEDY ROUTINE AT THE PARTY.
WHO'D WANNA SEE US DO *THAT?*
I WOULDN'T MIND SEEING IT.
A PARTING MEMORY!
NO THANKS!!
WE'RE GONNA BE PRETTY BUSY.

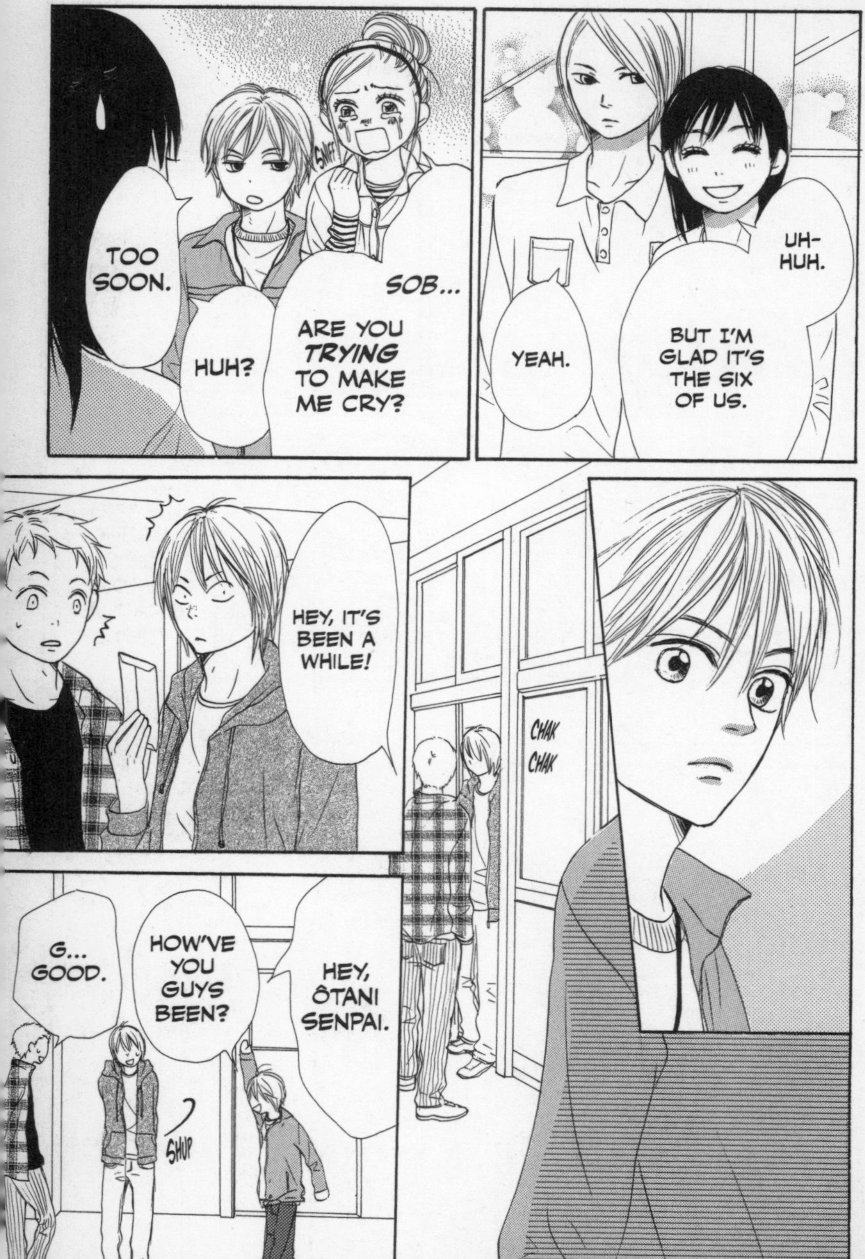
UH-HUH.
BUT I'M GLAD IT'S THE SIX OF US.
YEAH.
SNIFF
SOB...
ARE YOU *TRYING* TO MAKE ME CRY?
HUH?
TOO SOON.
CHAK CHAK
HEY, IT'S BEEN A WHILE!
HEY, ÔTANI SENPAI.
HOW'VE YOU GUYS BEEN?
G... GOOD.
SHUP

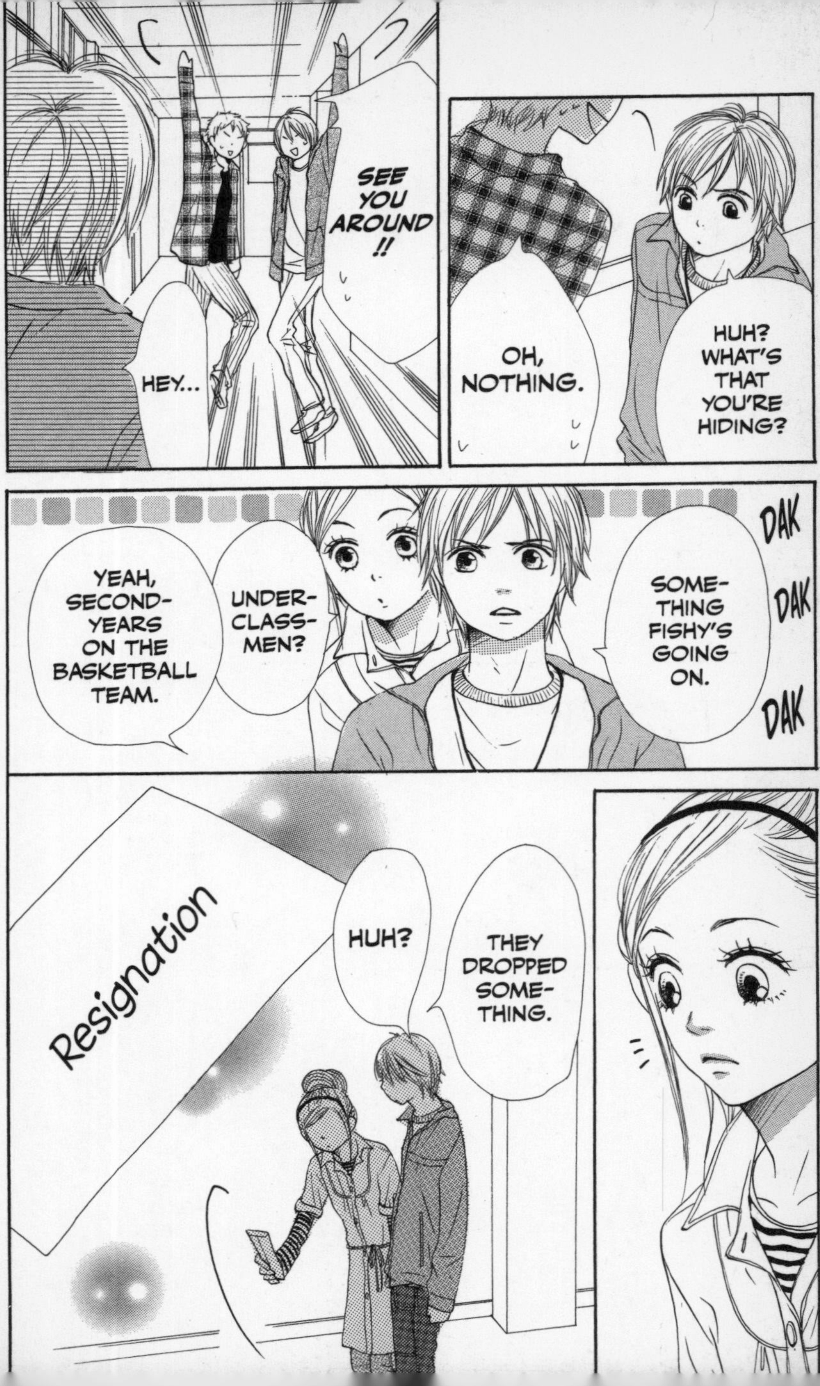
HUH? WHAT'S THAT YOU'RE HIDING?
OH, NOTHING.
SEE YOU AROUND!!
HEY...
SOME-THING FISHY'S GOING ON.
DAK
DAK
DAK
UNDER-CLASS-MEN?
YEAH, SECOND-YEARS ON THE BASKETBALL TEAM.
THEY DROPPED SOME-THING.
HUH?
Resignation

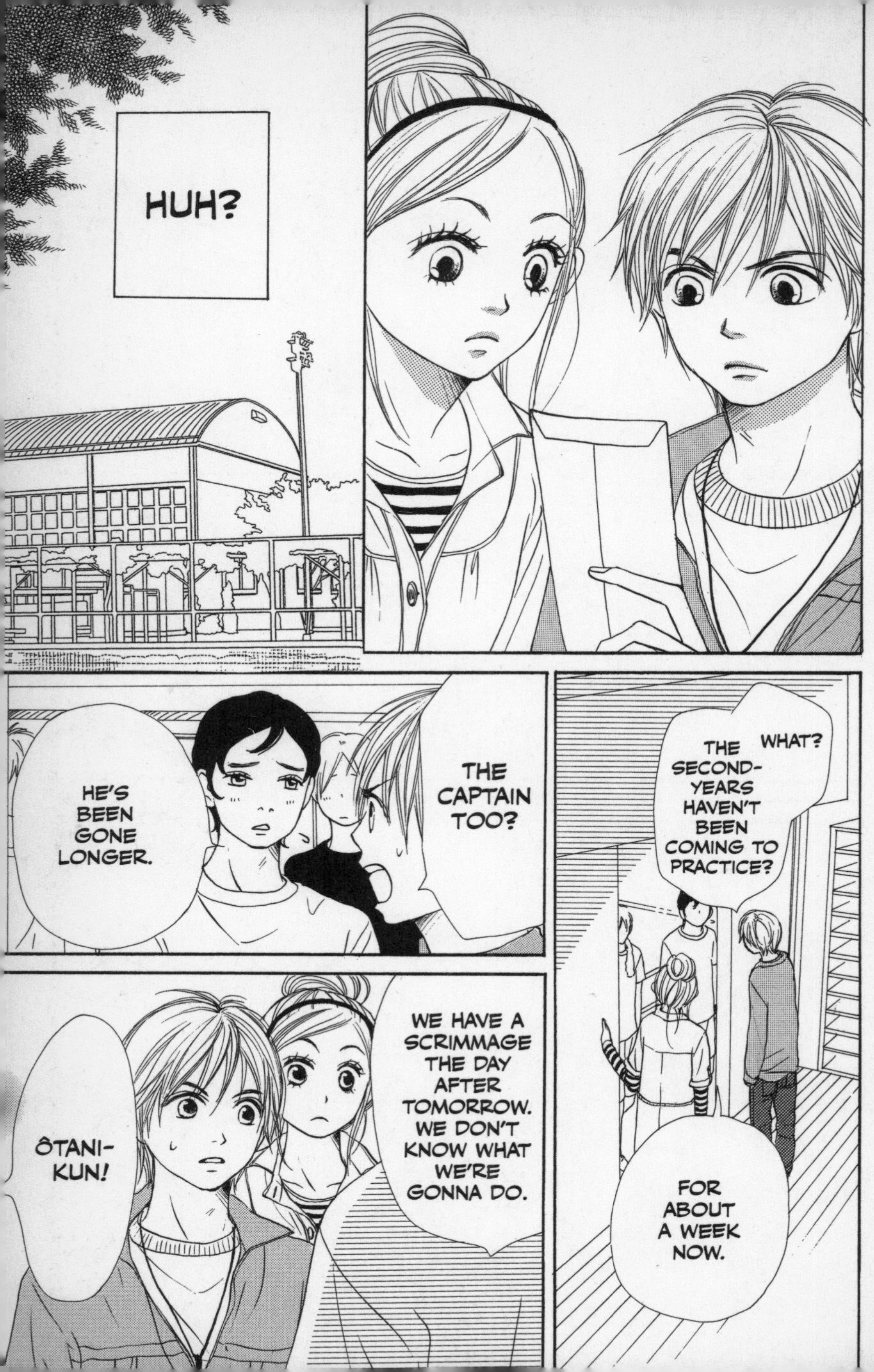
HUH?
WHAT?
THE SECOND-YEARS HAVEN'T BEEN COMING TO PRACTICE?
FOR ABOUT A WEEK NOW.
THE CAPTAIN TOO?
HE'S BEEN GONE LONGER.
WE HAVE A SCRIMMAGE THE DAY AFTER TOMORROW. WE DON'T KNOW WHAT WE'RE GONNA DO.
ÔTANI-KUN!

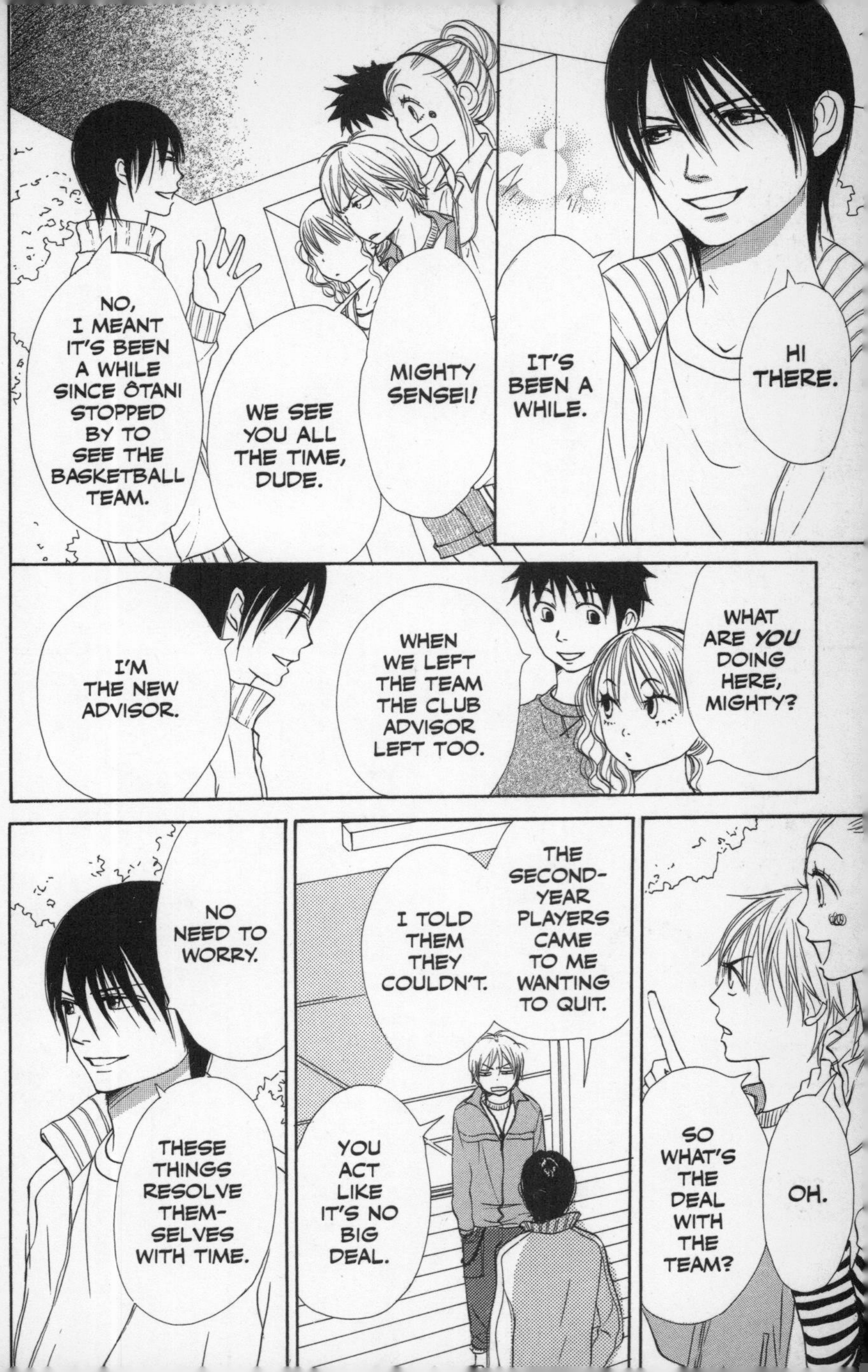
HI THERE.
IT'S BEEN A WHILE.
MIGHTY SENSEI!
WE SEE YOU ALL THE TIME, DUDE.
NO, I MEANT IT'S BEEN A WHILE SINCE ÔTANI STOPPED BY TO SEE THE BASKETBALL TEAM.
WHAT ARE *YOU* DOING HERE, MIGHTY?
WHEN WE LEFT THE TEAM THE CLUB ADVISOR LEFT TOO.
I'M THE NEW ADVISOR.
OH.
SO WHAT'S THE DEAL WITH THE TEAM?
THE SECOND-YEAR PLAYERS CAME TO ME WANTING TO QUIT.
I TOLD THEM THEY COULDN'T.
YOU ACT LIKE IT'S NO BIG DEAL.
NO NEED TO WORRY.
THESE THINGS RESOLVE THEMSELVES WITH TIME.

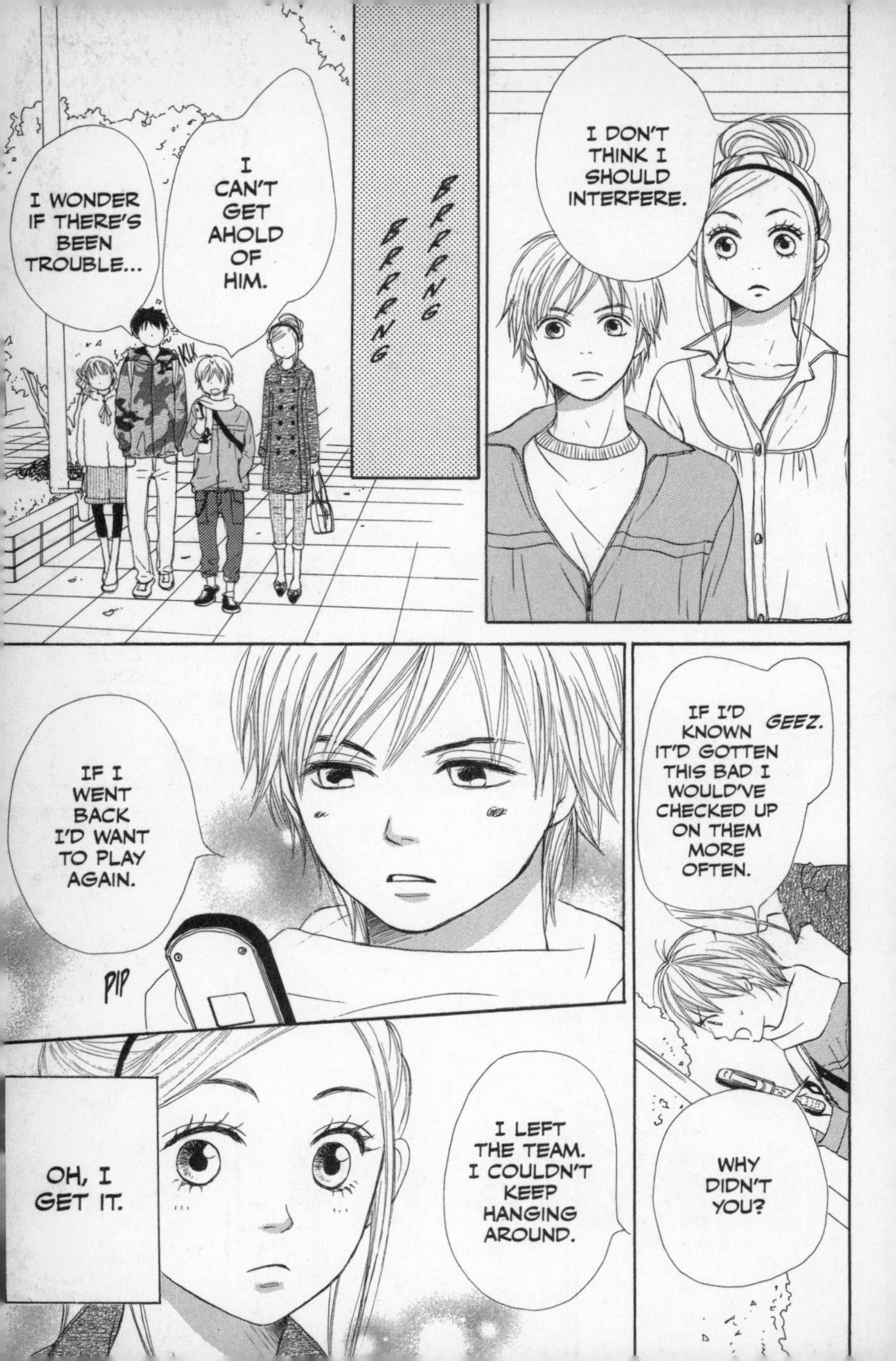
I DON'T THINK I SHOULD INTERFERE.
BRRRNG BRRRNG
I CAN'T GET AHOLD OF HIM.
KLK
I WONDER IF THERE'S BEEN TROUBLE...
IF I'D KNOWN IT'D GOTTEN THIS BAD I WOULD'VE CHECKED UP ON THEM MORE OFTEN.
GEEZ.
WHY DIDN'T YOU?
IF I WENT BACK I'D WANT TO PLAY AGAIN.
PIP
I LEFT THE TEAM. I COULDN'T KEEP HANGING AROUND.
OH, I GET IT.

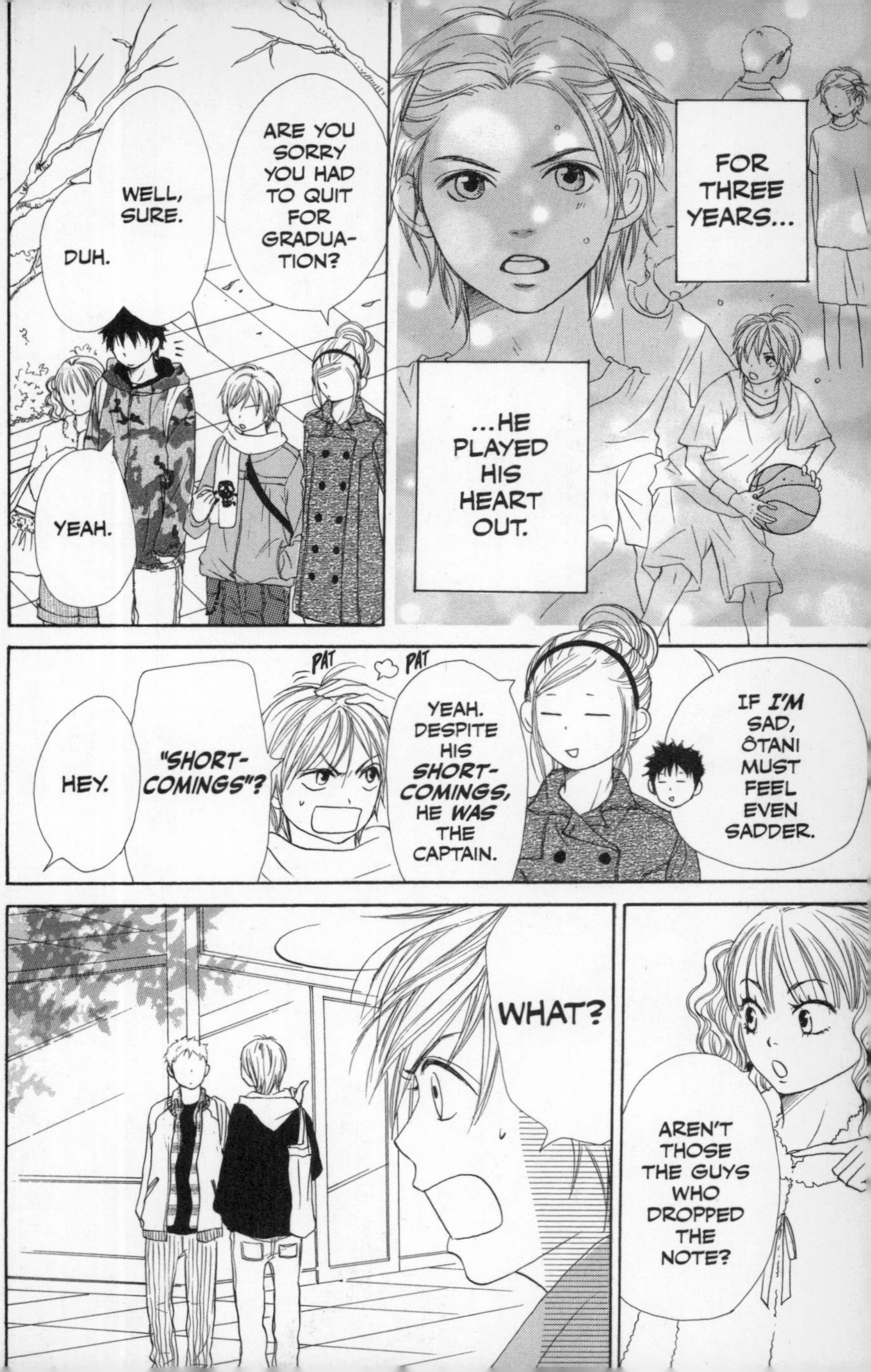

FOR THREE YEARS...
...HE PLAYED HIS HEART OUT.
ARE YOU SORRY YOU HAD TO QUIT FOR GRADUATION?
WELL, SURE.
DUH.
YEAH.
IF *I'M* SAD, ÔTANI MUST FEEL EVEN SADDER.
YEAH. DESPITE HIS *SHORT-COMINGS,* HE *WAS* THE CAPTAIN.
PAT
PAT
"SHORT-COMINGS"?
HEY.
AREN'T THOSE THE GUYS WHO DROPPED THE NOTE?
WHAT?

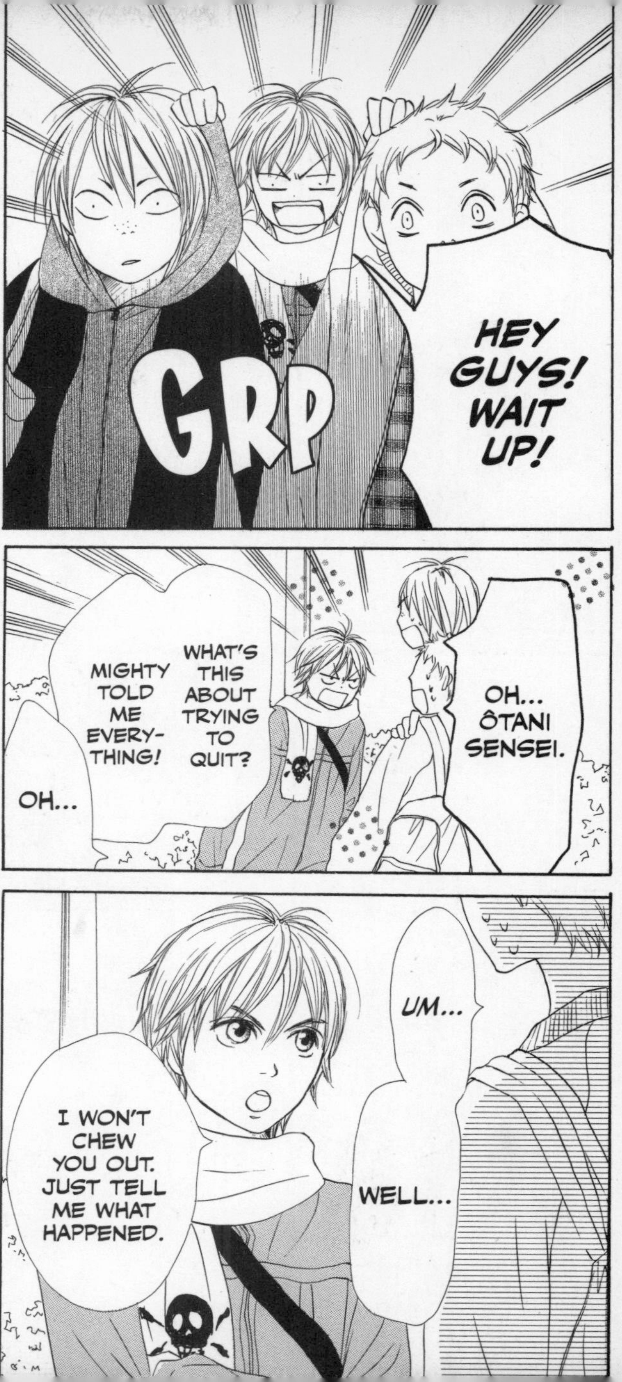
HEY GUYS! WAIT UP!
GRP
OH... ÔTANI SENSEI.
WHAT'S THIS ABOUT TRYING TO QUIT?
MIGHTY TOLD ME EVERYTHING!
OH...
UM...
I WON'T CHEW YOU OUT. JUST TELL ME WHAT HAPPENED.
WELL...

4

Hello! Nakahara here! I usually get into the flow of things at around the third author's note in each book. And then it's almost over! Ha ha...

The *Love★Com* movie is coming out on DVD on New Year's. Pick up a copy!

Really! Please take a look.

Please! Pretty please!

Please, please, please!

Please?

I'm so excited!!

Okay, I'll back off now. I hope we can meet again in volume 16.

Aya

November 2006

(*Love★Com the Movie* is available in the U.S. from VIZ Pictures—ed.)

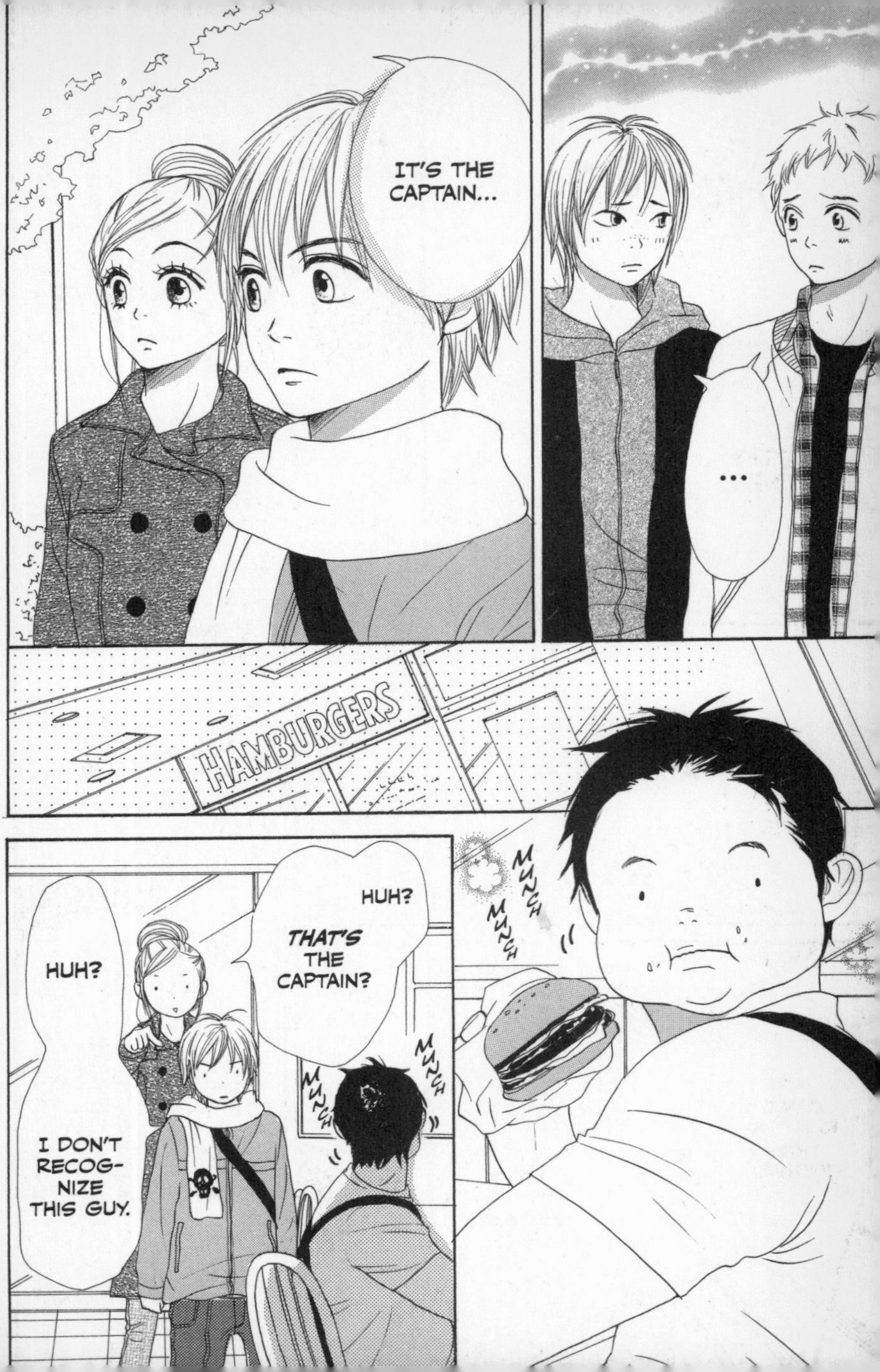
...
IT'S THE CAPTAIN...
HAMBURGERS
MUNCH
MUNCH
HUH? THAT'S THE CAPTAIN?
HUH? I DON'T RECOGNIZE THIS GUY.
MUNCH
MUNCH

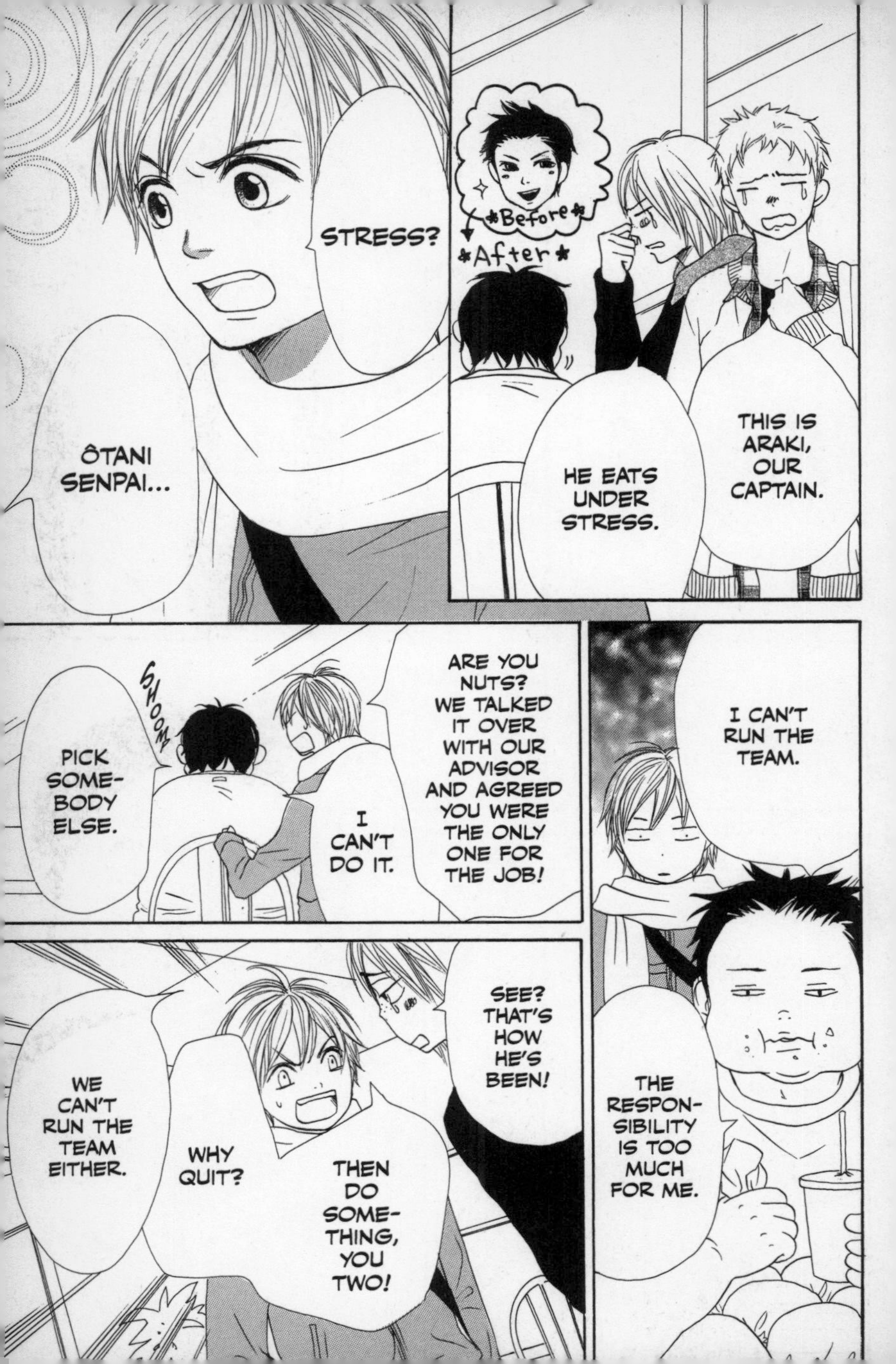

Before
After
THIS IS ARAKI, OUR CAPTAIN.
HE EATS UNDER STRESS.
STRESS?
ÔTANI SENPAI...
I CAN'T RUN THE TEAM.
THE RESPONSIBILITY IS TOO MUCH FOR ME.
ARE YOU NUTS? WE TALKED IT OVER WITH OUR ADVISOR AND AGREED YOU WERE THE ONLY ONE FOR THE JOB!
I CAN'T DO IT.
SHOOM
PICK SOMEBODY ELSE.
SEE? THAT'S HOW HE'S BEEN!
THEN DO SOMETHING, YOU TWO!
WHY QUIT?
WE CAN'T RUN THE TEAM EITHER.

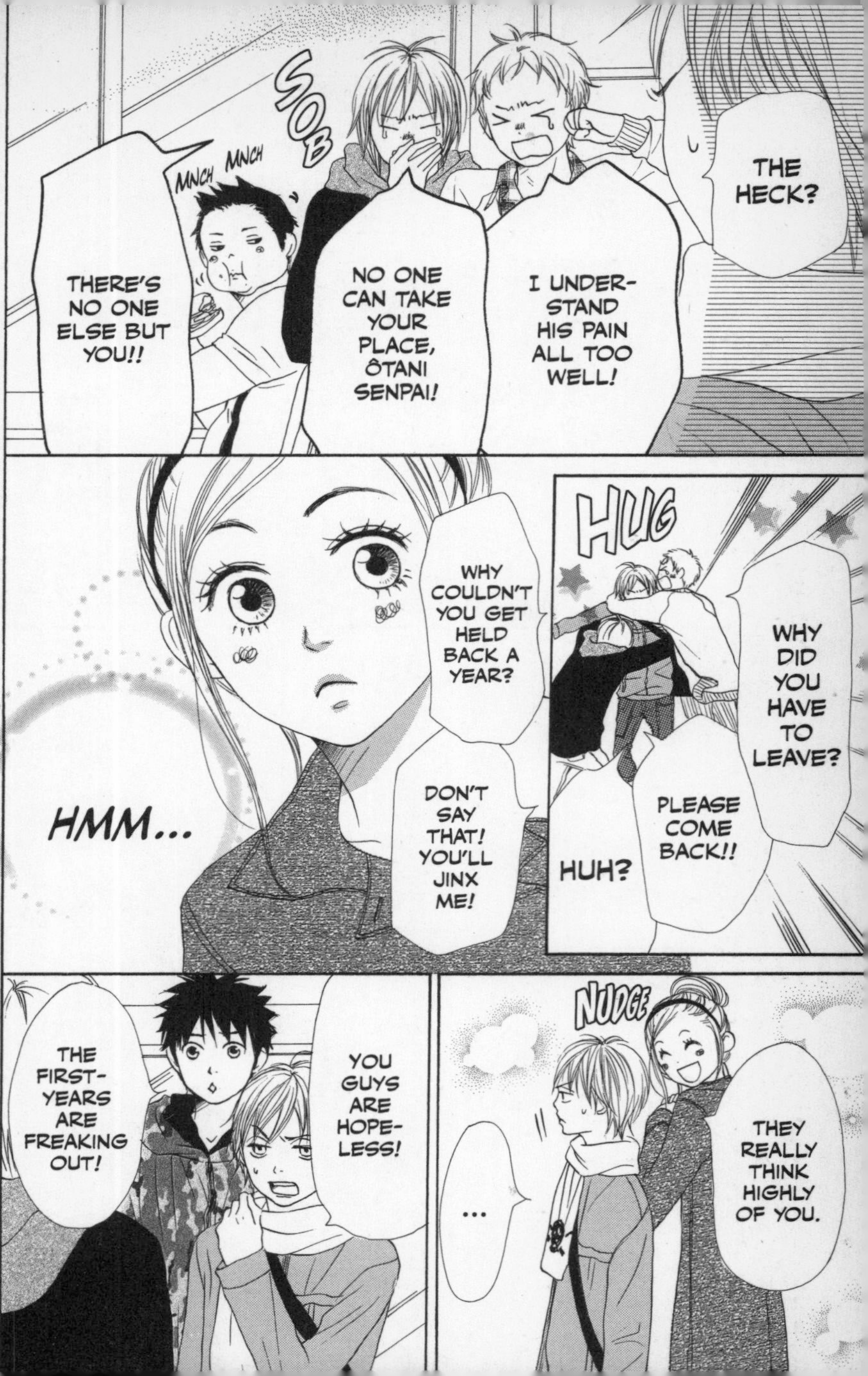
THE HECK?
SOB
I UNDER-STAND HIS PAIN ALL TOO WELL!
NO ONE CAN TAKE YOUR PLACE, ÔTANI SENPAI!
MNCH MNCH
THERE'S NO ONE ELSE BUT YOU!!
HUG
WHY DID YOU HAVE TO LEAVE?
PLEASE COME BACK!!
HUH?
WHY COULDN'T YOU GET HELD BACK A YEAR?
DON'T SAY THAT! YOU'LL JINX ME!
HMM...
NUDGE
THEY REALLY THINK HIGHLY OF YOU.
...
YOU GUYS ARE HOPE-LESS!
THE FIRST-YEARS ARE FREAKING OUT!

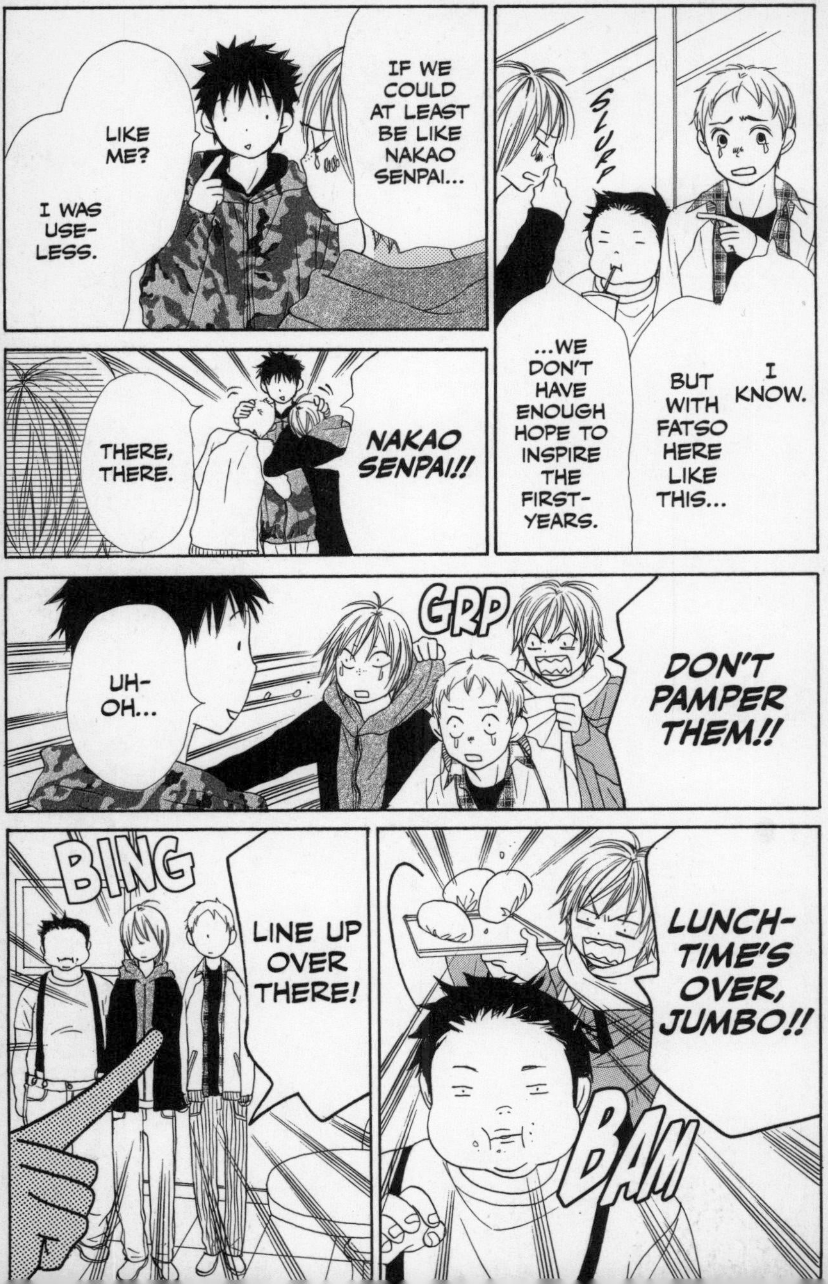
SLURP
I KNOW.
BUT WITH FATSO HERE LIKE THIS...
...WE DON'T HAVE ENOUGH HOPE TO INSPIRE THE FIRST-YEARS.
IF WE COULD AT LEAST BE LIKE NAKAO SENPAI...
LIKE ME?
I WAS USE-LESS.
NAKAO SENPAI!!
THERE, THERE.
GRP
DON'T PAMPER THEM!!
UH-OH...
LUNCH-TIME'S OVER, JUMBO!!
BAM
BING
LINE UP OVER THERE!

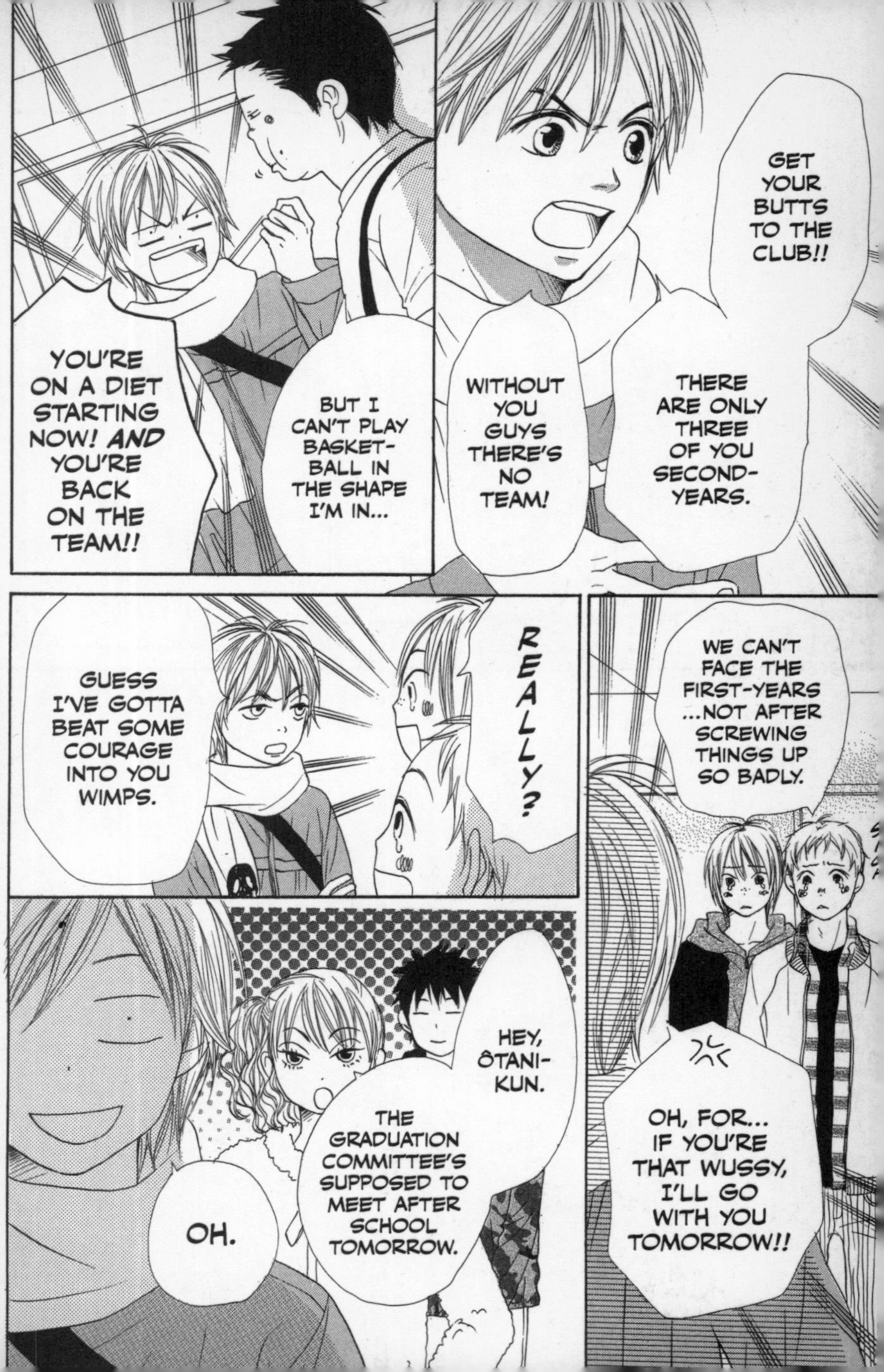
GET YOUR BUTTS TO THE CLUB!!
THERE ARE ONLY THREE OF YOU SECOND-YEARS.
WITHOUT YOU GUYS THERE'S NO TEAM!
BUT I CAN'T PLAY BASKET-BALL IN THE SHAPE I'M IN...
YOU'RE ON A DIET STARTING NOW! *AND* YOU'RE BACK ON THE TEAM!!
WE CAN'T FACE THE FIRST-YEARS ...NOT AFTER SCREWING THINGS UP SO BADLY.
OH, FOR... IF YOU'RE THAT WUSSY, I'LL GO WITH YOU TOMORROW!!
REALLY?
GUESS I'VE GOTTA BEAT SOME COURAGE INTO YOU WIMPS.
HEY, ŌTANI-KUN.
THE GRADUATION COMMITTEE'S SUPPOSED TO MEET AFTER SCHOOL TOMORROW.
OH.

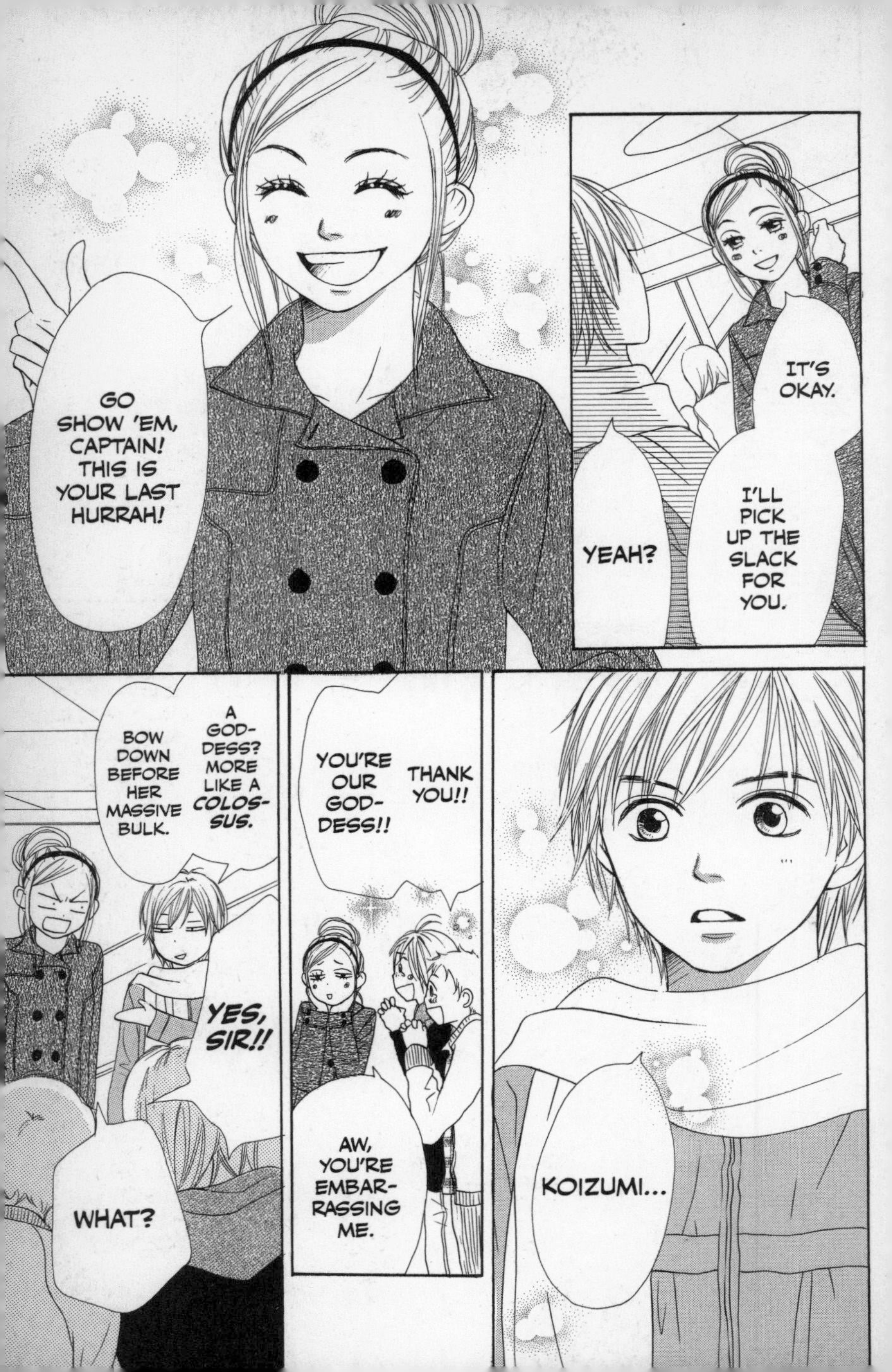
IT'S OKAY.
I'LL PICK UP THE SLACK FOR YOU.
YEAH?
GO SHOW 'EM, CAPTAIN! THIS IS YOUR LAST HURRAH!
KOIZUMI...
THANK YOU!!
YOU'RE OUR GOD-DESS!!
AW, YOU'RE EMBAR-RASSING ME.
A GOD-DESS? MORE LIKE A *COLOS-SUS.*
BOW DOWN BEFORE HER MASSIVE BULK.
YES, SIR!!
WHAT?

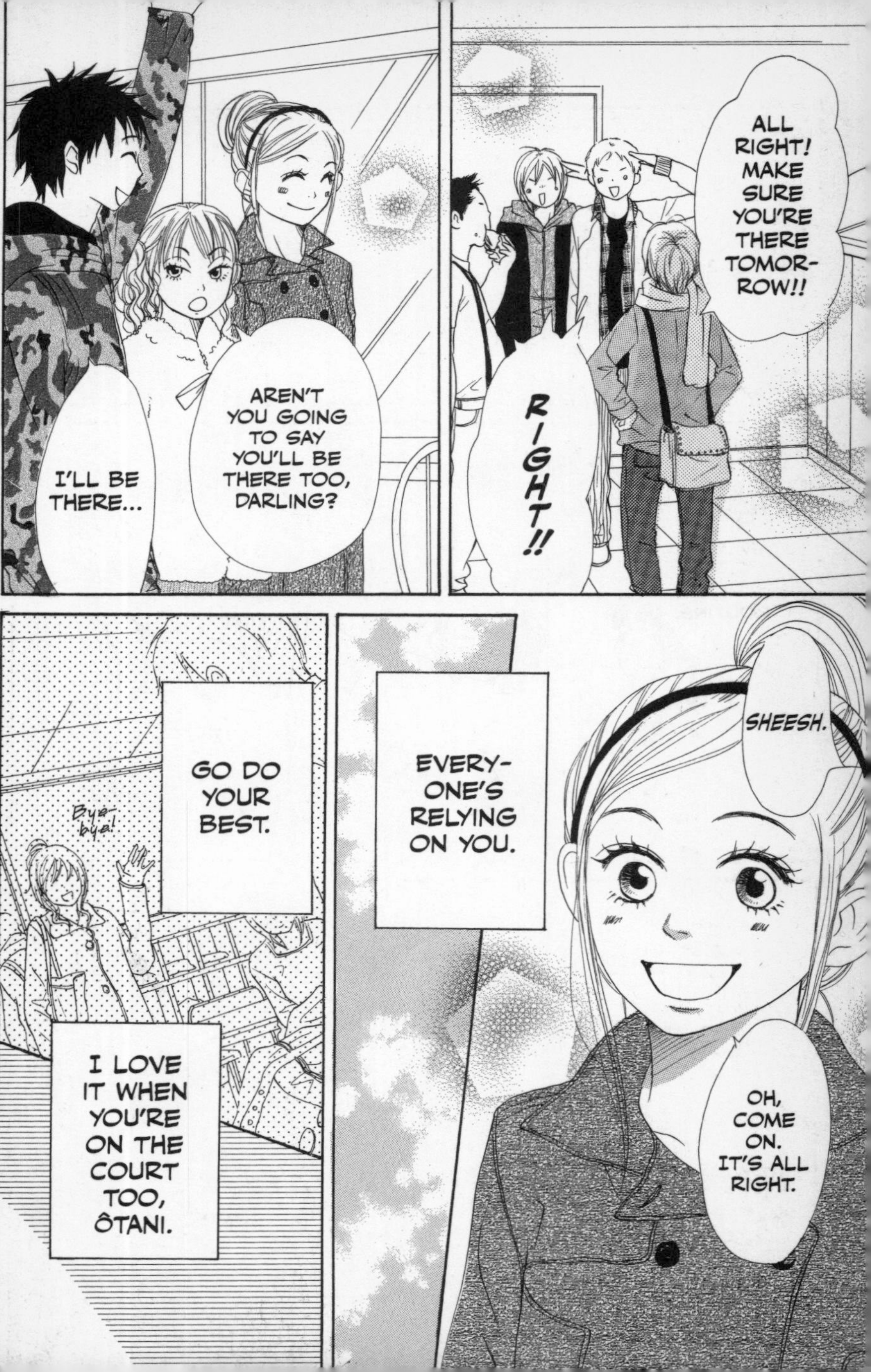
ALL RIGHT! MAKE SURE YOU'RE THERE TOMORROW!!
RIGHT!!
AREN'T YOU GOING TO SAY YOU'LL BE THERE TOO, DARLING?
I'LL BE THERE...
SHEESH.
OH, COME ON. IT'S ALL RIGHT.
EVERYONE'S RELYING ON YOU.
GO DO YOUR BEST.
Bye-bye!
I LOVE IT WHEN YOU'RE ON THE COURT TOO, ŌTANI.

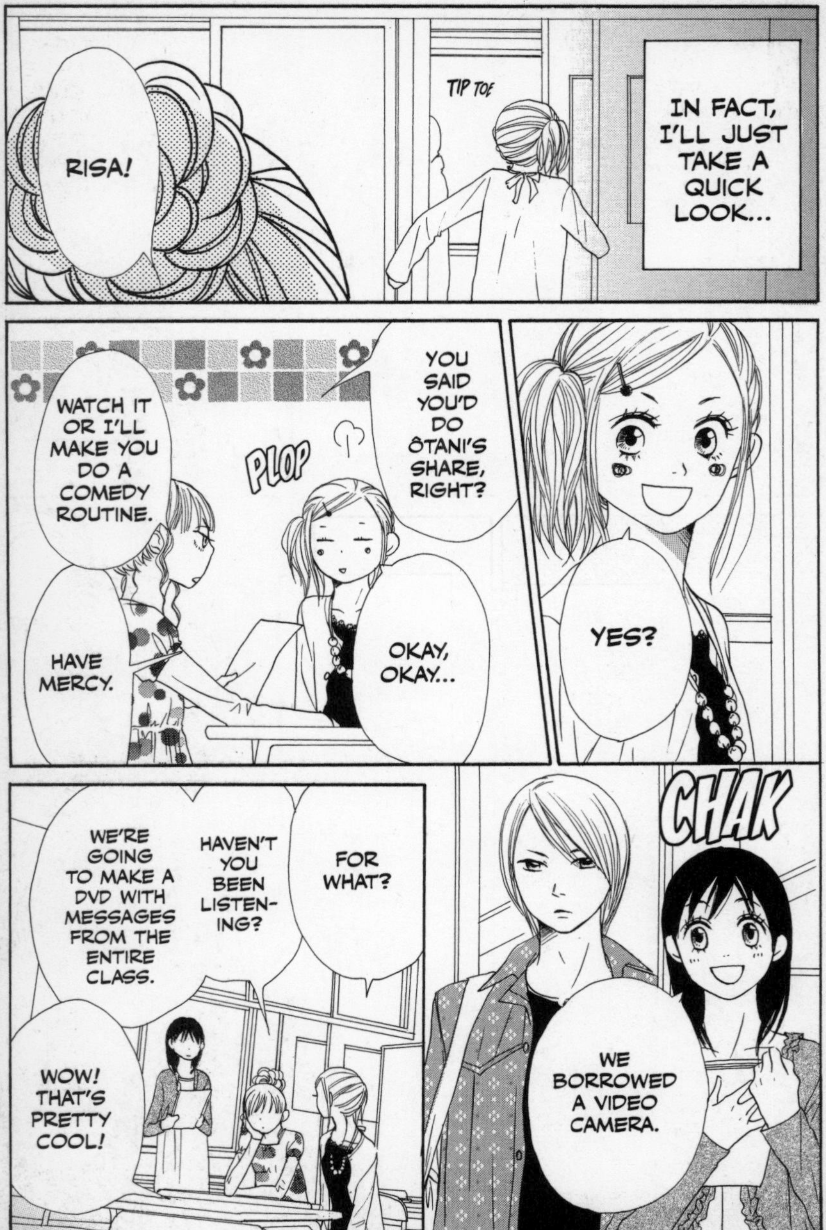
IN FACT, I'LL JUST TAKE A QUICK LOOK...
TIP TOE
RISA!
YES?
YOU SAID YOU'D DO ÔTANI'S SHARE, RIGHT?
PLOP
OKAY, OKAY...
WATCH IT OR I'LL MAKE YOU DO A COMEDY ROUTINE.
HAVE MERCY.
CHAK
WE BORROWED A VIDEO CAMERA.
FOR WHAT?
HAVEN'T YOU BEEN LISTENING?
WE'RE GOING TO MAKE A DVD WITH MESSAGES FROM THE ENTIRE CLASS.
WOW! THAT'S PRETTY COOL!

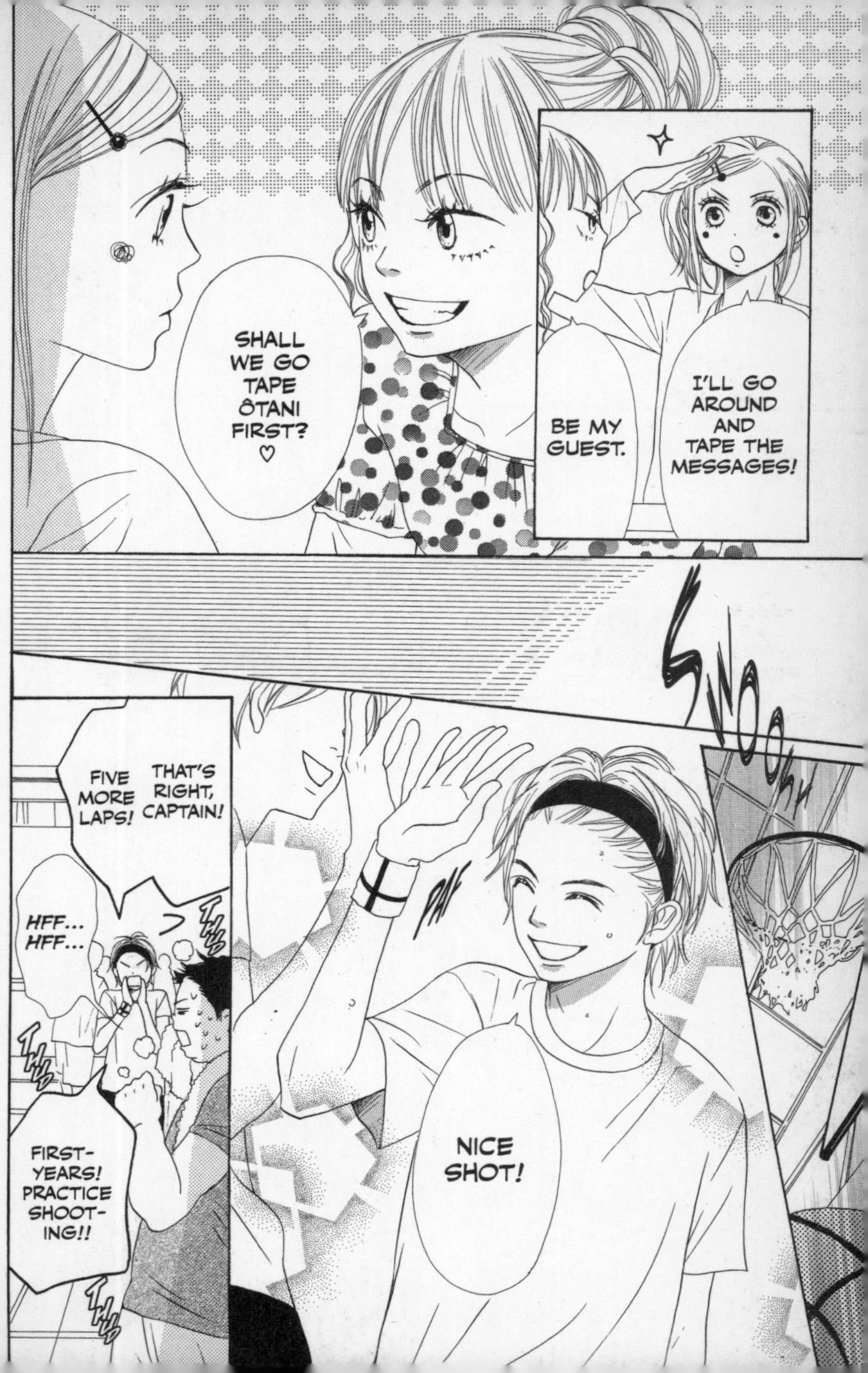
I'LL GO AROUND AND TAPE THE MESSAGES!
BE MY GUEST.
SHALL WE GO TAPE ÔTANI FIRST? ♡
SWOOSH
NICE SHOT!
THAT'S RIGHT, CAPTAIN!
FIVE MORE LAPS!
HFF... HFF...
FIRST-YEARS! PRACTICE SHOOT-ING!!

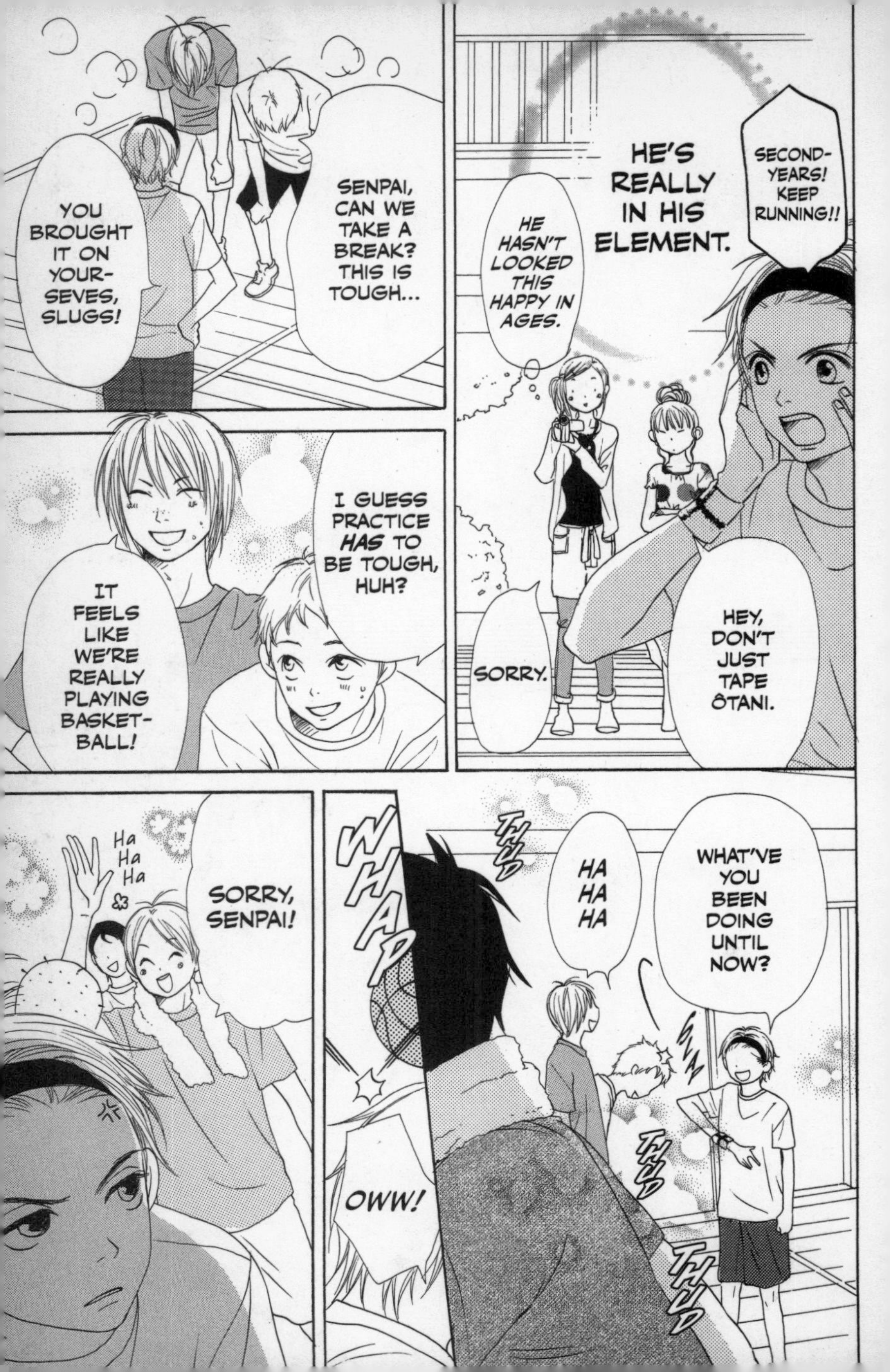
SECOND-YEARS! KEEP RUNNING!!
HE'S REALLY IN HIS ELEMENT.
HE HASN'T LOOKED THIS HAPPY IN AGES.
HEY, DON'T JUST TAPE OTANI.
SORRY.
SENPAI, CAN WE TAKE A BREAK? THIS IS TOUGH...
YOU BROUGHT IT ON YOURSEVES, SLUGS!
I GUESS PRACTICE *HAS* TO BE TOUGH, HUH?
IT FEELS LIKE WE'RE REALLY PLAYING BASKETBALL!
WHAT'VE YOU BEEN DOING UNTIL NOW?
HA HA HA
THUD
THUD
THUD
WHAP
OWW!
SORRY, SENPAI!
Ha Ha Ha

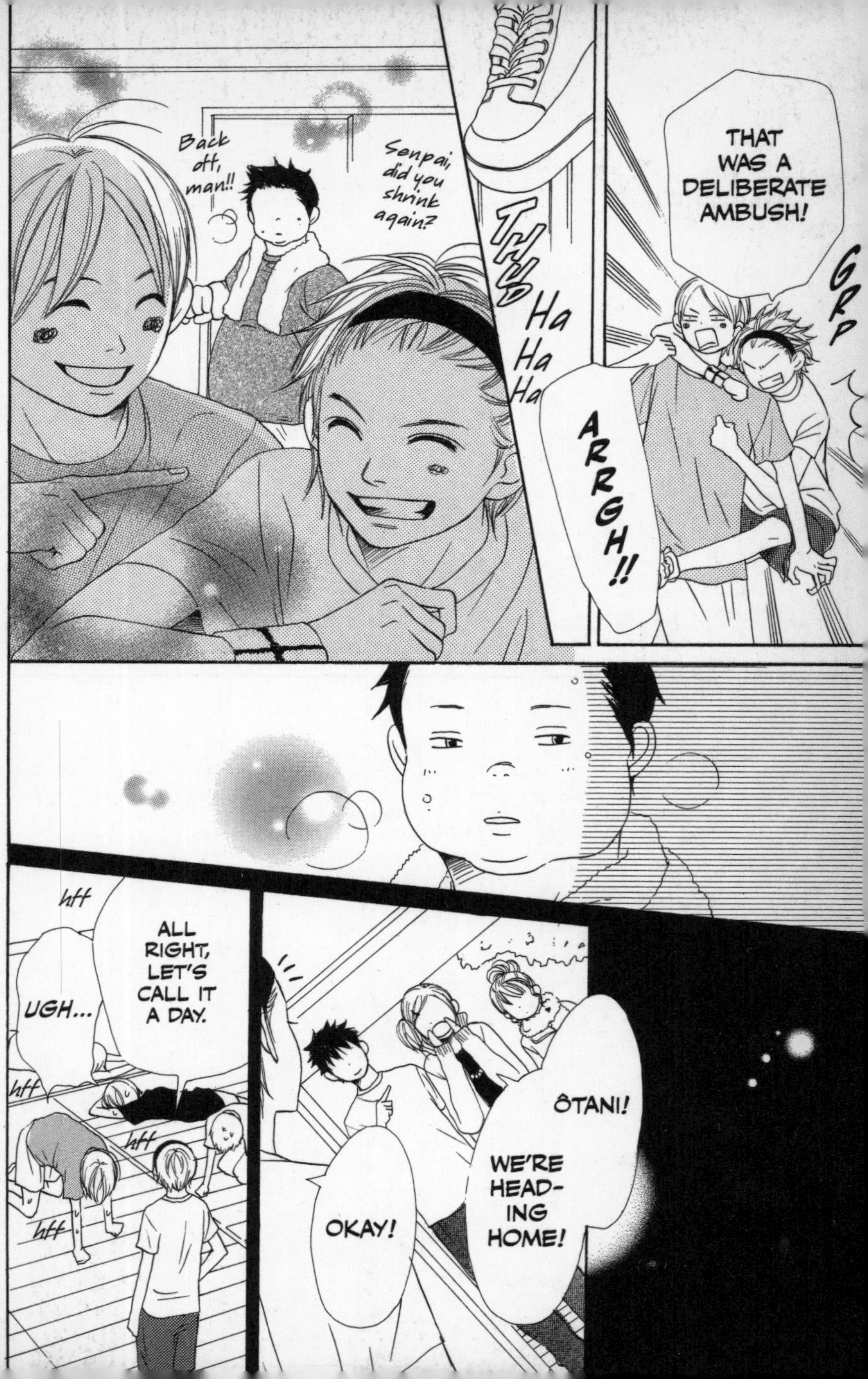
THAT WAS A DELIBERATE AMBUSH!
GRP
ARRGH!!
THUD
Ha Ha Ha
Senpai, did you shrink again?
Back off, man!!
ŌTANI!
WE'RE HEADING HOME!
OKAY!
ALL RIGHT, LET'S CALL IT A DAY.
UGH...
hff
hff
hff
hff

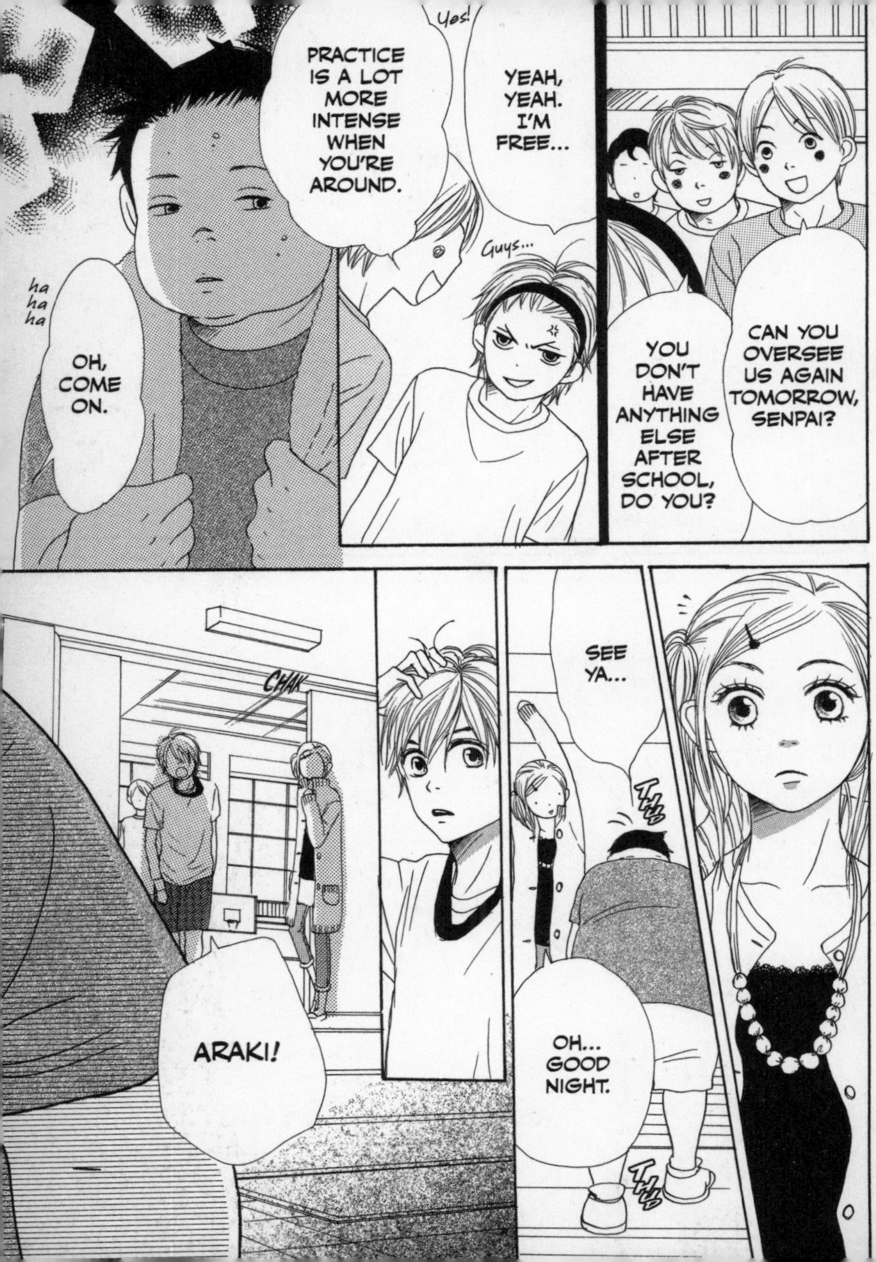
CAN YOU OVERSEE US AGAIN TOMORROW, SENPAI?
YOU DON'T HAVE ANYTHING ELSE AFTER SCHOOL, DO YOU?
Yes!
YEAH, YEAH. I'M FREE...
PRACTICE IS A LOT MORE INTENSE WHEN YOU'RE AROUND.
Guys...
ha ha ha
OH, COME ON.
SEE YA...
THMP
OH... GOOD NIGHT.
THMP
CHAK
ARAKI!

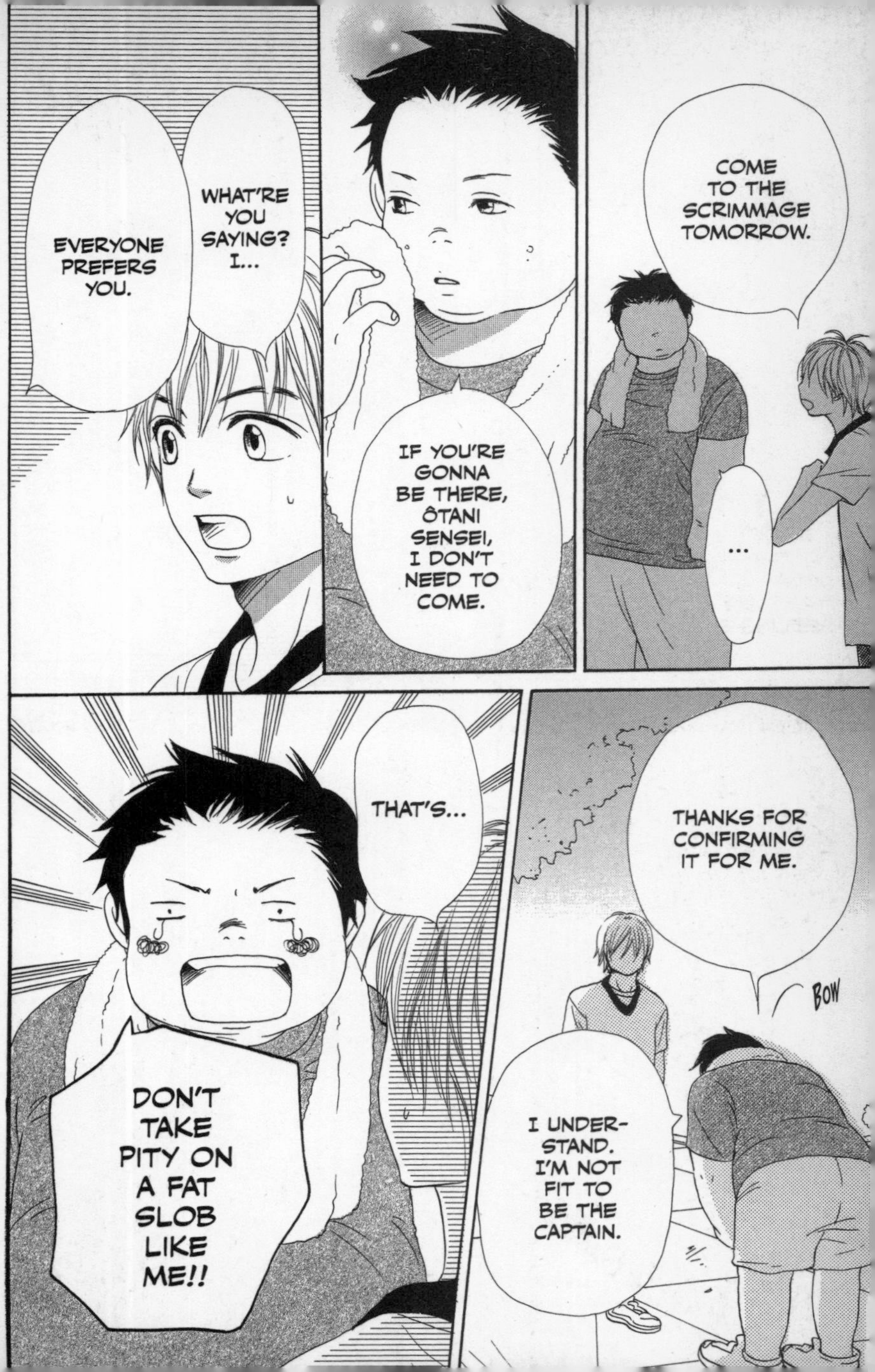
COME TO THE SCRIMMAGE TOMORROW.
...
IF YOU'RE GONNA BE THERE, ÔTANI SENSEI, I DON'T NEED TO COME.
WHAT'RE YOU SAYING? I...
EVERYONE PREFERS YOU.
THANKS FOR CONFIRMING IT FOR ME.
BOW
I UNDER-STAND. I'M NOT FIT TO BE THE CAPTAIN.
THAT'S...
DON'T TAKE PITY ON A FAT SLOB LIKE ME!!

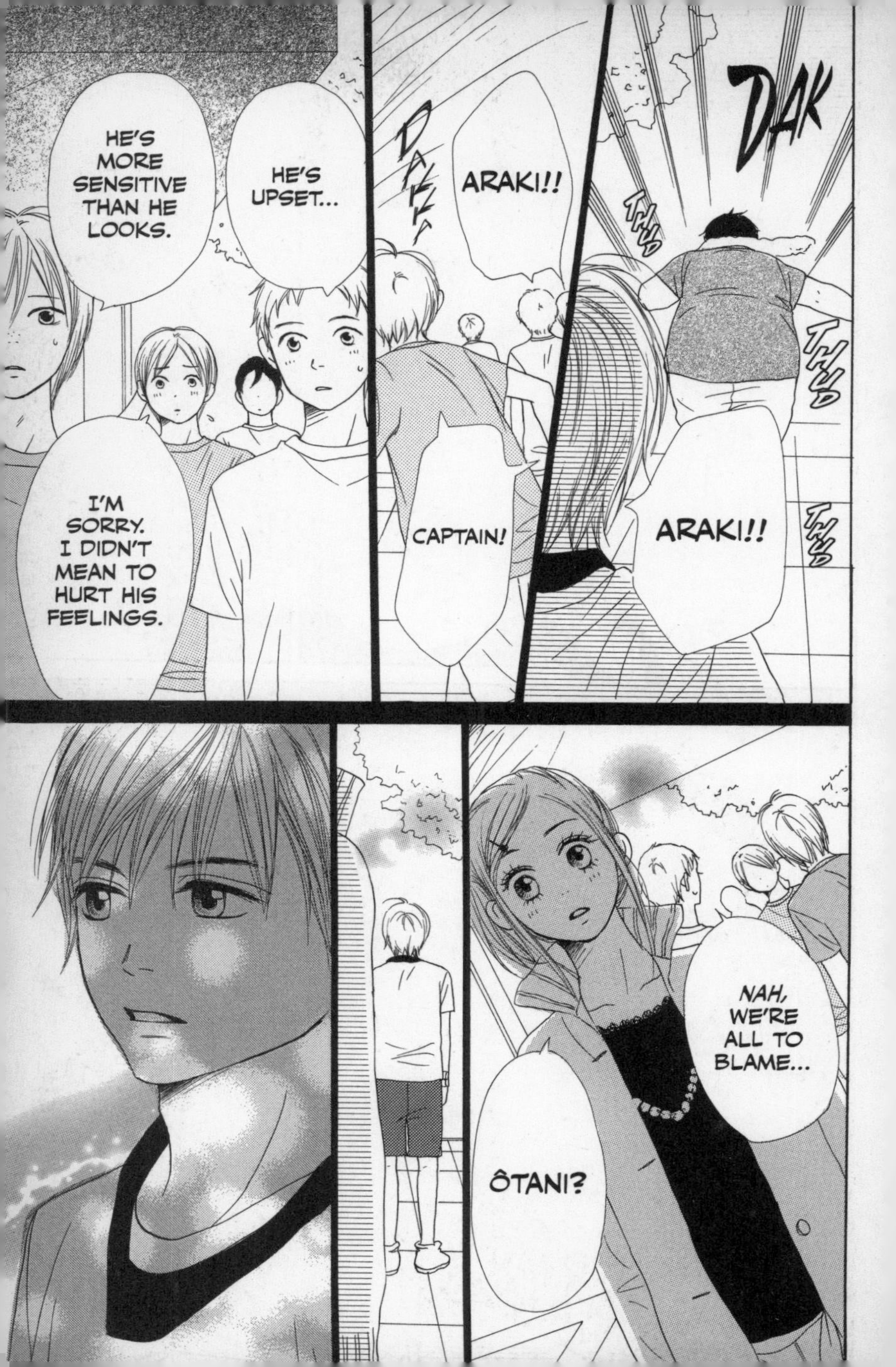
DAK
THUD
THUD
THUD
ARAKI!!
ARAKI!!
CAPTAIN!
HE'S UPSET...
HE'S MORE SENSITIVE THAN HE LOOKS.
I'M SORRY. I DIDN'T MEAN TO HURT HIS FEELINGS.
NAH, WE'RE ALL TO BLAME...
ÔTANI?

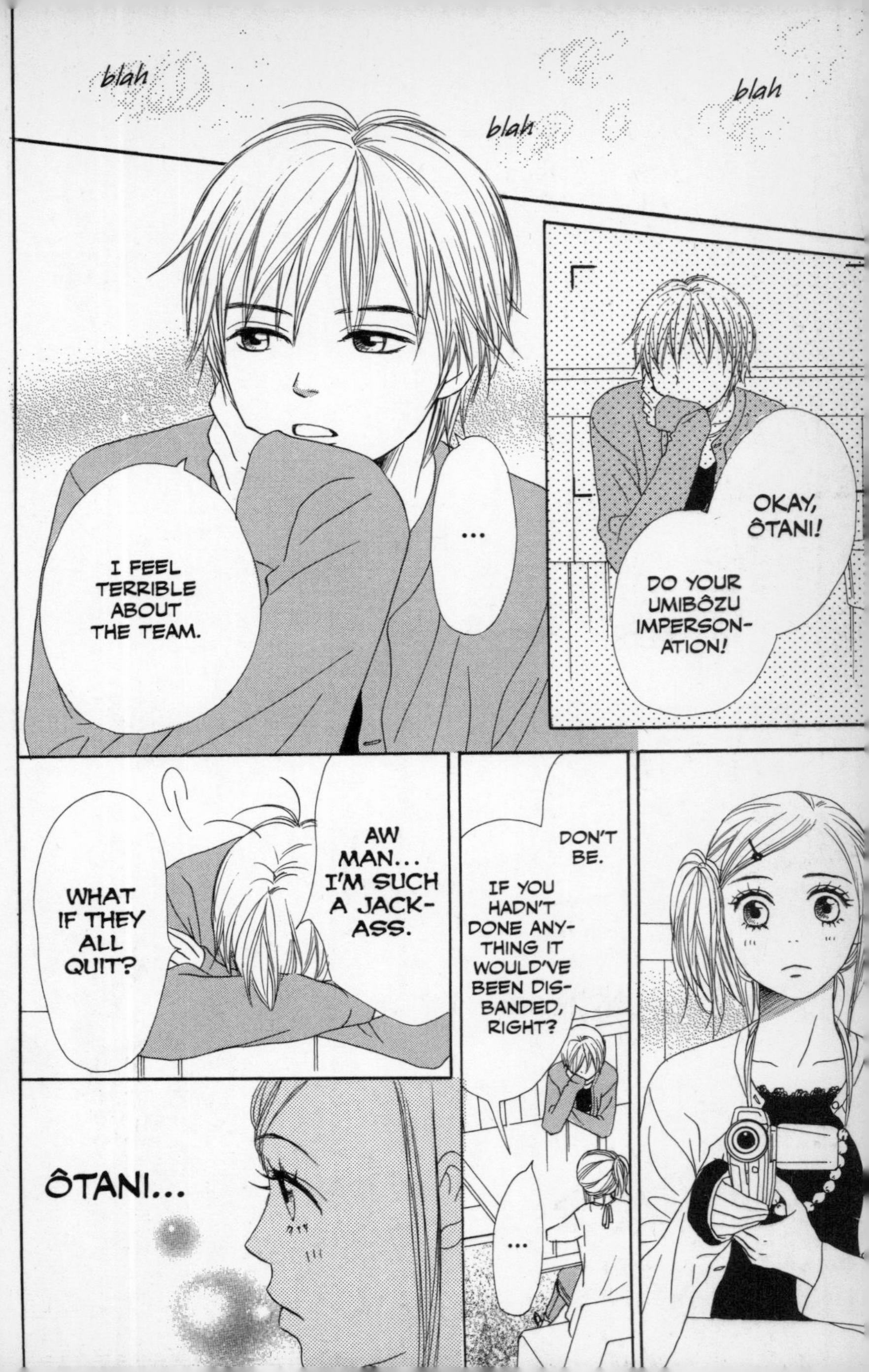
blah
blah
blah
OKAY, ÔTANI!
DO YOUR UMIBÔZU IMPERSON-ATION!
...
I FEEL TERRIBLE ABOUT THE TEAM.
DON'T BE.
IF YOU HADN'T DONE ANY-THING IT WOULD'VE BEEN DIS-BANDED, RIGHT?
...
AW MAN... I'M SUCH A JACK-ASS.
WHAT IF THEY ALL QUIT?
ÔTANI...

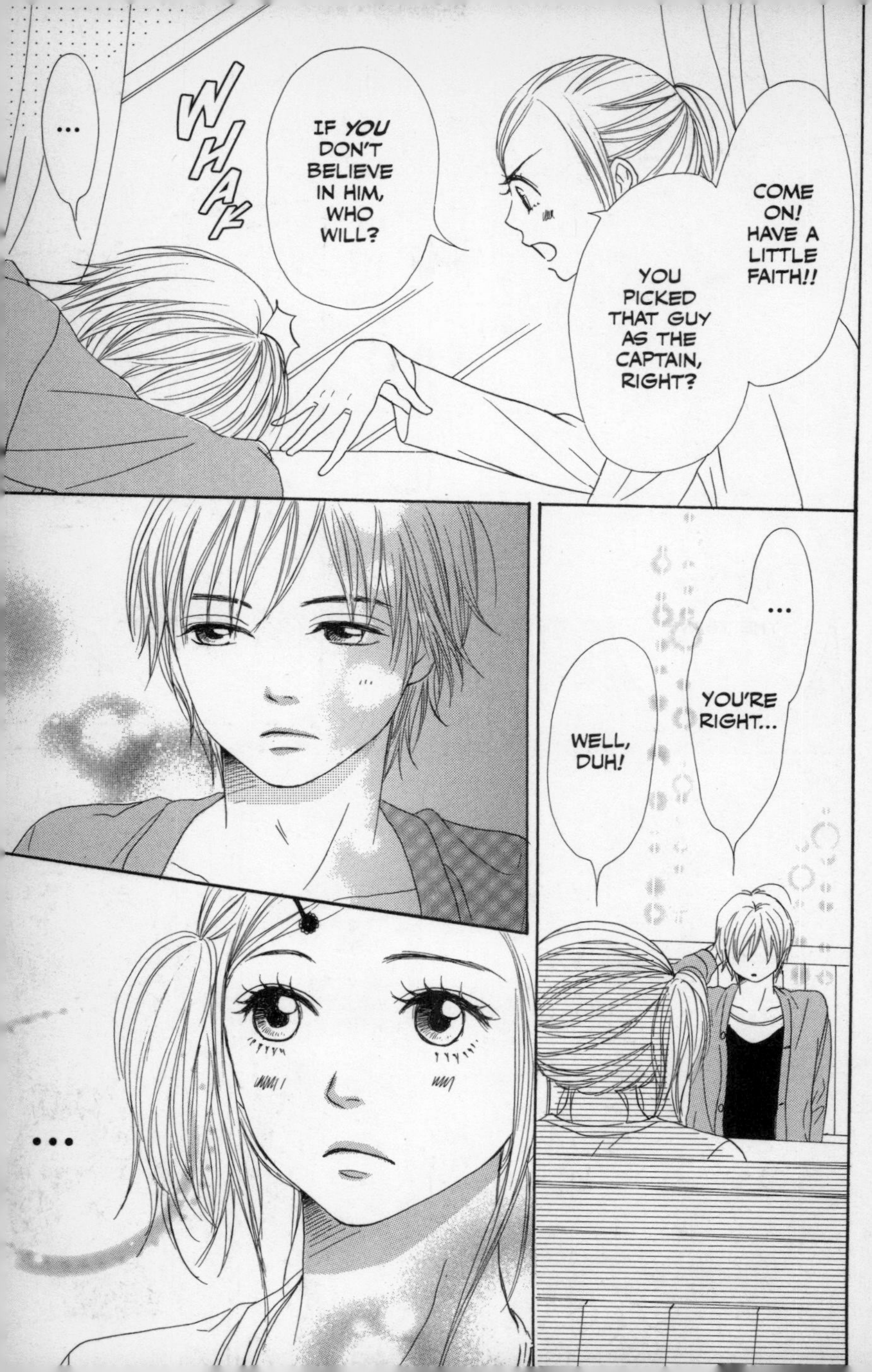
COME ON! HAVE A LITTLE FAITH!!
YOU PICKED THAT GUY AS THE CAPTAIN, RIGHT?
IF *YOU* DON'T BELIEVE IN HIM, WHO WILL?
WHAP
...
...
YOU'RE RIGHT...
WELL, DUH!
...

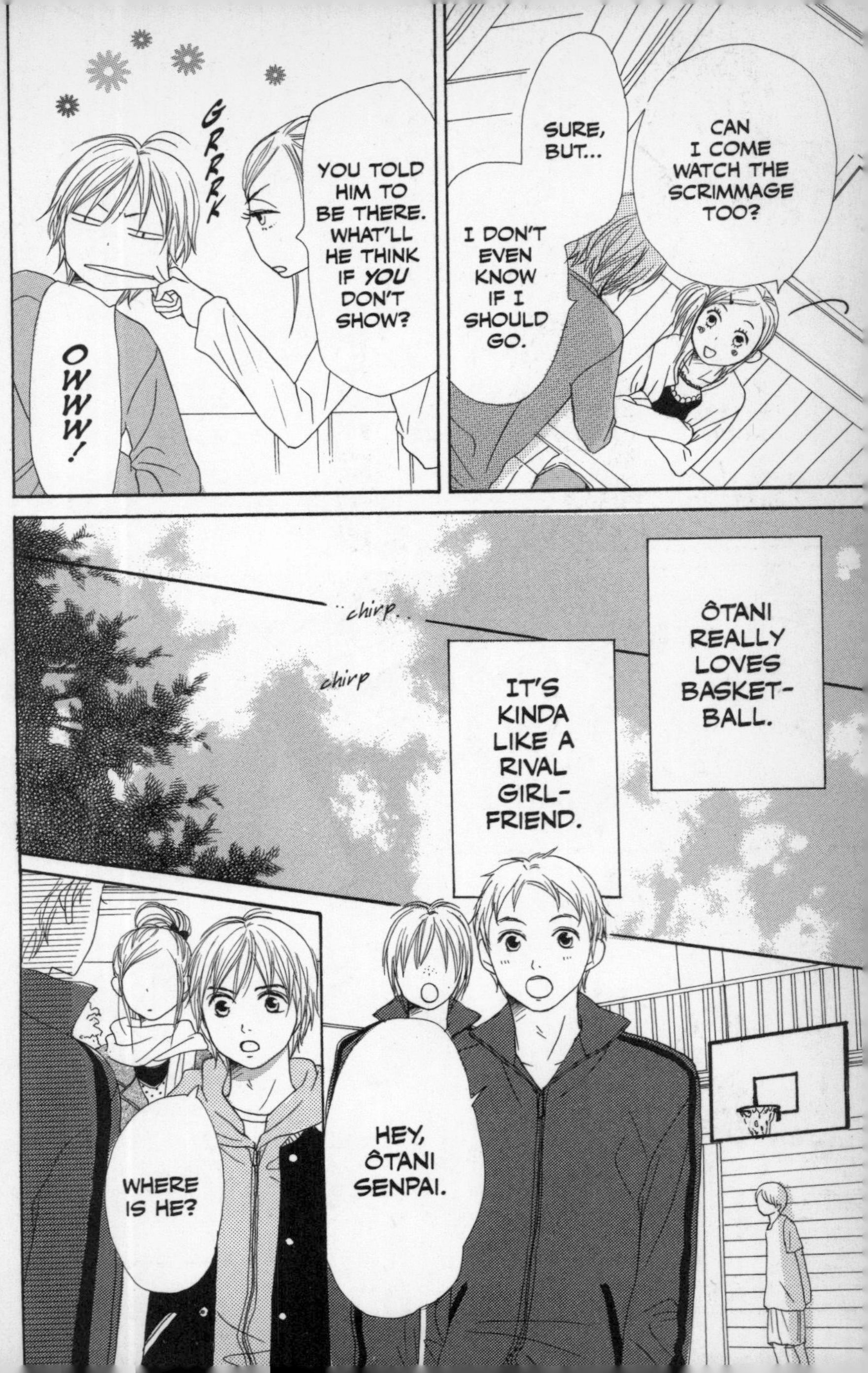
CAN I COME WATCH THE SCRIMMAGE TOO?
SURE, BUT...
I DON'T EVEN KNOW IF I SHOULD GO.
YOU TOLD HIM TO BE THERE. WHAT'LL HE THINK IF *YOU* DON'T SHOW?
GRRRK
OWWW!
ÔTANI REALLY LOVES BASKET-BALL.
IT'S KINDA LIKE A RIVAL GIRL-FRIEND.
..chirp..
chirp
HEY, ÔTANI SENPAI.
WHERE IS HE?

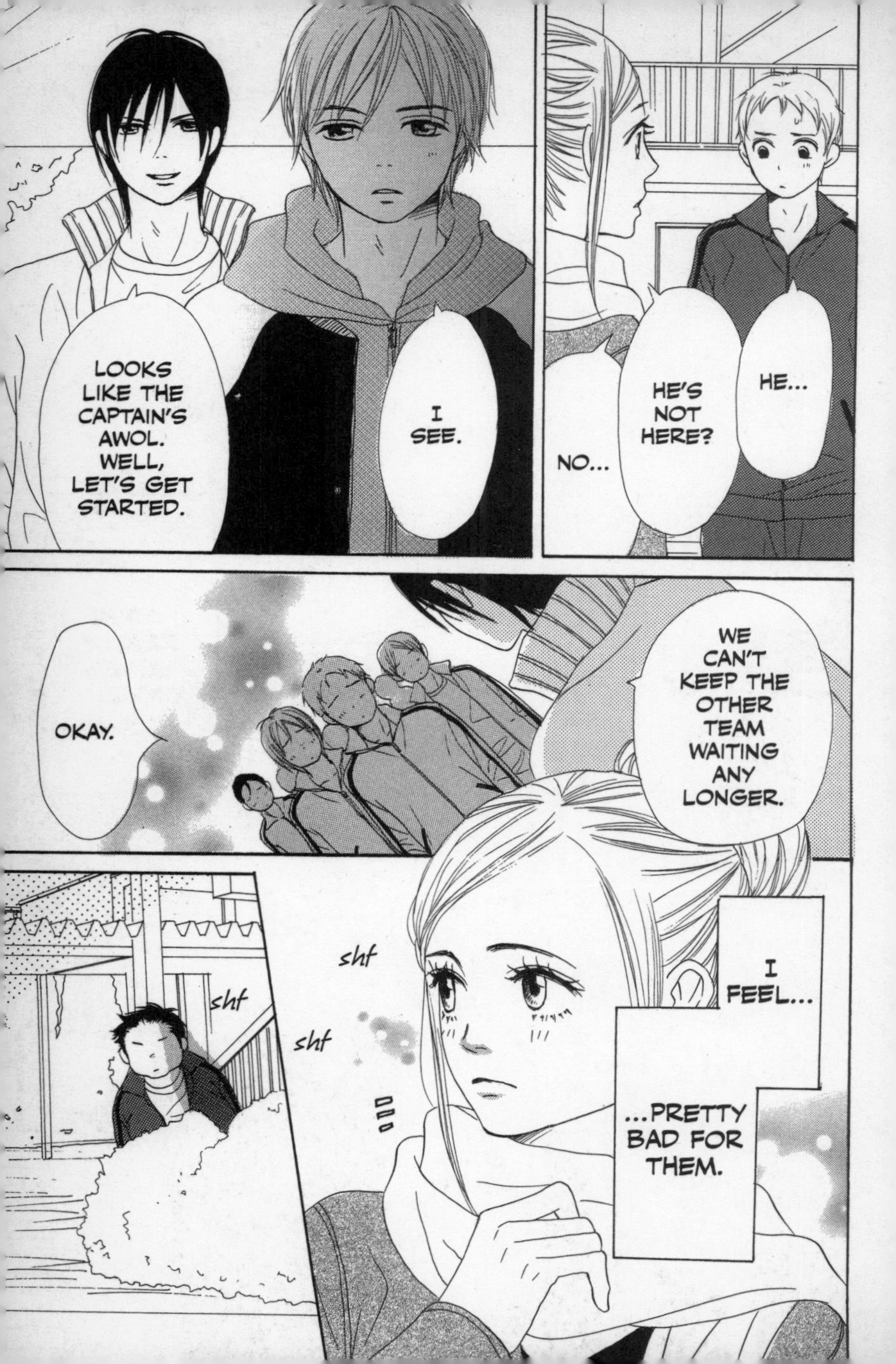
HE...
HE'S NOT HERE?
NO...
LOOKS LIKE THE CAPTAIN'S AWOL. WELL, LET'S GET STARTED.
I SEE.
WE CAN'T KEEP THE OTHER TEAM WAITING ANY LONGER.
OKAY.
I FEEL...
...PRETTY BAD FOR THEM.
shf
shf
shf

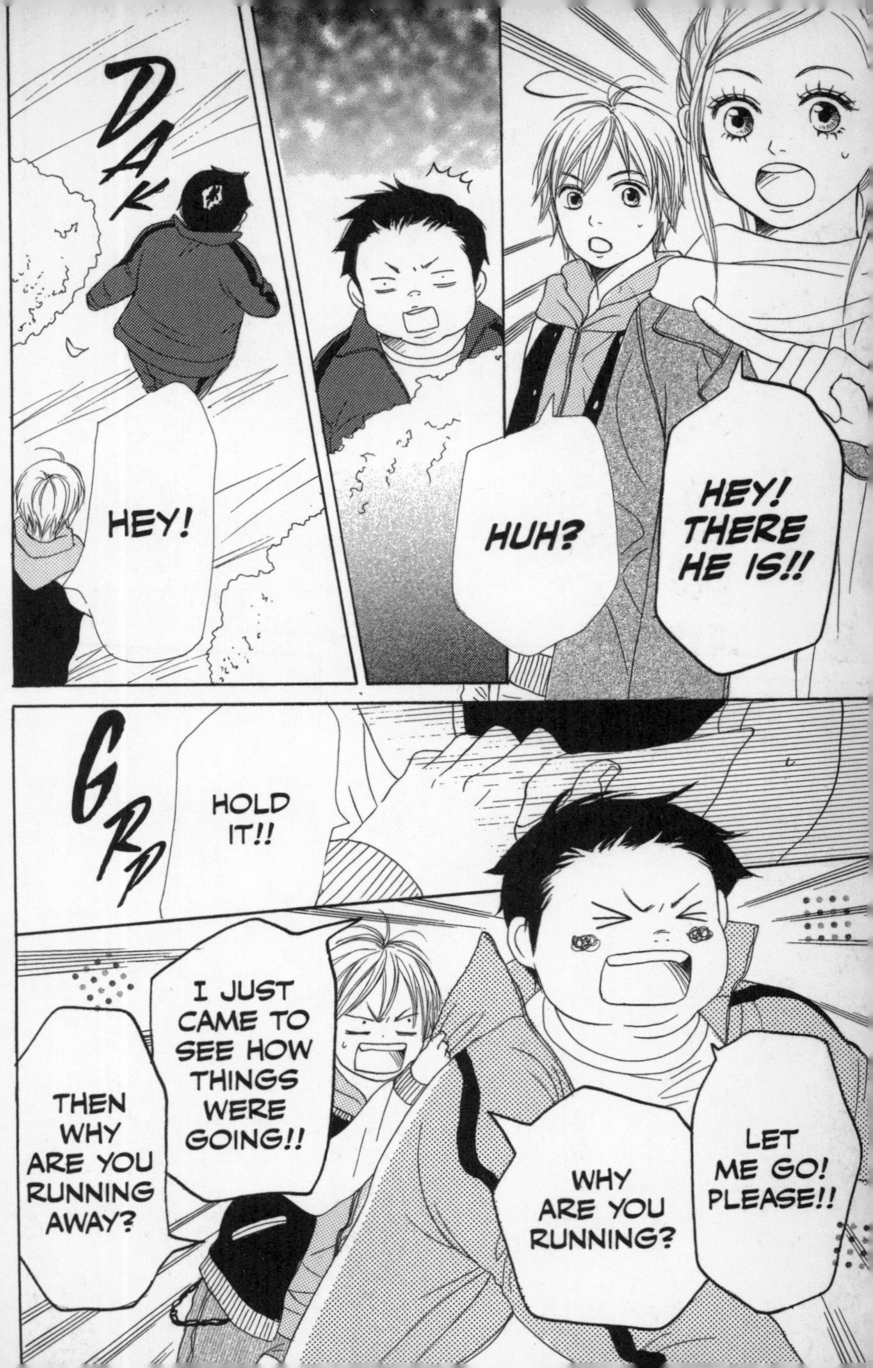
HEY! THERE HE IS!!
HUH?
DAK
HEY!
GRP
HOLD IT!!
LET ME GO! PLEASE!!
WHY ARE YOU RUNNING?
I JUST CAME TO SEE HOW THINGS WERE GOING!!
THEN WHY ARE YOU RUNNING AWAY?

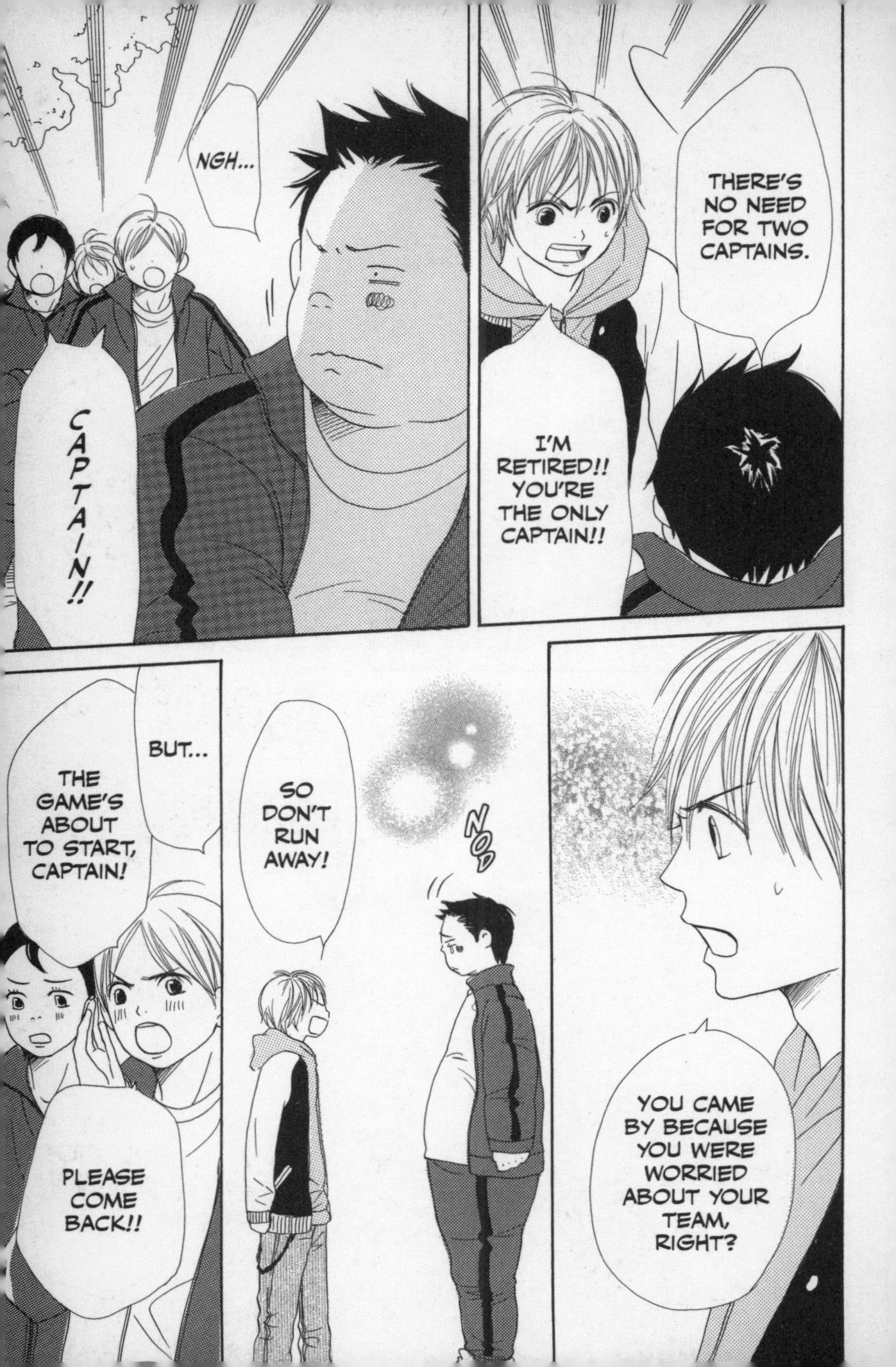
THERE'S NO NEED FOR TWO CAPTAINS.
I'M RETIRED!! YOU'RE THE ONLY CAPTAIN!!
NGH...
CAPTAIN!!
YOU CAME BY BECAUSE YOU WERE WORRIED ABOUT YOUR TEAM, RIGHT?
SO DON'T RUN AWAY!
NOD
BUT...
THE GAME'S ABOUT TO START, CAPTAIN!
PLEASE COME BACK!!

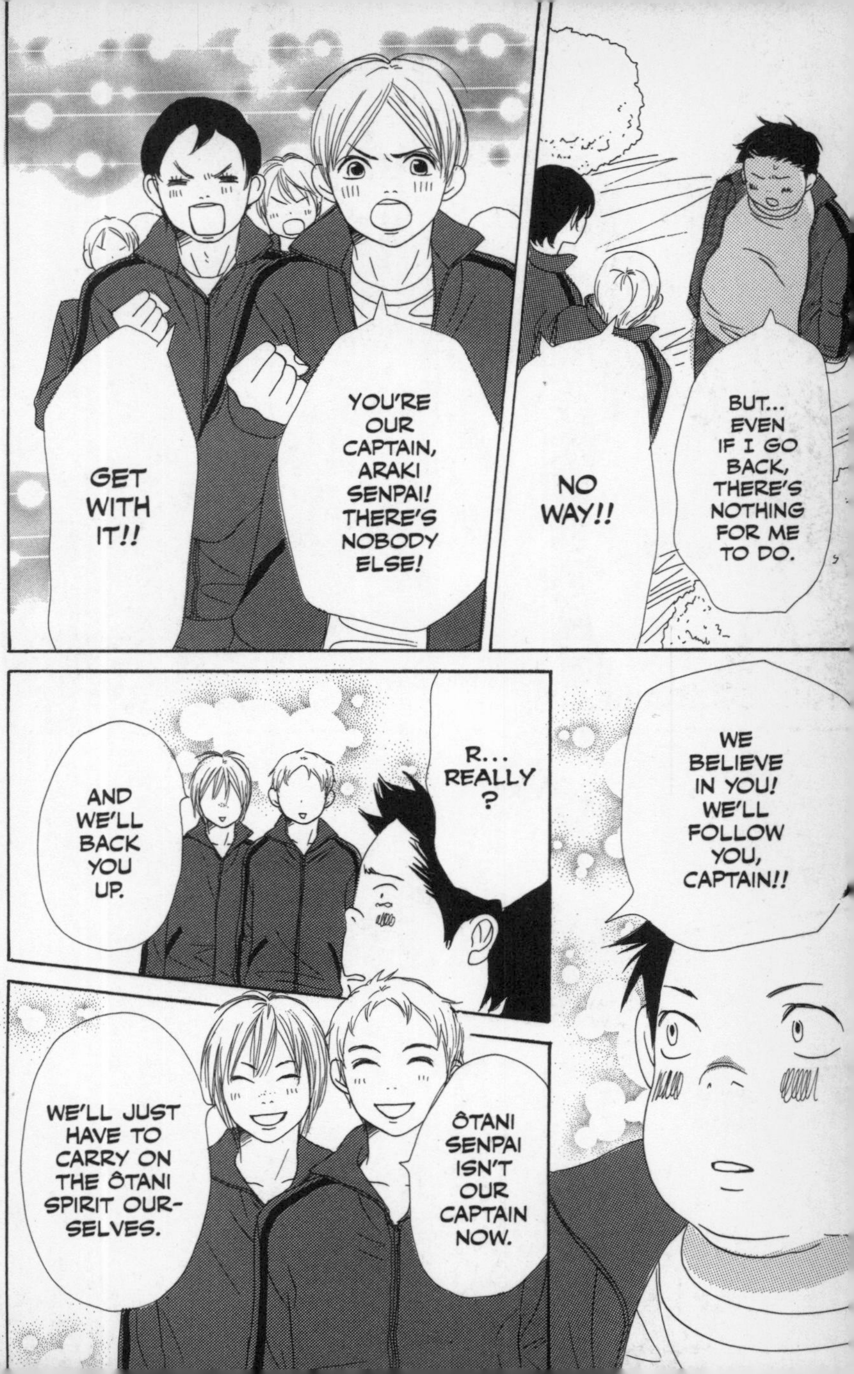
BUT... EVEN IF I GO BACK, THERE'S NOTHING FOR ME TO DO.
NO WAY!!
YOU'RE OUR CAPTAIN, ARAKI SENPAI! THERE'S NOBODY ELSE!
GET WITH IT!!
WE BELIEVE IN YOU! WE'LL FOLLOW YOU, CAPTAIN!!
R... REALLY?
AND WE'LL BACK YOU UP.
ŌTANI SENPAI ISN'T OUR CAPTAIN NOW.
WE'LL JUST HAVE TO CARRY ON THE ŌTANI SPIRIT OUR-SELVES.

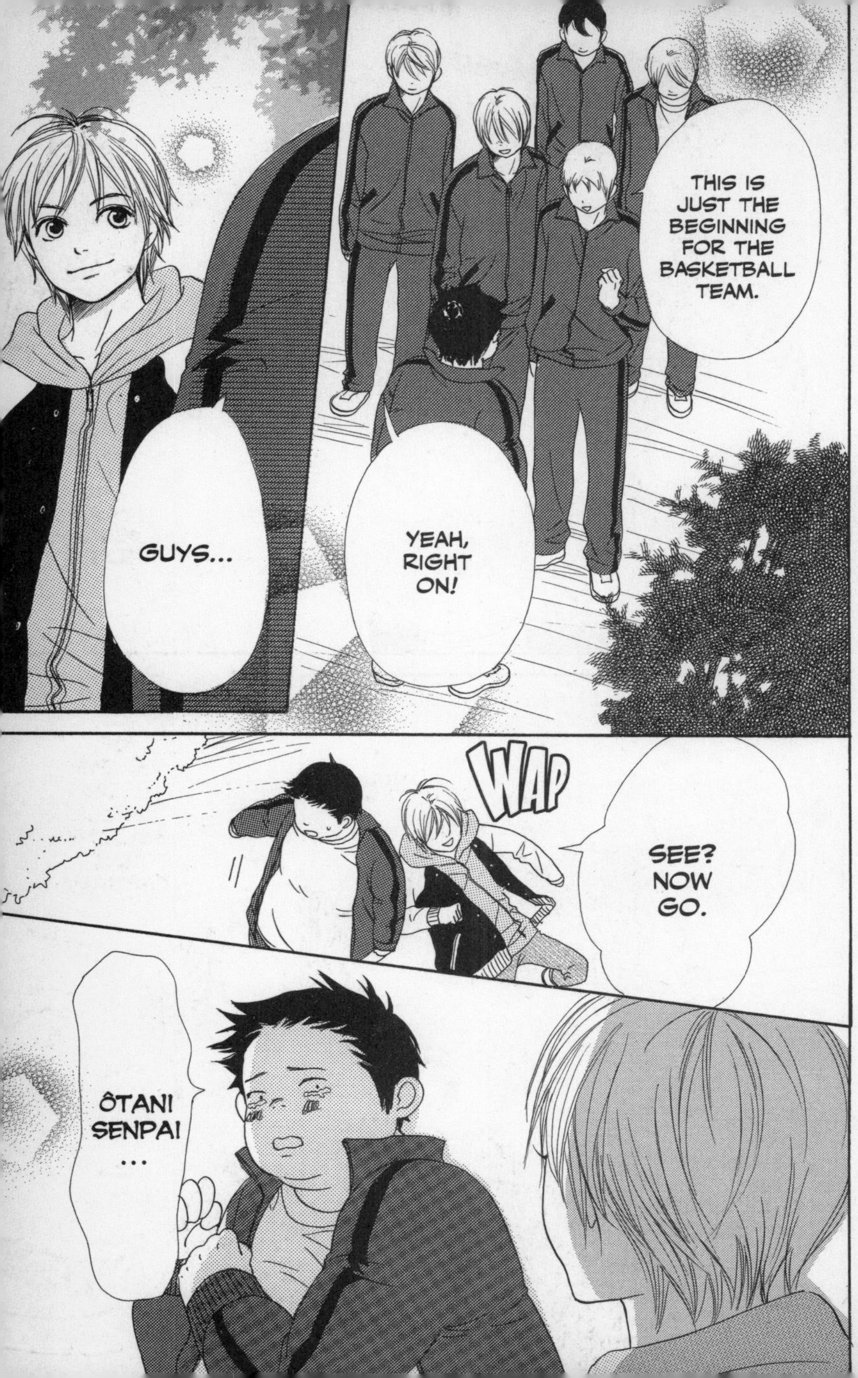
THIS IS JUST THE BEGINNING FOR THE BASKETBALL TEAM.
YEAH, RIGHT ON!
GUYS...
WAP
SEE? NOW GO.
ÔTANI SENPAI ...

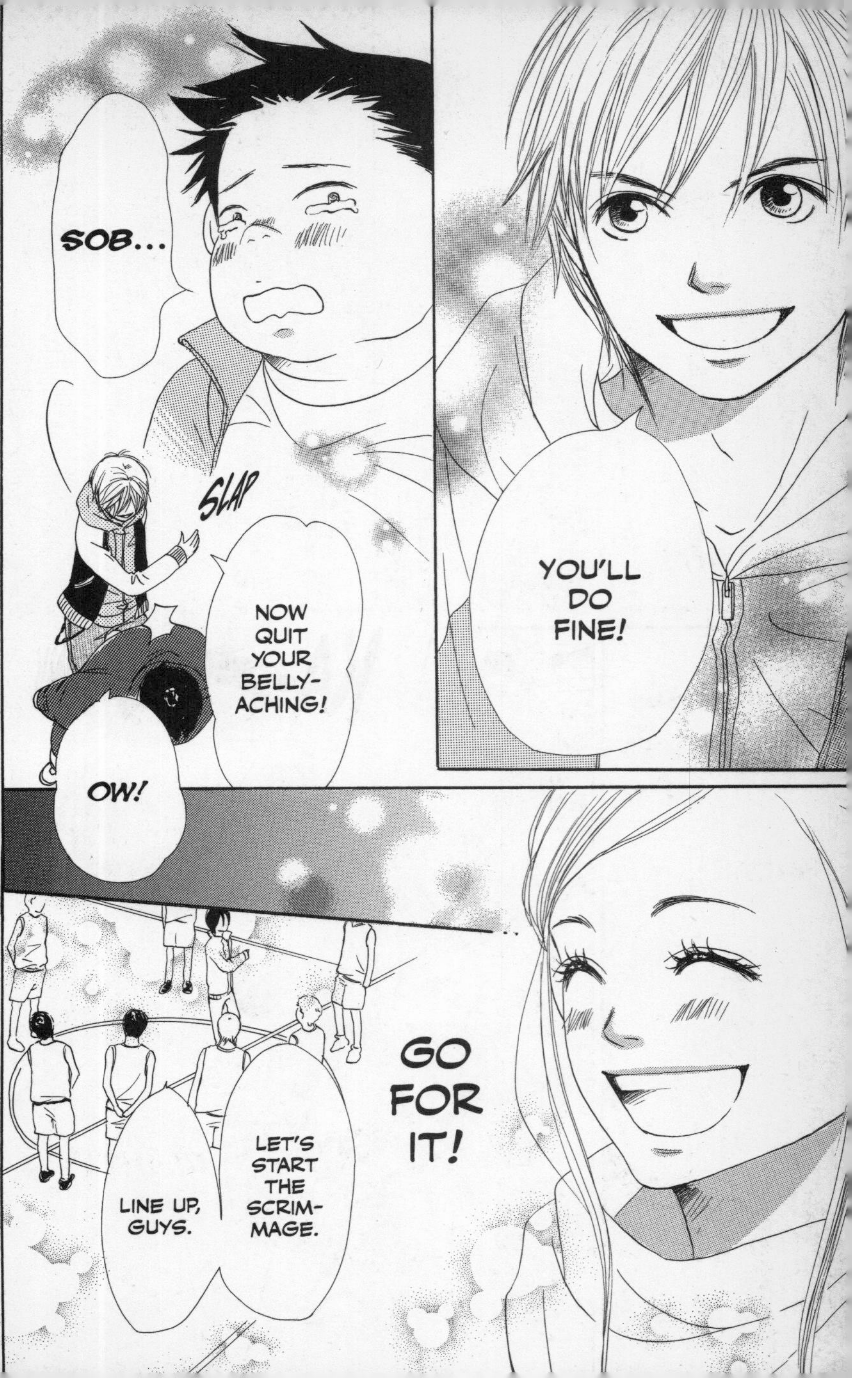
YOU'LL DO FINE!
SOB...
SLAP
NOW QUIT YOUR BELLY-ACHING!
OW!
GO FOR IT!
LET'S START THE SCRIM-MAGE.
LINE UP, GUYS.

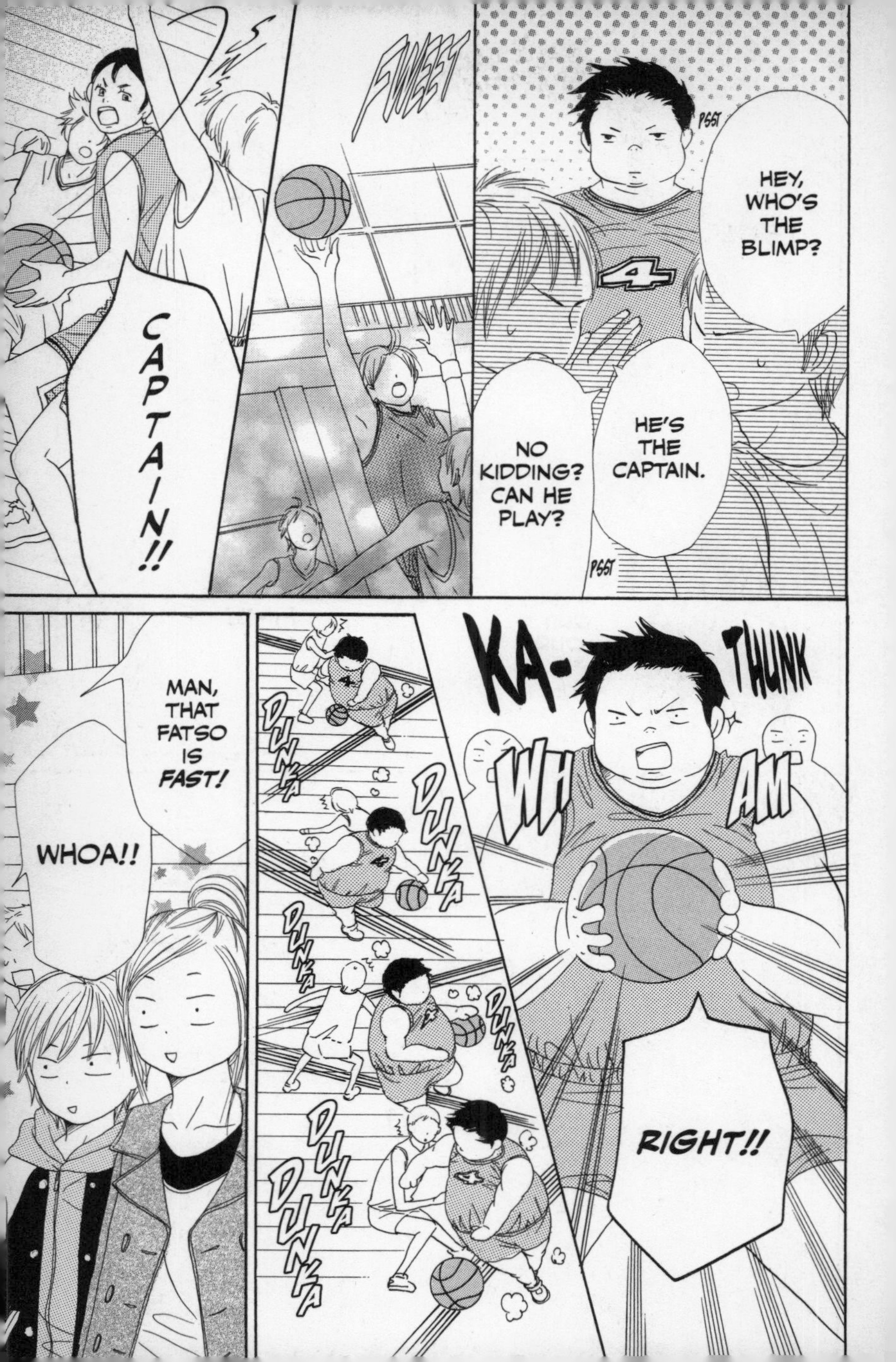
PSST
HEY, WHO'S THE BLIMP?
HE'S THE CAPTAIN.
NO KIDDING? CAN HE PLAY?
PSST
FWEET
CAPTAIN!!
KA-THUNK
WHAM
RIGHT!!
DUNKA
DUNKA
DUNKA
DUNKA
DUNKA
DUNKA
DUNKA
MAN, THAT FATSO IS FAST!
WHOA!!

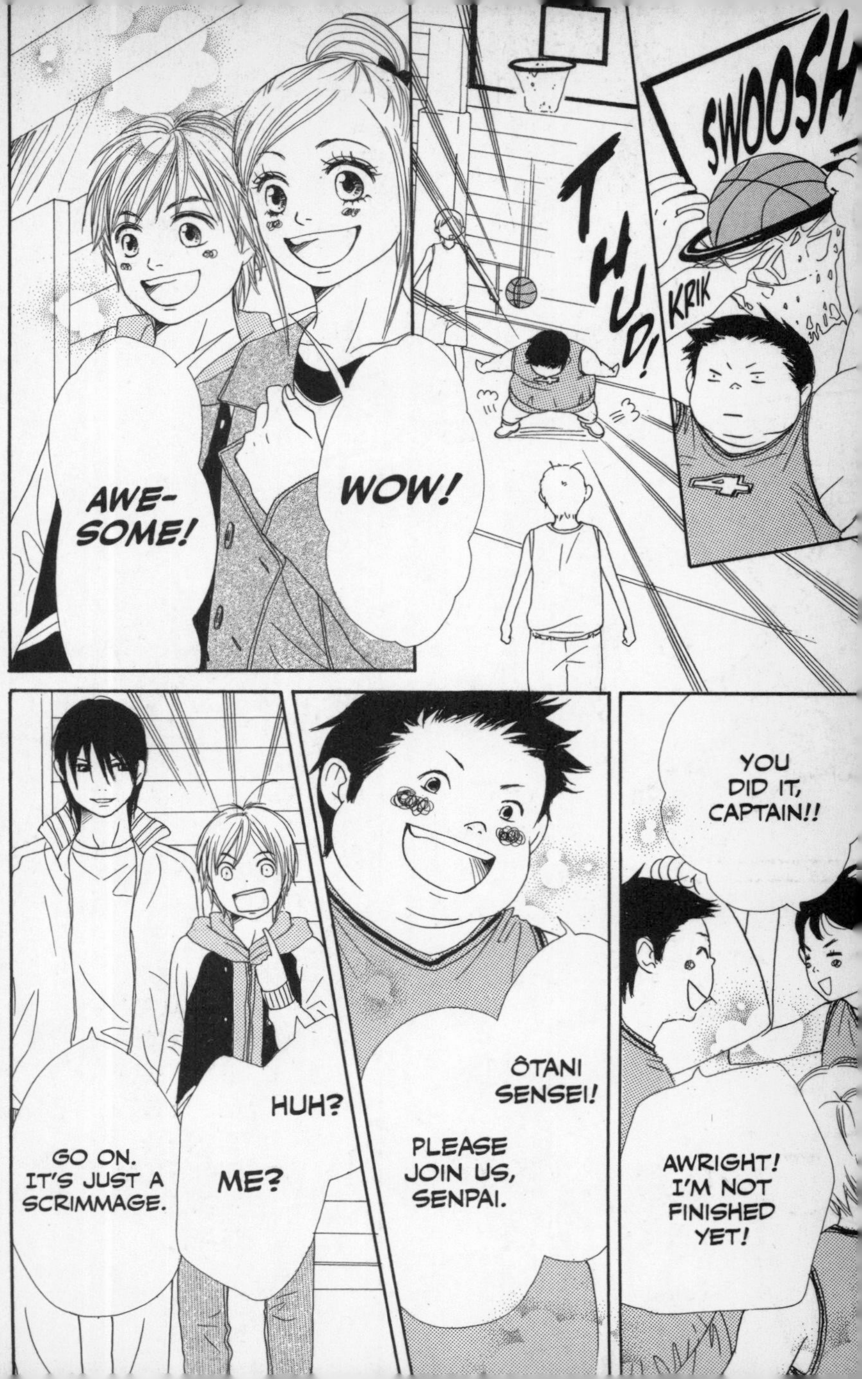
SWOOSH
KRIK
THUD!
WOW!
AWE-SOME!
YOU DID IT, CAPTAIN!!
AWRIGHT! I'M NOT FINISHED YET!
ÔTANI SENSEI!
PLEASE JOIN US, SENPAI.
HUH?
ME?
GO ON. IT'S JUST A SCRIMMAGE.

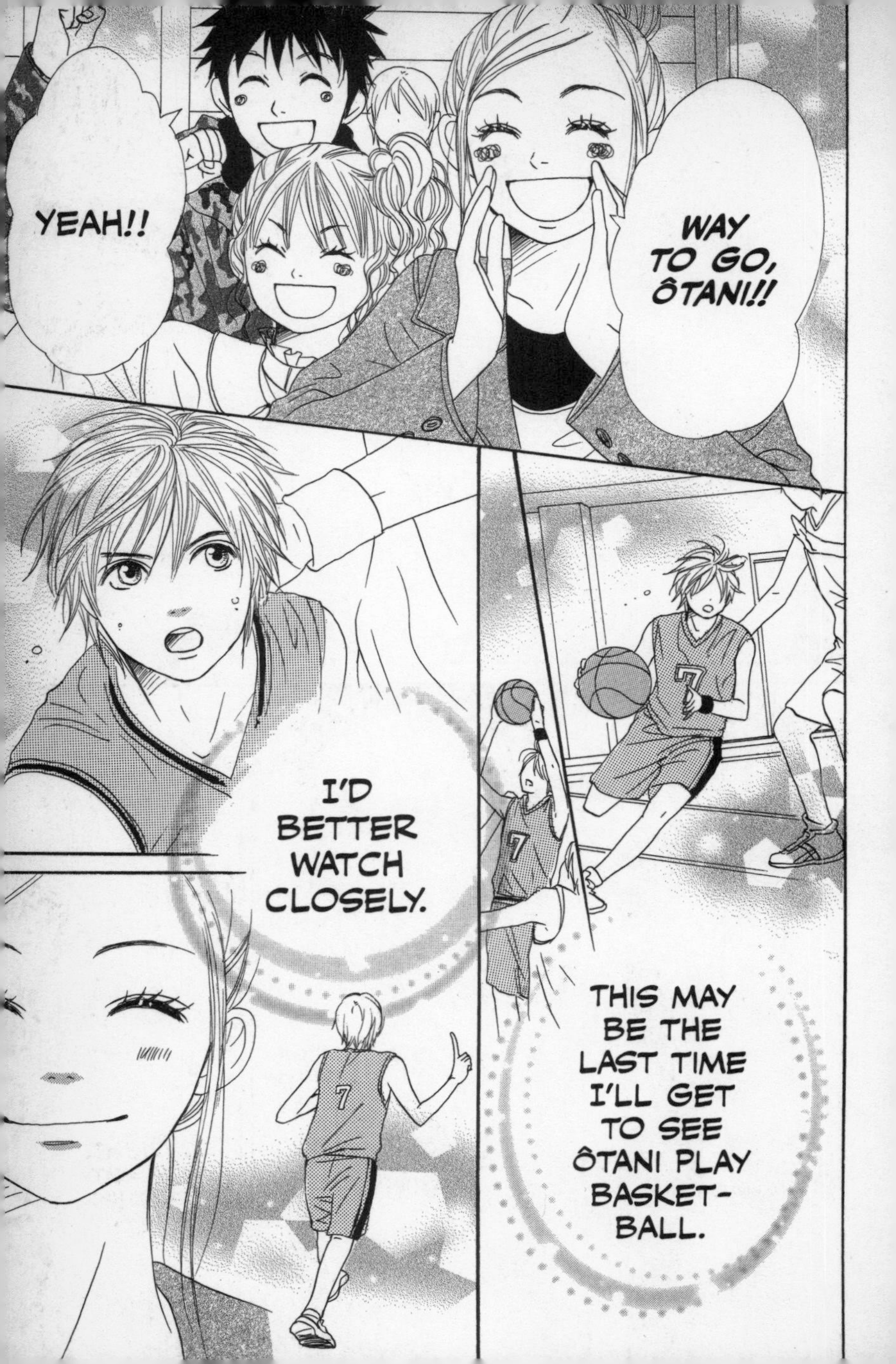
WAY TO GO, ÔTANI!!
YEAH!!
THIS MAY BE THE LAST TIME I'LL GET TO SEE ÔTANI PLAY BASKET-BALL.
I'D BETTER WATCH CLOSELY.

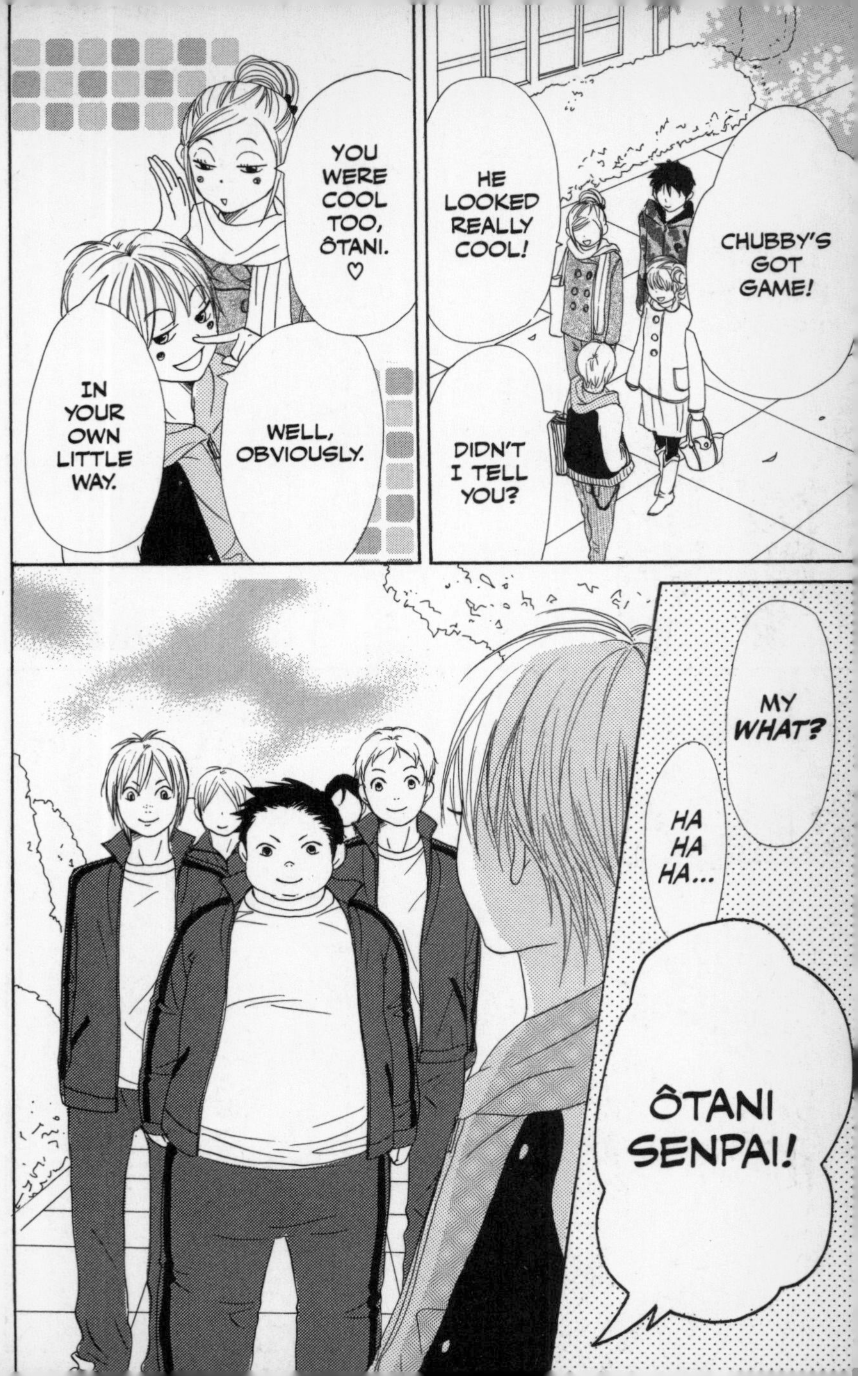
CHUBBY'S GOT GAME!
HE LOOKED REALLY COOL!
DIDN'T I TELL YOU?
YOU WERE COOL TOO, ÔTANI. ♡
WELL, OBVIOUSLY.
IN YOUR OWN LITTLE WAY.
MY *WHAT?*
HA HA HA...
ÔTANI SENPAI!

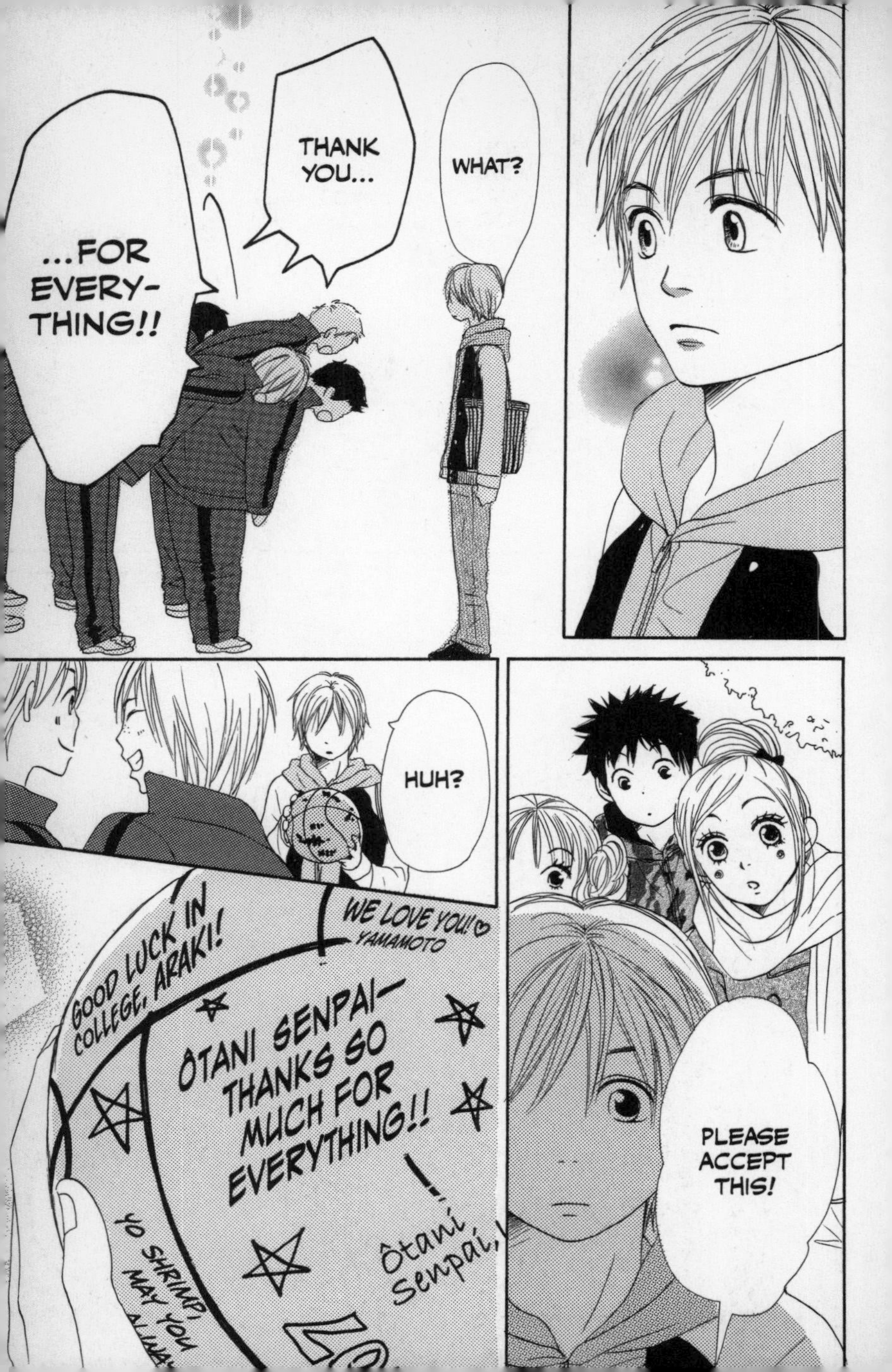
WHAT?
THANK YOU...
...FOR EVERY-THING!!
PLEASE ACCEPT THIS!
HUH?
WE LOVE YOU! ♡
YAMAMOTO
GOOD LUCK IN COLLEGE, ARAKI!
ŌTANI SENPAI— THANKS SO MUCH FOR EVERYTHING!!
Ōtani Senpai,
YO SHRIMP, MAY YOU

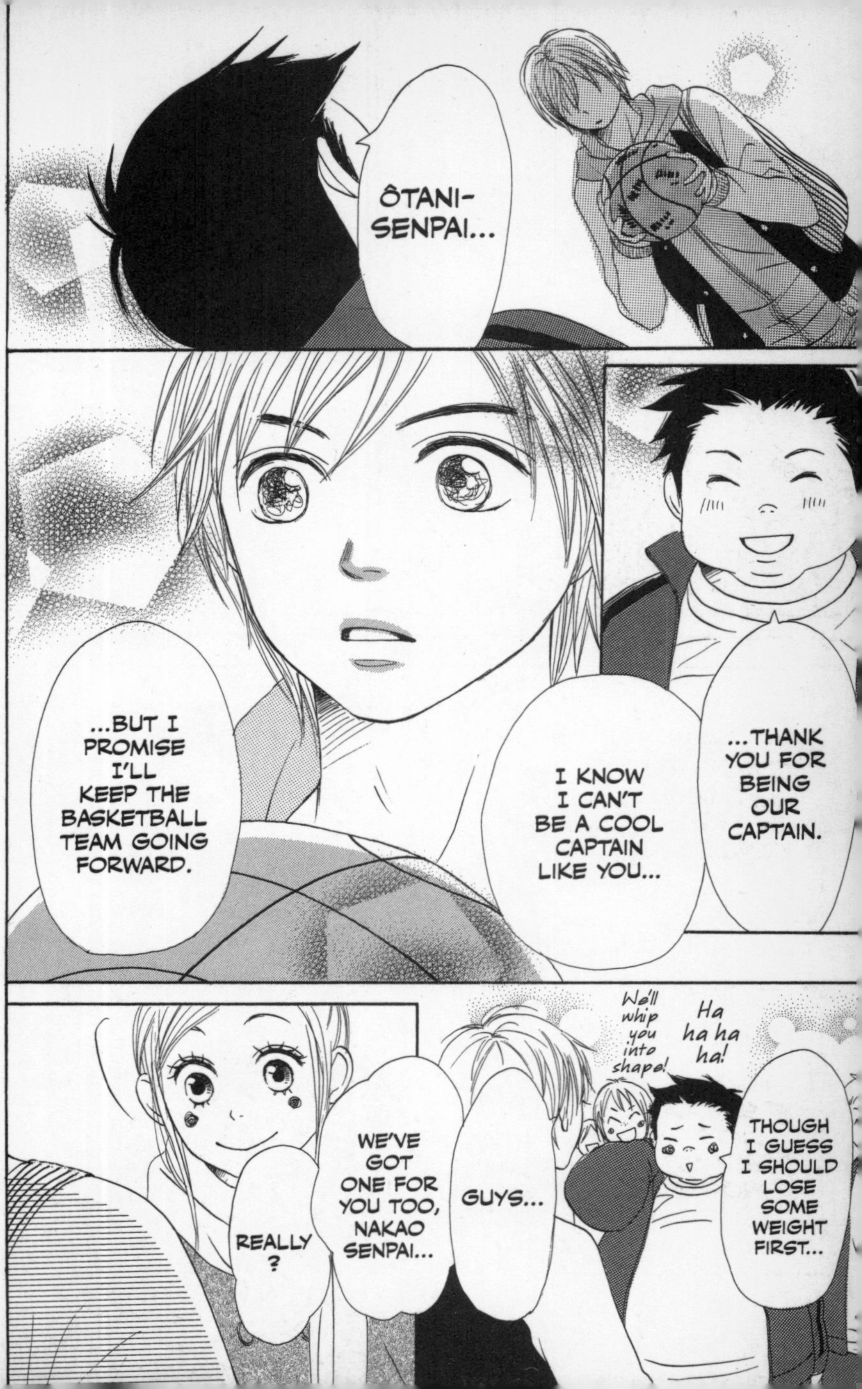
ÔTANI-SENPAI...
...THANK YOU FOR BEING OUR CAPTAIN.
I KNOW I CAN'T BE A COOL CAPTAIN LIKE YOU...
...BUT I PROMISE I'LL KEEP THE BASKETBALL TEAM GOING FORWARD.
THOUGH I GUESS I SHOULD LOSE SOME WEIGHT FIRST...
Ha ha ha ha!
We'll whip you into shape!
GUYS...
WE'VE GOT ONE FOR YOU TOO, NAKAO SENPAI...
REALLY?

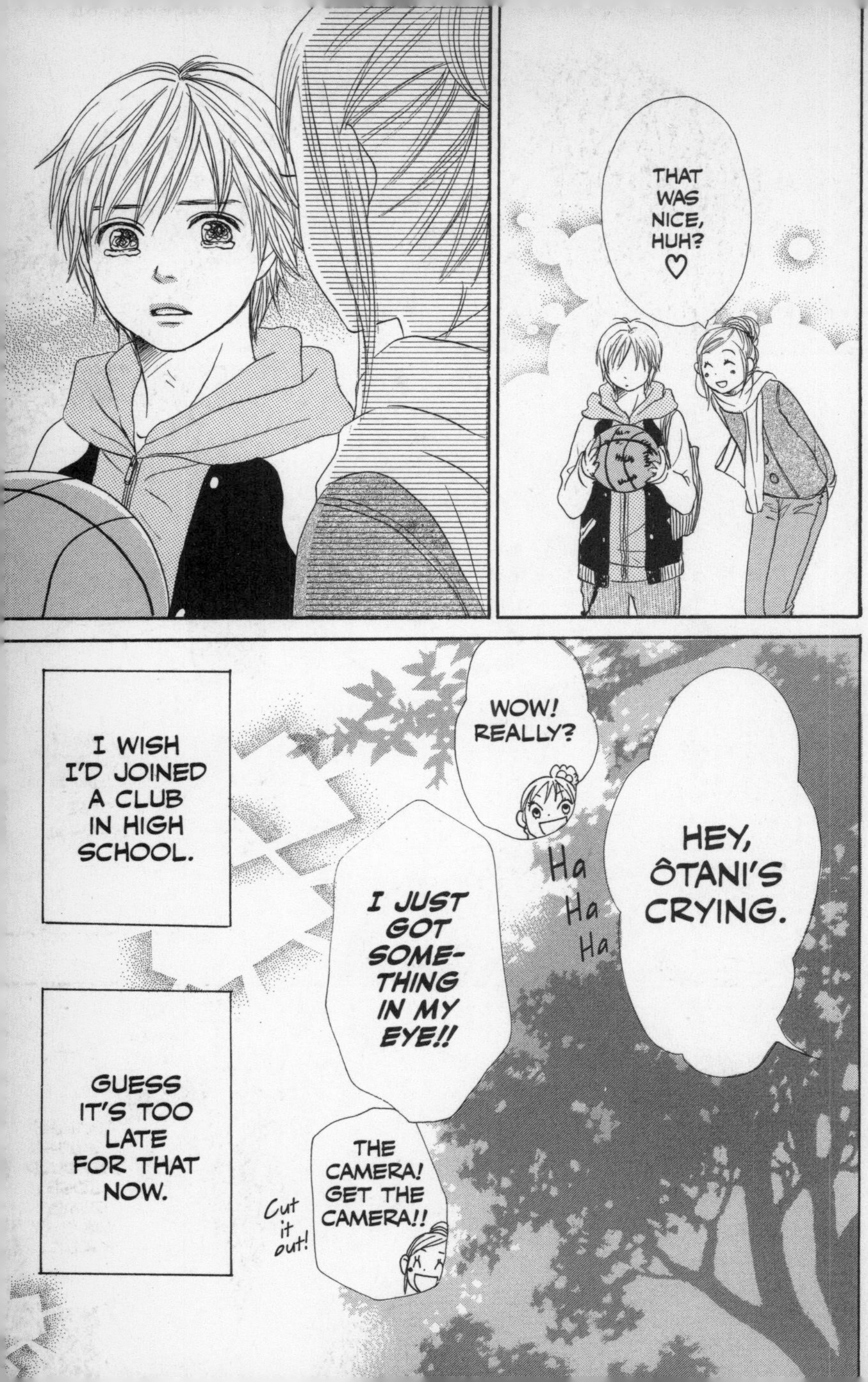
THAT WAS NICE, HUH? ♡
HEY, ÔTANI'S CRYING.
Ha Ha Ha
WOW! REALLY?
I JUST GOT SOME-THING IN MY EYE!!
THE CAMERA! GET THE CAMERA!!
Cut it out!
I WISH I'D JOINED A CLUB IN HIGH SCHOOL.
GUESS IT'S TOO LATE FOR THAT NOW.

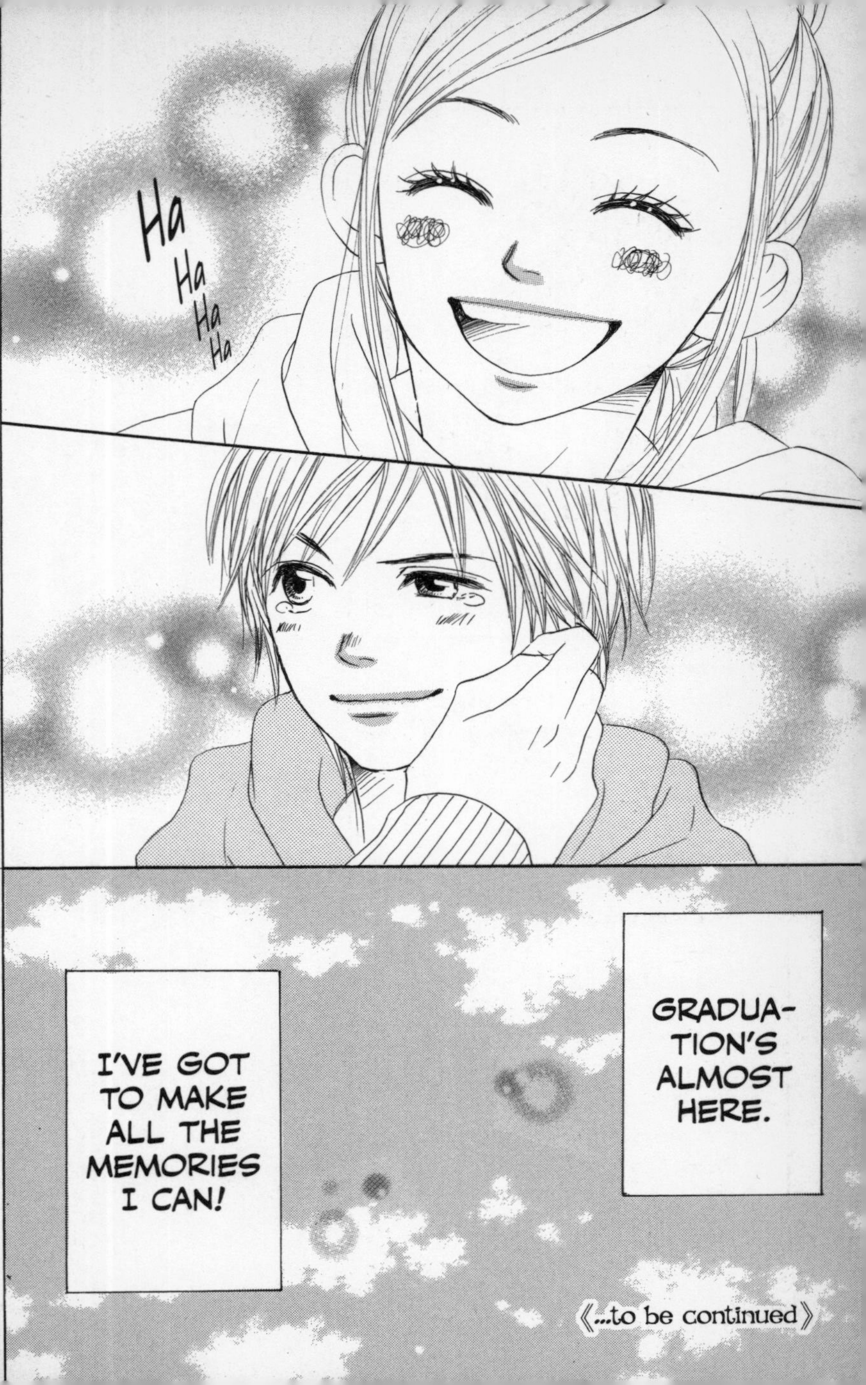
Ha Ha Ha Ha
GRADUA-TION'S ALMOST HERE.
I'VE GOT TO MAKE ALL THE MEMORIES I CAN!
《...to be continued》

My guitar playing was worse than I expected. I didn't realize I was so hopeless. I guess it was too much to believe I could do something now that I couldn't do when I was younger. As I gaze at the guitar I just bought, I'm filled with regret. It's become more of a room decoration than anything else.

Aya Nakahara won the 2003 Shogakukan Manga Award for her breakthrough hit *Love★Com,* which was made into a major motion picture and a PS2 game in 2006. She debuted with *Haru to Kuuki Nichiyou-bi* in 1995, and her other works include *HANADA* and *Himitsu Kichi.*

LOVE★COM VOL 15
Shojo Beat Manga Edition

STORY AND ART BY
AYA NAKAHARA

Translation/JN Productions
English Adaptation/Shaenon K. Garrity
Touch-up Art & Lettering/Gia Cam Luc
Design/Yuki Ameda
Editor/Carrie Shepherd

VP, Production/Alvin Lu
VP, Publishing Licensing/Rika Inouye
VP, Sales & Product Marketing/Gonzalo Ferreyra
VP, Creative/Linda Espinosa
Publisher/Hyoe Narita

Printed in Canada

Published by VIZ Media, LLC
P.O. Box 77010
San Francisco, CA 94107

10 9 8 7 6 5 4 3 2 1
First printing, November 2009

RATED T FOR TEEN
PARENTAL ADVISORY
LOVE★COM is rated T for Teen and is recommended for ages 13 and up.
ratings.viz.com

www.viz.com

www.shojobeat.com